On
FASTING
and
FEASTING

For
David, Robert, Gabriel, Emma, Dylan, Rachel,
and any brothers and sisters they may have
– a present for each of them
when they reach the age of twelve.

A Macdonald Orbis BOOK

© Macdonald & Co (Publishers) Ltd 1988

First published in Great Britain in 1988
by Macdonald & Co (Publishers) Ltd
London & Sydney
A member of Maxwell Pergamon Publishing Corporation plc

British Library Cataloguing in Publication Data

On Fasting and feasting.
1. Food
I. Davidson, Alan,   *1924–*
641.3

ISBN 0–356–15637–0

Filmset by MS Filmsetting Limited, Frome, Somerset
Printed and bound in Portugal by Printer Portuguesa

Senior Commissioning Editor: Joanna Lorenz
Art Director: Linda Cole
Designer: Ingrid Mason
Illustrator: Susan Alcantarilla

Macdonald & Co (Publishers) Ltd
Greater London House
Hampstead Road
London NW1 7QX

ALAN DAVIDSON

On
FASTING
and
FEASTING

A PERSONAL COLLECTION OF FAVOURITE WRITINGS ON FOOD AND EATING

ILLUSTRATED *by* SUSAN ALCANTARILLA

MACDONALD ORBIS

CONTENTS

641.3
ON

CHAPTER FOUR – FOOD from the WATERS

CHAPTER FIVE – On HOOF or WING

Chapter Six – Food *from the* Dairy

Chapter Seven – Fasting *and* Feasting

Chapter Eight – Here *and* There

CONTENTS

INTRODUCTION

This is a thoroughly personal choice of what I consider to be good writing on food and cookery. Its chief and simple aim: to give enjoyment to readers. I hope that it will also provide welcome information and inspiration.

During the last dozen years I have acquired and read, or dipped into, a very large number of books on this subject. I know which I recall with particular pleasure, and it is these on which I have drawn.

But that last statement needs a qualification. I really enjoy poking about among old books, especially those of the 17th and 18th centuries, and when I set about choosing items for the anthology I thought that I was going to pick out a lot from them. But no; the more I looked at them, and at works of the 19th century too, the more I realised that, however strong my own antiquarian tastes might be, these books are not a source of generally enjoyable reading. One or two shining exceptions are represented here. But most of the old cookery books are just collections of recipes prefaced by a promotional essay from the author, and they would only be meet for an anthology if it was to be an anthology of recipes, which this is not.

I have been intent on finding good writing *about* food and recipes, and after months of activity I have come to the conclusion (which others no doubt had already reached) that most of the really interesting material is quite recent. Standards have been rising: standards of accuracy, of detail, of style. New vehicles are available; the welling up in the 1980s of periodicals on the history of food and cookery and of semi-academic symposia on the same themes (Oxford, Leeds, Cambridge Massachusetts, Adelaide, Melbourne, Konya in Turkey) has tapped new springs of talent, which would never have come on stream if conventional recipe books and commercial magazines had remained the only outlets. In short, good things have been written in the past, but better things and more of them are being written now. We should rejoice.

Cookery is a global subject, and good writing about it is by no means confined to Western Europe and North America, or to the European languages. So I have chosen items from all five continents.

I have not devoted much space to the cookery of court and aristocratic circles in the past, and of the top restaurants today. These are potentially interesting matters, to be sure, but then so is the question of what ordinary people around the world have cooked and eaten, and are cooking and eating, or would cook and eat if they had it. As for myself, I certainly derive more pleasure from learning what Shetland fishing families do with fish livers† than from reading about some expensive banquet at which the flinty (or velvety-soft, or soft yet flinty, or purple and spongy) nose of the Château Quelquechose was a perfect match for the Délices de n'Importe Quoi cooked à la Nom Incompréhensible.

I have certainly not included anything because 'people would expect it to be there'.

8

On the contrary, I have aimed to introduce some less familiar, and often more vivid, writing in preference to the familiar prose of well-known gastronomic writers. In the same spirit, I have deliberately been sparing in my use of books which are current, well-known, and readily available; I would rather introduce readers to new things.

If all this sounds like careful dispassionate planning, I should repeat that this is a personal choice; adding that I am well aware that a person is, inescapably, a product of his/her heredity, history and environment, so that the activity of an anthologist must reflect, even lay bare, these things. Thus, in the unlikely event that anyone wished to probe into the matter, it would be easy enough to correlate many of my chosen items with experiences in my life so far: Scottish ancestry and my grandmother's high teas in a Glasgow suburb; Ireland my birthplace, and where I learned to cook potatoes; school in Yorkshire; the sea my habitat for four wartime years; the Arab world my home for four more; living in South-East Asia; making an annual ritual of marmalade-making wherever I have been; the birth in our home of Prospect Books, a real cuckoo in the nest; and so forth. Yet who could divine that the absence of Brillat-Savarin from these pages was caused by my being given a surfeit of him by fanatical Australians at Adelaide in 1984? And who would guess that ... But enough of this.

Naturally, I have had to leave out many items which I would have liked to include. It is fortunate that my publishers specified a book of manageable size; a surfeit of reading can be as vexing as a surfeit of food.

*　　　*　　　*

Although this compilation is my personal one, I did not place myself in a vacuum while putting it together. I am grateful to my wife Jane and my daughters Caroline and Pamela for their criticism; between them they were responsible for sparing the reader some unwise choices and some overlong bits of reading, and they all had good suggestions to make. The same applies to my editor, Joanna Lorenz, whose cheerful tact rendered quite painless some beneficial lopping and pruning of my material.

Of the other people who kindly gave thought to the matter, and who made suggestions which I gladly adopted, I would like to thank in particular Jane Grigson, Ian Jackson, Patience Gray, and Candida Brazil.

I am of course deeply grateful to all the authors and publishers who were good enough to give permission for work to be used, and equally to all those writers of previous centuries whose benevolent but posthumous approval I have assumed; see the bibliography and publishers' acknowledgements at the end of the book.

World's End, Chelsea
April 1988

† Anyone who is curious will find information in a volume of my essays, *A Kipper with My Tea* (Macmillan, 1988).

The Cook and the Kitchen

Without people who cook and kitchens for them to cook in, this book would have no content; so we start with them. M. F. K. Fisher, discussing why some people 'love to cook', strikes a disconcerting keynote. (Did Simulus the Roman ploughman and his kinky-haired assistant, the description of whose activities in the darkness before dawn constitutes a breathtaking scoop for the Bristol Classical Press, love to cook? I bet not.)

The art of recipe writing and the use (or disuse – see John Thorne) of recipes also belong here. Much can we learn from Elizabeth David's crystalline appreciation of Eliza Acton; and much from Raymond Sokolov's comparison of old-style recipes and new.

M. F. K. Fisher   1984

LOVING COOKS, BEWARE!

*Among the famous writers on cookery in North America one
stands apart, a star with her own share of the sky, a star
whose luminosity differs in kind from all the others: this is
M. F. K. Fisher. A quick look through her books will give the
impression that they are about food – as indeed, in a sense,
they are. But reading them reveals their transcendent quality;
they are really about life itself. This essay on people who 'love
to cook', which exemplifies her ability to put things in a wholly
new light, to amuse and yet disconcert. Most of it is here.*

Perhaps it is impossible to know how much most people 'love' to do something they do well, and how much they do it simply to feel powerful.

I learned this cruel truth when I was about fourteen, I think, and since then I have always taken with more than one grain of salt any flat statement that X really *loves* to do something he obviously does well, like play a fiddle, or write a book, or cook. If someone tells me X makes the most beautiful omelets in the world because he loves to, I cryptically say, 'Ah?!' Why, because his omelets are superb, is it assumed that he loves to make them? Why should he? And what does he really *love* about making one masterly omelet after another, year after year?

The reason I ask these basically unpleasant questions is that, when I was fourteen, I had to ask and then answer them all by myself about *me*. And it was painful.

Since I was very young I had courted flattery, fawned for praise, without realizing it. I felt warm and important when my parents would let me hear them say that I was the best child they'd ever known about, so skillful, so helpful in the kitchen on Saturdays, and on the cook's night off. I battened like a conceited little mouse on these crumbs. I 'really had a hand at the butter churn.' I was wonderful at beating eggs for the cook's famous sponge cakes. *Never* had such a young child proven so deft at carrying a tea-tray.

'Oh, yes,' Mother would say comfortably, 'I can always depend on her! She *loves* it.' All this was especially heady because as a family we were not given to undue praise, to flowery compliments. So I floated along, smug and hypnotized, for several years. Suddenly, when cold adolescence started to settle in, I asked myself why I was always the girl told to come home early from school when there were friends for tea. I knew that I could assemble the whole dainty farce better than anyone else. And Mother *counted* on me. And I loved that. But why in Hell couldn't my younger siblings give up an afternoon now and then? Why in Hell didn't Mother train the current kitchen slavey to wheel in the tea-wagon?

That was when I began to 'grow a little difficult,' as my parents later told me. My sisters said I was uppity. I know I was surly and sullen and generally disagreeable, because I was for the first time looking at myself as a fool, a dupe, a complete patsy who had thought for years that she loved to cook, when really all she wanted was to feel powerful, important, essential. It was a hard time, and not conducive to obedience and warmth, and fairly soon I was tucked into a kindly concentration camp for budding Christians, and other less gullible people made the cupcakes and churned butter and served tea, for *money*, not love. They were paid *cash*, not compliments.

By now, of course, I feel good about almost everything in my fine childhood. But I've not ceased speculating about loving to cook, since those first queasy realizations of how *used* I was, and why. And when people say flatly that I *must* love to cook, since I not only write about food but make it, I wince a little, I cringe, invisibly. Why must I 'love' it, just because I do it as well as I can? Are they really saying that I love myself?

Professional cooks, the great and famous ones who once ran famous kitchens (the Reform Club in London, the Paris Ritz) and cooked for kings, and who in our days fly everywhere giving 'demos' and opening wineries and crowning beauty queens, perhaps do not love cooking at all, as the word *love* is meant. They enjoy all the things that their skills and training have developed in them, to make them powerful and admired and even rich. Often they live as much for the inner satisfaction of turning out a perfect dish as they do for the praise it brings them. But love? I doubt it.

Amateur cooks, on the other hand, live more overtly for the compliments they need in order to act. They do not cook for money, of course, like an Escoffier or a Guérard, and their training is comparatively non-existent: perhaps a season in Lausanne at l'Ecole Hotelière, or a couple of courses with Beard in New York, with Child in Santa Barbara. . . . But they *LOVE* to do absolutely superb omelets, unforgettable spaghetti sauces, incredible hash-browns. . . .

And I ask, silently, Really? Or do they simply need the ineffable feeling of power, of warmth, of being appreciated, that made me so smugly happy when I was nine or eleven or even going on fourteen? Have they deliberately chosen to be purring patsies?

There is another category of people who 'must love to cook,' and I belong to it . . . It is the cooks of this third gastronomical world, who must be most careful about confusing the love to cook with the love to control and dominate. They/we can be a rapacious and ruthless lot, in the need to keep families undoubting and devoted. We must watch ourselves and our own skills and trickeries like wary buzzards, so that we stay honest . . . or at least overt.

It is probably fortunate that most of us practitioners of the art of making our loved ones believe that we love to cook, because we love *them*, can often watch our own kind at work.

We have all had the chance, for instance, to recognize how fallible people can be. Say that an Italian friend invites us to a 'strictly family' meal. 'If you haven't tasted my mother's spaghetti,' and he rolls his eyes ecstatically and spreads his hands outward in a slightly helpless gesture straight from either Milan or Genoa, 'Ah, *mama mia*, you have never tasted true spaghetti!'

So you go, as if to a Special Mass, to an intimate kitchen-table meal, which means that Papa is in his shirtsleeves and a sulky daughter-in-law has consented to drop in with a couple of howling babies, who are mercifully invisible in Grandma's bedroom. And Mama, in very high heels because this afternoon was her Society of the Daughters of the Circle of Holy St. Genevieve, teeters dutifully between stove and the big table where we all sit, tumblers of cheap rot-gut red on the ready, waiting for the platter of lukewarm overcooked packaged pasta that one of her boys carries dramatically ahead of her as she sinks, exhausted but beatific, into her chair. Somebody tosses the puddle of bottled tomato-mushroom sauce into the limp pasta; we all sprinkle it with imitation Parmesan cheese, and moan and grunt in voracious bliss. '*Mama Mia!*' the men mutter, rolling their eyes. Papa lifts his tumbler of Coke toward his wife (he has a bad stomach) and she smiles at us, drifty-dreamy after her afternoon with the Ladies of the Circle and their punch-laden Bingo. And there is a special treat from the son who let me intrude: a 'bought' cake thick with pink and green icing. We all toast Mama again, and she smiles blearily at us, serenely sure for that moment anyway that we worship her.

Of course it is not always mothers who command this blind if occasional devotion, but they seem dominant, at least in our Western society, and I can think of many I have known, here and in Europe and Mexico. In the Mid-West, for instance, I know a woman who honestly believes that The Kitchen is holy. It is the fountain-head of our whole society, and something never to be touched by doubting foreigners or the subversive anti-Christian elements that are trying to eat away our good American trust in Mom-the-Flag-and-Apple Pie. (This is not a humorous phrase to her. And of course Mom comes first, because without Mom ... without Mom what else is there, what else can there be to keep us one nation, indivisible? And anyway, *she* is Mom, and makes the best apple pie in the country. ...)

This woman, born in Indiana, but a resident for almost fifty years now of southern Iowa, because of her husband who is called Paw, believes almost ferociously that Home is where the heart is, and the Kitchen, *HER* kitchen, is the heart of the home. Furthermore, anybody who does not love to cook knows not love itself. This is her gospel, The Gospel According to St Mom.

When she is not filling her temple, her shrine, with the heady incense of fried chicken, and Aunt Jennie's recipe for corn-bread and Gramma Jenkin's mince-meat pudding, with a kettle of plum butter chucklin' on the back burner, she is energetically making plaques, dozens of them.

She sells them at the County Fair, to benefit her Church missionary activities. They are of varnished pine, and after many years of turning them out between stirring her peach conserve and making the best canned corn this side of Sioux City, she is a whiz at using the electric script-burner Paw gave her on their twenty-fifth anniversary.

Sometimes she puts a design of entwined hearts at the top, for newly married couples, but usually the plain ones are the best-sellers. They say

WELCOME TO MY KITCHEN
AROUND THIS TABLE
FAMILY AND FRIENDS SHARE
THE WARMTH
OF LOVE AND TOGETHERNESS

Sometimes she changes the words a little, but the message is always the same, that we are invited to worship at her kitchen and its stove. It is there that we will find real love, because *she* loves to cook.

At the risk of sounding sacrilegious, but always with the courtesy due any fellow-culprit, I think that people who have so candidly, even voluptuously, designated themselves as high priests at their own altars, are potential egomaniacs.

We must be wary of them, with all due respect of course if they prove to be good cooks in spite of, rather than because of, their love for cooking ... and whether they work their miracles in a king's kitchen or a diner on Route 22. So much the better if they manage to feed our souls as well as our bodies! But let us never fool ourselves that they must love to cook in order to be masters at it. The power to make us ask them to cook for us is what they love, and I see nothing wrong with that, as long as they themselves never confuse the reasons.

THE JOURNAL OF GASTRONOMY, *vol 1, summer 1984*

William Verral 1759

EQUIPMENT *for an* EIGHTEENTH CENTURY KITCHEN

William Verral of Lewes is one of the most (and one of the few) engaging cookery writers of the 18th century. Here, quite unmistakeably, is a real cook and a remarkable personality, addressing us in his own words. They tumble forth, unimpeded by paragraph breaks!

From a presumption of some small success from my friends I venture to publish the following treatise. To pretend to write for fame would illy become a person in my sphere of life (who am no more than what is vulgarly called a poor publican). 'Twould be an unparalleled piece of imprudence, and wholly incompatible to reason and the nature of things. 'Twill be sufficient for me that it meets with the approbation amongst my friends and acquaintances, as may just satisfy me for the pains I have taken to collect them (though small matters) together. The chief end and design of this part of my little volume is to show, both to the experienced and unexperienced in the business, the whole and simple art of the most modern and best French Cookery; to lay down before them such an unerring guide how it may always be well managed, and please the eye as well as the taste of everybody; and to show, too, by the notorious errors I have frequently seen, how of course it must for ever fail of being either good or pleasing, and a great many favourite morsels entirely spoiled.

First, then, give me leave to advise those who please to try the following receipts, to provide a proper apparatus for the work they take in hand, without which it is impossible it can be done with the least air of decency: and before I finish this, shall further show by maxims unexceptionable, that a good dinner cannot be got up to look neat and pretty without proper utensils to work it in, such as neat stewpans of several sizes, soup-pots, &c. to do it withal, though your provisions be never so good. I have been sent for many and many a time to get dinners for some of the best families herabouts; the salute generally is: Will, (for that is my name) I want you to dress me a dinner to-day; with all my heart, Sir, says I; how many will your company be; why about ten or twelve, or thereabouts: and what would you please to have me get, Sir, for ye? O, says the gentleman, I shall leave that entirely to you; but I'll show you my larder, and you'll be the better judge how to make your bill of fare; and a vast plenty of good provisions there was, enough to make two courses, one of seven, the other of nine, with an addition only of three or four small dishes for the second course; and a fine dish of fish there was for a remove. So it was agreed that should be the thing; but, says the gentleman, be sure you make us some good things in your own way, for they are polite sort of gentry that are to dine with me. I promised my care, and wrote the bill immediately; and it was vastly approved of. My next step was to go and offer a great many compliments to Mrs. Cook about getting the dinner; and as it was her master's order I should assist her, I hoped we should agree; and the girl, I'll say that for her, returned the compliment very prettily, by saying, Sir, whatever my master or you shall order me to do, shall be done as far and as well as I am able. But Nanny (for that I found to be her name) soon got into such an air as often happens upon such occasions. Pray, Nanny, says I, where do you place your stewpans, and the other things you make use of in the cooking way? La, Sir, says she, that is all we have (pointing to one poor solitary stewpan, as one might call it,) but no more fit for the use than a wooden hand-dish. Ump, says I to myself, how's this to be? A surgeon may as well attempt to make an incision with a pair of sheers, or open a vein with an oyster-knife, as for me to pretend to get this dinner without proper tools to do it; here's neither stewpan, soup-pot, or any one thing else that is useful; there's what they call a frying-pan indeed, but black as my hat, and a handle long enough to obstruct half the passage of the kitchen. However, upon a little pause I sent away post haste for my own kitchen furniture. In the meantime

Nanny and I kept on in preparing what we could, that no time might be lost. When the things came we at it again, and all was in a tolerable way, and forward enough for the time of day; but at length wanting a sieve I begg'd of Nanny to give me one, and so she did in a moment; but such a one! – I put my fingers to it and found it gravelly. Nanny, says I, this won't do, it is sandy: she look'd at it, and angry enough she was: rot our Sue, says she, she's always taking my sieve to sand her nasty dirty stairs. But, however, to be a little cleanly Nanny gave it a good thump upon the table, much about the part of it where the meat is generally laid, and whips it into the boiler where I suppose the pork and cabbage was boiling for the family, gives it a sort of rinse, and gave it me again, with as much of the pork fat about it as would poison the whole dinner; so I said no more, but could not use it, and made use of a napkin that I slily made friends with her fellow-servant for; at which she leer'd round and set off; but I heard her say as she flirted her tail into the scullery, hang these men cooks, they are so confounded nice. – I'll be whipt, says she, if there was more sand in the sieve than would lay upon a sixpence. However, she came again presently, and I soon coax'd her into good humour again; come, says I, Nanny, I'm going to make a fricasee of chickens, observe how I cut'em (for I'll show ye how to do any part of the dinner), and she seemed very attentive. When I had cut mine, there, says I, do you take that, and cut it in the same manner: and indeed the girl handled her knife well, and did it very prettily: then I gave her directions how to proceed; and it was done neatly, notwithstanding the story of the sandy sieve. I then took in hand to show her in what manner it was to be finished for the table. And now, dinner being dish'd up, Nanny was vastly pleased, and said, that in her judgment it was the prettiest and best she had ever seen. When 'twas over, the gentleman desired, if I had time in the evening, he should be glad I would come and get him two or three little matters for supper, for they all stay: and be sure, says he, make us just such another fricasee, for it was highly approved on; so I went and told Nanny she should do it; which was agreed to: but, Sir, says she, if I don't do right I hope you'll tell me. But it was done to my mind, and Nanny was now the cook; supper was sent in, and great praises ran from plate to plate, and they unanimously agreed that that fricasee was better than what they had for dinner. Before supper was well over out comes the gentleman to me. Will, says he, we hope you have this dish in the book you are going to publish. Yes, Sir, says I, and everything else you had to-day drest in the foreign way. But, Sir, says I, your cook did that you had for supper. My maid do it, says he, and away he went to his company. Nanny was immediately sent for, and after some questions something was given her for the care she had taken; so I wished the family a good night, and went home.

A COMPLETE SYSTEM OF COOKERY

Bridget Ann Henisch 1976

GOINGS-ON *in the* MEDIEVAL KITCHEN

*The fruits of scholarship are easier to digest if they are sauced
with wit. Bridget Ann Henisch's classic work on medieval
cookery provides the archetypal example of this felicitous
combination. Here she brings alive for us the medieval kitchen.
(See also pages 206 and 314.)*

As one peers down the tunnel of time, trying to catch glimpses of the medieval cook at work, there is at first disappointingly little to be seen. Neither he nor his equipment were considered worthy of a center-stage position, and so they must be hunted down patiently in the nooks and crannies of art and literature. Kitchen scenes are hard to find, but many a cauldron bubbles in exotic settings: devils tend their pots over the fires of hell in a Last Judgment, cooks stir their dinner on the back of a whale at the bottom of a page. A stewpot perched on the head of a rakish monster in a manuscript border, a stumpy little man carved on a bench end, clutching a ladle as long as himself, these are the scraps which make up the patchwork quilt of first impressions.

Such random clues suggest that cooks were exceedingly cross and their kitchens in perpetual uproar. Dogs were everywhere, looking for dinner. According to a proverb recorded in the sixteenth century, 'The cook is not so sone gone as the doges hed is in the porigpot.' Medieval dogs never deigned to wait for a back to be turned. A misericord in St. George's Chapel, Windsor, shows four enormous hounds piling into a cauldron, indifferent to the cook just poised to hurl his ladle. On another, at St. Mary Virgin Church in Fairford, Gloucestershire, a very fat dog is headfirst in the pot, while on a bench end at Sherborne Abbey, a woman has given up the unequal struggle and meekly holds out the bowl for her dog to lick.

When dogs are not the problem, a fox is running off with a hen, the distracted housewife is in hot pursuit, and the family pig left behind to a leisurely exploration of the pots and pans. In a fifteenth-century edition of Aesop's fables, two plump rats investigate the resources of a larder.

Animals may have been incidental irritations in the kitchen, but the cook's principal distractions were his fellow humans. The scene which appears most frequently in art shows the cook repelling boarders, beating off the tasters and nibblers who hover hopefully round his precious stewpot. A polished flirt knew exactly how to make defenses crumble. In a border of the fourteenth-century *Smithfield Decretals*, he has one arm round the cook, while deftly fishing a joint out of her cauldron with the other.

Only lovers can get away with such shameless depredations; husbands are clouted as soon as they creep within range. On a misericord in Bristol Cathedral, the husband has actually managed to get as far as lifting the lid of the stewpan, but his wife has him firmly by the beard, while a pot, shown by the artist in mid-flight past the poor man's ear, testifies to female bad temper and worse aim. When the vice of Discord was illustrated by the carvers of Notre Dame they merely showed a man and a woman squabbling. At Amiens Cathedral, whose thirteenth-century carvers drew inspiration for their own cycle of Vices and Virtues from Notre Dame, an overturned cooking pot has been added to the scene. The kitchen was a classic battleground for the sexes, although which was regarded as the aggressor depended naturally on the point of view. A sequence of border scenes in the *Smithfield Decretals* shows a husband toiling to please, fetching water, washing dishes, grinding corn, baking bread, but beaten up after every task by an implacable wife. In the fifteenth-century poem *A Young Husband's Complaint*, the henpecked victim is barked out of the kitchen in every verse, and hit on the head whenever he asks for dinner. On the other hand, a twelfth-century celebration of virginity looks at life through a wife's jaundiced eye: 'When she comes in she hears her child screaming, sees the cat at the flitch and the dog at the hide. Her cake is burning on the hearth stone, and her calf is drinking all the milk. The pot is boiling over into the fire, and her husband is grumbling.'

This particular treatise for women is a ringing call to celibacy, which grimly contrasts the horrors of home with the sweet serenity of monastic life. If other evidence is to be believed, however, bad temper could shatter the calm of a convent kitchen as easily as it soured the domestic scene. Indeed, when Langland wanted an appropriate setting for his personification of Wrath in *Piers Plowman*, he chose just such a kitchen, and made Wrath the convent cook. Predictably, the room seethes with malicious gossip, and the nuns are at each other's throats. Tempers were not sweetened by the cook's traditional weakness for the bottle. In popular belief, cooks were expected to be drunk: the medieval phrase 'a temperance of cooks' is heavy with sarcasm, and Chaucer's cook runs true to type by being so full of liquor that he falls off his horse.

When not actually quarreling, cooks seem to have had an alarming sense of humor and plenty of time in which to indulge it. Among the stories written down in the twelfth century about the Saxon outlaw Hereward and his guerrilla warfare against the Norman conquerors, one tells how he slipped into the King's camp disguised as a potter. His first stop was at the kitchen, to show his wares. There the cooks, inevitably, were drinking on the job while they prepared the King's meal. As spirits rose, one of them had the brilliant idea of shaving off the potter's beard with his chopping knife. Hereward had to fight his way through a suddenly menacing circle of kitchen staff, armed to the teeth with razor-sharp equipment. Being no mere peddler but a hero in disguise, he not only escaped but left behind him several concussed cooks and, doubtless, one King crossly roaring for his ruined dinner.

FAST AND FEAST

Anonymous *1st century AD*

The FIRST 'PLOUGHMAN'S LUNCH'

*This poem, at one time wrongly ascribed to Virgil but anyway
dating from that period, is a truly remarkable document; not
because it is about a 'ploughman's lunch' and can be seen as
the distant ancestor of the fare served under that name in
English pubs today, but rather because it seems to be the
earliest surviving detailed account of someone cooking.
Moreover, it is not about a cook in a wealthy household, but
about a humble countryman preparing the simplest of victuals
himself (albeit with the aid of Scybale).
The Latin title of the poem,* Moretum, *refers to the pounded
relish of herbs, garlic and cheese, which the ploughman
prepares.
The translation here reprinted comes from the edition prepared
by E. J. Kenney (Bristol Classical Press, 1984). Inter-
disciplinary communications being what they are, or rather are
not, we may suppose that by about 2000 the extraordinary
significance of the text for food historians will have become
generally known to them.*

Already the winter's night had completed its tenth hour and the watchman bird had
by its song heralded the day, when Simulus, the rustic cultivator of a tiny farm,
fearing grim hunger in the approaching day, rose, and slowly lowering himself from his
poor bed, with cautious hand groped in the blank darkness in search of the hearth,
which at length, painfully, he found.

There remained a little piece of kindling in the shape of a charred log, and the ash
hid the glow of the hot coals beneath. With his forehead bowed down low he brought his
lamp forward to the embers, teasing out with a spike the wick, dry of oil, and awoke the
sluggish fire with repeated breaths. At last, after much effort, the fire caught, and he
drew back, shielding the light from the draughts with his hand, to undo the door of his
closed store-cupboard.

On the ground had been dumped a miserable heap of grain; from this he took out
for himself as much as a measure holds that runs to twice eight pounds. Next he went
and took up his position by his quern and on a small shelf kept fixed to the wall for such
purposes he placed his trusty lamp. Then he freed his two arms from his clothing and
girt in a shaggy goatskin he swept with its tail the stones and the inside of the quern.
Next he called on his hands to assist the work, allotting it to this side and that: the left

hand was occupied with supply, the right with the hard labour. The right hand turned the round stone and kept it in swift incessant circular motion (the grain, crushed, ran from the rapid strokes of the millstones), and from time to time the left took over from her wearied sister and changed places, now he sang some country song and with uncouth strains beguiled his labour, from time to time calling for Scybale.

She was sole caretaker, African by race, her whole appearance bearing witness to her native land, kinky of hair, swollen of lip and dark of complexion, broad-chested, with breasts hanging slackly and flat belly, thin-shanked, well-endowed with roomy feet. To her he called, ordering her to put logs on the hearth to burn up and to heat cold water on the flame. When the revolving task had reached its appointed end, with his hand he swept the meal across and poured it into a sieve and shook; the black siftings stayed on the upper surface, the unmixed flour sank down and was strained purified through the holes. Next he promptly piled it on a smooth board, poured on the now warm water, mixed and blended flour and fount, working the mixture back and forth until by the action of hand and liquid it became firm and cohesive, occasionally sprinkling the heaps with salt.

Now the kneading was done, and with his hand he smoothed the dough and spread it out into regular rounds, marking each loaf with segments impressed at equal intervals. Thence he inserted it into the hearth (Scybale having first swept clean a suitable place for it) and covered it with crocks, heaping the fire on top.

Meanwhile, as heat and hearth were performing their functions, Simulus did not idly leave the time unoccupied, but went in search of another resource for himself, and so that bread alone should not be displeasing to his palate he gathered food to add to it. He had no meatrack hung up by the hearth with a salted chine of pork or ......, but only a round cheese pierced through the middle with a string and some old dill tied up in a bunch. So the far-seeing hero contrived another resource for himself.

A kitchen-garden lay next to his hovel, which a few osiers and re-used reeds defended with their slender stems – tiny in extent but fertile and richly stocked. He lacked nothing required by a poor man's needs; on occasion a rich man would ask for more from his poor neighbour. His little estate cost him nothing but his labour: if ever rain or a holiday kept him unoccupied at home, if by any chance there was a respite from ploughing, that time was spent in the garden. He was expert in ordering the different plants, in entrusting the seeds to the unseen earth and in leading the nearby streams as required around the crops. Here there flourished cabbage, beet with its widely spreading arms, sorrel in profusion, mallows and elecampane; here there grew *siser*, the 'headed' leek so-called, and lettuce that affords relief from rich foods, ... and the radish which grows to a point and the heavy gourd which grows swelling into a wide belly.

This produce, however, was reserved not for its lord – nobody could have been narrower than he – but for the public; and every eight days he would carry his bundles on his shoulder to sell in town, returning home light of neck but heavy with money, scarcely ever escorted by purchases from the town market: it was red onions and his patch of chives that subdued his hunger, or watercress which with its sharp bite screws up the face, or endive, or rocket which recalls flagging potency.

Then too it was with some such menu in mind that he went into his garden; and first with his fingers he easily unearthed and pulled up four heads of garlic with their closely packed insides, next he plucked some delicate leaves of parsley, bushy rue, and thin trembling stalks of coriander. Having collected these, he sat down by his bright fire and loudly called to the servant for mortar and pestle. Then he undid each head of the garlic from its knotty framework, stripping off the outer skins and scattering all over the floor and discarding what he rejected; the bulb with the leaves he kept and dipped in water, then dropped into the hollowed round stone. On it he sprinkled some grains of salt, and as the salt dissolved added hard cheese, then heaped on the herbs he had gathered, and with his left hand wedged the mortar into his shaggy groin; his right hand first mashed the pungent garlic with the pestle, then pounded everything so as to mix the juices evenly.

Round and round went his hand; gradually the original ingredients lost their own properties and one colour emerged from several, not wholly green, since the milky fragments held out, nor shining milk-white, being variegated by all the herbs. Often the sharp smell went right up the man's spreading nostrils and with uptilted nose he passed judgment on his dinner; often with the back of his hand he wiped his streaming eyes and in a fury cursed the offending reek.

The work went steadily on; and no longer in jolts, as before, but more heavily the pestle travelled in slow circles. So he poured in some drops of olive oil and on top added a tiny drop of pungent vinegar, and once again mixed and thoroughly remixed the mass. Finally with two fingers he wiped round the whole mortar and brought together the parts into a single ball, so as to produce a *moretum*, perfect in appearance as in name.

Meanwhile Scybale, also active, dug out the bread, which Simulus joyfully received in his hands, and with the fear of hunger banished, and free from care for that day, he wrapped his legs in a matched pair of leggings and with skin cap on head he mustered his obedient bullocks under the thonged yoke, drove them fieldwards and plunged the ploughshare into the earth.

Moretum

Anthony Trollope   *1848*
Maura Laverty   *1946*

IRISH KITCHENS

If it seems unkind to Ireland to quote the first passage, I plead
in defence that I was born in Ireland and love it, and that
what Trollope said was brought to my attention by one of
Ireland's most famous cooks, who commented ruefully that
there was still some truth in Trollope's devastating description!
Anyway, the second item, from a writer who treats Irish food
in a manner both romantic and practical, serves as a
counterweight (for more of her, see page 76).

The difference of the English and Irish character is nowhere more plainly discerned than in their respective kitchens. With the former, this apartment is probably the cleanest, and certainly the most orderly, in the house. It is rarely intruded into by those unconnected, in some way, with its business. Everything it contains is under the vigilant eye of its chief occupant, who would imagine it quite impossible to carry on her business, whether of an humble or important nature, if her apparatus was subjected to the hands of the unauthorised. An Irish kitchen is devoted to hospitality in every sense of the word. Its doors are open to almost all loungers and idlers; and the chances are that Billy Bawn, the cripple, or Judy Molloy, the deaf old hag, are more likely to know where to find the required utensil than the cook herself. It is usually a temple dedicated to the goddess of disorder; and, too often joined with her, is the potent deity of dirt. It is not that things are out of their place, for they have no place. It isn't that the floor is not scoured, for you cannot scour dry mud into anything but wet mud. It isn't that the chairs and tables look filthy, for there are none. It isn't that the pots, and plates, and pans don't shine, for you see none to shine. All you see is a grimy, black ceiling, an uneven clay floor, a small darkened window, one or two unearthly-looking recesses, a heap of potatoes in the corner, a pile of turf against the wall, two pigs and a dog under the single dresser, three or four chickens on the window-sill, an old cock moaning on the top of a rickety press, and a crowd of ragged garments, squatting, standing, kneeling, and crouching, round the fire, from which issues a babel of strange tongues, not one word of which is at first intelligible to ears unaccustomed to such eloquence.

THE KELLYS AND THE O'KELLYS

I may claim with a certain amount of justification to be a born cook. Consider the facts. Quite literally, I was born in a kitchen. What is more, I wasn't five minutes in the world when I was responsible for a new recipe.

It seems that I made my unobtrusive entry while my mother was in the middle of cooking four fine perch which my father had just caught in the mill-pond. Possibly, she had made some miscalculation concerning the date when she would require the ministrations of Nurse Cassidy, but I have always preferred to think that the perch had something to do with the way I hurried into the kitchen, and that this was the first evidence of the passionate interest in cooking which has never left me.

About that recipe which I invented at birth. My mother had always cooked perch by baking them in the pot-oven with a dollop of fat on the chest of each fish. On that particular day, she had the fish all ready except for their scapulars of fat. It appears that the pot-oven wasn't yet hot enough, so she filled in the time by cutting slices of bacon from the flitch for the following morning's breakfast, a job which could not be entrusted to Moll Slevin, our servant girl, because the poor creature had a bad cast in her eye. She had cut the fifth slice when she became the mother of an eight-pound daughter. In the confusion that followed Moll was left to deal with the cooking. It happened that on the table were a couple of bay leaves and some milk intended for a rice pudding. Moll went out of her mind and threw into the pie-dish with the fish everything she could lay hands on – bacon, bay-leaves, milk and all. The results were so satisfactory that from then out perch was never cooked in any other way in our house. By the time it was ready, mother and child were doing nicely. Indeed, I have been told the mother was doing so nicely that she called down from the bedroom demanding her share of the fish. I hope they gave it to her, for those mill-pond perch were as good as trout, particularly when cradled head to tail in a buttered pie-dish under a quilt of fat bacon slices monogrammed with a bay leaf or two.

Having chosen the kitchen to be born in, it was only natural that from the first I should have had a love for the scene of my birth. They tell me that from the time I could crawl I persecuted them by refusing to play anywhere but in the kitchen, and that nothing but the special protection of Holy Anne, the patron saint of housewives, could explain the way I daily escaped death from scalding or burning. The natural result was that I cut my first tooth on an egg-beater, learned my A.B.C. out of Mrs. Beeton and was making real pie at an age when most children content themselves with mudpies.

Not that there was anything very remarkable in my wanting to cook. Every little girl born into this world loves to help in the kitchen. What was remarkable was the kindness of our grown-ups in putting up with me. Now that I have cookery-conscious daughters of my own, I know how exasperating it can be to have a child getting in the way when meals are being prepared, how difficult it is not to cry, 'Have you no place in the house to stand but under my two feet, and I rushed to death?' With ingredients scarce and dear, it takes all one's forbearance and patience not to deny such pleas as, 'Can't I cream the butter and sugar? You said you'd let me if I didn't read in bed,' and

'Please let me stone the raisins – I promise I won't eat them.' On such occasions, a harassed woman's only chance of remaining sane as well as generous is to look backwards and forwards – back to her own childhood and the thrill that came from being allowed to help, forward to the day when her daughter will be grown up and when cooking will be as much a duty as a pleasure. Sometimes you'll hear a mother grouse, 'She's twenty years of age and can't boil an egg – takes no interest at all in cooking. All I say is, May God help the man who gets her!' It's ten to one said daughter's early culinary efforts were frustrated by a mother who believed in keeping her kitchen to herself.

MAURA LAVERTY'S COOKERY BOOK

Blanche S. Rhett   *1976*

PRICELESS ADVICE *from* MARTHA

There are many good things in Two Hundred Years of
Charleston Cooking *by Blanche S. Rhett and others. One of
the hero figures is William, a master of shrimp soup. But it is
the words of Martha, in the extract below, which I treasure
and unsuccessfully endeavour to follow in my own activities.*

Also from William's skilled hands comes shrimp soup. William never seems to hurry; yet in addition to his elaborate cooking, and in addition to running Mrs. Rhett's elaborate house, William is the leader of a famous quartet which sings spirituals in the old-fashioned way. He has a beautiful tenor voice. Colored people like William seem to accomplish enormous amounts of work without ever being in a hurry and always with time for courtesy.

Once I talked to an old cook down there who did all the work of a large house and then went home and did her own. I said, 'Martha, how do you manage to do so much?' And she said, 'I never does more than one thing at a time. I does a thing and when it's done I goes on to the next thing.'

TWO HUNDRED YEARS OF CHARLESTON COOKING

John Thorne   *1986*

COOKING WITHOUT COOK

*For years I have been receiving an idiosyncratic newsletter
called* Simple Cooking *from John Thorne in New England.
We had tea together once, in an improbable venue, where we
were both strangers, the Harvard Faculty Club. His gaze
darted to and fro appraising with intensity all the people who
went by. I had the feeling that he viewed everything sideways,
or from some other unusual angle, not from the front. The
vision expressed in his writing about cookery is similarly
intense and disconcerting. We know what he is talking about,
but we have never seen it quite the way he sees it. There is
something of the painter in him.*

To myself I never seemed to have grown up. This circumstance strikes me
most forcibly when I go into my kitchen. I perceive saucepans, kitchen
spoons, tin canisters, chopping-boards, egg-beaters, and objects whose very
name I do not even know. I perceive these objects, and suddenly it comes
into my mind – though I can hardly believe it – that these things actually
belong to me. I can really do what I like with them if I want to. I might
positively use the largest of the saucepans for making butterscotch, or I
might fill the egg-beater with ink and churn it up. For such were the
adventurous aspirations of my childhood when I peeped into the kitchen,
which was a forbidden and glamorous place inhabited by a forbidding moral
force known as Cook. And that glamour still persists, that feeling still
remains. I do not really very often go into my kitchen, although it and all it
contains, are my property. I do not go into it because, lurking at the back of
my head, I have always the feeling that I am a little boy who will either be
'spoken to' or spanked by a mysterious They.

Ford Madox Ford, Memories and Impressions (1911)

The butcher's paper torn open, four lamb shanks spill onto the counter, pink and
meaty, musky with the smell of sheep. Absently, I heft the largest of them, fingers
adhering to the waxy fell. I bought them to stew with a mess of pearl barley and
mushrooms, but the latter were picked over and shabby, and I came home without
them. So, taking the lamb shank with me, I wander around the kitchen, poking through
the shelves for some different meal. I pick things up and put them back ... the mind
refusing to turn over, the nose not catching any scent that fires appetite.

Impatient to get things rolling, I seize the box of rice and set it firmly on the counter next to the meat. Immediately, contrarily, a bag of white beans proposes itself. All right, down it comes, too. My hand reaches for the jar of capers and seizes the anchovies instead. They join the little group on the counter, and so do a bottle of olive oil, a jar of roasted peppers, a can of tomato paste.

I turn to the herb shelf, sniff at a bag of dried mint and put it back. There's oregano and rosemary growing in the living room window, refugees from the New England winter ... maybe some snips of them, but not until there is more coherence to what are so far only random choices. I am still fumbling around, waiting for a pattern to emerge.

I set the lamb shank back on the counter with its comrades so I can root free-handed in the fridge. There's not much there ... the usual eggs, part of a bunch of carrots, wilted parsley in a jug, half a cabbage, a couple of scallions. I pull out the carrots and the parsley and go back for a chunk of lemon I noticed on a rack of the refrigerator door.

I gather up a few more odds and ends ... some onions from the onion basket, a jar of black Greek olives, a head of garlic, the remains of a bottle of cheap red wine ... then swing the kitchen chair around so I can lean over the back of it, stare at all this stuff, and think. Like a chess player pondering a tough move, occasionally I reach over and almost touch a piece, shake my head, let my arm fall back.

There's no dearth of ideas – roll the shanks in crushed herbs and braise them in wine with a handful of olives ... simmer them in chicken broth with white beans, onions, parsley ... or with carrots and rice seasoned with tomato paste and nutmeg. Yes ... well ... maybe....

The reason no bell is ringing, I begin to realize, is that my mind is just flipping through random options like a finger through a cookbook ... and there already seem to be too many options entirely. It is my appetite I need to listen to ... stop thinking and sit still for awhile, stare at all this food and feel hungry. And, sure enough, once my mind stops flinging suggestions at my hunger like a waiter flogging the chef's daily specials, things start to sort out ... all on its own, my hand reaches over and takes possession of the carrots.

Well, all right, their sweet, bright taste would go well enough with the shanks ... maybe just the two of them, simmered in nothing more than the meat's own juices, seasoned with a little minced onion and parsley. But, no, it still doesn't seem right ... push the onions back, move up the garlic. A whole head of it, broken into cloves, peeled ... and the carrots cut down to little same-sized nuggets. And no parsley, a sprig of fresh rosemary ... and some anchovies.

Anchovies. But before I get to them, I want to say something more about this struggle to get a culinary conversation going with the stuff of my kitchen. This is nothing unusual – especially when I come without recipe or idea, looking to these things for inspiration. I have to take them down, shuffle them around, ponder them, plead with them before the juices of my imagination start to flow.

Of course, it isn't their fault, and it isn't that the ideas aren't there, either. But they have a forced feeling to them, like recipes you sometimes find in cookbooks that look all right but somehow lack that refraction of desire that tells us they sprang from genuine appetite, not the need to fill the page.

No, it is a strange and awkward hesitancy, even a shyness . . . exactly what Ford Madox Ford describes as the sensation of being a child in one's kitchen, afraid of being caught or at least caught out. Touch these things and if you don't know what you're doing, Cook will suddenly appear to administer a scolding and a slap on the hand with her spoon. It isn't cooking that intimidates me, it's Cook.

She can be foiled as happened here, by dogged persistence, but the usual solution to this dilemma is to decide instead to try to curry her favor. Turning to a cookbook, acting out a recipe, is to play at being cook while really being no more than Cook's little helper. Master these recipes, is her refrain, and someday you'll earn your right to cook on your own.

There must be some merit in this thought (or how could so many be convinced by it?) but it is in essence wrong. Kitchen ownership is no more earned than adulthood – it is something at some point you simply seize hold of and claim as yours, *diplômé de Le Cordon Bleu . . . ou non.*

Which brings us back to the anchovies. The moment that desire came to mind – and desire is what it was, not an idea – my first reaction was not to embrace it but to ridicule it. What made me think anchovies would do anything for this dish? Indeed, what made me think they wouldn't ruin it, make it fishy and off-tasting – or, conversely, dissolve away during the long cooking, flavor utterly evaporated?

These are all solid objections . . . and, given that, what should one do? Go and look through all one's cookbooks for a lamb shank and anchovy recipe? Not much hope there . . . even so-called cook's encyclopedias are geared to answer questions about already existing recipes, not potential ones. It's unlikely there's a cookbook anywhere with the index entry, 'Anchovies, effect of long braising with lamb.' And the same would have been true if I had chosen balsamic vinegar instead. I had to just go and find out.

And, as it happened, the dish turned out well. Carrots and garlic nicely balanced each other. The rosemary gave some stringency to what would otherwise have been too unctuous a richness. And the anchovies, which mostly did dissolve away and whose flavor mostly did meld into the whole, still left a mysterious tang to prickle the tongue's interest. I enjoyed every bite . . . but, even so, I doubt I'm cured.

SIMPLE COOKING, *winter 1986*

Dorothy Hartley

1954

My Kitchens

When Dorothy Hartley's massive book, Food in England, *was
first published, it was a real piece of pioneering work. The vast
store of knowledge which she had accumulated and her
enthusiasm for the subject shine through its pages. It is
probably safe to say that since then no one has written
anything serious about English food traditions without
consulting her – and probably quoting her. Here is part of her
description of her own successive kitchens.
(See also pages 124 and 133.)*

My first kitchen was a stone-floored cottage in the Yorkshire dales. It had a thick rag
rug on the hearth and a ceiling rack that held thin brown oatcake. When soft and
newly made, the oatcake hung in loops, which later dried out stiff and brittle. The stone
slab where it was baked made a little separate hearth at one side of the fireplace. The
high mantelpiece had a polished gun over it, and on it two china dogs and brass
ornaments. The window, almost blocked by red geraniums in flower-pots, was set deep
in the thick stone wall; and most of the light came through an open door that gave onto
the moor. Fresh mountain air and the smell of cooking always filled this brightly
polished kitchen. I can remember a basin of mutton broth with a long-boned chop in it.
A man reached up to lift down a flap of oatcake to crumble into the broth, and I
remember the warm, safe feel of the big sheepdog I leant against. I remember too, being
carried high on the farmhand's shoulder, and feeling him drop down and rise up as he
picked white mushrooms out of the wet grass. Once a week a wagonette ran to Skipton
to take people to market.

My next kitchen was in a convent of French nuns at Skipton. It had a high ceiling
and a sense of space and peace. The wooden tables were scoured white as a bone,
scrubbed along the grain with sharp river sand and whitening. The wide range shone
like satin; the steel fender and stands were rubbed bright with emery cloth. In the
wintry sunshine brass pans and silver dishcovers glittered on the cream plaster walls. To
prevent clogs slipping the flags were lightly sanded, and the hearthstone was white as
drifted snow. At one side of the fireplace stood an iron coffee-grinder; at the other sat a
black-gowned little Sister, with white coif and blue apron, slicing vegetables, her clogs
laid beside her and her white-stockinged feet on the rolled-back hearthrug.

All morning the kitchen was alive with stir and bustle, the clatter of clogs and pails,
and the aroma of breakfast coffee. The range fire roared away like an imprisoned dragon
behind his long bars, and the meat jack clicked and clicked as steadily as the rosary of

the old Reverend Mother who slept away her last days in the warm armchair by the window. From ten o'clock to twelve the jack clicked before the fire, while on top sizzled and bubbled the pans and the big pot. Interesting noises came from scullery and pantry: the clank of the soft-water pump by the sink, the gurgle of the new boiler, the whirr of beating eggs, the clonking thump of the heavy bread pancheons, and the scurried prayers and ejaculated responses with which the kitchen Sisters timed their cooking.

The long afternoon was still. The sunlight shone through the window, the opened range smoked gently, the clock ticked loudly, a cricket chirped. The woollen rug was spread out before the hearth and a yellow cat was asleep in the middle of it with the little 'vegetable Sister' asleep at the side. At five o'clock a bell rang, and the kitchen woke up. The big kettle began to sing, the rhythmical tump-tump of the bread slicer sounded, and a yellow bowl of butter was put to warm on the fender. Sometimes the big fire front was dropped right down, and around it sat the four or five lucky girls who had drawn lottery numbers for that honour. (Other's numbers allocated prayers for the Holy Souls, weeding the grotto, or cleaning the altar candlesticks.) The toasters, armed with long wire forks, handed the brown slices back to the kitchen Sister, who at once ran them through the mangle: it was more economical to crush the crusts than to cut them off, and it allowed the butter to soak in more easily. Then the slices were arranged in a line along the hotplate, held upright between two flannel-covered bricks that looked like book-ends. Afterwards they were buttered and piled on plates on the refectory table. In each urn the tea hung in bags, with an attendant basin behind, into which the bag could be lifted after 'three Hail Marys and grace' had been said, as it was bad to drink tea that 'had stood'. (When the first missionaries brought back tea from China they reported it should stand as long as it took to say the Pater Noster slowly.) The jugs of milk were rich with cream and crystallised sugar stood in stemmed glass bowls. When tea was over the 'charge girls' carried round a bowl of soapy water and a clean tea towel. We turned round to wash our knives and spoons, dried them and replaced them in our silver goblets rolled up in our napkins. In true mediaeval exclusiveness we each kept our own table-ware as the mediaeval people kept their 'Neps'.

Nightfall in the convent kitchen was redolent of broth. The big iron pot with the screwed-on lid (called a digester) which had chuckled unmoved at the back of the stove since dinnertime, was now laid, washed and empty, on a newspaper by the hearth. 'Piggy's dinner' was steaming in a bucket on the dying fire. The little 'vegetable Sister' had gone to chapel. The voice of Thomas the gardener called through the backdoor, 'Will you be wanting anything more tonight, Mother?' before he clumped off leaving the watchdog under the table for the night. ... The yellow cat and a long-legged child are drinking milk together on the hearthrug.

My largest kitchen, masculine and enterprising, was at a boys' school. Being 'northern' the bread was homemade, rising each week in a huge tub set before the fire. Piles of Yorkshire teacakes came daily from the baker, and a new gas-stove supplemented the oven range. It was here I first realised the specialities of England, for my enterprising mother sent away to her Welsh home for small Welsh mutton, as she thought the large Yorkshire sheep very coarse. We had bilberries from the mountains in leaking purple crates. From the east coast came barrels of herrings and boxes of bloaters, and cream cakes in wooden shelved hampers from 'Buzzards of London'. Apples came from Gloucestershire, and cream, in hygienic containers that weighed a ton, from Devon. From the north came sacks of oatmeal. Oxfordshire sent crates of wonderful fruit, Moorpark apricots, and apricot hams. The beef was local: all the pressed beef and brawn moulds were learned in that kitchen and are genuine Yorkshire recipes from the dale farms. At sheep shearings huge flat baskets of beef sandwiches were carried round, each with a mustard pot tied to the handle. No one eats mutton at a sheep shearing. At cattle fairs there were rounds of beef, snowy under tufts of shaved horseradish, and big tins of Yorkshire pudding, golden crisp, with tortoiseshell markings where dripping had splashed onto them. The Craven Heifer Inn served a massive Yorkshire tea with ham, game pies, apple pies, parkin and cheese, hot teacakes, jam and honey and black treacle, and tea ...

My next kitchen was in a country rectory in the shires between Nottingham and Leicestershire. A rambling Elizabethan house with a garden and orchard, pigsties and barns; more like a small farm than a rectory. It had an apple loft with slatted shelves, and a meat larder with a pulley to lift a carcase of mutton to the ventilated roof. Strange bleached frogs swam in the underground soft-water tanks; and all the water, which was as hard as iron and corroded the kettles, had to be pumped up. The kitchen, over thirty feet long and twenty feet wide, contained a Queen Anne dresser that had twenty-four brass handles and twelve knobs to polish. There were six steps down to the larder and five up to the scullery; three steps down to the dining-room and two up from the entrance hall. Counting coal-houses and outside pumps and passages you walked about a mile per meal. We had neither gas nor electricity, and during the dark winter months there were seventeen lamps a day to be lit and trimmed, and each night a dozen flat brass candlesticks were cleaned and ranged on the oak chest for the foot of the stairs. A lovely old house with every mediaeval inconvenience ...

Today I live on the Welsh border where the mutton is good, the beef bad, and the best fruits are the wild ones. Here there are a profusion of small fine damsons, and the blackberries hang like bunches of grapes over the Dee. Welsh cookery is based on the mountain grazing farm, the Hafod; only in the valleys do you get rich food. But now a noisy chemical works has invaded our peaceful valley. Our old big house has been divided and let, and I have lived for twenty years in a workman's cottage, with a gas-stove in one room and a log fire and pot crane in the other, and cooked – as convenient – on each. It's been a happy time, for –

'Better is the life of a poor man in a cottage ... than delicate fare in another man's house; and better a dry morsel and quietness therewith, than a house full of sacrifices with strife' (Ecclesiasticus).

FOOD IN ENGLAND

Elizabeth David 1968

The EXCELLENCE *of* ELIZA ACTON

The word 'unique' is often misused. But no one, I think, will
fault me for applying it to Elizabeth David's work, and to the
beneficial results thereof for attitudes to food and cookery in
Britain and elsewhere. Searching for special jewels of her writing to set
in this anthology, and for ones which will not already be familiar to many
readers, I lit upon this passage, in which she analyses with characteristic nicety
the excellence of Eliza Acton's recipes. (See pages 114 and 232 for the
others.) Eliza Acton's Modern Cookery for Private
Families, *first published in 1845, has been summed up by*
Elizabeth David as 'the greatest cookery book in our language'.
Here she explains why. It is both pleasant and fitting to associate,
in this way, the great name of the 19th century with the
great name of the 20th.

Miss Acton knew, and by instinct and sheer intelligence rather than by experience (this was her first cookery book, she must have worked on it for the best part of seven years, and apart from a somewhat enlarged and very cheaply produced, popular edition of *Modern Cookery*, her only other cookery publication was a crusading little work about bread making) that many people who use cookery books tend to pay attention only to the broad outline of a recipe, rejecting, because they think it of no importance, just some finer point which makes the whole difference. So she set about making as sure as she could that the smaller details were rammed home. Having learned from her failures (anybody who does not care to admit them could not, or should not, write a cookery book) she uses them as warnings. Appended to her instructions for *Superior Pine-Apple Marmalade* is a paragraph explaining how, by placing the preserving pan on a trivet which raises it above direct contact with the burning coals or charcoal, to avoid turning your jam to 'a strange sort of compound, for which it is difficult to find a name, and which results from the sugar being subjected – when in combination with the acid of the fruit – to a degree of heat which converts it into caramel or highly boiled barley sugar'. Nobody could so accurately describe this unnerving occurrence if they had not actually seen it happening; and the preventative is still applicable today.

One example of the Acton technique which I have always admired is demonstrated by the simplest possible recipe for sole cooked in cream. After first preparing some very fresh middling sized sole with 'exceeding nicety' you are to simmer them for two minutes only in boiling salted water; you lift them out, drain them, and put them in a wide pan with as much sweet rich cream as will nearly cover them; the dish is seasoned with pounded mace, cayenne, and salt. You cook the fish 'softly, from six to ten minutes or until the flesh parts readily from the bones.' She directs then that you at once 'remove them to the serving dish, stir the juice of half a lemon to the sauce, pour it over the soles and send them immediately to table'. She gives an alternative flavouring for the sauce, 'some lemon rind may be boiled in the cream, if approved', and says that you can thicken it should you think necessary (Miss Acton, one fancies, did not) with a small teaspoonful of arrowroot very smoothly mixed with a little milk *before* the lemon juice is added. Now, in two lines, comes a recapitulation of the whole recipe: 'Soles, 3 or 4; boiled in water for 2 minutes. Cream, $\frac{1}{2}$ to whole pint; salt, mace, cayenne; fish stewed 6 to 10 minutes. Juice of half a lemon.'

These summings up at the end of a recipe, entirely Miss Acton's own invention and at the time quite revolutionary in English cookery writing, were subsequently copied by Mrs Beeton, who chose to place them at the head of each recipe, where they carry much less impact. What Miss Acton then does, in a final brief paragraph, is to throw out a fresh piece of information. 'In Cornwall, the fish is laid at once into thick clotted cream and stewed entirely in it' – and uses it to bring the reader back to what she considered the vital initial instruction – 'but this method gives to the sauce, which ought to be extremely delicate, a coarse fishy flavour which the previous boil in water prevents.'

Those final lines provide a clue to what makes good cookery instruction. The author's little piece of knowledge about Cornish regional recipes opens up new possibilities for us; she lets us know that she has tried variations and tested the Cornish cream recipe, she warns us that she thinks it slovenly, she prefers her own, she tells us why. If we can't be bothered with the processes she recommends, we know what to expect.

Over and over again, reading *Modern Cookery* – for twenty years the book has been my beloved companion – I have marvelled at the illuminating and decisive qualities of Miss Acton's recipes. Remark these directions for beating egg whites for a sponge cake:

> The excellence of the whole depends much on the manner in which the eggs are whisked; this should be done as lightly as possible, but it is a mistake to suppose that they cannot be too long beaten, as after they are brought to a state of perfect firmness they are injured by a continuation of the whisking and will at times curdle, and render a cake heavy from this cause.

There you have, in under one hundred words (Madame Saint-Ange, in some ways the twentieth-century French equivalent of Eliza Acton, devotes eight closely written pages to the explanation of these little facts of kitchen life) the simple explanation of a million leaden sponge cakes – and for that matter of several million failed soufflés ...

How was it then that this peerless writer came to be superseded by imitators so limited in experience, and in capacity of expression so inferior?

I think that Miss Acton's eclipse came about because, born in 1799, she was in taste and in spirit, a child of the eighteenth century. Although so masterly an innovator in style and method she was, in full mid-nineteenth century, living in the manner and writing of a style of English domestic life already doomed. Her book was the final expression, the crystallization, of pre-Industrial England's taste in food and attitude to cookery. The dishes she describes and the ingredients which went into them would have been familiar to Jane Austen and Lord Byron, to Fanny Burney and Tobias Smollett. They would have been served at the tables of great political hostesses such as Lady Melbourne, and of convivial country gentlemen like Parson Woodforde.

By 1845, when Eliza Acton's book first saw the light of day, this rural England was vanishing fast. Radical changes were about to overtake English cooking. To some of them, such as the influence exercised by Baron Liebig's chemical and nutritional theories, Miss Acton paid admiring tribute when in 1855 she revised her book. Others, less edifying, she ignored. In 1840 for example, there had been launched a commercial product called Birds Custard Powder. What we know as modern cookery, and it had little to do with Eliza Acton's version, was on its way.

THE BEST OF ELIZA ACTON

Nicholas Kurti   *1969*

The PHYSICIST *in the* KITCHEN

This was the title of Professor Kurti's address to the Royal
Institution of Great Britain on 14 March 1969. He began by
pointing out that it was almost exactly 170 years since 'the
proposals for forming the Institution, as published by Count
Rumford' had been adopted; and by recalling the Count's
high reputation as a culinary innovator. As a tribute to
Rumford, this was appropriate; as an apologia for addressing
the Institution on the subject of cooking it was unnecessary.
The audience was fascinated by the lecture and by the
demonstrations with which the Professor and his daughter
accompanied it. An excerpt is given here.

Let me now turn to another aspect of the physicist's influence on kitchen practice, namely the introduction of new tools and techniques. Physicists are usually on the lookout for equipment designed for entirely different purposes which might come in handy in their own work. How invaluable are the dentists' drill, and the dentists' fantastically shaped scrapers and files in laboratories and workshops. So why not introduce new and seemingly out of place instruments into the kitchen? I give you an example. One of the pleasantest items of traditional Christmas fare is the mince pie, especially if, just before serving, a small amount of rum or brandy is added to it. The normal procedure is to prize up the lid, as my daughter will demonstrate, then pour a little rum on to the mincemeat and replace the lid. This is not always easy, especially not if the pastry is made to perfection and just crumbles away. How much easier it is to use a well-known and cheap instrument, namely a hypodermic syringe; a deft jab at the crust, gentle pressure on the plunger, and the mince pie is infused with rum. This method of treating mince pies is also more economical. If you use the traditional method your guests will regard you as rather mean if you give them only a small teaspoonful, but approach them with a 2 millilitre hypodermic syringe filled with rum and they will shrink back with horror and cry out 'That's too much' – and yet, a small teaspoon contains more than 2 millilitres.

While on the subject of hypodermic syringes I might mention another good use to which I was led through contemplating possible scientific reasons for some of our culinary habits. Pork and ham are very often served with pineapple. Why? Is it simply because the taste of the pineapple goes well with the taste of pork? Or is there some other explanation? Everyone who has tried to make a jelly or a gelatine-based cold soufflé with fresh pineapples will have discovered to his own cost that it will not set. The reason is that fresh pineapple contains the proteolytic enzyme bromelin which, similarly to papain found in papaw leaves, splits protein molecules. Could it be that just as papaw leaves have been used as meat-tenderizers in South America so the original purpose of pineapple slices was to make tough and dry pork more tender. To test this hypothesis I took a loin of pork; injected *fresh* pineapple juice into one half of it (tinned pineapple juice is useless since the enzyme decomposes during the canning process), then roasted it and compared slices cut from the two halves. The difference was remarkable; the meat from the treated half was so tender that it could almost be spread. I've brought a similarly prepared roast loin of pork along so that the audience may judge the beneficial effects of fresh pineapple juice.

Incidentally, I should like to make it clear that the use of the hypodermic syringe as a variant or alternative to marinade is not my own invention. I saw many years ago a recipe which calls for the injection into a leg of lamb of an infusion of herbs and garlic in brandy, and the dish is suitably named 'gigot de mouton Pravaz' after the inventor of the hypodermic syringe. All this shows that a hypodermic syringe in a kitchen is not necessarily the sign of a drug addict – it could equally be that of a progressive cook.

Let us now turn to some physical processes or conditions which have so far barely been used in the kitchen. Our cooking is almost entirely based on the chemical changes that occur when heat is applied. Heat is occasionally used not so much to produce chemical changes but to remove certain ingredients, for instance to remove water from sweetened whipped egg-whites to turn them into meringues. But there are other ways of drying things, e.g. one could expose the meringue mixture to a continuous stream of dry air or simply pump away the water vapour. In the following simple demonstration of making vacuum meringues, the mixture is placed under a bell jar which can be evacuated and, as you see, the meringue greatly increases in size as the pressure drops. Now as the water evaporates the meringue cools – this is the basis of the process of freeze-drying – so gentle heating is applied by an electric heater to keep the temperature inside the meringue, as indicated by a small thermocouple thermometer, at about $50°C$ ($122°F$). It takes about 15 minutes to make a meringue in this way compared with an hour or two by the traditional method. But saving of time is not the only thing; the product is different from the standard meringue. It is much lighter, and eating it one has the uncanny sensation of biting into hard 'nothing', so quickly does it melt away in one's mouth. There are other possible applications of vacuum to food preparation in the home, and maybe before long we shall see small vacuum pumps become just as much standard kitchen equipment as are mixers or blenders.

How about the application of low temperatures as a culinary aid – not only to preserve food or make ice-cream but also to alter the composition of the ingredients. Many of you may have heard the story of how in Canada where the temperature during the winter drops to about $-40°C(=-40°F)$ they have developed a simple and cheap method for making applejack, a potent liquor similar to the Calvados of Normandy. A barrel of draught cider is left in the open round early December. As the weather gets colder, the contents of the barrel freeze gradually from the outside and since water freezes preferentially, the remaining liquid becomes enriched in alcohol, and by the time the temperature has dropped to $-40°C$, the liquid in the centre of the barrel will be a mixture containing 60 per cent alcohol or 120 proof.

I am not familiar with the Canadian liquor laws, but quite a few years ago when I thought of doing this type of experiment in Oxford, using artifically produced cold, I was under the impression that our laws only forbade the possession of stills and the production of spirits by distillation, and that, provided one did it only for one's own consumption the enrichment of alcohol by freezing was permissible. I consulted a distinguished lawyer, the late Dr. Stallybrass, Principal of Brasenose College, Oxford, and he advised me that I would be within my legal rights in doing this, but fearing that the Board of Excise might get wise to this trick, enjoined me to make forthwith a few bottles for his personal use before it was too late. I did not pursue the matter at that time and it was not until I began preparing this lecture that I looked into the question again and found that Dr. Stallybrass was alas wrong and that the relevant provisions of the Spirits Act of 1880 were amended by the Finance Act of 1921, and as a result the manufacture of spirits by any process, not only by distillation, became prohibited except by licence.

PROCEEDINGS OF THE ROYAL INSTITUTION OF GREAT BRITAIN, *42, no. 109*

Charles Pierce 1863

QUALITIES *of a* COOK

*The choice of this item was partly dictated by the mysterious
reference to Woodger, 'The late Carême of England', and
apparently the coolest-headed cook of his time. I have seen no
other reference to this paragon.*

A cook, to be perfect, should know a little of most sciences, have a taste for the fine arts, and be capable of modelling and drawing; then by daily practice he becomes familiarized with culinary chemistry, and with the medical properties of the viands at his command.

Though many say that a good dinner can be dressed without the cook possessing the foregoing knowledge, yet it is also said the artist in whom these qualifcations are combined becomes the most perfect in his art. To these qualities are to be joined those of activity, cleanliness, cool-mindedness, vigilance, firmness, and discretion.

In fine, the culinary art, as practised by the *artiste*, calls for such knowledge as is not often to be found in other professions ranking higher than his in the social scale.

Coolness should never abandon him, since during his work the accidents he may have to endure are numerous. His dinner is clearly not of the order of those works which admit of being postponed till the morrow; his assistant may, in an excess of zeal of duty, casually overturn a dish; or a servant may slip, and destroy some tasteful preparation: still, it is expected that this artist should have, at all times resources which he can immediately call into action, and so cover the failures of those about him.

It should also be well remembered that an ill-tempered man can never succeed as a master in the culinary art, since the derangement of his gastric juice destroys the peculiar excellence which should govern his palate: it leaves it vitiated and tasteless. It is remarked in England, that the best *chefs de cuisine* enjoy the best tempers; and amongst men of this quality, it must not be forgotten to name the highly-respected and much-lamented Woodger, the late Carême of England. Poor fellow! – Some say he never thoroughly recovered his spirits after the death of his greatly-esteemed master, the late Mr. Chaplin, of the Clarendon.

THE HOUSEHOLD MANAGER

Grimod de la Reynière   *1805*

PURGING *the* COOK

To put it mildly (very), Grimod de la Reynière was one who
strove for effect, in deeds (such as inviting friends to a
mourning dinner on the occasion of his death, while he was
still very much alive) as well as words. His writings can be
seen as striking an unfortunate and pretentious note at the
very start of the dread era of French 19th century gastronomic
prose (and, worse, poetry). But this passage appeals to me as
much for its implicit and guileless assumptions about values
as for the jest which it embodies.

In cookery, as in nearly all the other arts, theory is nothing if not accompanied by practice. Thus a man, well versed in the rudiments of cookery, who has learned by heart the best studies on the culinary art, will be unable to make a decent fricassee if he has never tied an apron round his waist. A blind routine, bereft of knowledge and study, will doubtless never make an artist. Similarly, theory without practice will never yield the wherewithal to produce a stew. In this respect the most incompetent of chefs can upstage a member of the French Institute.

Yet the practice of cooking is attended by so many distasteful, disagreeable and perilous procedures, that we should honour those who embrace it, and recompense them with care, consideration and glory itself, for money alone cannot suffice to reward a great chef.

We are speaking here not of the noxious vapours emitted by coal which are quick to undermine the soundest of constitutions; nor of the intense heat and brightness of the fire so pernicious to the eyes and the chest; nor indeed of the smoke, so harmful to the sight and to the freshness of the complexion etc. These are constantly recurrent dangers from which there can be little respite. A cook must live with them just as a soldier lives with bombs and bullets, the difference being that for the former every day is a day of active combat, and that this combat is virtually always without glory. For the name of the most dexterous of chefs is nearly always unknown to these who most frequent a sumptuous table.

It is for the master of the house, jealous of the pre-eminence of his table, to remedy such injustices. If he wishes his food to be prepared with style, distinction and excellence in all respects, his cook must be his best friend. He must keep a gentle watch over his health, responding to his every need as only those of high birth and refinement know how. And above all, he must have his cook purged at regular intervals.

We sense that, on hearing this word, several of our readers will recoil in horror, not seeing the connection between the delicacy of one's table and the care one takes to have cook take a regular dose of medicine. One or two words of explanation should serve to make the point.

We began this article by stating that no art, particularly the culinary art, is complete without its being put into practice. Tasting, as is well known, and continual tasting at that, is part of the practice. The index finger of a good cook must travel ceaselessly from saucepan to mouth, and only by dipping it every other minute in his stews can he tell when they are done. His palate must therefore be extremely delicate, almost virginal, responding to the slightest influence, warning him of any mistake.

However, the constant smell of the ovens, the need to drink at frequent intervals (often poor quality wine) to wet a parched throat, the smoke fumes, his humour and his bile, which are in constant flux, affecting the faculties, all contrive to vitiate a cook's taste buds. The palate becomes, as it were, encrusted; it loses the delicacy, finesse and exquisite sensitivity which had made it so responsive to the nuances of flavour. It ends up as callous and insensitive as the conscience of an old judge.

The only way of restoring to him the bloom he has lost, of helping him to recover his suppleness, strength and sensitivity is to purge the cook, however much he should resist the idea (for there are those who, deaf to the voice of glory, see no need to take medicine when they are in good health).

How is one to decide precisely when to administer the purgative and for how long? There can be no hard and fast rules on this: all depends on the work and temperament of the subject, on nature, on his cooking and on a thousand and one other elements which cannot even be mentioned here. However, as a general rule, when you sense that your cook is becoming lax, when his stews are too spicey and over seasoned, when his cooking has become a little too piquant, then you can be certain that his palate has lost its sensitivity and that it is time to call an apothecary to your assistance. Simply prepare the subject with two days of dieting and cleansing; have a purgative administered which has as its base 'Calabriar manna', senna, cassia and seidlitz salts, the dosage to be varied according to the degree of insensitivity of his palate. Allow him to rest for one day and then repeat the treatment so as to finish the purging of his humours. Two days of complete rest should follow the second course of treatment and you can then flatter yourself on having a completely new man.

This recipe for maintaining the even quality of your table is by no means a jest. It is practised in all houses where the host is jealous of the high esteem in which his hospitality is held. All great chefs subject themselves to it without complaint, which can be avoided if it is made a condition of their employment. Whoever refuses proves that he is not destined for greatness, and this indifference to fame places him squarely in the ranks of those simple artisans who will never be anything other than obscure scullions.

You who would maintain a delicate, refined and distinguished table, have your cooks purged regularly. There is no other way to achieve it.

ALMANACH DES GOURMANDS, *seconde année*

Raymond Sokolov *1984*

A Recipe Transformed:
Peach Ice Cream

*If you take a kitchen and put a cook in it, and food,
something more is still needed to produce action. This
necessary catalyst is a recipe, whether on paper or in the
cook's head.*
*This extract from a symposium paper demonstrates
vividly how much change there has been in recipe-writing
during this century. Sokolov led up to the passage I quote by
explaining that he had been studying a recent facsimile
reprint of* The Settlement Cookbook *(1903), edited by Mrs
Simon Kander; and how severely its style of recipe
presentation can be criticised from the vantage point of the
1980s.*

As so often with matters of fundamentally daily importance in human life, recent progress in the art of writing recipes has gone, so far as I know, completely unrecorded. And yet, one of the few undoubted steps forward in cooking in our time has been the evolution of a rational and clear mode of presenting directions for the preparation of a dish.

Without question, the modern cookbook is a response to great social change. People who need to cook no longer find themselves living in multigenerational households where older and experienced cooks are always available to show them what to do. New arrivals to American cities, whether refugees from other countries or from our own rural areas, have needed help in coping with unfamiliar foods, customs and kitchen equipment. *The Settlement House Cook Book* aimed to be a guide to the perplexed and uprooted. And so it was.

But looked at in the light of eight decades of subsequent culinary publishing, it is fair to say that the first edition falls far short of the standards now routinely enforced by professional cookbook editors. [Here follows a detailed criticism of the 'Settlement' recipe for Pumpkin Pie.]

The ideal cookbook would, in addition, do more than give reproducible directions. It would set a folkloric dish like pumpkin pie in its ritual context. It would talk about the American pumpkin as a special case among squashes. But more than anything else, the ideal cookbook would be written with verve and humour. I think we have only begun to explore the historical, ethnographic and literary possibilities of the cookbook form. So far, almost all the good and pioneering work has aimed at giving cooks clear directions. But so much more is possible.

As an experiment, I append two versions of a brief recipe for peach ice cream, the 'Settlement' original and my own 'ideal' revision of it.

1903 PEACH ICE CREAM

6 yolks
1 cup hot milk
1 quart cream
1¼ cups sugar
6 yellow peaches

Stir yolks and sugar together, add milk, grated peaches, and cream: freeze.

1984 PEACH ICE CREAM

6 egg yolks, lightly beaten
1¼ cups sugar
1 cup milk
6 ripe peaches, peeled and pitted
1 quart (4 cups) heavy cream

1. Whisk the egg yolks and sugar together in a bowl until the mixture turns light yellow.
2. Combine the yolk-sugar mixture with the milk in a heavy bottomed saucepan and set over medium-low heat. Whisk gently or stir with a wooden spoon until the mixture thickens. You are in fact making a custard. Thickening occurs well before boiling, at just over 160°. If you are in physical contact with the potential custard, you should be able to tell easily when thickening occurs, as you stir. Stirring helps spread heat evenly through the mixture. As the right temperature is reached, the mixture will be very hot to the touch, hotter than normal tap water.

When the custard thickens, plunge the bottom of the pan into a basin of cold water to stop cooking. Push the custard through a fine (chinois) strainer to purge any particles of scrambled yolk. This will save a custard that has started to boil. Nothing will save a custard that never thickened in the first place. Boldness is crucial the first time you try this. It is almost worth letting a custard scramble completely, once, so that you will forever know what egg yolks do across the whole possible range of cooking temperatures.

Let the strained custard cool to room temperature.

3. Meanwhile, chop the peaches very finely, by hand or in a food processor, with the metal blade. If you use the processor, do this in small batches, with short bursts of power, so as not to liquify the peaches. Or use the grating blade. The idea is to leave shreds or specks of recognisable peach flesh in the ice cream. If the peaches are too large, they will freeze solid because of the water they contain.

4. Combine the custard, cream and peaches. Pour into the canister of your ice cream freezer. If you are using the old-fashioned hand-cranked variety, follow these uncharacteristically complete instructions from the original 'Settlement' cookbook:

Scald and then chill can cover and dasher before using. Adjust can in tub, put in mixture, then the dasher and cover; adjust the crank, and pack with finely chopped ice and rock salt; this must be higher around than the mixture is inside. Use three parts of ice to one part of rock salt for freezing, and use four parts of ice and one part of salt for packing afterwards. Ice cream must be frozen slowly and steadily ... Let stand five minutes, turn again five minutes; repeat until frozen. When mixture is frozen, remove ice and salt from the top of the can, wipe top and cover; uncover and remove dasher, scrape it; beat the frozen mixture with a wooden spoon. Place the heavy paper over it, put on cover and place a cork in the hole. Do not strain off the water until the mixture is frozen. Repack the freezer, putting ice on the top, cover with carpet or newspaper, and stand in a cool place several hours.

A tightly covered tin can and a wooden pail may be substituted for an ice cream freezer, using a wooden spoon to scrape the mixture from the sides and bottom of the can as it freezes.

The ice must be finely crushed. Place in a burlap and give a few blows with the broad side of an ax or hatchet.

Yield: approximately 2 quarts.

I have eaten coconut sherbet made by hand in a wooden pail. The old woman who had laboriously scraped it together with a wooden spoon sold it proudly in Savane, the main square of Fort de France, Martinique. It was perfection, almost melting but not quite. I understood then why Tortoni, the man who invented modern ice cream, became an international celebrity and was lionised in an Offenbach operetta.

The first person I ever saw make ice cream in a mechanical freezer was my father. He went to all the trouble of cracking ice and finding rock salt in midsummer in

Michigan. And then cranked away until his arm ached. So did mine, since I helped a little. As a reward, I got to lick the dasher. For the benefit of the young, the dasher is a sort of multi-tiered paddle that is attached to the crank and circulates the ice cream in the freezer's canister. When it won't turn easily any more, you conclude you have finished the job. At this stage, the ice cream is not really frozen, but it is solid enough and what is left on the dasher after it has been scraped, is a special treat indeed, and the only taste of ice cream anyone gets until the cranked mass really has frozen hours later.

My father performed this feat in unfamiliar ground, at a friend's summer home, by the shore of the lake. Totally absorbed in the messy and sweaty task, he bumped a great toe on a rock and broke it. This did not dampen his enthusiasm for ice cream then or now.

Today, there is no need to go through all that ice-smashing and cranking and waiting. Several motorised ice cream freezers do the work for you. Some fit into the refrigerator freezer compartment. The best, and most expensive, have their own freezing units. They take up considerable space, but this is a small sacrifice for the confirmed ice cream fan.

'Cookery: Science, Lore and Books'
OXFORD SYMPOSIUM DOCUMENTS 1984/5

Karl Friedrich Freiherr von Rumohr   *1822*

GERMAN *and* FRENCH KITCHENS
CONTRASTED

Rumohr's book on gastronomy appeared several years before the publication of the more famous work (quoted almost to death, but not here) by Brillat-Savarin, but is hardly known outside Germany. A pity, since in some ways it is the better book, meatier and less pretentious. I constantly search for a volunteer to translate the whole work into English.

Perhaps I might be permitted here to include some comments on the literature of French cookery. First it should be mentioned that the Italians, the forerunners of modern thought in so many fields, also showed the way ahead in the field of cooking.

Italian cooking had already achieved a high degree of refinement as early as the sixteenth century. Perhaps even earlier, to judge from various sources, principally that of the Italian novella. The Italians had translated all their artistic taste and sense of beauty to the table, as is instanced by the banquets of the Golden Age and the heraldic arms emblazoned on aspic which all but poisoned the Pope's envoy in Siena (cf. Novelle Sinesi). The most distinguished of Pius the Fifth's chefs, Bartolo Scappi, published an excellent and instructive cookery book in 1570, which is littered with valuable insights, even if the taste of the period inclined towards mannerism. Nowadays we tend to prize only popular Italian cooking.

The aesthetic refinement of earlier Italian cookery reached the French court via the Medici princesses, together with the Italian taste in art and the rather unsuccessful aping of Italian and Spanish poetry. It quickly spread from France to Germany, as the cookery books printed in Frankfurt around 1600 shows us, and as is seen in the rules Commander von Hanau gives his guests in Simplicissimus, that peerless depiction of social mores during the Thirty Years War. Yet in the north, the barbarous tendency towards gluttony which had still not entirely yielded to a much needed moderation, militated against the development of a more refined cuisine. After all, drinking like an animal ruins the stomach; and without a healthy digestion, a sensitive palate becomes quite inconceivable.

Whatever influence Italian cooking may have had on French cuisine in days gone by, we are indebted to the French for establishing meat stock as the foundation for all recipes based on liquids and for thus making an infinite number of dishes tastier and more nutritious. Italians, both ancient and modern, made virtually no use of meat stock. Greeks and Romans had large reserves of olive oil of different quality, and this served as a standard agent for binding liquid and moist ingredients, and also led to the excessive use of hot spices as is still the case today in Southern Europe and as was noted with disapproval by Pliny the Elder. Where such fatty substances were a little bland, liquamina was added, a liquid jelly once made from seasoned pears, and soon to be made exclusively from expensive fish, as in the Orient. Jura and Juscula would appear, from the description Apicius gives us, to be meat stock, no less, and yet they were in fact a clever mixture of oil, acids, spices and plant juices.

In the north, however, instead of oil, heavy use was made of lard, butter and other animal fats. The French, who had access to good quality oil only in the extreme South, and access to butter only in the extreme North, found themselves in the position of having to make up for the lack of fats. This forced them, as so often happens in other areas of life, to make use of the delicious meat stock which was to herald in a new era in the history of cooking. It was a development which the majority of Europeans nowadays take so much for granted that the refined cuisine of the ancients, as well as its descendents in modern Spain, Italy and Greece, appears barbaric in comparison.

I have in my possession, dated 1756, the original housekeeping records of Louis the Fifteenth, from which it can be seen that the royal family of the time ate somewhat moderately. Only eight or nine courses were served. Two thirds of the meat alone was transformed into strong stock for use in the other dishes. Admittedly the use of stock on such a scale was only possible in royal kitchens. However, it does indicate with uncommon clarity what the trend in modern cooking was at the time.

With the French Revolution, the third estate and its pot au feu (an old type of family stew) was promoted to a position of honour. It was justifiably the pride of the French nation. The national palate which had been gradually weened off spicey food, became more sensitive and discerning. The new style of cooking became, no small thanks to the French, more widespread. At the same time, a love for the English, particularly in their North American incarnation, led to the adoption of the English method of roasting meat, which had been sadly lacking in French cookery. At this time, French cuisine was on its way to achieving the state of perfection I consider the ideal. Signs of the direction it was taking can be found in extracts from La Cuisiniere Bourgeoise. After a brief period of heady political frenzy, the French, with their ever spirited taste for living were forced to sharpen their minds on less important matters. They concentrated on the culinary art, on which more ingenuity and inventiveness was squandered over several decades than on other areas of French literature. The tendency of these works is towards over-refinement; therefore I advise budding masters of the art to follow them with caution.

French cooking has thus been from an early stage (and is again today) guilty of too much sophistication. Yet if one compares French cookery books with the majority of German books, one finds the latter more overloaded than their French models. This is because in every aspect of human enterprise, slavish imitation contrives to exaggerate the foibles of the original. In fact, one would be hard pressed to find in the better French books the supposed originals for many of ther German recipes which are, frankly, reminiscent of the pharmacy. In a Viennese cookery book for example I found a recipe for mushrooms, shallots, lemon peel, and basil mixed with other less piquant herbs in the same meat casserole. Anyone who hasn't permanently ruined his palate by smoking tobacco, or who is not totally bereft of imagination, will shudder at the thought of combining these subtle, pungent, sharp and cloying tastes together.

GEIST DER KOCHKUNST

The ORCHARD

The claim of fruits and nuts for primacy among human foods, on which I think both the Bible and anthropologists (or, at least, many of them) agree, is fortified by the manner in which they have been celebrated by writers, including poets. There is only one poem here, but many of the items are tinged with poetry; indeed three writers – Jane Grigson, Ian Jackson, Paul Popenoe – have chosen to quote poems in their prose.

Edward Bunyard   *1929*

On PLUMS *and* APRICOTS

Given my concept of this book (picking out the plums of
cookery writing), there has to be an item on plums. I have
chosen Edward Bunyard's survey of them, as his well-rounded
prose seems to suit these handsome fruits; and have appended
for good measure the opening paragraphs of his essay on the
apricot, in which some of his comments have a wider
application.
Bunyard was the son of an eminent Victorian nurseryman,
and carried on the family business at Maidstone. His literary
bent and his love of good food and wine were strongly
apparent; and nothing else has been written quite like The
Anatomy of Dessert, *from which these extracts come.*
Dr Joan Morgan has pointed out to me that it was in the
Bunyard catalogue of 1927 that Golden Delicious apples,
described as 'the most highly advertised fruit of modern times',
seem first to have been offered to the British public, as an
interesting American variety. If Bunyard could have foreseen
how this imperialist variety would eventually swamp the
market and suppress interesting minorities, he might have
decided to avoid association with it.

PLUMS

In no fruit, except the Cherry, do the shops treat us so scurvily: Greengages from
Southern countries, usually as hard as golf-balls, and orchard-grown specimens,
small, unripe, and stony, are the best we can find; the result is that the poor townsman
usually considers Victoria the best plum, and it is usually the best he can procure. The
choice gages are known to garden-owners only, and not all of these realise the length of
season and wealth of flavour which is at their disposal.

The distinction between a 'Gage' and a plum is only British, and arose from the
fact that a greengage, known in France as Reine Claude, was imported by a member of
the Gage family, and, owing to a lost label, was renamed in honour of its introducer.
Generally a plum with a good flavour is called a gage in this country, and our selection
will be mainly confined to this group; the Victorias and their like may well remain in the
kitchen, very welcome when cooked, but hardly up to the best standard of the dessert.

In August we may expect the season to open with Oullin's Gage, a large, round, creamy yellow fruit of merit, firm as to flesh, and fair – only fair – in flavour, except in a hot, dry summer, when it imagines itself at home in the 'Midi' climate and answers with a rich sweetness not usually given us in our average year. In dull years its destiny is the bottle, whence it comes excellently in winter months with a firm yellow transparent flesh and a faint ratafia flavour.

The early August days see the ripening of the Early Transparent Gage, that worthy descendant of the Old Transparent Gage, the King of all Plums, whose royal potency has descended in no small degree to his offspring. The Early Transparent may be quite large, but if overcropped is small and flavourless. Its great fertility has caused it to be placed rather below its merits in many hands, as no fruit more than the Plum depends on its best flavour for a judicious thinning. At its best this earliest member of its family is first-rate and has the true 'gage' consistency with the richness which this family alone provides.

In mid-August comes Denniston's Superb, an excellent fruit which we owe to America, and it now approaches its centenary and retains its merits unimpaired. An oval fruit, inclining to a certain rotundity, its yellow skin is washed with pale green stripes, as if painted on with a light water-colour wash. The transparent flesh is of an admirable texture, firm but not tough, and its flavour irreproachable. A little later we may find Golden Esperen ripening its golden fruit and blushing slightly under the sun. Here is a real sweetmeat, a *bonne bouche* for any August dinner, and a pleasing reminder of Major Esperen, one of Napoleon's generals, who devoted his latter years to the raising of fruits at Malines. His name is better remembered as the raiser of the pear, Bergamotte Esperen. Both are worthy.

With the last days of August comes the Queen of Plums, the Greengage, a variety which is quite probably a wild Caucasian species which has wandered (as so many fruits) to us through Italy. In France it is always known as Reine Claude, and the legend runs that it is thus named after the wife of François I.

Whether the Greengage of to-day is that of the sixteenth century no one can say, and as this fruit comes very nearly true from seed there are several pretenders to the throne.

The memories of the 'Old' Greengage are often a careless rapture which is hard to recapture, and there are some who think that the modern fruit is not of the Royal line. There are so many factors which influence flavour; over-cropping, exposure, soil, manure, and the age of the tree being a few; but I think that there is no doubt that we are growing the fruit of a century ago, and at its best it is so good that it is hard to imagine the supposed deterioration. In no fruit is supreme ripeness more necessary; a slight shrivelling around the stalk, a deepening of the claret dots, indicate that the moment has arrived. Alas! the wasps are not often so patient.

If we may call this the Queen of Gages – what of the King? Appropriately enough at the same season comes the incomparable Transparent Gage, often called the 'Old' to distinguish it from its worthy sons. If there is a better gage than this, I know it not, and certainly there is none more beautiful. Its French name, Reine Claude Diaphane, exactly describes its clear, transparent look; a slight flush of red and then one looks into the depths of transparent amber as one looks into an opal, uncertain how far the eye can penetrate.

The flesh is firm, short of toughness, and in it are blended all the flavours that a plum can give in generous measure. Larger than a greengage, suffering less from a sunless summer, with a more robust constitution, well may we call this the King of Gages. *Ave Imperator!*

In early September we welcome Jefferson, another emigrant from America, a President among Kings, and with the characteristic Jeffersonian tenacity. It hangs long on the tree without losing its flavour, and is apt to be a little tough in fibre, a virtue in Presidents and quite pardonable when accompanied with real merit ...

There are some interiors so delicately balanced that the Plum is to them a source of inquietude and regret, though I doubt if it is always so culpable as it is supposed.

Perhaps one reason may be the ferments which reside on the skin of every fruit as it ripens, waiting for the moment when it is their proud duty to turn the sugar within to the alcohol of man's desire. These ferments may be unwelcome intruders into that mysterious warfare of bacilli and phagocytes which rages unseen in us all. Rightly or wrongly, I fancy the peeling of plums is advisable, and pass on this valuable hint to all who fear or suffer.

APRICOTS

'Apricots', said the 'ever-famous Dr. Muffet', 'are Plums concealed beneath a Peach's coat', and of their virtues, medical and otherwise, he had much to say which was permissible in the seventeenth century but which cannot be repeated in the twentieth.

Let us pass to another epoch and to a writer who, even in his most intimate moments, always remains quotable. 'The apricot, shining in a sweet brightness of golden velvet.' Ruskin – of course you guessed.

There is a satisfying richness about a tree of apricots in fruit; the dark leathery leaves serve as an admirable background to the fruits. Here and there a fruit will be marked with a vinous flush and some darker freckles, indications of richness slowly maturing within. For the complete picture we need an old brick wall, mellowed by sun and rain to a rose tint, and we have a colour effect which the flower garden will not easily surpass, and the added charm of anticipation leading to that complete absorption of the subject which Samuel Butler thought to be love's highest expression. It is in this quiet carnal anticipation that much of the charm of fruit-growing rests – as we watch the slow process of development, the fugitive flower, its hopes and fears, the slow swelling of the fruit and the dangers it runs, until we have for the survivors an almost maternal love; and at the last – how much is our enjoyment enhanced by this accumulated weight of anticipation!

There is a universe between the meal set brusquely before you and that on which thought and careful planning have been spent.

But the perfect Apricot is not easily come by; too often we find a mealy cotton-wool texture where we looked for a translucent and melting flesh.

Too much water, lack of sun and air, are two of the faults which require correction. At its best the Apricot has a certain Eastern lusciousness, a touch of the exotic which comes strangely into our homely country. In some Persian Palace whose quiet garden hears only the tinkle of a fountain it would seem to find its right setting, fitly waiting on a golden dish for some languid Sharazade. But even in the sun-warmed Midi it is not always grown to perfection, and much of the fruit which enters this country from abroad is quite unworthy. Gathered too early, they do not even look like apricots. Pale cream is their wear, in place of the wine-stained gold that they should show. Those from Angoumois are often good, and in their native country supreme. We can, however, produce as good fruit in England, given a warm wall, thoughtful culture, and a favourable season. THE ANATOMY OF DESSERT

Paul B. Popenoe 1913

DATES

*When I lived in Tunisia I became so enthusiastic about dates
that I contemplated writing a booklet on the subject. It was
just as well that I stayed in contemplating mode, for it would
have been hard to add anything much to Popenoe's book,
which I only discovered much later. This was based on
extensive travel in the date-growing regions of the world, and
gave generous space to the uses of the date-palm and its fruit
as well as to their cultivation.*

As a general rule the Arab eats his dates raw, out of hand, just as the American does. In this way he can dispose of astonishing quantities day after day: – the explorer Nachtigal tells of natives who often ate six pounds between sunrise and sunset, in Tripolitania, and thousands of Arabs, whose principal food during half the year is dates, consume several pounds a day regularly throughout their lives, and are among the healthiest and most vigorous members of the human race. It will usually be found, when a traveler reports Arabs suffering from too many dates, that their troubles are due solely to the fact that they eat the fruit when it is half ripe, in which case it tastes something like a green persimmon. It is not dates, but tannin and free organic acids that are to blame in these rare instances.

51

Nevertheless, it is natural that the Arab should seek to vary this diet in such a way as to make it less monotonous, and to add to it the protein element which the date lacks. In the Sahara, ever since the middle ages, there has been in some regions a superstitious idea that the meat of dogs was the ideal accompaniment to a diet of dates, and dogs are even today fattened for food purposes in parts of Morocco and Tunis and in the Zíbán of Algeria. Such a habit could hardly have originated, or persisted, among a more purely Arab race, for the dog is to the orthodox Muslim an unclean animal, and Muhammadan geographers notice this habit with unconcealed scorn. Even today the gamins of Biskra take all the conceit out of a pompous visitor from the Záb by a piece of doggerel which they shout at him in the street, taunting him with the loathsome nature of his diet.

On the authority of Muhammad, cucumbers are also considered a particularly good accompaniment for dates. The prophet is quoted in the Traditions as saying, 'the cold of the one counterbalances the heat of the other and the heat of the one diminishes the cold of the other,' a piece of absurdity typical of popular Arab medical lore. As a matter of fact, the only advantage cucumbers might have would be to dilute the sugar in the dates, which water would do just as well. Probably the universal habit of drinking milk with dates is principally due to this same need – anyone who eats a lot of sugar will realize that nature calls for a drink. Milk has also the advantage of adding a little fat and protein to the dates and making a well-balanced diet; accordingly it will be found that most of the Arab methods of using the fruit are based on this principle.

The simplest way, and one of the most popular in the Sahara, is to split the fruit, remove the seed, and then fill the cavity with a chunk of butter; this is usually done at the table as they are eaten. Of course the butter for this purpose must be unsalted. This manner of eating the date has been popular throughout the Arabic world for centuries, so that it has even been recognized by the poets; a well-known stanza contains the lines:

'I placed some butter upon a date,
And both the food and the condiment
were rendered delicious.'

At Baghdád and in other regions where buffalo cream is available, it is allowed to clot thickly, and used as a substitute for butter.

The names of dishes made in this manner are numerous, and not worth repeating here, but one of them is too famous in literature to be ignored – it is called khabís, and its invention is ascribed to the time of Muhammad. His friend 'Uthman b. Affar is named as the inventor; it appears to have consisted of dates, butter, and honey, and the merit claimed for it is that inferior dates taste as good as the choicest when prepared with these accompaniments. When the amateur chef had concocted this dish he carried it to Muhammad, who sampled it and, lifting up his hands, cried, 'O God, set aside thy best favors and accord them to 'Uthman!' The word khabís has accordingly taken on the figurative meaning of 'complete happiness.'

DATE GROWING

Alfred Wallace   1869
F. N. Howes   1948

DURIAN *and* BRAZIL NUT

An odd pair? Yes, but they have this in common, that you
have to be careful they don't drop on your head. A falling
apple could give one a mild bonk, but a falling durian or
shellful of Brazil nuts would be quite a different matter.
Alfred Wallace was a travel writer, but he kept his eyes open
and his pen ready for interesting food items.
Howes was the author of a compact and readable volume
on nuts, still the handiest one to consult on the subject.

The old traveller Linschott, writing in 1599, says:– 'It is of such an excellent taste that it surpasses in flavour all the other fruits of the world, according to those who have tasted it.' And Doctor Paludanus adds:– 'This fruit is of a hot and humid nature. To those not used to it, it seems at first to smell like rotten onions, but immediately they have tasted it they prefer it to all other food. The natives give it honourable titles, exalt it, and make verses on it.' When brought into a house the smell is often so offensive that some persons can never bear to taste it. This was my own case when I first tried it in Malacca, but in Borneo I found a ripe fruit on the ground, and, eating it out of doors, I at once became a confirmed Durian eater.

The Durian grows on a large and lofty forest tree, somewhat resembling an elm in its general character, but with a more smooth and scaly bark. The fruit is round or slightly oval, about the size of a large cocoanut, of a green colour, and covered all over with short stout spines, the bases of which touch each other, and are consequently somewhat hexagonal, while the points are very strong and sharp. It is so completely armed, that if the stalk is broken off it is a difficult matter to lift one from the ground. The outer rind is so thick and tough, that from whatever height it may fall it is never broken. From the base to the apex five very faint lines may be traced, over which the spines arch a little; these are the sutures of the carpels, and show where the fruit may be divided with a heavy knife and a strong hand. The five cells are satiny white within, and are each filled with an oval mass of cream-coloured pulp, imbedded in which are two or three seeds about the size of chestnuts. This pulp is the eatable part, and its consistence and flavour are indescribable. A rich butter-like custard highly flavoured with almonds gives the best general idea of it, but intermingled with it comes wafts of flavour that called to mind cream-cheese, onion sauce, brown sherry, and other incongruities. Then there is a rich glutinous smoothness in the pulp which nothing else possesses, but which adds to its delicacy. It is neither acid, nor sweet, nor juicy, yet one feels the want of none of these qualities, for it is perfect as it is. It produces no nausea or other bad effect, and the more you eat of it the less you feel inclined to stop. In fact to eat Durians is a new sensation, worth a voyage to the East to experience.

When the fruit is ripe it falls of itself, and the only way to eat Durians in perfection is to get them as they fall; and the smell is then less overpowering. When unripe, it makes a very good vegetable if cooked, and it is also eaten by the Dyaks raw. In a good fruit season large quantities are preserved salted, in jars and bamboos, and kept the year round, when it acquires a most disgusting odour to Europeans, but the Dyaks appreciate it highly as a relish with their rice. There are in the forest two varieties of wild Durians with much smaller fruits, one of them orange-coloured inside; and these are probably the origin of the large and fine Durians, which are never found wild. It would not, perhaps, be correct to say that the Durian is the best of all fruits, because it cannot supply the place of the subacid juicy kinds, such as the orange, grape, mango, and mangosteen, whose refreshing and cooling qualtities are so wholesome and grateful; but as producing a food of the most exquisite flavour it is unsurpassed. If I had to fix on two only, as representing the perfection of the two classes, I should certainly choose the Durian and the Orange as the king and queen of fruits.

The Durian is, however, sometimes dangerous. When the fruit begins to ripen it falls daily and almost hourly, and accidents not unfrequently happen to persons walking or working under the trees. When a Durian strikes a man in its fall, it produces a dreadful wound, the strong spines tearing open the flesh, while the blow itself is very heavy; but from this very circumstance death rarely ensues, the copious effusion of blood preventing the inflammation which might otherwise take place. A Dyak chief informed me that he had been struck down by a Durian falling on his head, which he thought would certainly have caused his death, yet he recovered in a very short time.

Poets and moralists, judging from our English trees and fruits, have thought that small fruits always grew on lofty trees, so that their fall should be harmless to man, while the large ones trailed on the ground. Two of the largest and heaviest fruits known, however, the Brazil-nut fruit (Bertholletia) and Durian, grow on lofty forest trees, from which they fall as soon as they are ripe, and often wound or kill the native inhabitants. From this we may learn two things: first, not to draw general conclusions from a very partial view of nature; and secondly, that trees and fruits, no less than the varied productions of the animal kingdom, do not appear to be organized with exclusive reference to the use and convenience of man.

THE MALAY ARCHIPELAGO

The tree yielding the Brazil nut is one of the largest in the Amazon forests, reaching a height of 100–150 feet and a trunk diameter of 3–6 feet, branched only in the upper part as a rule. The nuts are borne in a large spherical fruit or container up to 6 inches in diameter, in appearance not unlike a large coconut, with a hard woody outer casing about half an inch in thickness. From a dozen to two dozen nuts or seeds are developed in each 'container'. They are closely packed together with the thin edge inwards, in more or less the same way as the sections of an orange. When the fruits ripen they fall or rather crash to the ground where they are gathered by the native collectors and the nuts extracted. The collection of these fruits is not without risk to those engaged in the work and often serious or fatal accidents occur, for it has to be remembered these hard woody fruits weighing from 3 to 4 pounds and falling from a height of a hundred feet or more strike the ground with considerable force. If one should happen to strike the head of a collector the dire consequences can well be imagined. For this reason it is usual for the collectors not to venture forth under the nut trees in windy weather. There is also less danger from falling fruits in the morning than after midday. When the ground is soft or muddy it is not unusual for the fruits to become completely buried on striking the ground and lost to the gatherer, the impact being so great.

It is usual for collectors to work in parties of three to six. Temporary shelters with roofs of steeply pitched palm leaves are erected in the collecting areas. These provide shelter for the workers and serve to store the nuts until they are removed to the nearest depot. After carrying the fruits in from the forest in baskets the nuts are extracted. When the wind is so strong as to render it dangerous to be under the trees the time is often spent in this work of extracting the nuts. This is accomplished by breaking the woody shell of the fruit with a machete or small axe. To an ordinary person this would not be an easy task but the experienced collector or 'castanheiro' accomplishes it with three or four blows deftly applied at points near the extremity of the shell which is its weakest part. The nuts are then washed in order to give them a cleaner or more attractive appearance. Nuts

Gavin Brown   *1949*

GOOSEBERRY COMPETITIONS

A uniquely English institution, these began in the 18th century, reached their zenith in the 19th, and survive on a much reduced scale in the 20th. Reading the essay from which this extract comes was part of my preparation for attending the one at Egton Bridge, Yorkshire, a few years ago.

The gooseberry was not cultivated to any extent in this country until the time of the Reformation, and for many years was not considered to be worthy of much attention. Thomas Hitt, writing in 1757, describes it thus: 'The gooseberry is a dwarf fruit tree, but of the meaner sort. I suppose there are many people who will think it not worth the expense to make any alteration in the soil for so common a sort of fruit.'

This was the attitude in the gardens of the large private estates, but, in the second half of the eighteenth century, with the advent and subsequent development of the cottage garden, considerable interest was taken in the cultivation of the gooseberry. This was particularly so in Lancashire, Cheshire, and the Midlands, where the moist climate seems to have suited the gooseberry, for there it was grown better than anywhere in the world. About this time cottage gardeners were starting to take an interest in growing flowers and fruit for exhibition and in breeding new varieties for this purpose. The gooseberry, with it variation in colour and shape, was a plant which until then had not been greatly improved from the wild kinds and was therefore ideal material for breeding and selection. Great enthusiasm sprang up for the growing of gooseberries for exhibition, large-fruited gooseberries, and the larger the better. Hundreds of new varieties were raised and Gooseberry Clubs were instituted to hold annual shows where the largest fruits were awarded prizes. No attention was paid to flavour or cropping; it was only the size of individual fruits that was considered of importance . . .

The majority of the gooseberry growers were handloom weavers, a class who earned a great reputation, not only in raising gooseberries, but in producing many new kinds of the so-called florists' flowers and many new varieties of potatoes. They were extremely enthusiastic and no amount of labour or sacrifice to personal comfort seems to have been too great in their efforts to produce a fruit capable of the premier award at the local show.

The methods of cultivation used to produce these exhibition fruits were really extraordinary and elaborate, and, although the general methods of cultivation are known, most growers had their own special practices to which they attributed their success, and which were kept as closely guarded secrets from their fellow competitors . . .

The first anxious period for the gooseberry-grower was when his plants were in flower, for then they had to be protected from possible frost damage, and the bushes had to be covered nightly with mats. If there was any likelihood of damage by wind the sides of the framework were also covered in. Only three or four of the best fruits were allowed to remain on each bush and most of the young growth was pinched off during the summer to throw all the energy into the developing fruits. Many unusual methods were used to try to increase the size of the fruits, and one, known as 'suckling', was to have saucers of water under the pendant fruits so that the calyx of the fruit just dipped into the water. Another way was to encourage a lush growth of chickweed under the bushes to create a cool, moist atmosphere round the berries. The most anxious time of the year for the grower was when the fruits were reaching maturity, and most dreaded was heavy and continuous rain which would cause the fruits to burst. Small portable tents were kept in readiness to be placed over the bushes at the first sign of rain. One Middleton silk weaver seems to have been less well prepared, for it is said that one night a thunder-storm impending, he lay awake, and with the first spatter of rain on his window he rushed from his bed to protect his precious berries with his quilt.

The culmination of the grower's efforts was, of course, the annual show, which was usually held in the clubroom of the local inn, and in the 1845 Gooseberry Grower's Register no less than 171 shows are reported. These were not shows as we know them to-day, where all the exhibits are open for inspection, for the fruits were kept hidden in boxes or baskets and were taken out only at the time of weighing. An excellent description of the proceedings at one of these shows is given in the *Midland Florist* 1854:

'By a very wise arrangement the gooseberry growers are left to settle among themselves which of the berries are entitled to the prizes. This is done by weighing them against each other in a very delicate pair of scales. The refreshment tent was used for accommodation of the weighers and during the operation of weighing it certainly presented a picturesque and striking appearance. The gooseberry men sat or stood round a large table. One, a grave and sober-looking individual held a pair of apothecary's scales in his hand, into which the gooseberries were put and carefully balanced. Every man had a small box or basket containing his fruit, which was carefully enveloped in moss or paper. The countenances of the group were expressive of deep earnestness and anxiety. Each man kept his box or basket close to himself and when he opened it to get out a gooseberry he did so with extreme care, lest the extent of his treasure might be seen. One would take out a monster berry, and holding it tenderly by the stalk, would place it on one of the scales, and watch as it lay there lest it should come to harm. Then another would fumble in his receptacle for a minute and bring out a berry and with the same care place it on the opposite scale. It would perhaps be too light for its opponent, then another search followed and another berry was produced. "No go," the weigher would say solemnly. Somebody else would produce another berry. "Try him." Perhaps the new one would outweigh the former and then the anxiety of the group of weighers would deepen whilst researches were made for the largest in the baskets. Thus the respective merits of Thumper and Whack'em, and Tallyho, and Turn'em out and other Brobdignarian Gooseberries were ascertained. The tent was rather dark and the light being admitted by a small aperture only, the faces of the weighers were marked with intense light and shade, such as we see in the picture of Rembrandt. A painter skilful enough to transfer the group to canvas would have immortalised himself by doing so.'

Fruits which were entered and weighed were topped and tailed to disqualify them from further competition, but, as will be seen a competitor might not have to produce his heaviest fruits if he managed to win a prize with a lighter one. These fruits could then be taken to another show. Probably the greatest and certainly the most famous gooseberry club was the one at Harborne, where at one show some 450 berries were weighed and 95 prizes awarded, the whole proceedings lasting about four hours.

Although many money prizes were awarded at these shows the most usual trophies to be won were either copper kettles or brass pans. A story is recounted in the November 1850 issue of the *Florist* of a clergyman who, on entering the cottage of a spinner, was surprised to see a number of bright copper kettles hanging in a row. He expressed his astonishment and begged to be informed whether the spinner was dealing in copper kettles as a sideline to his trade, as he could have no possible use for so many vessels of a similar character. With considerable pride the clergyman was informed that these were prizes won at the local gooseberry shows.

THE FRUIT YEAR BOOK 1949

Jane Grigson   *1982*

FIGS

In her introduction to her fruit book, Jane Grigson commented
that her feelings about fruit had made this book more fun to
write than any of her others. This is apparent to the reader too.
As a reviewer wrote at the time, the work deserves (in
Michelin language) four stars and six place settings. (See
also pages 104 and 294.)

Every time I am in London and pass, or visit, the National Gallery and see the fig trees so nicely growing against its walls, I feel a resentment at our climate and our greengrocery trade. Not to live in a country where figs grow or can readily be bought in the season, seems to me a deprivation. Although I could not quite say that figs are my favourite fruit, they are the fruit I most long for, that I have never had enough of. Times I have eaten them remain clear. One year we happened still to be at Trôo when a friend had a basketful from a neighbour's tree, and he gave us a dozen of them. The other fig tree in the village should do well, growing against the heat of the rock: but it also grows by one of the steep public paths down to the river and the children pick the tiny fruit as they go to school.

The fig tree is one of those mythical ideas that one grows up with in the north. I heard about it first at school in County Durham – 'When her branch is yet tender and putteth forth leaves, ye know that summer is nigh' – because it was the first tree mentioned in the Bible. Adam and Eve pulled fig leaves to make skirts and hide their nakedness. That kind of role has clung to it, with patrons of art worrying about male nudity. All right for them of course, but bad for the public – you and me – and shocking for the ladies. This has always puzzled me. We give birth and clean up the messes of infancy and illness: are we not strong enough to look at marble nudity? Were we not strong enough in those even messier days? Apparently not, fig leaves were slapped on, round the galleries of the world, with elegant curves and exaggerations of size.

With that Genesis story, the fig acquired an aura of lovemaking, as a direct symbol of female sexuality. This I came to understand in a most embarrassing way. We were having lunch one day at a *pensione* in Florence – I was a student learning Italian. A basket of fruit was handed round, and there were figs in it. I had never tasted them, but knew the word for fig tree, *fico*. I also knew that, in general, fruits were the feminine form of the tree name, *melo* apple tree, *mela* apple. '*Una fica, per favore.*' The dining-room shook with laughter. A kind neighbour said, 'Cut open the fig, and you will see why they stick to the masculine.' Well, yes. There inside is the brilliant deep mass of flowers, which later, in dried figs of certain varieties, has turned to seeds; there's a secrecy and flare of red warmth inside the discreet skin, as in Gide's poem:

> Now sing of the fig, Simiane,
> Because its loves are hidden.
>
> I sing the fig, said she,
> Whose beautiful loves are hidden,
> Its flowering is folded away
> Closed room where marriages are made:
> No perfume tells the tale outside.

The fig, with the olive tree, the vine and wheat, provided the four basic foods of Mediterranean eating until modern times. The uninterrupted enjoyment of them was every man's desire and dream. With them, he could live. All the tales and myths around these four foods reflect their central place.

In view of the deep Greek and Roman appreciation of figs, I was surprised to learn that the tree was not a native either of Italy or Greece but that it was most likely domesticated in Asia Minor. The best figs came from there in Roman times, and Smyrna figs have a reputation still. One night in France, the door banged open and an unrecognizable bearded young man fell across the threshold under the weight of his pack and the rain. As he asked for our daughter and at the same time brought a heavy necklace of dried figs out of the pack behind his head, we knew who it was. He had been in Turkey. They were Smyrna figs, bought outside Izmir, the right place, five days before, from the man who had grown and dried them.

Smyrna figs have travelled farther than that. Cuttings arrived in California in 1880, and the resulting fig, ambered and succulent, is known as the Calimyrna. The famous purple-black Mission Fig was taken there in the eighteenth century by Franciscan friars from Mexico where they had been given it by Spanish missionaries. A fig we all know from cans is the Kadota, a little translucent green fig in too-sweet golden syrup. I wish they produced it without added sugar, as they do so many different fruits these days. The name is difficult to understand – could it come from its plump resemblance to a Greek pot known as a *kados*?

My feeling towards dried figs is ambivalent – they remind me of the syrup of figs I once spat out on the nursery carpet and all over a blue dressing-gown. It must be the smell. Yet when I do have to eat one, whether dry or reconstituted, it always surprises and delights me. One member of the family eats a dried fig every night before he goes to bed. That is a ritual I have come to admire, since tackling dried figs for this book.

How *to* Choose *and* Prepare Figs

Most figs are thin-skinned and need no special preparation, unless it is just to rinse them and remove the stalk. Choose unbruised fruit, lifting each one out of the nice little paper they are often wrapped in. A good way of showing them off, is to arrange them on fig or vine leaves on a white dish with a low pedestal. Leave them in the sun for a while before serving them; warm figs are the best of all.

As far as the sweet course goes, avoid presenting them in ways which blur their shape, or which mean you have to chop them up. Shape is a good part of the fig's delight: any cooking should be gentle enough to maintain it undamaged. It should not be lost in a fruit salad but presented on its own.

The fig's allies, for sweet dishes, are nuts (excluding peanuts), candied peel or citrus fruits, fortified wines and orange liqueurs, cream and coconut cream. Caramelized figs – lightly caramelized – are lovely, or figs served with *crème brulée*, or figs scattered with praline.

I do not think it matters whether figs are black or white – or purple or brown or greenish or green-gold. Figs vary from region to region in taste, though they may look much the same.

Dried figs can be soaked in boiling water or steamed – the latter is particularly successful if you want to fatten them back into shape and stuff them with nuts.

Ham *with* Figs

In Assisi – very hot – on 9 July 1874, Ruskin wrote, 'Catherine brought me up as a great treat yesterday at dinner, ham dressed with as much garlic as could be stewed into it, and a plate of raw figs, telling me I was to eat them together!'

The usual hors d'oeuvre in Italy these days is figs with Parma ham – *prosciutto crudo di Parma* – which has been cured but not stewed. When figs are not around, melon is served instead. To me, it is the perfect summer lunch, beauty and freshness, sweetness and a salty bite.

JANE GRIGSON'S FRUIT BOOK

Richard Bradley 1732

The FIRST PINEAPPLE RECIPE

*Richard Bradley, the first Professor of Botany at Cambridge
University, left behind him scores of botanical works and two
cookery books. Here, from the second of these, is something
which points up his happy combination of interests: the first
pineapple recipe in English. I do not reproduce it as a mere
curiosity; it produces excellent results.*

*The pineapple first reached England in the 17th century,
but it was not until 1719 that one was induced to bear fruit,
by Sir Matthew Decker's gardener at Richmond in Surrey.
For more of Bradley, one of my favourite authors, see
page 186.*

To MAKE *a* TART *of the* ANANAS, *or* PINE-APPLE *from* BARBADOES

Take a Pine-Apple, and twift off its Crown: then pare it free from the Knots, and cut it in Slices about half an Inch thick; then ftew it with a little Canary Wine, or Madera Wine, and fome Sugar, till it is thoroughly hot, and it will diftribute its Flavour to the Wine much better than any thing we can add to it. When it is as one would have it, take it from the Fire; and when it is cool, put it into a fweet Pafte, with its Liquor, and bake it gently, a little while, and when it comes from the Oven, pour Cream over it, (if you have it) and ferve it either hot or cold.

MARMALADE *of* PINE-APPLES, *or* ANANAS

When you have fmall Pine-Apples in Fruit, which are not noble enough to be brought to the Table, twift off their Crowns, and pare them; then flice them, and put them into a Syrup of Water, Sugar, and Pippins; and boil them with half their quantity of Sugar added to them, with a little White Wine, breaking them with a Spoon, as they boil, till they come to a Mafh, or are a little tender. Then take them from the Fire, and put the Marmalade into Glaffes to keep, and cover every Glafs with white Paper, preferving them in a dry Place.

THE COUNTRY HOUSEWIFE AND LADY'S DIRECTOR, *Pt II*

John McPhee   1967

ORANGES

The New Yorker *magazine often commissions a really good*
writer to produce a full, not superficial, study of something –
a piece so long that it has to be run in instalments and can
then be turned into a book. So with John McPhee and
Oranges; *by far the best book on the subject and one which, in*
typical New Yorker style, weaves into a single pattern
information about the tree, its fruit, the growers, the processors
and the market. The whole is so coherent that is almost seems
a shame to pluck out two passages and present them by
themselves.

The color of an orange has no absolute correlation with the maturity of the flesh and juice inside. An orange can be as sweet and ripe as it will ever be and still glisten like an emerald in the tree. Cold – coolness, rather – is what makes an orange orange. In some parts of the world, the weather never gets cold enough to change the color; in Thailand, for example, an orange is a green fruit, and traveling Thais often blink with wonder at the sight of oranges the color of flame. The ideal nighttime temperature in an orange grove is forty degrees. Some of the most beautiful oranges in the world are grown in Bermuda, where the temperature, night after night, falls consistently to that level. Andrew Marvell's poem wherein the 'remote Bermudas ride in the ocean's bosom unespied' was written in the sixteen-fifties, and contains a description, from hearsay, of Bermuda's remarkable oranges, set against their dark foliage like 'golden lamps in a green night.' Cool air comes down every night into the San Joaquin Valley in California, which is formed by the Coast Range to the west and the Sierra Nevadas to the east. The tops of the Sierras are usually covered with snow, and before dawn the temperature in the valley edges down to the frost point. In such cosmetic surroundings, it is no wonder that growers have heavily implanted the San Joaquin Valley with the Washington Navel Orange, which is the most beautiful orange grown in any quantity in the United States, and is certainly as attractive to the eye as any orange grown in the world. Its color will go to a deep, flaring cadmium orange, and its surface has a suggestion of coarseness, which complements its perfect ellipsoid shape.

*   *   *

The oranges in the Indian River packinghouse I visited had been gassed and were being washed in warm soapy water, brushed with palmetto-fiber brushes, and dried by foam-rubber squeegees and jets of hot air. Brushed again with nylon bristles to bring out their natural shine, they were coated with Johnson's Wax until they glistened like cats' eyes. The wax, which is edible, replaces a natural wax that is lost when the oranges are cleaned. Apples, cherries, and the rest of the pip and stone fruits look much the same when they enter a packinghouse as when they leave, but when oranges arrive they are covered with various things, from sooty mold to dust smeared by heavy dews. They have to be washed, but without their surface wax they would breathe very rapidly and begin to shrivel within hours. The natural wax therefore has to be replaced. Packers replace it and then some – but if they apply too much wax, the orange will suffocate and its flavor will become, at best, insipid.

Oranges are graded after they are waxed. Eight ladies stood beside a conveyor of rolling oranges, taking out the ones whose skins were blemished by things like wind scars, oil blotches from petroleum sprays, hail damage, and excessive russeting on the blossom end. The oranges they eliminated would go to concentrate plants. Eliminations, as they are called, are something quite different from culls – split or rotting oranges that are taken out before the beautifying process begins. The ladies who do the grading wear gloves, because a light pass of a fingernail over the surface of an orange can rupture oil cells, causing peel oil to well out onto the surface and not only discolor the orange but also nurture fungi that destroy it.

Oranges do not bruise one another the way apples sometimes do, and an orange, in fact, can absorb a blow that would finish an apple. Oranges can actually be bounced like rubber balls without damage, except that when they are dropped more than a foot they will start to breathe too rapidly. Truck drivers who bring them into the packinghouses from the groves wade along through rivers of oranges while they are emptying their trucks, taking care to slide their feet along the bottoms of the chutes, like trout fishermen moving upstream. Government inspectors, who work every day all day in packinghouses and concentrate plants, squeeze a standard boxful – an average of about two hundred oranges – from each truckload, and they order the entire lot destroyed if the sample is not about ten per cent sugar and does not amount to at least four and a half gallons of juice.

Oranges that happen to be going to New York cross the Hudson River on barges and enter the city at Pier 28 at the western end of Canal Street. All fresh fruit of any kind that is shipped to New York City for auction is sold at Pier 28. The pier's interior is like the inside of an aircraft hangar, and fruits from everywhere are stacked in lots in long, close rows – oranges and grapefruit from the Ridge, California oranges, apples, avocados, pears, plums, cherries, lemons, grapes, pomegranates, and so on. Over at one side, separated by a wide area from all the other crates and boxes, is the fruit of the Indian River. A man from the Indian River is always there to look after it, and he has no counterpart elsewhere on the pier. Buyers walk around making notes, then they go upstairs into a room that could have been built as the auditorium of a nineteenth-century high school. The walls are made of tongue-and-groove boards and the wooden seats are set on frameworks of cast iron, which are bolted to the floor. The room seems to contain about ninety men and ninety lighted cigars. In London in the eighteenth century, oranges were auctioned 'by the candle.' A pin was pushed through a candle not far from the top, and when the candle was lighted, the bidding began. When the pin dropped, the most recent bidder got the oranges. In New York in the present era, oranges appear to be auctioned by cigar. The air in the auction room gets so heavy with smoke that if anything as light as a pin were to drop, it would probably stop falling before it reached the floor. The auctioneer sits on a stage, usually alone. The man from Indian River sits next to him when he auctions the fruit of the Indian River.

ORANGES

Christopher Driver 1985

PRUFROCK'S PEACH

*Christopher Driver's books and articles on food are well
known, especially to readers of the* Guardian. *His poetry has
attracted less attention, but it is from a private press edition of*
Twelve Poems *that I have chosen a piece to represent him. It
exemplifies his skill as wordsmith and his propensity to come
up at something from an unexpected angle.*

J. ALFRED'S APPETITE

Prufrock, as he takes a peach,
Fingers the bloomy fuzz, and peels.
When fruit is ripe, the skin is trash:
He needs a knife throughout his meals.

Banqueting tycoons demand
Unnatural skin, an apricot glaze;
So women, sticky-fingered, spend
At kitchen heat their working days.

The cafe gleams in white and gold
Where couples order scone and butter.
Haste has brought your cheek to bloom,
And envious looks like waiters glide
About the surface of the room.
But can a glance or clicking shutter
Pierce beneath the bloom to bone –
Or crimson, corrugated stone?

TWELVE POEMS

Ian Jackson   *20th century*

PECULIAR QUALITIES *of* PEARS

*It is odd that, so far as I can find out, there has been no book
on the history of pears. Ian Jackson's work, when published,
will handsomely remedy this gap. The extracts printed here
deal successively with the longevity of the pear tree, its
appearance, and the scent of pears.*

Pears are not so ornamental as other fruit trees in blossom; their flowers are smaller than those of the apple and less fragrant, indeed at times unpleasantly sweet or foetid. Pear trees in spring often look as though thunderclouds had become lodged in their branches: Samuel Palmer, preoccupied with the fullness of things, made flowering pears the theme of several of his paintings. His case, however, was exceptional, for the beauty of flowering fruit trees appears to have touched seventeenth-century gardeners far more than those of the nineteenth, who were apt instead to remark on their appearance in fruit. The pear was understandably a favorite, for when ripe, as the Manchester botanist Leopold Grindon (1818–1904) observed, 'the clusters are prone to hang in a peculiar mantling way, very beautiful, the pear being one of the trees which always give an impression of easy grace of carriage as well as of opulence'. Although the fruit did not stand out against the leaves as sharply as the apple, there were a few pears, the Beurré Clairgeau, 'one of the most gorgeous of fruits, coloring with a peculiar gold bronze tint, shading into a brilliant red blush', and the Frederic of Wirtenberg, 'the most beautiful object that has been colored by the pencil of nature – it hangs upon the tree like a drop of gold and crimson, its tints deepening day after day' – which led pomologists to quote Herrick's golden lamps in a green night along with the usual verses from John Philips' *Cyder* (praised by Philip Miller for its descriptions of apples).

Perhaps the earliest praise of the pear for the decorative aspects of its autumn coloring appears in Thomas James' *The Poetry of Gardening*, an essay first published in *The Carthusian* (1839), a miscellany by the alumni of Charterhouse. His opinion that 'the rich mulberry color of the foliage of the pear-tree in September is by far the finest of autumnal tints' shows him to have been an incidental, albeit discerning, amateur of fruit, for the coloring of the pear in fact ranges from the pale yellow of Joséphine de Malines and Bergamotte d'Espéren, the dirty mustard of Clapp's Favorite and bright orange of Nouvelle Fulvie, to the rich crimson of the Bartlett and Beurré Bosc, the ruddy brown of the Seckel, the chocolate leaves of Charles Ernest and the black of the Chaumontel. Pear leaves in their autumn coloring were recommended along with the crimson leaves of certain grapevines as suitable ornaments for a dish of fruit at dessert in place of the usual, rather less appropriate, poinsettia, coleus or caladium. The

Reverend William Wilks planted pears on his lawn for their fall color, for even when exposed somewhat to the wind, the tree retains its foliage long after the apple has become bare. The beauty of dying leaves in the crowded experimental gardens of the Belgian and American breeders must have been remarkable, for not only was the coloring reputed to be more vivid and pronounced in closely pruned trees, but as Thomas Andrew Knight remarked in his *Treatise on the Culture of the Apple and Pear* (1797), seedling trees displayed a markedly picturesque gradation of tints in autumn, as could be seen in comparing any artificial plantation with self-sown forest trees.

The pear cannot be said to provide the winter garden with any color, and thus its beauty when quite stripped of leaves has seldom been acknowledged. Walter Savage Landor, well known for caring more for the survival of his violet bed than for the safety of the cook whom he had thrown out the window onto it, was an early admirer of, amongst many other unfashionable things, the pear in wintertime, and in one of his poems:

> ... when the wintry lamps were spent,
> And all was drear and dark,
> Against the rugged pear-tree leant
> While ice crackt off the bark.

In modern times, it is perhaps to amateurs of bonsai that the pear tree appears most picturesque without its leaves; H. B. Tukey's description of the pear in his admirable *Dwarfed Fruit Trees* (1964) is some reflection of his catholic taste in dwarfs. 'Dark in color, irregular or even angular in shape, they develop an interesting framework that shows to best advantage in winter. On a cold, clear midwinter night when a full moon casts shadows upon a clean white blanket of snow, a pear tree is a most fascinating object.'

The pear is one of the most highly perfumed of fruits and the different scents of the various varieties have been a point of careful discrimination since classical times. The elder Pliny, whose *Natural History* furnishes the most extensive list of ancient varieties of fruit, including 41 pears, refers to several Roman kinds distinguished by their scents, the Laurea or bay leaf pear, the Myrapia or myrrh pear and the Nardina which smelled of spikenard. (The latter two were in fact old Greek varieties which had been described by Theophrastus in the third century BC.) The perfume of the older breaking pears, in which juice and flesh were not so exquisitely intermingled as they were to be in later years, was easily expressed, isolated and identified: the fruits seem often to have been eaten like perfumed confits. Raising fruits was indeed a kind of confectionery. Early gardeners hoped to influence the flavor of seedling fruits by the use of perfume in their cultivation, steeping the seeds in aromatic infusions and watering the young plants with them, a practice which was probably based, as Knight noted, on the observation that the milk and flesh of animals often retained the flavor of the herbs on which they fed. Venette remarked that some people preferred the breaking to the melting pears 'because these for the most part are odiferous, and the others are not'.

The anonymous Englishman to whom Bunyard alludes in his *Anatomy of Dessert* (1929) must have had similar fruits in mind when he divided pears into two classes, those that taste of hair wash and those that do not.

The French, who wrote dramatically of the 'parfums excitants' and 'enivrants' in their pears, took to giving other fruits an artificial scent so as to rival them. Louis Bosc (1759–1828), director of the Jardin des Plantes in Paris, perfumed apples with dried elder flowers; others preferred truffles. Contemporaries noted a pronounced fondness for perfume among Americans, a taste which still persists, in a modern love of varieties that are merely deodorant or a sweet scent and nothing more. Dr. Lister wrote in 1780: 'Most of the American fruits are exceedingly odiferous, and therefore are very disgusting at first to us Europeans: on the contrary, our fruits appear insipid to them, for want of odour.' The Bartlett pear, which is widely grown both in Europe and America, was appreciated for somewhat different qualities on either side of the Atlantic, its muskiness delighting American tastes, and at times, when too pronounced, repelling European amateurs, who seem to have enjoyed the variety almost in spite of its perfume.

There is scarcely a scent in the flower garden which one pomologist or another has not been able to discover in the pear. Zéphirine Grégoire had 'a peculiar and powerful aroma similar to that which is imparted to wines by elder flowers'; Andrews, 'the delicate perfume of new-cut hay, which in September carries one agreeably back to the freshly mown fields of June'; Ambrette d'Hiver, 'an agreeably musky perfume resembling ambergris'; Joséphine de Malines, 'a most delightful aroma which, in some specimens ... resembles that of the rose, and in others the hyacinth'; and the Fusée d'Automne, 'a particular perfume rather savoury and strong, somewhat like rue'. When, in 1839, the Massachusetts Horticultural Society was presented with an unknown French pear, newly fruited in America, they took the scent as the distinguishing characteristic and named it the Pond Lily pear 'from a resemblance in odor to that of the water lily'. The scents of many others were simply indescribable or, to quote the curious name of an old Flemish pear, Incommunicable, but to those who knew them each announced its period of ripeness. The scent of the rose appears most often in the juice of the pear, in the Winter Nélis, Beurré Hardy, Knight's Ickworth, Thompson's, Duchesse de Bordeaux, Bergamotte Crapaut, Beurré Audusson, the Bavarian Rosenwasserbirne and the Bergamotte Gaudry, to name but a few.

History of the Pear

MARMALADE

*One thing I definitely do in the kitchen – whether the kitchen
is in England, Tunis, Brussels, or Vientiane – is make
marmalade each year. How to simplify this task and perfect its
execution has engaged my attention since boyhood, as has –
more recently – the history of marmalade. How happy I was
when the foremost historian of food in England, Anne
Wilson, brought out a whole book on the subject! The part
reproduced here deals with the climactic period when 'beaten'
marmalade gave way to what the Scots called 'chip'
marmalade (recognisable as the prototype of our modern
marmalade), and marmalade took up its rightful place at the
breakfast table.*

The first English printed recipe for orange marmalade, unassisted by pippins or pippin-juice, was probably that published by Mary Kettilby in 1714, and it was for beaten marmalade, with the orange-peel and pulp boiled soft and pounded in a mortar. The earliest Scottish printed recipe, 'To make marmalet of oranges and lemons', in Mrs McLintock's *Receipts* of 1736, is also for beaten marmalade (the lemons do not appear anywhere in it, so probably the original recipe, like several others, once terminated with words to the effect that 'Thus also may you make marmalade of lemons'; but the sentence was dropped owing to the rarity of lemon marmalade in Scotland).

In England, the shredded-peel orange marmalades were also made throughout the eighteenth century and their popularity was reflected by their frequent appearances in the cookery-books. Eliza Smith in 1727 had one for which the Seville orange skins were to be cut 'as thin as palates' (a fricasee of ox-palates is a delicacy described elsewhere in her book) and boiled clear and tender before being reboiled into marmalade with the orange-pulp and lemon-juice. Her second orange marmalade, which included pippin jelly, also had the rinds cut 'very fine'. Hannah Glasse's version of orange marmalade (1747) was made with 'peel that is shred'; and Elizabeth Raffald (1769), who had one recipe for beaten orange marmalade, had another for transparent marmalade, with the peels cut in very fine slices and marmalade boiled until both peels and jelly were clear and transparent.

The Scottish cookery-books soon followed suit. Elizabeth Cleland in the 1750s had both beaten and shredded-peel marmalades made from a single composite recipe, with the oranges given a preliminary boiling and then divided into two groups for separate treatment; and she called the slivers of shredded peel for her second kind of marmalade 'chips'. Susanna MacIver, whose *Cookery and Pastry* was first published in 1773, gave separate recipes for both types under the titles 'smooth marmalade' and 'chip marmalade'.

These early Scottish recipes naming the shredded orange-peels as 'chips' show how this word was already becoming the favourite Scottish term for the finely-cut peels of marmalade-making. It may have originated with candied orange-peel chips, a separate item of confectionery prepared on both sides of the border and well liked even before the days of shredded-peel marmalades. In England marmalade with finely-cut peel, set by its own pectin, was known for a long time as transparent marmalade, following Elizabeth Raffald's use of this name for her recipe of 1769. In Scotland it was called chip marmalade. Its fame spread to such an extent that Richard Abbott, in *The Housekeeper's Valuable Present* published in London about 1800, put in a special instruction under the heading 'Scotch marmalade': 'When you make your orange marmalade [his recipe is for beaten marmalade], put a little by; then cut some orange-peel into fine strips, and giving them a boil in a little clarified sugar, mix them in the marmalade, and put them into pots.'

The most striking contribution of the Scots to the history of marmalade is not, however, to be sought in the realm of recipes. It lay in the transferring of the conserve to a new mealtime position, as part of the first meal of the day. The medicinal virtues of orange-peel 'condite with sugar, and taken fasting in a small quantity', as recommended by Sir Thomas Elyot, had not been forgotten. Both the peel and the sugar were warming to the cold early morning stomach.

The Scots had their own way of warming the stomach at the beginning of the day, by drinking a dram of whisky, and following it up with ale with a toast swimming in it. This pattern of breakfasting was disturbed when tea-drinking began to grow popular in Scotland, early in the eighteenth century. Some people continued with the customary dram, but replaced the ale with tea. Others replaced the dram as well, and ate warming sugar-preserved orange-peel or orange marmalade in its stead.

It was William Macintosh of Borlum who first published a complaint about the new practice in 1729. 'When I came to my friend's house in a morning, I used to be asked if I had my morning draught yet? I am now asked, if I have yet had my tea? And in lieu of the big quaigh [drinking-cup, originally of staved wood] with strong ale and toast, and after a dram of good wholesome Scots spirits, there is now the tea-kettle put to the fire, the tea-table, and silver and China equipage brought in, with the marmalet, cream and cold tea.' The rest of the passage makes it quite plain that the writer disapproved of the innovation.

Others were more complimentary. Later in the century Scottish breakfasts became famed for their excellence among English travellers. Oatcakes and toasted bread, butter, honey and preserves made from local berries were added to the marmalade; and sometimes there were cold meats and potted meats, or newly-caught fish as well. The dram of whisky was often retained, too. Samuel Johnson partook of it during his journey to the western islands of Scotland in 1773. He gave an enthusiastic report on the Scottish breakfast:

'Not long after the dram, may be expected the breakfast, a meal in which the Scots, whether of the lowlands or mountains, must be confessed to excel us. The tea and coffee are accompanied, not only with butter, but with honey, conserves, and marmalades . . .'

It has long been a tradition that Janet Keiller, wife of a Dundee grocer, was the inventor of orange marmalade. F. Marian McNeill tried to identify Janet more closely and found two Janet Keillers, an earlier one, née Pierson, who was married to James Keiller in 1700 (the record of her marriage is in the Dundee register); and a later Janet, née Matthewson and wife of John Keiller, a descendant of the original James, who with her son, also James, established the firm of James Keiller and Son in 1797. The story runs as follows:

The husband of one of the Janets (Miss McNeill believed it was the first, but the Keiller Company's own account suggests it was the second) bought a load of Seville oranges cheaply from a storm-driven ship which had taken shelter in Dundee harbour, at an unknown date in the eighteenth century. Janet was able to turn the oranges into marmalade with the help of her husband's stock of sugar; and it sold so successfully in his shop that in due course the firm of James Keiller and Son was established to manufacture and sell such marmalade as a full-scale commercial enterprise. The firm was founded in 1797, presumably not too long after Janet's original marmalade sales had demonstrated that the market was ready for her conserve (which again points to the second Janet, the mother of James, as the maker).

It is most unlikely that she needed to invent a recipe to cope with her abundance of oranges, for so many were in circulation at that period. She, and her friends, would surely have had their own family marmalade recipes. Even if that had not been the case, then somewhere in Dundee there must have been available one or two copies of the recipe books of McLintock, or Cleland, or MacIver, or Frazer, or of such English counterparts as E. Smith, Glasse or Raffald; and any of these could have supplied viable recipes. The presence of the oranges themselves is sufficient guarantee of the popularity of Seville orange marmalade in Scotland at the time. The lost and storm-tossed ship was not apparently heading for Dundee in the first place; but it could have been bound for Leith, its stock of oranges intended for the markets of Leith and Edinburgh for the use of marmalade-makers there.

Janet Keiller did not invent orange marmalade. But she contributed to the establishment of the 'chip' version as Scotland's very own marmalade. The eighteenth-century Scottish cookery-books carried recipes for both beaten, alias 'smooth', marmalade and for chip marmalade. Janet, faced with vast numbers of oranges, had to make a decision about which type to prepare, and she perhaps found it marginally less laborious to shred or 'chip' the peels than to pound them to a pulp in a mortar. For chip marmalade was the type for which James Keiller and Son became known and there is no reason to doubt that the company's choice in this matter followed Janet's initiative.

Again, Janet and her husband John were not the first people to offer marmalade for sale, for pots of marmalade were almost certainly on the shelves of eighteenth-century confectioners' shops in Scotland, as well as in England. But it was perhaps the size of Janet's operation which made her son James realise that a large-scale market for manufactured marmalade could be found, not only in Dundee but very soon also in Edinburgh and before long in distant London and other English cities.

THE BOOK OF MARMALADE

Sir Francis Hastings Doyle 1886

CHERRIES PROVOKE *a* MORAL STRUGGLE

I often forget what it is like to be a child. This item, about a child in the year of Waterloo, pierces the thick adult hide I have grown and brings it all back. It is curious (although not surprising, if one thinks about it) that children face far more moral problems than grown-ups.

In the course of the Waterloo year, I think, I remember with perfect distinctness undergoing my first moral struggle. I came down to dessert one evening, and applied myself to some cherries greedily enough, I daresay, when somebody asked me, in one of those jesting moods so terrible to children, whether, if my papa was turned into a cherry, I would eat him or not? Had the question been put to me some years later, when my natural truthfulness had been shaken to pieces under the grinding tyranny of Monsieur Clément my Chelsea schoolmaster, I have no doubt I should have made a very proper and decorous answer, indefensible on this ground only, that it would not have been true. In my then state of mind however, it was impossible for me to tell a lie, and though I felt all the time that what I had to say sounded discreditable to me, and would probably displease my hearers (and how bitterly children do feel such things is seldom remembered, I think, by grown-up people), out it had to come. I answered thus: 'Well, if my papa was going to be turned back again from the cherry into my papa, of course I wouldn't eat him; but if he is to keep always being a cherry, why shouldn't I?' Everybody laughed, to my surprise, and I went to bed relieved in mind, and thinking I had got off cheaply enough.

REMINISCENCES AND OPINIONS

Dr Joan Morgan *1985*

APPLES

*Morton Shand was one of the apple enthusiasts who were
concerned at the loss of old varieties when many English
orchards were pulled up during the Second World War. This
passage from an essay, 'In Praise of Older Apples' by Joan
Morgan, includes some of an eloquent broadcast on this theme
which Shand made in 1944. Joan Morgan has herself now
become one of the most prominent connoisseurs (and guardians)
of old apple varieties; a true scion of Shand, one might say.*

Whether it was in the design of a bridge or wine from a small vineyard Morton
Shand's main concern was quality. English apples he felt had quality and almost
inexhaustible shades of flavour. 'It is in no sense an exaggeration to say that except for
the world's few really great wines nothing we eat or drink presents such fascinating
diversity of savour within the compass of a single generic type, or afford such a rare
delight to the epicure,' he claimed in a lecture to the Royal Horticultural Society in
1948. During the last war, seeing orchards pulled out to make way for food crops,
Morton Shand became concerned that many of the old varieties that he remembered
from his childhood might disappear altogether. He made a number of broadcasts and
apples came flooding in to be identified. With fellow enthusiasts Sir Leslie Martin,
Gerald Finzi and Miss Holliday he grafted and planted trees, giving nearly 100 'missing'
varieties to the National Fruit Collection. The following extract is from Shand's first
broadcast entitled 'Apples – Going, Going . . .' which went out on 15 September 1944.

I started to collect disappearing and apparently doomed apples in 1941. At
that time some 50% of my skeleton list of about 50 names could still be got
in ones and twos from a few older firms scattered about the country. By 1942
the percentage had dropped to 35, and by 1943 it had dropped to well under
25. This year the number of the old varieties still offered has fallen to less
than 10% of my list. Well, strings of names are dull things to have to listen to
so I shall mention no more than five included in that list of mine, and these
will have to be representative of only one region: The Wessex apple I shall
single out rather invidiously won't be the charmingly named and subtly
spiced Cornish Gilliflower; it won't be its even older fellow countrymen, the
peerless Cornish Aromatic – although I could be lyrical about both of them.
It won't be either of those now extinct Somerset apples, the Pomeroy and
Court of Wick which I was never lucky enough to taste. Those who have
tasted them speak of them reverently with shining eyes, drawing in their

breath with a gasp of keenly remembered delight. No, my choice is that glorious Ashmead's Kernel. It was raised by a Doctor Ashmead of Gloucester about 1720, and I chose it because it was my father's favourite apple and he was no mean judge. He happened upon Ashmead's Kernel quite by chance and without ever having heard of it after 50 years unquestioning loyalty to Ribston, Blenheim and Cox, with occasional imperialistic interludes of those splendid Tasmanian Sturmer Pippins. It was his considered opinion that Ashmead's Kernel was just perceptibly superior to any of those august four. What an apple; what suavity of aroma. Its initial Madeira-like mellowness of flavour overlies a deeper honeyed nuttiness; crisply sweet – not sugar sweet but the succulence of a well-devilled marrow-bone. Surely no apple of greater distinction or more perfect balance can ever have been raised anywhere on Earth.

PETITS PROPOS CULINAIRES (PPC) 20

Claire Clifton 1984

SEARCH *for the* BLUE VIOLET SALAD

This culinary detective story is a good example of what happens when a diligent mind applies itself to a recipe which clearly enjoyed some sort of existence, but whose details are elusive. On how many tables did it actually appear? Claire Clifton still doesn't know. Probably no one will ever know.

Choosing a favourite recipe is almost as difficult as describing an ideal book. As an example of the various forms a single recipe can take on I have tried to trace the history (and did hope to discover the *ur-text*) of one easily identifiable recipe. I picked one I find especially appealing. So did M. F. K. Fisher and she is the best one to introduce it: 'I remember deciding once, long ago and I believe after reading Ellwanger's *Pleasures of the Table* for the first time, that the most exquisite dish I had ever heard of was a satiny white endive with large heavily scented Parma violets scattered through it. It meant everything subtle and intense and aesthetically significant in my private gastronomy, just as, a few years earlier, a brown-skinned lover with a turquoise set in one ear lobe epitomized my adolescent dream of passion'. She went on, in 'E for Exquisite' in *An Alphabet for Gourmets* (1949), to say that when the salad was served to her it was a crushing disappointment. It is a pity the dish did not live up to expectations but as a reader I love what the brown-skinned lover with a jewel in his ear tells you about M. F. K. Fisher.

73

George H. Ellwanger first wrote about 'The Blue-Violet Salad' in *The Story of My House* (1892). It is a tedious book but here is what M. F. K. Fisher read:

There was a great bunch of double violets on the table, the lovely dark variety (*Viola odoratissima* fl.pl.) with their short stems, freshly plucked from the garden, and the room was scented by their delicious breath.

A bowl of broad-leaved Batavian endive blanched to a nicety and alluring as the siren's smile was placed upon the table. I almost fancied it was smiling at the violets. A blue-violet salad, by all means! There are violets, and to spare. On a separate dish there was a little minced celery, parsley and chives. Four heaped saladspoonfuls of olive oil were poured upon the herbs, with a dessertspoonful of white wine vinegar (the best in the world comes from Orléans), the necessary salt and white pepper, and a tablespoonful of Bordeaux. The petals of two dozen violets were detached from the stems, and two-thirds of them were incorporated with the dressing. The dressing being thoroughly mixed with the endive, the remaining flower petals were sprinkled over the salad and a half-dozen whole violets placed in the centre.

The lovely blue sapphires glowed upon the white bosom of the endive. It was the true sequence of the salmis.

A white-labelled bottle, capsuled Yquem, and the cork branded 'Lur Saluces', was served with the salad. You note the subtle aroma of pine-apple and the fragrance of flower ottos with the detonation of the cork – the fine vintages of Yquem have a pronounced *Ananassa* flavour and bouquet that steeps the palate with its richness and scents the surrounding atmosphere.

Now try your blue-violet salad.

Is it fragrant? is it cool? is it delicious? is it divine?

Ellwanger was obviously fond of that piece of purple prose as he repeated it in *The Pleasures of the Table* (1901) in the chapter 'Sallets and Salads'. 'And when the endive is nicely blanched, and the first dark-blue double violets appear in the greenhouse – though skies lower and storms frown without – what in the varied round of the seasons presents itself more delicious than a blue-violet salad, with a flash of some noble vintage worthy to bear it company! The recipe, which cannot be too widely known, has been presented at length in a previous volume'. He then quotes from his earlier book.

Dr. W. T. Fernie, an altogether different, and I think more likeable, writer published *Meals Medicinal* in 1905. In his chapter on salads he wrote:

A 'Salade des Violettes' is a delicious dish, fit for the table of Apicius, or Lucullus: 'Take Batavian endive, finely curled celery, a sprinkling of minced parsley, a single olive, and the petals of a couple of dozen blue Violets; these several ingredients are to be mixed with the purest olive oil, salt and pepper being the only other condiments; add a dash of Bordeaux wine, and a suspicion of white vinegar.'

Dr Fernie is scrupulous about putting material from other sources in quotation marks but in common with a maddening number of other writers gives neither chapter nor verse. Ellwanger never says the salad is his invention, and I feel sure that he would have said so if it was. With the exception of Fernie's 'single olive' and Ellwanger's chives, the ingredients are identical.

'*A Housewife's Notebook*, 1909' is the credit Florence White gave in *Flowers as Food* (1934) for the Fernie version. Mrs Leyel calls it 'Dr Fernie's Salade des Violettes' in *Green Salads and Fruit Salads* (1925). Charles Cooper in *The English Table in History and Literature* (1929) in the chapter 'Flowers in Old Time Cookery' gives the same recipe with slight variations; he leaves out 'and these being the only condiments' and 'soupçon' instead of 'suspicion'. *Flower Cookery* (1967) by Mary MacNicol, a book upon which no steely-eyed editor ever gazed, gives the Ellwanger version on page 224 and the Cooper on page 232.

This search has been fraught with dead ends. Feverishly turning the pages of cookery books, herbals and magazines, I kept coming close but, as they say, 'no cigar'. In *The Table*, Mrs E. G. Marshall's 'weekly paper, social and gastronomical' which started in 1886, flowers abound. Society hostesses are described wearing them, decorating their elaborate tables with them and eating them. In 1887 the Paris correspondent, who signed his column '*Qui Dine, et Qui s'Amuse*', Maître Friand, wrote for the March 12 issue, 'There are in Paris hard and fast rules as to the decoration of various salads. These be few; endive salad is crowned with borage leaves, or with slices of beetroot; lettuce salad with garlands or marguerites formed of the yellow and whites of hard-boiled eggs; wild endive, or chicory salad (*barbe de capucin*) is decorated with violets, either loose or in the form of a wreath'. On March 26 he wrote that a gourmet friend gave him the details of a Lenten menu which included 'volga sterlet, surrounded with a garland of primroses and served with cavier sauce ... *buisson* of crawfish arranged with alternate bouquets of white violets'. April 16 brought news of the fashionable way of serving *brochet*, on a dish surrounded with a garland of cowslips, but 'brill on the other hand is garnished with parsley intermingled with wood anemones, while salmon should be "framed" in white or pale violets, or in the flowers called periwinkles'. On May 7 he wrote ' "Will you come and eat salade with me?" is modern Parisian for "Will you take pot-luck with me?" or "Will you dine with me?" The salad is either the too-dreadfully boring Japanese salad, or the Ardennes, Madagascar, Normandy, Gascony or Bourbon ...'

The rules for garnishing salad may have been strict in 1887, but more than a decade earlier Alexandre Dumas, in his letter to Jules Janin which was published as part of his *Grand Dictionnaire de Cuisine* (1874), suggests, although it may sound 'bizarre', putting not only violet flowers in a salad of *barbe de capucin*, but also a pinch or two of Orris root which has a faint scent of violets and was used at the time for making sachets for linens. Dumas borrowed from almost every writer on gastronomy and doesn't say where this idea came from.

The frontispiece of *La Cuisinière de la Campagne et de la Ville* (1847) by M. Audot is a charming illustration of a *Salade de Romaine* and a *Salade de Chicorée* decorated with flowers which look very much like violets and borage. There is a brief chapter on salads which gives directions for making salads in the country and says to place flowers on them as indicated in the picture. It advises flowers which are not harmful, 'La Capucine, la Bourrache, les Mauve et Guimauve, la Chicorée sauvage, la Buglosse, la Pervenche et le Bouillon-blanc'.

Two writers I admire but who sometimes make me want to scream with frustration who have mentioned violets in salad are Waverley Root and Alice B. Toklas. Mr Root stated baldly in *Food* (1980), 'Violet, whose petals were added to Louis XIV's salad'. I want to know a lot more about that. It is probably the fault of the publisher that the entry is so terse. According to a letter that Mr Root wrote to Craig Claiborne quoted in Claiborne's *Memoir with Recipes* (1982), only a third of the million words he wrote were published in *Food*.

Miss Toklas wrote in *Aromas and Flavors of Past and Present* (1958), 'The Empress Marie Louise and the last Empress of Russia had a weakness for violets, not only for flavoring desserts – for here is a recipe where they are the ingredients in a salad' – with corn, potatoes and eggs. Oh! Miss Toklas, how I wish you were still alive. I would so like to ask you, please, where did you ever get that fascinating piece of information?

'Cookery: Science, Lore and Books'
OXFORD SYMPOSIUM DOCUMENTS 1984/5

Maura Laverty 1946

PICKING RASPBERRIES

We met Maura Laverty on page 23. There is an appealing wildness about her writing on cookery. Never under control, that one.

Wild raspberries grew in the fox covert. Nobody, except maybe the tinkers, knew they were there until the day I mitched from school. There was no real reason for me to mitch. I was not in trouble with any of the nuns. The night before, I had gone to bed completely at peace with school-life. My spellings and Catechism were learned, my sums were done and my Irish transcription written out without a blot. My shoes were polished and my clean ribbon ready. There was nothing at all to warn me that I was about to fall. It was waking at four in the morning that did it. There was a thrill in being the only one awake at that hour. The air was full of thrill. It was in the colour of the thick gold wedge of light that came through where the curtains wouldn't meet. It was in the queer careful way the birds were singing. They seemed to be bursting with some marvellous news that mustn't be told too soon. I went to the window. The sun was doing things to the fields and river and bog, making them look as if they had all been made half-an-hour before. The whole world had the clean ready look I had noticed on my sister Peg, when she was going over to the chapel to make her First Holy Communion.

I went a little mad and began to feel that this was all mine since there was no one but myself to see it. I went madder, and got the notion that I could do as I liked with it. Then I went stark, staring mad and decided to go and pick mushrooms instead of going to school. I took the three quart can and sneaked out.

It was early for mushrooms and though I walked far beyond the Commons, I found none. The sun began to get hot and strong, so I went into the wood that fringed the Commons. The fox covert was deep in the heart of the wood. Only once before had I been this far. It was here I found the raspberries. At one minute, I was looking at what seemed an ordinary tangle of long stemmed bushes. The next minute, I saw the fruit. The canes were heavy with beaded blood berries. Here and there among them were white raspberries like clusters of seed pearls. I picked and ate, but mostly ate. Even so, I filled the can. Raspberries are not filling, and when the twelve o'clock Angelus rang, hunger drove me towards home and food and retribution.

I met my father on the road. He had been sent to look for me. I was glad to see him. No one was ever afraid of my father. 'Is she mad at me?' I asked him. 'She'll take your life,' he told me. 'When the three-quart can was missing, she knew well you were out after mushrooms. Weren't you the mad poor eejut of a child to do the like?'

I recognised that as a rhetorical question, so I made no answer. My father pulled at his lip and looked at me. 'The Curragh Races are on to-day,' he said. 'Jim Payne offered me a lift. He'd take you, too. We'd still be in time to catch him. If we doubled around the Pound to his house, your mother wouldn't see us. Come on.' I had trust in my father's maxim that one should never meet the devil half-way. He said that if you hang back long enough it sometimes happens that you don't have to meet him at all. He gave a child a penny to tell my mother we'd be home some time, and we made for the Pound.

We left the raspberries in Jim Payne's house for safety, and had a great day at the Curragh. I didn't get into trouble after all, for my father had had four winners and he gave my mother three pounds. Besides, she was delighted to get the can of raspberries, for she loved making jam.

Maura Laverty's Cookery Book

Geraldene Holt   1987

OLIVE OIL

The fruit of the olive tree and its oil have been the subject of
much fine prose, in many languages. My choice falls on a
book published very recently, by an author who combines
unobtrusive erudition with an artist's eye.

Nothing in the south seems older than the olive. Neither the smooth symmetry of the arena of Nîmes, nor the fretted outline of the Pont du Gard, nor even the rocks themselves, bleached white by the sun. Olive trees have grown here since before the Romans came. It's thought that the Phocaean Greeks introduced the olive to Provence around 650 BC. To northern eyes, accustomed to a sappy verdure, the olive tree appears almost dead; its dull grey-green sabre leaves rustle like paper even when new, and its twisted and contorted limbs seem beyond life. But in fact, the lifespan of an olive tree is immense – most live from three to six hundred years, and a few span ten centuries.

Olive trees have an almost hypnotic effect on me; I cannot remain unaware of them. Whether I see one or a hundred, my attention is held. It's an odd yet peaceful feeling. And while for me this experience is a personal and private celebration of a venerable tree and its life-giving fruit, the people of the south are gloriously public about it.

On the first Saturday in July, in Nyons, ten men dressed in white, their green waistcoats trimmed with red, raise trumpets to their mouths and a fanfare echoes across the square to announce the start of the olive festival. These are the *Chevaliers des Olives*, an association founded by the mayor a generation or so ago to protect and propagate the appreciation of the olive. ·

Nyons, itself, sheltered from the *mistral* wind by the low hills of Les Baronnies, is home to the most delicious olive in France. Small, oval and black, its dry yet buttery flavour has an intensity and almost wine-like taste unequalled anywhere. And, of course, the oil produced from these olives is superb. No matter that the oil has collected prizes and accolades for a century, your tongue and your palate will tell you that this is a classic among olive oils. It's not just a liquid that you slurp over salads or mix with lemon juice or wine vinegar; it is also a food with a flavour and consistency to be valued in its own right. One of my grandfathers swallowed a teaspoonful every day of his life when olive oil was kept in the medicine cupboard. Thank heavens that today, in Britain, this generous liquid has made its way on to supermarket shelves and into grocers' shops. And although you can still buy olive oil at the chemist's, it is now on the food counter.

It is an old country custom that olives should be picked with a waxing moon. The first olives are picked green and unripe in September; these are known as *olives d'été* or *olives amères*, because they will still have a slightly bitter flavour when eaten the following summer. The bitterness is not leached out as is necessary with other green olives. They are simply put into a 10 per cent solution of brine with some Provençal herbs and are cured for 6–8 months before serving.

In October the main crop of green olives is picked. They are soaked in an alkaline solution, sometimes made by mixing wood ash with water to remove some of the bitterness, and are then pickled in brine for a month or so. A few olives are picked when they are turning purple and on their way to acquiring the brown-black colour of the fully ripe fruit. Ripe olives need only to be soaked in cold water for twenty-four hours before brining.

There are a few varieties of olive which remain green when fully ripe. The Verdales variety grown around the village of Beaumes de Venise is picked, when green, specially for pressing to produce one of the finest *vierge extra* olive oils in France.

The olive oil cooperative La Balméene has sixty-four members and they each bring their olive crop – sometimes only a few kilos but for others a trailer load – to the mill at the crossroads in Beaumes as soon as the olives are ripe enough to press. Here they are stored at room temperature for three to four days until very slightly fermented. After the dust of the countryside has been washed away the olives travel down a chute into the mill itself. Every stage of the operation is carried out at as low a temperature as possible in order to retain the fine bouquet and flavour of the oil. And because olive oil attacks iron, every piece of equipment at the mill must be stainless steel . . .

In many villages in Provence the older, stone oil mills are still to be found. There is a particularly fine example which is easy to view in the Syndicat d'Initiative in Carcès – an attractive small town in Var. Here you can see the huge stone wheel which tracks round the circular trough, crushing the olives in its path. The design is remarkably like that of a stone cider mill still in use in our Devon village. A stone conduit led the oil and water mixture to a vat which was heated by a small fire lit underneath. The heat evaporated the water from the mixture and the oil – which was once also a source of heat and light in Provence – was run into wooden barrels. These then travelled back to the farms and cottages set amongst the olive groves.

The best olive oil is cold pressed and the finest oil is graded as *vierge extra*, or virgin extra, and it contains no more than 1 per cent oleic acid. But a *vierge* or virgin oil with a slightly higher acidity of up to 4 per cent is still a fine oil. Although oils are graded by their acidity, the really important test is performed by the palate. On occasions one prefers an oil with a pronounced bouquet, at other times the feel of the oil with its sensation of buttery fatness takes preference. All olive oil should be kept just below room temperature and out of sunlight, preferably in a dark cupboard.

To my mind, the finest salad in France is dressed with the olive oil from Provence. It is served in a bowl made from the wavy light and dark shaded wood of the tree itself, a tree which also gives us the symbol of peace – the olive branch.

FRENCH COUNTRY KITCHEN

Elisabeth Luard 1985

CLOUDBERRIES

*Going about my business in the Swedish Ministry of Foreign
Affairs – a placid place – many years ago, I was amazed to
find that they had a desk officer assigned to 'the cloudberry
wars'. It seemed that the inhabitants of the far north of
Norway, Sweden and Finland, in their (understandable)
enthusiasm for this fruit, would sometimes go so far as to
fight over it. Elisabeth Luard's essay 'Berried Treasure of the
Vikings' helps to explain how such passions are aroused.*

The end of August, advised the late Ethel B. Tweedie, is the appropriate time to
visit the Land of the Midnight Sun for the berry harvest. For instance, take
cloudberries. If you do any such thing, I discovered, you must expect to be battle-axed
by an irate native with the blood of the Vikings hot in his veins and his winter larder on
his mind. You may pinch a Viking's bilberries and snaffle his Arctic bramble, but you
may not cull his cloudberries.

The Scandinavians are not normally mean with their moors. They can, after all,
afford to be generous: half a million square miles – five times the area of the United
Kingdom – is a lot of land for a population of 20 million. There is no law of trespass in
Scandinavia. Unrestricted access is the rule. Townsmen and tourists are free to roam the
mountains and valleys at will. With, that is, the exception of the cloudberry-patch. That
is something quite other. Blows have been exchanged by normally mild-mannered good
neighbours when faced with marauders during the ripening season at the end of August.
Woe betide he who is found skulking with bulging knapsack high on the hills in the
twilight.

The cloudberry, *Rubus chamaemorus*, is listed in Fitter and Blamey's *Collins
Guide to the Wild Flowers of Britain and Northern Europe* as a 'shy flowerer in Britain'.
The fruit of the Vikings needs the twenty-four-hour sunshine within the Arctic Circle to
set its reproductive processes aflame. Cloudberry blossom is a single, pearl-white, five-
petalled flower – every bit as beautiful as a member of the rose family should be. It is a
vulnerable plant, unprotected by the usual tangled mass of thorny stems. It grows low in
the heather, and the thick palmate leaves make solid dark patches, clearly visible among
the feathery fronds of the moorland vegetation. The fruit forms quickly after flowering.
At first it looks like a large hard orange blackberry, striped with scarlet where the flesh is
exposed to the sun by the separating sepals. Then, as the fruit ripens, it swells and grows
paler. When it is fully ripe, the berry is a mass of sunny golden globelets – plump and
fragrant and full of thick amber juice. The berries have one extraordinary property:

they do not, as does other soft fruit, go bad. They have a built-in preserving agent. Cloudberry jam needs minimal sugar and very little cooking. It is possible to pick the berries straight into a storage-jar and keep them in a cool cellar all winter. They will still be miraculously fresh in the spring.

To return to the late Ethel B. Tweedie: the lady was an intrepid traveller in nineteenth-century Scandinavia. She found and sampled eleven species of edible berry and gave cloudberries top billing: 'The cloudberry grows in the extreme North in the morasses during August. It is a *most delicious* fruit with a pine tree flavour.'

I have a Norwegian friend with a small-holding 200 miles inside the Arctic Circle. Her farm runs from the mountain ridge above her steading to the lake-shore beneath. She harvests meadow hay for her cows, and the fish from the lake for her supper. But her most prized crop by far is the cloudberries on the moor which runs up to the ridge above the birch-wood behind her fields. Beneath her pretty wooden farmhouse she has a deep storage-cellar. In it she keeps her year's supply of potatoes, her rhubarb wine (clear and dry and packing a 15 per cent proof punch), bilberry cordials, bramble jellies and all her winter pleasures. Beyond, in a special secret place, is her shelf of cloudberry conserve, golden as the best caviare, hoarded against invaders. She brought a jar out for our supper. It was wonderful. The fruit is neither sharp not sickly and has a thick rich texture. I could see what Ethel meant about the pine-tree flavour.

The problem is how to acquire this elusive treasure. Perhaps this year will be a good year for cloudberries on the northern moors of Britain. Or you might care to brave the Vikings and make a clandestine dash to the uplands of Scandinavia. There is one other possibility – although it is only an echo of the real thing. The Finns make and export under the state label, Lapponia, a liqueur made from cloudberries. The Scandinavians like theirs on the sweet and sticky side, but the flavour of the berry in their Cloudberry Liqueur is still discernible. Should you be fortunate enough to find a handful of the ripe berries, restrain yourself from eating them (it requires resolve of steel), and slip them instead into a bottle of vodka or plain *eau de vie* such as the French sell for home-made fruit brandies. Keep the bottle hidden away securely until the long dark nights of January or February. Then open it and raise a glass of the pale gold nectar to the memory of Ethel B. Tweedie, who brought the good news from the Arctic tundra.

THE PRINCESS AND THE PHEASANT

The VEGETABLE GARDEN

*The items in this section range from Émile Zola's
splendid depiction, akin to a painting by one of
the Impressionists who were his contemporaries,
of the vegetable market, back to Sir Hugh Plat's
17th-century parsnip cakes and forward to Rena
Salaman on Greek greenstuff. Claudia Roden's
account of the djinns which inhabit vegetables is
related to the Middle East, but presumably the
djinns are in vegetables everywhere, not just
there, so look out.*

Émile Zola   *1873*

DAWN *over the* VEGETABLES

The French novelist Emile Zola set his novel Le Ventre de
Paris *in Les Halles, the famous market area which has now
been displaced to a distant suburb. His descriptions of the
various parts of the market are of unrivalled felicity. Here we
have dawn rising over the vegetables. (See also pages 120
and 158.)*

In a burst of enthusiasm Claude had climbed onto the bench and was urging his
companion to admire the sun rising on the vegetables. Before him was a seascape. It
stretched from the Pointe St. Eustache to the Rue des Halles, between the two sections
of the covered market. And at either end by the crossroads, the swell increased still
further, vegetables drowning the flagstones. Day dawned slowly with a faint grey light,
lending to the composition a delicate wash effect. Waves breaking one on top of the
other, the rising vegetable tide seemed to make the road its river bed, and like a violent,
autumn downpour, the flood took on a delicate, pearly shading, soft blues, pinks tinged
with milk, greens thinned with yellow, a complete range of pastels turning the sky into a
shot-silk canvas at break of day. And as the morning took hold, flames licked the far end
of the Rue Rambuteau, so the vegetables stirred further to life, leaving the blue shadows
which were strewn upon the ground. Lettuce, endive, chicory, open and still caked in
leaf-mould, showed their bursting hearts; bunches of spinach, bunches of sorrel,
clutches of artichokes, piles of beans and peas, heaps of Cos lettuce, tied up with lengths
of straw, sang chromatic scales of green from the delicate lacquered green of the pods to
the rough green of the leaves; a sustained chord sung morendo, fading into the streaked
green of a clump of celery and a clutch of leek. But the top notes, sung loud and clear,
were provided by the bright patches of carrot, and the pure patches of turnip, strewn in
prodigious number the length of the market, setting it alight with their motley of gaudy
colour. At the junction with the Rue des Halles rose mountains of cabbage; enormous
white cabbage, tight and firm like pale metallic cannonballs; brassica, their large leaves
like bronze bowls; red cabbage, transformed by dawn into spectacular blossoms,
blotches of ruby and deep purple.

At the other end of the street, at the junction with the Pointe St. Eustache, the
entrance to the Rue Rambuteau was blocked by a barricade of orange pumpkins, set out
in twin rows, displaying their swollen bellies. A basket of onions, their skin like polished
bronze, a pile of blood-red tomatoes, a mound of faded yellow cucumbers, a brace
of purple aubergines added intermittent flashes of colour. Meanwhile, fat, black
radishes, draped as if in mourning, cast a funereal darkness amid this vibrant scene of

joyous awakening.

Claude clapped his hands at the sight. He found 'all this blessed veg' wildly extravagant, unreal. And he was convinced they were not dead, but rescued from death the day before, waiting for the new day to dawn, so that they could say farewell to him, here on the floor of the arcades. To him they were living, opening their leaves, as if still peacefully rooted in hot compost. He claimed he could hear the last gasps of every dying plant in the neighbourhood.

Le Ventre de Paris

Claudia Roden   *1968*

Meeting *the* Chickpea Djinns

Ever since Middle Eastern Cookery *was first published, Claudia Roden has occupied a special niche as the author to whom everyone turns for information on the subject – and, of course, for recipes. In the score of years which have passed since then it has become much more common for cookery writers to set their recipes in context and to provide good reading as well as good recipes; but this happy development should not result in our failing to honour the pioneers. I have observed that, not surprisingly, many cookery books reflect the personalities of their authors. This is certainly true of Claudia Roden, whose style is always reader-friendly and witty. To borrow words from the passage I have chosen, her* own djinn *is both gentle and piquant.*

*D*olma to the Turks, *dolmathes* to the Greeks, *dolmeh* to the Persians, and *mahshi* to the Arabs, stuffed vegetables are the great family favourites, the party pieces and festive dishes of the Turks, the Uzbeks, the Azerbaijanis, Armenians, Greeks, Egyptians, Persians, Syrians, Lebanese, Saudi Arabians and North Africans. Adopted by all, each country has developed its own variations.

Their origin is not certain, though both the Turks and the Greeks claim them as their creation. They do not appear in the very early Persian and Arab manuscripts, but seem to have been known at the time of the Ottoman Empire, and were served at the lavish banquets of the Sultans. Perhaps they were developed at this time; but they may equally well have been adopted from the vanquished Greeks, who claim a rich culinary tradition stemming from their early civilization.

However, stuffed vegetables were obviously developed as a 'court cuisine',

85

invented and prepared for a rich and powerful leisured class to excite their curiosity and titillate their palates, as well as to satisfy their desire for ostentation. The long, elaborate preparation required for these dishes, and the experienced and delicate handiwork that goes into the making of them are proof of the number of dedicated cooks employed in the huge kitchens, while the subtle harmony of the vegetables and their fillings demonstrates the refined taste and deep culinary knowledge of their masters.

Today, poorer people can usually afford vine leaves, courgettes, onions and aubergines; and although they have had to make the fillings simpler and cheaper, they count their own time as cheap as their masters deemed it, and spend it lavishly on rolling and filling their beloved *mahshi*.

As well as the love for different, subtle flavours, for the exciting fusion of vegetables and their fillings, the traditional wish to take pains and give of oneself is satisfied by the trouble one takes in making these dishes. So is the wish to impress by one's culinary expertise. And how the guest loves to be surprised by an intriguing parcel, the contents of which are always slightly unpredictable!

In the past, Arabs have been – and in certain places still are – obsessed by their belief in the existence of numerous spirits of *djinns*, several *djinns* per person in fact, who inhabit both things and people whenever they get a chance. Their tales give a fascinating picture of vegetables inhabited by *djinns* – rice *djinns*, meat *djinns*, chick pea *djinns* – seasoned and spiced, and given piquant, naughty or gentle personalities, like the *djinns* who inhabit humans.

A very common filling for any stuffed vegetable is a mixture of chopped onion, minced meat, rice and chopped parsley, sometimes with chopped tomatoes as well, seasoned with salt and pepper. Sometimes raisins, pine nuts and chopped walnuts are added to the mixture. Persians favour the addition of well-cooked yellow split peas. An Armenian filling is made with burghul (cracked wheat) flavoured with aniseed and garlic.

In the past, stuffed vegetables were customarily fried gently in oil or *samna* (clarified butter) before being stewed. Today, since the tendency is to make dishes lighter and less rich, this step, though an enhancement to the flavour of the dish, is omitted.

Almost any vegetable can be, and is, stuffed.

A BOOK OF MIDDLE EASTERN FOOD

Anonymous   *c. 1879*

BEETON *on* HORSERADISH

The Beeton whose name appears on this book was Mr not Mrs,
and he was publisher not author.

HORSE-RADISH (*Cochlearia armoracia*). Horse-radish is looked upon as an almost essential accompaniment to roast beef, either scraped or in the form of horse-radish sauce, the latter being made from grated horse-radish mixed with cream and seasoned with vinegar. In some districts it is much more extensively used than in others, and is but little known out of England, except to English residents in foreign countries, who have been the means of introducing the root abroad.

Horse-radish is perennial, and once it has taken firm hold of any situation, it is very hard to extirpate it; and as the smallest piece takes hold of the earth and flourishes, it is apt to spring up in inconvenient places in a garden, where it often becomes a nuisance. The writer was once making a pedestrian journey in South Wales, and saw a small field, near Caerphilly Castle, of horse-radish growing luxuriantly. Upon making inquiries about it, being struck with its appearance in that out-of-the-way place, curiosity having been excited (for there were few eaters of roast beef in that part of the country who would make it a *sine qua non* to have horse-radish whenever they partook of it), the information given was that nothing was done with it, and the field was utterly useless – the owner had endeavoured to plough it up and destroy it more than once, but it had sprung up again and again, and the trouble it occasioned made him give the field up as a bad job, and there it was allowed to remain. It might, of course, have been profitably disposed of, made up in bundles and sent to London, but there was no railway then near it, being about 35 years ago. The Taff Vale line had certainly been completed from Cardiff to Merthyr Tydvil, but the only way of sending would have been thence to Cardiff, continuing by packet to Bristol, and on to town per Great Western Railway, or *viâ* Newport.

Those days were just about the ending or finish up of the old coaching days, before the South Wales line was completed; and the *route* used to be either per Great Western Railway to Gloucester, and thence by a well appointed four-horse coach through Monmouth, Ross, and Abergavenny – a charming ride – or else by the *route* previously indicated to Bristol, and thence by packet to Cardiff.

We fancy that no fields of horse-radish would now be allowed to stand idle and unremunerative, but that it would be soon neatly made up into bundles, and sent to Covent Garden, if no nearer market could be found for it.

FIELD, FARM AND GARDEN

Louise Andrews Kent   *1942*

Mrs Appleyard's Pumpkin Pie

Many a cookbook has sprouted in New England soil.
Mrs Appleyard's Kitchen by Louise Andrews Kent is one of
the most attractive. In the introduction, Mrs A is quoted as
saying that 'the trouble with most cookbooks is that they
assume that people live the way they don't live'. She's a great
one for tossing out independently-minded observations of this
sort, and a great one for detail in recipes.
Her dust jacket blurb, straying off the usual tracks, remarks
that she likes other people (but not herself) to have curly hair,
and that she 'starts conversations with complete strangers'.

The best pumpkins for pie, she says, are the small ones. They have less string and more sweetness than the jack-o'-lantern style. Cut them in halves, take out the seeds and string, cut them into large pieces and steam them until they are tender. Separate the pulp from the shell and put the pulp through a fine strainer.

Mrs. Appleyard has often gone all through this process, and she has on other occasions opened a can of pumpkin. Mr. Appleyard disapproved of anything but the home-grown product – never having tried anything else. He is, however, a man of reason, so when his mother and his wife conspired against him and made two pies – one of canned pumpkin and one of fresh – and he, poor innocent, voted for the canned one as being a trifle the more utterly delicate of the two, he simply beamed upon the plotters when they confessed, and had another piece of each pie. He has never since been so crude as to inquire which kind Mrs. Appleyard was devoting to his nourishment this time, and if he can't tell, no one can.

However you acquired your cooked pumpkin, either by steaming and straining it yourself or by opening a can, you have really only just begun. You take a large iron frying-pan, butter it lightly, put in the pumpkin, and cook it down until it is dry and brown. This cooking, plenty of cream, a delicate accuracy in seasoning, rich flaky crust, are the essential things in turning out a good pumpkin pie. The cooking in the frying-pan is well worth the trouble of standing over it and stirring it constantly. It will scorch if it is not stirred often, and what you are trying to do is to dry the moisture out of it and just slightly caramelize the natural sugar that is in the pumpkin. If this is done right, turning the whole mass over so that it all comes in contact with the hot pan from time to time, it brings out the flavor and sweetness of the pumpkin. Drying out the pumpkin in the oven is *not* a substitute for cooking it in the pan on top of the stove. In the oven it is likely that the pumpkin will simply dry on the outside and still be moist inside. Keep turning it over as the steam puffs out of it. It will take about twenty minutes and at the end of that time it should be a rich golden brown all through instead of orange, and thick and smooth instead of watery. There should be about one and a half cups if you are planning to make two large pies.

PUMPKIN PIE (B. H. K.)

1½ c. cooked and browned pumpkin

2 t. flour

2 eggs

1 t. salt

1 c. sugar

1 t. cinnamon

½ t. ginger

⅛ t. mace

3 c. rich milk

1 c. cream

Put the pumpkin in a bowl, sprinkle it with the flour, and stir in the flour thoroughly. Butter the bottom of a saucepan and scald the milk in it. Add the cream and the seasonings. Pour it over the pumpkin mixture and add the eggs – well beaten. Get pie shells ready, built up around the edge, and nicely fluted or crimped. Do not have the pie shells too full of the mixture; three quarters of an inch deep is about right. If your tins are only of medium size this will be enough for another small pie tomorrow. Bake only what you are going to eat within twenty-four hours. Both pastry and filling will keep in the ice chest until you need them. Cut cheesecloth into inch strips or use one-inch strips of gauze, moisten it a little and put it around the edge of your pies. This will keep them from browning too fast at first.

Bake the pies in a fairly hot oven – 450°F for forty-five minutes, reducing the heat to 325°F if they seem to be cooking too fast. They are done when they will just shake in the middle when moved.

To leave out some Vermont cheese when you serve the pie is a serious offense in the Appleyard family.

If you want to make squash pie, go right ahead, but don't expect any help from Mrs. Appleyard, who would rather speak about Lemon Meringue.

It is not true that Mrs. Appleyard has the digestion of an anaconda. Her constitution is really an organism of peculiar delicacy; for instance, she is allergic to cornstarch. Anyone who wishes to make lemon pie – or anything else, such as that pudding that tastes like slate pencils – had better carry on his researches somewhere else.

MRS APPLEYARD'S KITCHEN

Joyce Conyngham Green   1947

CABBAGE EVERYWHERE

Despite its culinary title, Joyce Conyngham Green's
Salmagundi is a book about life in the country (just after the
Second World War) rather than about cookery. But there are
some lively bits about food. What she says here about cabbage
is a refreshing antidote for anyone who has had a surfeit of
reading about country establishments where everything in
kitchen and pantry is perfect.

And halting at a few paces from it [the shop], as he sees a soldierly-looking woman, with her outer skirt tucked up, come forth with a small wooden tub, and in that tub commence a whisking and a splashing on the margin of the pavement, Mr. George says to himself, 'She's as usual, washing greens. I never saw her, except on a baggage-wagon, when she wasn't washing greens!'

Charles Dickens, Bleak House

Your mother has vitamins again rather badly; we eat little but carrots, generally raw.

John Galsworthy, The Silver Spoon

Without having vitamins at all badly we eat little but raw carrots plus shredded raw cabbage, because there is nothing else here. Offal, poultry, game, rabbits, have all entirely vanished these four years, and fish is seldom obtainable. Mercifully we have always had a light salad-and-coffee lunch, so compulsory almost-vegetarianism has not hit us as hard as it has our two-meat-meal-a-day friends. But now that vegetables have disappeared as well, with the exception of spring cabbage, cooked beetroot, and potatoes, we are on the point of starvation.

And what spring cabbage! About four edible leaves in each cabbage to a great mass of tough outside greenery which is about as chewable, cooked, as deck-chair canvas, and not, I should think, as flavoursome. As they are sold by the pound it is quite costly to get enough 'inside' for one small salad or cooked dish; and the amount of water has to be seen to be believed. I feel quite worn out and blighted just coping with the washing of cabbage.

It is no exaggeration to say that from Friday's, Saturday's, and Sunday's salads alone there was: (*a*) an outsize enamel bucket full of outside leaves to give to Mrs. Convallaria's hens: (*b*) a ditto shopping-basket ditto ditto; (*c*) a large basin of not-quite-so-far outside leaves (Saturday's); (*d*) a large pile on the scullery windowsill of ditto (Sunday's), the two latter for Dee to look over in the faint hope that fresh eyes, so to speak, might discover some that were cookable; (*e*) one very small basin of reasonably tender just-outside-the-heart – heart, huh! – that could be cooked, and, what is more important, *eaten* when cooked.

All of these were quite apart from salad leaves and one molehill of outside which I had 'souped' before the sight of mountains of more or less unusable cabbage had begun to unnerve me entirely; and two large bucketfuls which had previously gone up to Mrs. Convallaria. Dee swore he could smell the huge pile of decaying relics of Monday's, Tuesday's, Wednesday's, and Thursday's salads which had had to be dumped on the compost heap in despair – after all, we have some war-work to do apart from rushing unwanted and unemployable brassica about – not only all over the garden, but all over the village as well, as well.

A dreadful belief is arising in our bosoms that our house is becoming – like the Tite Barnacles' – a sort of bottle, only instead of being filled 'with concentrated provisions and extract of Sink from the pantry' it is pervaded by the effluvia of ancient and modern cabbage, and that when the stopper is taken out, i.e. the front door is opened, a great gust of *Brassica oleracea capitata* will burst into the face of the waiting visitor.

SALMAGUNDI

Myrtle Allen *1981*

EILEEN *and* IRISH POTATOES

Ballymaloe, where Myrtle Allen and her husband Ivan preside
over a whole complex of family enterprises (hotel, restaurant,
farm and farmshop, gift shop, wine business, cookery school,
cafe), is not far from Youghal, where Sir Walter Raleigh had
his Irish estate and where the first potatoes grown in Ireland
(fateful tubers!) may have been planted. While there, we
heard the tale of Eileen from Myrtle's own lips, and while
eating the potatoes whose virtues Ivan glowingly described.

I found it really impossible to keep a house this size and look after six children single-handed. Fortunately, somebody always turned up to help. One year it was Eileen. She was cheerful, quick and intelligent, I became dependent on her. One week she asked for her half day on a Wednesday instead of a Thursday and I didn't see her again for some while. Neither did her mother. We didn't know where she was, but on Wednesdays the

91

boat sailed for England and someone saw her at the quays. A month later, she turned up as unexpectedly as she had left and tearfully came to see me. 'Well if you went to London,' I said 'Why did you come back again?' 'I couldn't eat the potatoes', she sobbed.

Potatoes are really important to Irish people. British Queen are the ones we like to eat in summer and Kerr's Pink followed by Golden Wonder in winter. They are very floury and inclined to break in the cooking water. They should never be peeled before cooking and if they still break, the water must be poured off before they are cooked and they are finished cooking in their own steam. They are peeled at table and (ideally) eaten with a big lump of golden butter.

There are a great many Irish potato dishes and some confusion about their names. The two we usually serve are Colcannon which is made with cabbage, or stelk or champ made with chives or spring onions.

COLCANNON

6–8 potatoes
2–4 oz butter
1 head of cabbage
about 1½ cups milk
salt and pepper

Scrub potatoes and put down to boil in salted water. Quarter, core and finely shred cabbage. Put down in a very little boiling water. Boil rapidly, turning occasionally until cooked, and the water has all evaporated. Peel potatoes and mash with milk. Stir in cabbage immediately and beat very well. Taste for seasoning. Serve in a warm dish, hollowing the centre a little. The butter is placed in the hollow to slowly melt into the vegetables.

CHAMP OR STELK

6–8 potatoes
1 cup chopped spring onions or ½ cup chopped chives
about 1½ cups milk
2–4 oz butter
salt and pepper

If onions are used, cook until soft in the milk. Peel and mash freshly boiled potatoes and mix with milk and onions or with hot milk and raw chives. Season to taste.

THE BALLYMALOE COOKBOOK

Tabitha Tickletooth   1860
Edouard de Pomiane   1932

POTATO COOKERY

Two contrasting items.
Tabitha Tickletooth was the nom de plume of a male author
whose book contained some serious and sensible advice about
cookery, but was also a jest. A glance at its frontispiece, an
engraving of the bulky and forbidding Tabitha, is enough to
establish the latter point. What 'she' says about potatoes is an
example of the former. (See page 210 for more of her.)
De Pomiane, a prominent French writer on cookery of the
1930s, often adopted a scientific approach to the subject; he
declared that, while Gastronomie *was an art, it rested on a*
scientific base which he termed Gastrotechnie *(a term which*
has failed to catch on). In the book from which an extract is
given here, published in 1932 by the Paris Gas Company, he
foreshadowed the work of later authors by emphasising
techniques which are of general application. These were
exemplified by highly specific and exact recipes, such as that
for Pommes de Terre Soufflées.

This appears at first sight to be, next to boiling the tea-kettle, the easiest of all culinary efforts; but daily failures, or 'perishings in the attempt,' show us that in dealing with this tuberous root, we often parallel the proverb of 'one man can lead a horse to the water, but a hundred cannot make him drink;' for although a child may put it into the saucepan, a brigade of the most illustrious '*chefs*' that ever wore white caps, men who, like '*le Grand Vatel,*' would die for the honour of their profession, cannot force or coax it to boil well, *if nature has determined otherwise.*

This is the cause why so many good housewives are often in despair when, in spite of plain boiling, steaming, with or without their jackets, drying, &c. &c., the cleanest, smoothest, and best looking farinaceous warranted Yorkshire regents, pink eyes, cups, or apples, turn out 'waxy, sad, or bony,' and dropsical. 'To begin with the beginning,' then, in your efforts to merit the reputation of a good cook, let your first care be to procure good materials, for without good quality your greatest skill will prove unavailing; but experience will teach you that there are many sorts of potatoes which will 'steam' although they wont boil, others which require quick boiling, others slow, others which should be peeled, and others which should retain their skins.

No certain rule can be laid down to be generally adopted among the various methods I have detailed; nothing but constant practice will enable you to judge of the 'natures of the craytures,' and how to deal with them accordingly. The best guide I can offer is to select those with rough skins, and eschew those with numerous large eyes; and if you have doubts of their soundness, break off a small piece, and if the inside be spotted or honeycombed, reject them as worthless. To proceed with my receipt. Buy your 'fruit' in the mould, for the scrubbing and washing as practised by the potato merchants several days before use, greatly injure their crispness and freshness. Scrub them well with a hard brush, but do not cut out the eyes, or partially pare them, as by so doing you will let the water into the heart, and produce all the bad boiling qualities you desire to avoid. Carefully select them of an equal size, and put them into a saucepan with a tablespoon of salt, and just sufficient cold water to cover them; for if there be too large a quantity they must necessarily remain in the water long before they boil, and consequently break before they are done. When they have boiled five minutes, pour off the *hot* water and replace it with *cold** and half a tablespoonful of salt. Neither simmer nor 'gallop,' but boil steadily (with the cover on) three-quarters of an hour, some kinds (which you will discover by watching, and gently testing with a fork, *if they be not cracked*), will not require more than half an hour. When you are sure that they must be done (if you are in doubt, probe them with a fork) drain them dry, and put a clean cloth (kept for the especial purpose) upon them, cover closely with the lid, and let the saucepan stand on the hob until you are ready to serve your dinner, when you must take them out with a spoon, for if you use a fork for that purpose, you will in all probability break them if they are floury.

N.B. The sooner a potato is eaten after it is done the better.

Cooking and serving in the skins is unquestionably the best method, if the quality of the vegetable will warrant it; but, when peeling is necessary, on the Irish principle of 'killing a sick pig to save its life,' you must make the most of it.

THE DINNER QUESTION

---

* The reason for this innovation on the general practice is, that the heart of the potato being peculiarly hard, the outside, in the ordinary course, is done long before it is softened. By chilling its exterior with cold water, the heat of the first boiling strikes to the centre of the vegetable, and as its force gradually increases when the water boils again, by the time the outside has recovered from its chilling, the equilibrium is restored, and the whole potato is evenly done.

What then is a souffléd potato? It is potato sliced in rounds whose sides have distended due to the expansion of gases within. However, to get a potato to swell in this way it must:

1. be soft enough on the inside to break up easily
2. not be overcooked, crusty or caramelised on the outside so as to prevent it swelling. In other words, the inside has to be well done, while the outside has to remain underdone. A cruel dilemma.

I'll tell you what I am going to do before I begin.

First I shall cook the potato rounds in slightly heated fat. Frying them will soften the insides, but the temperature will not be enough to harden the outsides. I shall then remove the potatoes from the pan. Then I shall increase the heat until the fat begins to smoke. After that I shall pop the cooked potatoes back in the hotter fat. The hot fat will make the vapour inside expand, forcing the limp outsides to swell. They will rise like a soufflé. Then the outsides will caramelise.

Here we go.

The frying pan containing the oil is beginning to smoke on the cooker. It is on a low heat. I shall leave it for a few minutes. Meanwhile I shall cut fifteen or so potato rounds from some enormous Dutch white potatoes. As you will appreciate, the bigger the surface area, the more flexible the outside will be, and the more easily they will expand.

I shall then wipe the potato rounds and line them up, side by side, on a dry cloth.

Meanwhile back at the stove, the fat has cooled.

Step 1. I immerse the potatoes in the fat and give the pan a shake to stop them sticking. Then I'll leave them for four minutes.

Step 2. I turn off the heat and leave the potatoes to cook another seven minutes in the cooling fat.

Step 3. I turn the heat right up and continue shaking the pan as much as possible, holding it by the handles. One or two potato rounds are already rising. I continue to cook them until the potatoes begin to turn red at the edges.

Step 4. I remove the potatoes and strain them. Then I heat the fat further until it smokes.

Step 5. The fat is letting off smoke. I immerse the potato rounds and they nearly all swell up.

When they have turned a rich, golden brown, I take them out with my fish slice or scoop. I drain them ... salt them ... taste them.

They are exquisite.

LA CUISINE POUR LA FEMME DU MONDE

INSTANT SALAD

The first book, at least the first in English, to be devoted to salads was John Evelyn's Acetaria *(1699). It is full of information and advice which is as pertinent today as it was then; and Evelyn often gives us useful reminders – of herbs which are now little known, or of the use of flowers in salads. The short extract from his book which I have chosen may seem less useful (it is hard to credit that salad plants could be grown to edible size in two hours, though I admit that I have not tried), but it serves both to pique curiosity and to exhibit his fine style of writing.*

Now, becaufe among other things, nothing more betrays its unclean and fpurious Birth than what is fo impatiently longed after as *Early Afparagus*, &c. Dr. *Lifter*, (according to his communicative and obliging Nature) has taught us how to raife fuch as our *Gardiners* cover with nafty *Litter*, during the Winter; by rather laying of Clean and Sweet *Wheat-Straw* upon the Beds, *fuper-feminating* and over-ftrowing them thick with the powder of Bruifed *Oyfter-Shells*, &c. to produce that moft tender and delicious *Sallet*. In the mean while, if nothing will fatisfie fave what is rais'd *Ex tempore*, and by Miracles of Art fo long before the time; let them ftudy (like the *Adepti*) as did a very ingenious Gentleman whom I knew; That having fome Friends of his accidentally come to Dine with him, and wanting an early Sallet, Before they fate down to Table fowed *Lettuce* and fome other Seeds in a certain compofition of Mould he had prepared; which within the fpace of two Hours, being rifen near two Inches high, prefented them with a delicate and tender *Sallet*; and this, without making ufe of any naufeous or fulfome Mixture; but of Ingredients not altogether fo cheap perhaps. *Honoratus Faber* (no mean *Philofopher*) fhews us another Method by fowing the Seeds fteep'd in *Vinegar*, cafting on it a good Quantity of *Bean-Shell* Afhes, irrigating them with *Spirit of Wine*, and keeping the Beds well cover'd under dry Matts. Such another Procefs for the raifing early *Peas* and *Beans*, &c. we have the like Accounts of: But were they practicable and certain, I confefs I fhould not be fonder of them, than of fuch as the honeft induftrious Country-man's Field, and Good-Wife's Garden feafonably produce; where they are legitimately born in juft time, and without forcing Nature.

ACETARIA: A DISCOURSE ON SALLETS

Flora Thompson   1939

TOMATOES ARRIVE *at* LARK RISE

Flora Thompson's trilogy, Lark Rise to Candleford, *is rich in
information about food in an English hamlet at the turn of
the century. A more substantial passage appears later (page
159), but I particularly like this short one from* Lark Rise, *the
first of the three books. Yes, one knows that the tomato, which
arrived from the New World centuries ago, was slow to win
acceptance, but the knowledge only took root properly in my
mind when I read this vivid account of its first appearance in*
Lark Rise.

It was on Jerry's cart tomatoes first appeared in the hamlet. They had not long been
introduced into this country and were slowly making their way into favour. The fruit
was flatter in shape then than now and deeply grooved and indented from the stem,
giving it an almost starlike appearance. There were bright yellow ones, too, as well as the
scarlet; but, after a few years, the yellow ones disappeared from the market and the red
ones became rounder and smoother, as we see them now.

At first sight, the basket of red and yellow fruit attracted Laura's colour-loving eye.
'What are those?' she asked old Jerry.

'Love-apples, me dear. Love-apples, they be; though some hignorant folks be a
callin' 'em tommytoes. But you don't want any o' they – nasty sour things, they be, as
only gentry can eat. You have a nice sweet orange wi' your penny.' But Laura felt she
must taste the love-apples and insisted upon having one.

Such daring created quite a sensation among the onlookers. 'Don't 'ee go tryin' to
eat it, now,' one woman urged. 'It'll only make 'ee sick. I know because I had one of the
nasty horrid things at our Minnie's.' And nasty, horrid things tomatoes remained in the
popular estimation for years; though most people today would prefer them as they were
then, with the real tomato flavour pronounced, to the watery insipidity of our larger,
smoother tomato.

LARK RISE

Dr Henri Leclerc   *1927*

JERUSALEM ARTICHOKE

*Dr Leclerc's book on vegetables is matched by another on fruit
and a third on spices, using the same formula of historical,
nutritional, medical and culinary information. I have the
impression that he particularly enjoyed writing about the
topinambour, as the French call it.*

In the early days of April 1613 people strolling through the streets of Paris, always a regular feature of the capital, were able to feast their eyes on a sight never before seen, and one for which they paid absolutely nothing. The sight was that of six authentic savages, Tupinambu Indians from the coast of Brazil, who, thanks to the loyalty their forefathers had shown to France ever since the sixteenth century, were given such a welcome that Malherbe, in a letter to Fabri de Peiresac, was moved to record the following episode:

> This day my lord of Razilly, who is recently returned from the island of
> Maragnon, presented to the Queen six Tupinambus Indians whom he had
> brought hence. Passing via Rouen, he had them dressed in French clothes,
> for, as is the practice in their own land, they go about quite naked, except for
> a black cloth which is worn to cover their private parts; the women wear
> absolutely nothing. They danced a *kind branle*, though they did not join
> hands and neither did they change position. Their violins were made of
> gourds similar to those used by palmers for drinking and to these had been
> affixed nails and pins.

This new kind of saraband scored a great success with the Parisians; indeed it might even have found its way into current choreography if hadn't been for the fact that, two months after their arrival, three of the dancers passed away. The survivors were hastily baptised and the King himself was appointed godfather, though there was soon to be no recollection of the hapless Tupinambus apart from the name of a vegetable; for it was since their fleeting appearance that the people of Paris had given the name of *topinambour* to the tuber whose use had been pointed out to the colonials of New France (Canada) by other savages, Hurons and Algonquins, several years previously. Champlain, who had seen them in the hands of Canadian Indians in 1603, compared their taste with that of the artichoke and, several years later, Lescarbot was referring to them in these terms: 'There is a certain kind of root tuber in this country, about the size of a turnip or truffle, which makes excellent eating and whose taste is reminiscent of the artichoke, if anything more pleasant; they grow in great abundance, as if from spite, and it really is most startling to see.'

Lescarbot, who had eaten these roots either cooked beneath ashes or raw with an oil-based sauce with vinegar and pepper, brought some back to France, where they caught on with extraordinary speed.

The Jerusalem artichoke was given a varied reception by the inhabitants of the old world. Claude Mollet sang their praises in 1615: 'The large tubers make excellent eating during Lent, cooked in the embers like pears and mashed and made into a sauce as one would with artichokes; in fact they taste just like artichokes.' Philip Guybert on the other hand makes no pretence of the loathing he feels for them: 'Another bulbous root is cultivated here which goes by the name of *topinambour*, owing to its country of origin. In my judgement it is no different from the truffle, being no better in taste and giving rise to dizziness, headaches, biliousness and wind in those who use it; for which reason I am persuaded that this barbarous food should be left to those so foolish as to favour only that which comes from afar and who are willing to cross the ocean to find what they consider superior; in my estimation we have healthier, tastier roots in France.' This is precisely what de Combles thinks, declaring that, even though the populace consumes it, the Jerusalem artichoke is 'by common consent the least favoured of vegetables'. It wasn't until Parmentier, undertaking its defence, as he did for the potato, emphasised the benefits it would bring both to nutrition and agriculture, that the Jerusalem artichoke was rehabilitated. Parmentier reminded his readers that, boiled or steamed 'it has a taste similar to that of the artichoke which made it highly sought after by those who favoured the latter', going on to suggest ways of eating it with a white sauce, or in a stew with butter and onions, and pointing out that its blandness could be improved upon by adding a little mustard. He showed that its leaves could be fed to cattle and its more shapely stems used 'as a trellis to support the vine and to perform a similar function in the garden with peas and beans...'

Very close to the artichoke in terms of its organic structure and its constituent elements, the Jerusalem artichoke is put to the same use in the kitchen, and also performs a similar dietary function. It is usually eaten boiled, sautéed in butter and sprinkled with fine herbs or seasoned in a salad as is done with potatoes. The connoisseur to whom such culinary practices may appear a little plain and simple might like to try a recipe suggested to me by one of my friends, a man of wide reading and culture with an original turn of mind, and a gourmet of note. He calls the dish '*strophes de topinambours à la parmentière*' (Jerusalem artichoke sliced into stanzas in the style of Parmentier): 'Prepare slices of veal liver, bacon, potatoes and Jerusalem artichokes of the same shape and size; place them on a skewer, alternatively, following the same pattern each time; place in the oven for 30 to 40 minutes, basting regularly with the meat juices enriched with a little Madeira; add pepper, salt, chervil and a hint of finely chopped shallot; serve and savour.'

Many restaurants serve Jerusalem artichoke as a substitute for artichoke hearts, given the low cost of the former and I have seen even the most experienced of palates taken in by this ruse. When I was the staff medical officer under General Foch, I attended a dinner given for Colonel Weygand, who had recently been awarded the *Légion d'honneur* (this was during the Yser campaign). The crowning glory of the meal was roast beef garnished with artichoke hearts. We were only informed about the precise nature of the dish's vegetable content the day our mess chef, my amiable and learned friend, Dr Briand V. S., having consulted the grease-stained accounts book, came across a paragraph concerning the 'purchase of a kilo of Jerusalem artichokes for artichoke hearts.'

LES LÉGUMES DE FRANCE

Sir Hugh Plat 1594

Of PARSNIPS *and* OTHER MATTERS

Sixteenth century English recipe books may glitter with interesting points for the scholar, but they are heavy going for the non-specialist reader. But there is one book, of inventions rather than recipes, which anyone can dip into with pleasure. This is Sir Hugh Plat's Jewell House of Art and Nature (1594), a delightful jumble of ideas in which some aspects of cookery appear. In the extracts below I have alternated cookery and non-cookery to show with what agility Plat explored everything at once.

SWEET *and* DILICATE CAKES *made* WITHOUT EITHER SPICE *or* SUGAR

Slice great and sweet Parsnep rootes (such as are not seeded) into thin slices, and having washed and scraped them cleane, then drie them and beate them into powder, searching the same through a fine searce [sieve], (Qre. if there might not be som means found out for the grinding of them, whereby to make the greater riddance or quantitie,) Then knead two parts of fine flower with one part of this powder, and make some cakes thereof, and you shall finde them to taste verie daintilie. I have eaten of these cakes diverse times with verie great good liking.

HOWE *to* CLARIFIE HONIE *so that the* TASTE THEREOF *shall be much* ALTERED

Put a gallon of water blood-warme to a gallon of honie, put in your honie first, and with a sticke take the depth thereof in the vessell wherein you boile it, and then put half an ounce of beaten cloves bound in a linnen cloth therein, and let them boile with the water and honie on a gentle fire till all the water bee consumed, which you shall ghesse at by the marke on the sticke. Your hony must be pure and simple not mingled with woort, flowre, or other bad composition, even as it is gathered upon the breaking up of the hives. It is a work of two or three hours, and the elder the honie is the better it serveth for this purpose. You must remember to take away the skum as it riseth. Som boile this honie a little higher to a more consistencie, and preserve fruit therein instead of sugar. These two receits I had of an Oxeford scholer, who assured me that hee had often made proofe therof in the Citie of Oxford, and I know the man to be both of good conceipt, and verie carefull in the commendation of any secrete to his friend otherwise then may well stand with his own credite.

HOW *a* MAN *may* WALKE SAFELIE *upon a* HIGH SCAFFOLD *or* PEECE *of* TIMBER, WITHOUT DANGER *of* FALLING

This is easilie performed by wearing of a paire of spectacles, whose sightes must be made so grose, as that he which weareth them may not discerne any thing a farre off, but at hand onely. For it is the sight onely of the steepenesse of the place, that bringeth the feare, and overturneth the braine....

A CONCEIPTED CHAFINGDISH *to* KEEP *a* DISH *of* MEATE LONG HOTE *upon the* TABLE WITHOUT *any* COLES THEREIN

Let the Dish be somewhat deepe, and cause the Chafingdish to bee made of such shape as may best receive the same, into the which you may convey a peece of yron red hote, the same beeing of an apt forme to lie in the bottome of the Chafingdish. This will continue his heate a long time, and if you have one other spare iron to heat as the first cooleth, you may keepe any dish of meate warme as long as you thinke good.

THE JEWELL HOUSE OF ART AND NATURE

Alexandra Hicks 1985

The CHEMISTRY of GARLIC

What a daunting subject chemistry has become! Even looking
at a page on which the names of chemicals appear is usually
enough to quell the lay person's appetite. But there is
fascinating knowledge to be distilled from the technical works,
and Alexandra Hicks (she who was the first to identify in
public the 'pink peppercorns' which recently had a vogue – but
that is another story) has succeeded here in making
comprehensible to us certain facts, pertinent to cookery, about
the chemistry of garlic.

Although garlic has been used therapeutically for thousands of years, its efficacy has been little understood until quite recent times. In fact, it was not until it was brought into the modern laboratory and assayed that its chemical principles were deciphered and its action understood. Until this time its 'power to cure or alleviate' has been attributed, in great part, to 'magic'. Because garlic is one of the few plants that has such a strong, pungent, effusive odour (one merely needs to rub the soles of one's feet with it in order to make one's breath reek offensively of garlic) the magic surrounding garlic and its effectiveness has been throughout the ages largely concerned with its odour. It was the odour of garlic, then, that entranced and intrigued primitive man and, as far as he was concerned, cured his maladies. Interestingly enough, substances that have strong odours, sharp tastes and marked physiological effects have also long attracted professional chemists. It is not surprising then that chemists brought garlic into their laboratories for investigation. Investigations made by chemists over more than nine centuries establish that cutting a garlic bulb releases a number of low-molecular weight organic molecules that incorporate sulphur atoms in bonding forms that are very infrequently encountered in nature. These molecules are extremely reactive and spontaneously change into other organic sulphur compounds, which in turn continue in further transformations. Furthermore, the molecules display a remarkable range of biological effect. Certain extracts of garlic are antibacterial and antifungal. Other extracts are antithrombotic, that is they inhibit the clotting of blood. It was the reasons for these and other biological effects that chemists were seeking and are now finding. It appears that the answers lie at the molecular level among the substances in garlic.

[The author describes early experimental work before coming to the important discoveries made by the American chemist C. J. Cavallito in 1944.]

It is interesting that although allicin accounts for the odour of garlic, a garlic bulb exhibits little or no odour until it is cut or crushed and it was not until 1948 that science knew why. The reason was discovered by Arthur Stoll and Ewold Seebeck in Basel who found that allicin develops in garlic only when an enzyme, known as allinase, initiates its formation from an odourless precursor molecule, which Stoll and Seebeck identified as Allicin [(+)-s-allyl-1-cysteine sulphoxide, or $CH_2 = CHCH_2S(O)CH_2(NH_2)COOH$]. The (+) and the (l) signify a particular spatial arrangement for the sulphur atom and for the carbon atom attached to nitrogen. This precursor, which was named by Stoll and Seebeck, accounts for .24% of the weight of a typical garlic bulb and can be formed by attaching an allyl group and an oxygen atom to the sulphur atom in the amino acid cysteine. This will enable allicin to be made synthetically in the laboratory. Simply stated, when a clove of garlic is cut or crushed, its extracellular membrane separates into sections. This enables an enzyme called allinase to come in contact and combine with the precursor or substrate alliin to form allicin, which contains the odoriferous constituent of garlic. However, the reaction of the enzyme allinase does not stop with the formation of allicin but continues to act on a number of molecules, showing that it has a number of substrates. These substrates are sulphur-containing substrates synthesised in garlic by chemical sequences that start with the sulphur-containing amino acid cysteine. Allinase enzymes then produce several sulphenic acids and two by-products of the reactions, namely pyruvate and ammonia, from them. Furthermore, the reactions require the participation of another substance, or cofactor, namely pyridoxal phosphate. The pyridoxal phosphate and the substrate then interact, converting the substrate into an activated form. A basic proton-capturing group in the enzyme then initiates the release of sulphenic acid. These sulphenic acids are very unstable and, in turn, spontaneously undergo further reactions, thus decomposing the allicin ...

In a nut shell, the garlic bulb contains an odourless, sulphur-containing amino acid derivative called alliin. This parent compound has no antibacterial properties but when the bulb is cut or broken, alliin comes into contact with an enzyme known as allinase which converts the alliin into allicin. Allicin is not only a potent antibacterial agent but is also the carrier of the potent odour. Allicin is extremely unstable and breaks down, depending on the method used, into various other useful and therapeutic compounds, including the lastest discovery of the antithrombotic ajoene.

Finally, garlic's mystique has been solved and although it is definitely still associated with its odour, it can no longer be attributed to the odour, nor to the Devil, nor to any other form of previous magic. Rather the answer lies in garlic's various components such as the rather magical allicin (as we have seen it is here one moment and gone the next) and others. It stands to reason that now that the chemical components have been isolated, analysed and identified they could be successfully synthesised in the laboratory and that is precisely what is happening. Researchers at the University of Minesota in the USA, and others, have successfully synthesised the major chemical constituents of garlic with the result that the useful applications of garlic's antifungal, antibiotic, antigermicidal and 'antisocial' factors could become very important and diversified.

At the University of Washington, Washington State, USA, scientists have cooked up a garlic surprise for animals that damage forest and orchard trees and vines. The surprise lies in a time release capsule that gives trees garlic breath. Pellets, filled with *dimelimine selenide*, are planted with the trees, gradually dissolved by water, absorbed by the roots and taken up by the tree. The tree then eliminates the compound dimethyl selenide, which is the very same garlicky odour one emits after eating garlic bread or any other form of garlic. the trees showed no growth impairment when companion-planted with the garlicky pellets but even the hungriest of rabbits and deer were repelled. Apparently, humans can detect a garlicky odour on a warm day, but the researchers claim that the people 'do not generally find the smell overpowering'. One wonders what it will do to the flavour of the fruits and berries. Anyone for garlic-flavoured grape, apricot or apple?

> Garlic then have power to save from death
> Bear with it though it maketh unsavoury breath,
> And scorn not garlic like some that think
> It only maketh men wink and drink and stink.
> *The Englishman's Doctor, Sir John Harington (1609)*

'Cookery: Science, Lore and Books'
OXFORD SYMPOSIUM DOCUMENTS 1984/5

Jane Grigson   1978

PEAS

Every vegetable receives its due in Jane Grigson's Vegetable Book, *but none fares better than the pea. (See also pages 58 and 294.)*

Everybody loves peas. East and west, it's the world's favourite vegetable. Peas were the first vegetable to be canned, the first to be frozen. They are the gourmet's delight – and the only green vegetable that most children will eat. As far away as Peking, boys and girls listen for the pea vendor's bell in early summer. They rush out with their bowls when he trundles his car into the street, watch their ladle of peas being cooked, then run home picking at them as they go.

The peas of long antiquity were prized as an important part of winter's diet, not as summer's delight. Dried and grey, they could not be compared, even in their youth, with our modern garden peas, green, sweet, succulent.

For this we have to thank Italian gardeners of the late Renaissance, who developed better varieties of pea. No longer a case of cottager's pease pudding, lenten fare, but the courtier's pleasure. At Versailles the new *piselli*, or *petits pois*, the little peas from Italy, became an object of secret gluttony. Ladies who had eaten with Louis XIV – and eaten some of the best food in Europe – might be found gobbling peas last thing at night in the seclusion of their bedrooms.

No such orgies are recorded at the English court, when marrowfat peas were first developed at the beginning of the nineteenth century (the name describes the tenderness of these peas, which are wrinkled with sweetness). But they had their little drama. Do you remember the conflict between peas and politesse at Mr Holbrooke's party, in Cranford? Mary, the young narrator, recalls that –

'When the duck and green peas came, we looked at each other in dismay; we had only two-pronged, black-handled forks ... Miss Matty picked up her peas one by one, on the point of the prongs ... Miss Pole sighed over her delicate young peas as she left them on one side of her plate untasted, for they *would* drop between the prongs. I looked at my host; the peas were going wholesale into his capacious mouth, shovelled up by his large, round-ended knife. I saw, I imitated, I survived!'

Would she, I wonder, have imitated Mr Holbrook if he'd chosen another way –

> I eat my peas with honey,
> I've done it all my life.
> It may taste kind of funny,
> But it keeps them on the knife.

In these more relaxed days, our problem is not how to eat peas, but how to find good peas in the first place. People with gardens are able to pick them at just the right moment, and cook them within a couple of hours. This is perfection. The rest of us have to chase round greengrocers' shops, trying to find peas which haven't been picked too large, or kept too long.

Often one is driven back ineluctably to frozen peas, even in June. Professional eaters-out may scoff, but if they lived in the country and had to endure their neighbours' podded bullets, they would conclude that frozen peas are sometimes the only honest choice. They can be delicious, particularly the *petits pois*, if cooked with care. I reflect that we have been trying to beat winter starvation for centuries and centuries. I think we should be grateful, and not guilty, when we buy frozen peas – particularly in December – reflecting that a hundred years ago one subsisted for six or seven months of the year on root and dried vegetables.

I refuse, though, to feel any gratitude for canned peas, British style. Why can't our manufacturers lose their dye-bags, and study the methods of European firms? The tiny French peas stewed with onion and carrot are a vegetable no one need be ashamed of putting on the table.   JANE GRIGSON'S VEGETABLE BOOK

The BEST PICKLED GHERKIN

*Here is a Janus-like author, one side of him facing fearlessly
up to philosophy (G. E. Moore and the Cambridge Apostles,
1979), the other disgorging lively writings on food (collected
in* Out to Lunch, *1986). In the latter capacity he is described
as 'funny, contentious, authoritative and opinionated – when
Paul Levy speaks, teacups rattle'; so I have chosen a funny
and authoritative opinion from him, which may or may not be
contentious.*

What I am about to divulge is the best recipe in the world – I write this without
conscious hyperbole – for one of the classic dishes. And if anyone should object
that a pickled cucumber does not, in itself, constitute a 'dish', I shall simply have
to quibble.

It is true that man cannot live by pickled cucumbers alone, or even make a
complete meal of them without accompaniment. But it is equally true that there are
some noble gustatory experiences that would not merely be incomplete, but almost
unthinkable, without their pickled cucumber garnish.

The dreaded salt beef sandwich, of course. But what about coarse *terrine, pâté de
campagne, rillettes d'oie* and *de porc*, and all kosher products of the charcutier's art?

My recipe for pickled cucumber is not only suitable for putting up the *cornichon*
that is indispensable to the enjoyment of the above, but it produces a superior gherkin
to any you can buy. For mine is pickled in brine, and has very little vinegar. Of course,
the recipe is not, strictly speaking, mine, although I tracked it down.

The search for the perfect pickled cucumber was a relentless one. It took me to
Manhattan more times than I would care to recount. In the service of the quest I ordered
and consumed incredible, sick-making quantities not only of salt beef, but of (much
nicer) pastrami.

My researches took me to the further reaches of Florida, where I should not care to
return. And to neighbourhood delicatessens in Chicago. I combed the East End, not for
a perfect pickled cucumber, merely for a *good* one. Even some well-known establishments not a million miles from Baker Street could not satisfy my questing palate.

In the end, I found the recipe in my own backyard. It belonged to the mother of my
best friend from childhood. This tale may seem unbelievable to those who cannot credit
the existence of a large colony of people of Russian-Jewish descent in Lexington,
Kentucky, where I was born.

Yet truth will out. One day, down there on a visit, Ada Gail, the mother of my friend, a renowned cook and a good painter, gave me a pickled cucumber. And I instantly knew that *that* was the pickled cucumber of my youth, the taste I was seeking to recapture. (And, incidentally, it was so literally. For my own mother told me that Ada's pickled cucumbers had been among the most precious of gifts, frequently bestowed in my infancy and youth.)

You can plant dill and even cucumbers – though seed for the sort used in America and Russia is difficult to get here, and you would be well advised to buy a case of the short, stubby Israeli or Cypriot cucumbers if you ever see them at your greengrocer.

In each large sterilised storage jar (Kilner or Le Parfait) place sprigs of fresh dill; three peeled cloves of garlic; one chilli; six black peppercorns; a pinch of mixed pickling spices; and, to keep the pickle crisp, a pinch of alum (obtainable from the chemist).

Fill the jar with scrubbed *cornichons* or gherkins about three to four inches long, and pour *hot* brine, made by boiling 10.5 litres (14½ pints) of water with 340 g (12 oz) coarse salt and 120 ml (4 fl oz) cider vinegar. Place a vine leaf, if available, over the contents of each jar and seal. Wait for the brine to ferment, after two or three days, and top up with the boiling brine that you have reserved for this purpose. You can start eating the pickle four or five days after fermentation has ceased.

In the same sugarless brine, following the same procedure, you can pickle almost anything. But do try French beans, shallots, tiny cobs of sweetcorn, small sweet peppers and, especially, green tomatoes.

OUT TO LUNCH

Rena Salaman   *1983*

GREEK GREENS

*Rena Salaman lives in London, but escapes to her other home
on a Greek island at the beginning of every summer. In her
books the passages about the foodstuffs and the people
compete with the recipes for attention. Here she brings alive for
us the whole matter of hand-picked wild greens, one of the
central features of Greek ways with food.*

It is inevitable in a country like Greece, where vegetables constitute a major part of the national diet, that salads should be taken for granted as they are. They are as much part of the everyday table as knives and forks. They are not just something to nibble at; on the contrary, very often they are the main course coupled with some delicately fried fish, squid or sweetbreads. Their arrival at the table, even at restaurants, is never questioned; it is expected. Always seasonal, they vary from the most ordinary, such as tomatoes, cucumbers and lettuces to the most eccentric and esoteric of hand-picked wild greens (*horta* as they are collectively described) from nearby hills and fields, or at their most unusual, made of wild plants which grow in the cracks of gigantic rock formations by the sea. These are called *kritama* in Greek, or rock samphire (*Chritmum Maritimum*) as it is known commonly in England. It is a short, soft, fleshy, spiked-leaf plant of a cactaceous appearance and grey-green colour.

Rock samphire was best known as a pickle in seventeenth-century England but very popular as a vegetable in the nineteenth century, boiled and strained and served with butter. This is very popular on our island. From March onwards the short leaves are collected in quantities and treated like any other wild greens. They are first boiled and then strained and dressed with olive oil and lemon. Apart from valuing it as a salad the local people believe that it also has medicinal qualities against rheumatism. It has quite a definite bitter, slightly sour taste of aniseed and it takes some time to get used to and become a believer. Since I was introduced to it, quite late in my life, I still haven't become one! In the Pilion villages they pickle it and offer it as a *meze* with *ouzo*.

In no other country have I seen such an affinity for wild hand-picked greens as well as their specially cultivated counterparts, as in Greece. '*Agria horta tou vounou*', wild greens from the mountains or '*Imera horta*' (strictly translated 'tame greens') were street cries that we grew up with.

There is an enormous variety of the wild greens that appear with the first autumnal rains, such as all kinds of dandelions and delicious *vrouves* in the spring (a kind of mustard with tiny yellow flowers).

There is a wonderful description of *vrouves* growing in one of the most unlikely places in Athens, none less than the Acropolis, in William Miller's *Greek Life in Town and Country* (p. 194). 'The sacred rock of the Acropolis produces a mustard plant from which an excellent salad is made and in February numbers of women may be seen collecting herbs and digging up roots on the Pnyx and near the monument of Philopappos, which they cook and eat . . .'

I am sure *vrouves* as well as the other wild varieties of *horta* are still growing around the foot of the Acropolis and the hill of Philopappos, along with soft carpets of chamomile with the first rays of spring. I am also quite certain that you will not see anyone collecting them, as in the past two years the pollution in Athens has reached such unacceptable standards that it has alarmed even the Greeks, though optimists by nature.

There are also young poppy plants which are collected before they flower and are not only used as a salad like the rest but on the island are also used as a filling to a delicious pie.

Then there are their cultivated counterparts, *radikia*, a spinach-leafed-like plant, another variety called *italika* which resemble rhubarb plants on a micro-scale, with their unusually red slender stems (perhaps this is the reason I still cannot get used to eating rhubarb as a dessert in any form), there are curly endives (*andithia*) which are also used in a lamb fricassee, and the most delicious of all, *vlita*, which no visitor to Greece should miss an opportunity of trying in the spring and early summer. *Vlita* has a sweet but also faintly sour taste that one can get addicted to. It seeds itself so easily that on our island it is not even cultivated; it just comes back every spring here and there, in people's gardens or disused fields, and there it really thrives unless it is a particularly dry spring and summer. Then consequently all the crops suffer, since most of them do not rely on irrigation systems but on God's good will!

All these greens are always first boiled, covered in salted water, then strained and dressed with a refreshing olive oil and lemon dressing. There is a great tradition of collecting wild greens in Greece, as the extract from W. Miller so picturesquely reaffirms. Very often in the autumn or the spring, a Sunday family outing from Athens would be a *horta*-picking expedition to the nearby countryside of Penteli, Marathon, Tatoi, or slightly further on the way to Delphi with the breathtaking mountain views and the wonderful amphitheatre along with the other archaeological treasures waiting at the end. These outings would always be followed by an exquisite lunch in some small, isolated place with huge barrels of wine and a roaring fire.

Sometimes, one could see hillsides dotted by the colourful *horta* pickers, since whenever a good spot was discovered it would soon attract other cars to stop and join in with singing and joking and laughing echoing and bringing the deserted hillsides to life. Sometimes we would hold competitions among the family of who could collect the largest amount. These were all rituals that brightened our childish lives and gave them a sense of continuity, as all rituals do, and I still get an enormous joy out of similar expeditions.

I remember how proud I was when, while on a school outing for the day, I spent the entire morning gathering *horta* with my little blunt knife and storing them in my jacket and how proud I was when I presented my grandmother with my trove at the end of the day.

During the German occupation and the terrible famine of the years 1943–4, wild greens saved a lot of lives and if the favourites could not be found, there was always an abundance of nettles, which even the Germans could not stop from growing. Friends a little older than myself can clearly remember eating boiled nettles quite often.

In the villages and, of course, in our village on the island, gathering *horta* is almost done routinely at the end of a working day in the fields or the olive groves along with the other essentials – that is a pile of firewood for the home hearth and a huge bunch of greenery for the goats' daily meals. One of the goats' favourite bushes is a large evergreen shrub with small glossy leaves called *koumaria* in Greek, *Arbutus Unedo* or as it is known commonly in the west, a strawberry tree. This grows wild in abundance in the Greek countryside and on the hillsides of our island. This was also a favourite of our childhood years, not for its shiny leaves but for its brightly red-orange and perfect round berries that achieved magical qualities, to our eyes at least, ripening as they were in the autumn amidst a season of discipline and fading colours, coinciding with the opening of our schools. I remember particularly the familiar smell of our brand new books covered neatly in dark blue paper by our mother, our new stiff dark blue uniforms ready for the 'battle' and above all the remote autumnal melancholy that vibrated in the air.

GREEK FOOD

Patience Gray 1986

La SALSA: *Tomato Sauce*

The remarkable book Honey from a Weed, *on which I worked as editor and publisher with the author for two years, is the fruit of twenty years' experience of life and food in simple surroundings in the Mediterranean – Tuscany, Catalonia, Naxos, and now Apulia, which is the home of La Salsa. Because she does herself what she describes, writing always 'from inside' and not as a mere observer, passages such as this have an exceptionally vivid quality. (See also page 281.)*

The sauce that many Apulian householders prepare for winter is made on a large scale, involving the whole family and at least a hundred kilos of Leccesi tomatoes grown for this purpose, but often far more.

In the first weeks of July the ripening tomatoes are picked at dawn with their short stems, then laid out in a covered space to ripen further (in a garage, spare room, or wine-making place, *il palmento*). During this time bottles, elegant old liqueur bottles or mineral water bottles, are assembled, washed, laid upside down to drain in the hottest sun. Cauldrons are scoured, glazed earthenware vats are washed and turned upside down, firewood (olive) is prepared, corks or metal caps lined up, the tomato machine examined, herbs gathered, packets of sea salt acquired.

One day at 6 in the morning, the operation begins. While the man of the house prepares the outdoor fires and sets the iron tripods, the women, crouching over a deep scarlet sea of tomatoes on the floor, at speed remove the stalks and carry basins of fruit to the now filled vat, pouring them in, then lightly squeezing the tomatoes under water to release some of the seeds and some of their acid, and rapidly fill the cauldrons. Into each cauldron half a purple onion is sliced up, some sprigs of thyme and rosemary are added and a handful of salt, together with a cup of water. The man then bears the cauldrons away and sets them on the fires, putting on their lids. While the contents of the cauldrons cook, every domestic vessel is being filled with more slightly crushed tomatoes, taken from the water vat. The cauldrons are stirred from time to time and, once they come to the boil, cooked (10 minutes) till the contents acquire a deeper colour and are soft.

Near the fire is a large tin bath with over it a beautiful circular rush mat, a kind of sieve. The man, protecting his hands with rags, pours the contents of the first cauldron onto the rush mat. The juice runs through and a dense tomato mush remains. The mush is carefully poured into another earthenware crock, placed on a table, to which the tomato separating machine has been affixed, under a tree. By now, it is 8 o'clock and already hot.

Someone starts putting the tomatoes into the top of the machine with a cup and someone else winds the handle and prods. The seeds and skins spill out onto a plate on one side, and the sauce pours into an earthenware vessel on the other. Meanwhile ever new cauldrons are being boiled up.

Some of the liquor of the last cauldron can be added if the sauce is too thick. The aim is to get a sauce which is very dense, but not so dense that once in the bottle it will refuse to come out. By this time everyone is covered with tomato juice and their hands which have been yellow turn black, the effect of the acid.

In the end there is a huge vat of dense sauce on the one hand, and a mountain of skins and seeds on the other. The seeds released into the water vat are removed with a fine sieve and dried in the sun against next year's planting, when they will be sown on heat in February covered with plastic sheets.

The sauce now has to be measured; this is done by transferring it by litre measure from one vat to another. Supposing the outcome of this operation is 60 litres of sauce, a measured quantity of salicylic acid is going to be added: 1 gram for each litre of sauce, plus 2 grams for every 10 litres – total 72 grams of salicylic acid.

Two or three handfuls of sea salt are added to the sauce and stirred in; it is then transported indoors to an aerated room and covered. At dusk the salicylic acid, precisely calculated, is poured in, the stirring repeated, and the sauce left to rest overnight, then stirred at dawn.

BOTTLING *the* SAUCE

Using a funnel and some kind of jug, you fill each bottle leaving a little space at the top, the space being filled afterwards with a sprig of basil and a covering of olive oil. But first you have to 'bump' the bottles to get the air bubbles out. You then with a clean white rag clean the inside neck of each bottle, and line them up on a table, insert the leaf of basil, fill up with olive oil, and put in the corks. After two or three days you drive them in, and now have more than enough tomato sauce for winter, which is good, because you can give some of it away.

There are two other ways of making *la salsa:* (1) *sotto la manta*, under the cloak;

(2) sterilising the freshly bottled sauce, by packing the bottles in straw and fitting them into a gigantic petrol bin, and boiling again. I have described the method we always use imparted by our neighbour Teresa because it is good. Without her help and instructions we might never have got down to it. Once the operation is mastered it is possible at the same time to prepare some *pomodori pelati*, a conserve of plum tomatoes, and *la salsa secca*, probably the most healthy conserve in existence.

The tomato concentrate *par excellence* is most simply made on the same day as *la salsa*, by abstracting a quantity of freshly passed tomato sauce before its transfer by litre measure to the second vat, as already described

At this point you line up as many plates as you can find, say 30, and rob the vat, using a breakfast cup – a cup of sauce goes into each plate. A little salt is sprinkled on the surface, and the plates are transported onto the parapet of the roof. Please note: the paste only dries with the help of the north wind, and if the *scirocco* is blowing it is of no use.

In any case, one has to keep on stirring the paste, with a wooden spoon, and later, with a knife, one pares off the little fragments that dry at the edge of each plate. If it is extremely hot (38–40°C) and a good wind is blowing, by nightfall the paste will have so reduced that you can combine the contents of two plates and use the vacant ones to cover the others for the night. Next day: scrape away at these plates, working the dried bits into the thickening paste. You do this 4 or 5 times a day. By nightfall the contents of the 15 plates can be reduced to 7, covering them again and taking down the spare plates to wash them. On the third day, by stirring and scraping, the paste may have dried sufficiently to be amalgamated onto one large dish, which you cover. Next day: critical inspection, the mass should be convincingly dry and of a deep red colour. If in doubt, continue to work it from time to time until mid-day. Then take it down, cover with a cloth, let it rest.

Next day you massage this lump of rich red concentrate with the best olive oil until it shines. Then oil some litre or $\frac{1}{2}$ litre jars lavishly inside, rolling the oil around, stuff in the paste and cover with $2\frac{1}{2}$ cm (1″) of oil.

This is used in winter in preparing legumes; is spread on a bread; enriches the bottled tomato sauce for pasta and in cooking *pezzetti*; is added to a poultry braise; i.e. is employed in a thousand ways.

Honey from a Weed

EAT MORE MUSHROOMS

The Reverend Badham wrote one of the most engaging of the
numerous Victorian treatises on mushrooms, and did not fail
to implore his countrymen to be more open-minded about
eating them. Here, after dwelling on the delights of
mushroom-gathering in Italy, he comes to the peroration with
which his book concludes. (In a footnote he tells how he
himself ate 31 different species in a single year. But this
record seems puny beside that of William Delisle Hay, who
states in his boringly-titled Elementary Text-book of the
British Fungi, *1887, that he had eaten over 200. And an*
Italian author of the 20th century has claimed 1250.)
Badham wrote on fish too: see page 125.

Not only in Italy, in our own country also, the Collector in Mycology will have to traverse much beautiful and diversified scenery; amid woods, greenswards, winding lanes, rich meadows, healthy commons, open downs, the nodding hop-grove and the mountain sheep-path; and all shone upon by an autumnal sunset, – as compared with Southern climes 'obscurely bright,' and unpreceded by that beautiful rosy tint which bathes the whole landscape in Italy, but with a far finer background of clouds to reflect its departed glories: and throughout all this range of scenery he will never hunt in vain; indulgent gamekeepers, made aware of what he is poaching, may warn him that he is not collecting mushrooms, but will never warn him off from the best-kept preserves. In such rambles he will see, what I have this autumn (1847) myself witnessed, whole *hundredweights of rich wholesome diet rotting under the trees; woods teeming with food and not one hand to gather it;* and this, perhaps, in the midst of potato blight, poverty and all manner of privations, and public prayers against imminent famine. I have indeed grieved, when I reflected on the straitened condition of the lower orders this year, to see pounds innumerable of extempore beef-steaks growing on our oaks in the shape of *Fistulina hepatica, Ag. fusipes* to pickle, in clusters under them; Puff-balls, which some of our friends have not inaptly compared to sweet-bread for the rich delicacy of their unassisted flavour; *Hydna* as good as oysters, which they somewhat resemble in taste; *Agaricus deliciosus*, reminding us of tender lamb-kidneys; the beautiful yellow Chantarelle, that *kalon kagathon* of diet, growing by the bushel, and no basket but our own to pick up a few specimens in our way; the sweet nutty-flavoured *Boletus*, in vain calling himself *edulis* where there was none to believe him; the dainty *Orcella*; the *Ag. heterophyllus*, which tastes like the craw-fish when grilled; the *Ag.*

ruber and *Ag. virescens*, to cook in any way, and equally good in all; – these were among the most conspicuous of the *trouvailles*. But that the reader may know all he is likely to find in one single autumn, let him glance at the catalogue below. He may at first alarm his friends' cooks, but their fears will, I promise him, soon be appeased, after one or two trials of this new class of viands, and he will not long pass either for a conjuror or something worse, in giving directions to stew *toadstools*. As soon as he is initiated in this class of dainties, he will, I am persuaded, loose no time in making the discovery known to the poor of the neighbourhood; while in so doing he will render an important service to the country at large, by instructing the indigent and ignorant in the choice of an ample, wholesome, and excellent article, which they may convert into money, or consume at their own tables, when properly prepared, throughout the winter.

A TREATISE ON THE ESCULENT FUNGUSES OF ENGLAND

Elizabeth David 1981

MAD, BAD, DESPISED *and* DANGEROUS

This free-ranging exploration of the history of the aubergine
in Europe embodies, as Elizabeth David says, 'quite a
collection of oddities'. (See also pages 32 and 232.)

The attractive proposition that aubergine and auberge might have some connection was recently put to me. It opened up some glorious possibilities. The game had to be resisted. There are already plenty of garblings of the Indian *badinjan* without my weaving an *aubergiste* or a *jardinier de l'auberge* or other such fancy into the rich confusion. So I turned instead to a few remembered cookery book and other references, early and late, to the aubergine, badinjan, berenjena, melanzana, or egg plant. Quite a collection of oddities could be put together. The present one is more than a beginning.

The first book I turned to was a modern one, Dr. Henri Leclerc's *Les Légumes de France*, undated but circa 1930. Dr. Leclerc, a physician on General Foch's medical staff during the 1914 war, subsequently produced some entertaining and original works about vegetables and fruit, their origins, their history, and how best to cook them. He was keen on vegetarian diets, but – being possessed of a sense of humour – never over-persuaded. His comments on the derivation of aubergine provide a good example of his touch:

The word aubergine is among those which must fill with joy the souls of those numerous philologists whose innocent mania it is to claim that every term in the language derives from Sanscrit; without in the least being forced

114

into the tortuous acrobatics which such exercises usually entail, they may elegantly and painlessly prove that *Vatin Gana*, name of the aubergine in Sanscrit, gave birth to the Persian *badingen*, from which the Arabs derived *albadingen*, which via the Spanish *albadingena* became the aubergine.

The Spaniards appear to have accepted *berenjenas*, as they were called in the early Spanish cookery books, without difficulty. In the 1529 edition of *Libro De Guisades Manjares Y Potajes*, Ruperto de Nola for example, gives four recipes for them, including one for *berenjenas en escabeche* and one for *berenjenas espesas*, peeled aubergines cooked in meat broth with onions and pounded almonds, sieved, and made into an egg-thickened custard spiced with nutmeg, cinnamon, cloves, dried coriander 'softened', and Aragonese cheese.

In Italy *berenjenas* had a bad press. They were variously called *mala insana* and *pomi disdegnosi*, and also had some garbled names such as *molegnane moniache* (Cristofaro di Messisburgo, *Libro Novo*, 1557) indicating that they were in some way associated with Armenia, like apricots. Antonio Frugoli, an early seventeenth century steward who wrote a hefty work on the art and practice of stewardship, published in Rome in 1631, calls them *marignani*, and says they are low class food, eaten by Jews. This curious piece of folklore – did it have some relation to the provenance of the plant? – was repeated two and a half centuries later by Pellegrino Artusi in his *Scienza in Cucina*, ca. 1880, asserting that 'forty years ago they were scarcely to be seen in the Florence market, being held base Jewish food'. He calls them *petonciani*. We are almost back to *badinjan*. At what period *petonciani* turned into the modern Italian *melanzane* I have no idea. Probably both names, with local and regional variations coexisted for a long time. Certainly Scappi in 1570 uses both *molignane* and *melanzane*, so does Castore Durante in his *Herbario Novo* of 1585. As for those *pomi disdegnosi* of the fifteenth and sixteenth centuries, a recipe for candying them in the Genoese fashion appeared in Alexis of Piedmont's *De Secreti* published in 1557. In the English translation of this work, done from the French published in 1558, the recipe was omitted. The translator was probably baffled by those mad, bad, despised, noxious apples. I don't know if candied aubergines were still made in Genoa or anywhere else, but I do remember many years ago in Greece buying, out of curiosity, a tin of aubergine jam, one of those very sweet and heavily syrupy confections you get given in Greece in spoonfuls, as a token of hospitality. The aubergines were tiny little things, and could just as easily have been infant melons or cucumbers as aubergines. The confection was a strange one, but then the aubergine *is* strange, in appearance, in texture and in taste. Its capacity to absorb olive oil, butter or whatever cooking medium is used is also notorious. One way and another, early resistance to this odd fruit is understandable.

The sixteenth century Roman physician Castore Durante, in his *Herbario Novo* mentioned above, said *petonciane* or *melanzane* were really not of a very agreeable taste, they were windy, hard to digest, and not a healthy food. Although they are eaten in

Italy like mushrooms, boiled, with oil, salt, and pepper, or boiled in slices and eaten as a salad with oil, pepper and vinegar, or again prepared in a pickle, if you eat them too often they generate melancholy humours, cancer, leprosy, headaches, hardening of the liver and the spleen, and induce long fevers and a bad complexion in the whole person. However, prepared and eaten as he had described 'they are less harmful'. In Germany, says Durante, *melanzane* are called *Dollapffel*, and in Latin *melengena* or *mala insana*, in French 'pomes demoers, which is to say *pomi d'amore*'. A fine piece of confusion, not helped when you find that Durante also calls tomatoes both *pomi d'oro* and *pomi d'Amor*, but in Latin *aurea mala*. They are a kind of *melanzane*, he says. Some were red as blood when they are ripe, others the colour of gold; some call them *pomi d'etiopia*, Ethiopian apples. They are eaten in the same way as *melanzane*, with pepper, salt, and oil, but they provide little and poor nourishment. Interesting, that reference to tomatoes being known as Ethiopian apples. They must have already been cultivated in Africa some while before Durante, who is supposed to have been one of Pope Sixtus V's physicians, was working on his Herbal.

Perhaps I should also mention that the tomato, like the aubergine, was at one time dubbed *mala insana*, at any rate according to Doctor Leclerc. As for the *pommes d'amour* confusion, that one persisted for quite a while in France. La Quintinye in 1695 mentions *melanzane* or *pommes d'amour* in his list of plants which dislike the cold, others being Indian pepper, summer savory, and the *pomme d'orée*. Evidence of how the French cooked aubergines in the seventeenth and eighteenth centuries is singularly lacking. Doctor Leclerc says they didn't. What the Doctor seems not to have known is that in the Catalan language the aubergine is *alberginia*, surely an indication that aubergines had crossed the Spanish Catalan frontiers into southern France long before the time they were first launched on the Paris market which, again according to Doctor Leclerc, was not until 1825, when they were introduced by a specialist in *primeurs* called Decouflé, whose business was in the rue de la Santé. Whether by that time European cooks had discovered that the two kinds of *pommes d'amour*, both of the Solanaceae family, had a certain affinity for each other, I am none too sure, but what is certain is that in our own times the aubergine began to get submerged in tomato purées and sauces, and modern French recipes became rather repetitious. But Doctor Leclerc offers the following variant of the Turkish *Imam bayeldi*, which has one or two original features, with the tomatoes kept under control ...

AUBERGINES *à* L'ATHENIENNE

Split a dozen aubergines in quarters lengthwise and without completely separating them. Prepare a mixture of vegetables as follows: coarsely shred 5 skinned and deseeded tomatoes, a handful of sorrel and 2 onions; add 6 chopped cloves of garlic and a little fennel, likewise chopped; season with salt, pepper, and cayenne. Stuff the mixture into the quartered aubergines, which you press back into shape and tie with string. Arrange them in a baking dish. Pour over them the juice of 5 lemons and a quarter of a bottle of olive oil. Put into the oven for 35 to 40 minutes, then leave them to cool in their sauce, if possible on ice.

Arrange the aubergines in a vegetable dish and pour the cooking juices over them. This is served cold and as an hors-d'oeuvre.

'In savouring the preparation,' Doctor Leclerc adds, 'in which so many different flavours have harmonised, it is difficult not to feel compassion for the centuries of ignorance and darkness in which the aubergine, the aubergine with its amethyst skin, confined in dispensaries between the pallid marshmallow and the perfidious hemlock was reduced to the subaltern and humiliating role of anodine poultice.' This last remark is explained by an earlier paragraph in Doctor Leclerc's essay in which he quotes from Valmont de Bomare's *Dictionnaire raisonné universelle d'histoire naturelle*, 1776. According to Valmont de Bomare the aubergine was used only in the form of anodine and resolvative poultices in the treatment of haemorrhoids, cancers, burns and inflammations. Doctor Castore Durante, who was of the opinion that *mala insana* or *melanzana* could cause cancer, would probably have thought it very proper to use the same offending fruit in its treatment.

PETITS PROPOS CULINAIRES (PPC) *9*

FOOD *from the* WATERS

*Why do molluscs and crustaceans seem to
inspire more fine writing than fish? Reading
William Warner on the blue crabs of
Chesapeake Bay and Eleanor Clark on the
oysters of Locmariaquer is enough to prompt
this question. And it is noticeable that one
of the most engaging bits of writing by
Alexandre Dumas for his encyclopaedic work on
cookery is about the hermit crab.*

Émile Zola 1873

The FISH MARKET

*The author who described for us dawn breaking over the
vegetable market (page 84) found further, perhaps even
greater, inspiration in the fish market. It is almost as though
he was wielding an artist's brush instead of an author's pen.
(See also page 158.)*

O n the first morning Florent turned up at seven o'clock, lost, confused, afraid. Fishwives stalked about the nine stalls at which the auction would be held, while clerks arrived with ledger books, and transport company reps, leather satchels slung round their necks, leant back in their chairs inside the sales offices, waiting to see how much they would make. The fish was unloaded, unpacked and set out inside the enclosure formed by the stalls, spilling over onto the pavement. Lined up along the floor were piles of little baskets, non-stop consignments of crates and cases arriving to join them, sackloads of mussels heaped one on top of the other, making the gutters awash with water. The men who checked the catch, busily straddling the piles of baskets, grabbed their straw handles, emptied the contents, and cast them negligently to one side, spreading out each lot on top of the large round crates with a single movement, presenting the fish to advantage. When the crates were all displayed Florent half believed he was looking at a fish-stall which had just run aground, here on the pavement, the fish still gasping, with pink abalone, milk white pearls, blood-red coral and all the rainbow silk reflections and all the grey-green dullness of the ocean.

Pell-mell, wherever the men had chanced to cast their net into the dark world of slumbering mysteries, the green depths had yielded up their riches: cod, haddock, plaice, dab, dirty grey run-of-the-mill fish, their bodies dappled with white; conger eels, like huge muddy blue grass snakes with squinting black eyes, so slimy they seemed to slither as if still alive; wide winged skate, their pale bellies hemmed with soft red flesh, the knots of their spines running the length of their superb backs, marbled to the pliant, ribbed wing-tips, with flecks of vermilion streaked with florentine bronze, a dark motley somewhere between a natterjack and a rotting flower; dogfish, hideous, their round heads and the mouths gashed wide like Chinese gods, their fins like fleshy bat-wings, barking monsters which guard the treasures of underwater caverns. Then came beautiful fish, placed singly on each wicker tray: salmon of chequered silver, each scale chiselled into the gleaming metallic skin; mullet, their scales thicker, as if a wider chisel had been used; large turbot and barbel, their white grainy skin like curdled milk; tuna, smooth and polished like bags of black leather; oval shaped bass, their enormous mouths open as if some unfortunate overweight soul in its death throes were gasping its last in full-throated, paralysing agony. And everywhere soles in pairs, grey and white, were in abundance; thin, stiff sand-eels like pewter shavings; herrings, slightly twisted, their lamé dresses stained with blotches from their bleeding gills; fat dolphins with a slight ruby hue; gilded mackerel, their backs streaked blue-green, their gleaming mother-of-pearl flanks changing with the light, and white bellied gurnet, heads stacked in the centre of the crates, tails radiant, sprouting strange, flowery spines, bright vermilion mixed with pearly white. There were yet more red mullet, their exquisite flesh flushed the colour of a goldfish, cases of opaline whiting, baskets of sparling, spick and span little baskets, pretty as baskets of strawberries, which exuded the powerful scent of violets. The pastel evanescence of a hamper filled with shrimps and prawns was studded imperceptibly with the myriad jet black buttons of their eyes; meanwhile spiny crayfish and lobsters streaked with black, still living, limping on their splintered legs, made cracking sounds.

Florent was not really listening to M. Verlaque's explanations. A shaft of sunlight coming through the glass ceiling high above the arcades lit up its sumptuous colours, washed and softened by the wave of light, prism'd and melting into the flesh tones of the shellfish, the whiting's opalescence, the mackerel's mother-of-pearl pallor, the gold of the mullet, the lamé of the herrings, the large pieces of silverware that were the salmon. It was as if a mermaid had emptied her treasure chest upon the ground, strange, exotic ornaments, shimmering necklaces, in heaps, monstrous bracelets, gigantic brooches, pagan jewels, whose purpose was obscure. On the backs of skate and dog-fish, fat, dark stones, emerald and ruby hued, were set in blackened metal; and the thin strips of the sand-eels, the tails and fins of the sparlings, possessed the finesse of delicate jewellery.

And yet what struck Florent was a fresh breath of wind, a familiar sea breeze, bitter and salty. He recalled the coasts of Guyana and the fine weather on the crossing. He sensed a bay at low tide with seaweed steaming in the sunshine; the exposed rocks wiped clean, the shingle exhaling the heavy scented breath of the sea. All around him the fish, as fresh as fish can be, spread their welcome smell, a tart and slightly irritating smell which corrupts the appetite.

That morning there was a particularly large consignment of German crayfish in baskets and boxes. White fish from Holland and England also cluttered the market. Rhine carp were unpacked, a burnished bronze with russet metallic markings, their scales like cloisonné enamels; large pike pointing their ferocious snouts, tough, iron-grey river highwaymen; tench, dark and magnificent, copper stained with verdigris. Amid all this severe gilding, the crates of gudgeon and perch, loads of trout, piles of bleak, flat fish caught in castnets, took on a vivid white, the steel blue of their backs gradually fading into the transparent softness of their bellies. Fat, young barbel, white as snow, lent highlights to this colossal still life. Sacks of young carp were gently poured into the aquaria; they turned, keeled over a second, tweaked, then darted out of sight. Baskets of tiny eels were emptied in a wriggling mass, falling to the bottom of a crate like a huge knot of snakes, while fatter ones, thick as a child's arm, lifted their heads and slid beneath the water with the smooth movement of a grass snake retreating into a bush. Lying on top of soiled, wattle boxes, fish, which had been gasping towards a long drawn out death since morning, neared their last amid the din of the market. Their mouths opened, sides taut as if to suck some moisture from the air, hiccuping silently every other second in an exaggerated yawn.

LE VENTRE DE PARIS

Julio Camba 1937

A SEA BREAM SALUTED

*Books about food which successfully combine an interesting
content with a good dose of humour are rare. The inhabitants
of Spain (I choose my words, meaning both Spanish and
Catalan) seem to be better at this than other people.
See pages 149–50 for more of Camba.*

One day a friend of mine came into a certain restaurant. Passing by a table where a whole family was united around a roasted sea-bream, he took his hat off and bowed politely. The one who seemed to preside over the group of parents, sons, grandparents, uncles and cousins, stood up and answered him.

'Excuse me', he said to my friend, 'but I can't remember. Could you please tell me, when did we meet?'

'When did we meet?' exclaimed my friend. 'The truth is I don't think we ever did.'

'Ah! Then you were saying hello to my wife or one of my daughters?'

'No, I wasn't.'

'Then, who were you saying hello to?' asked the man, more and more intrigued. And my friend, modestly, said:

'I said hello to the sea-bream.'

'To the sea-bream?'

'Yes, to the sea-bream. Are you surprised? This sea-bream that you are going to eat so thoughtlessly is an old friend of mine. For more than two weeks I've been watching him every day, in this same plate, with these same parsley decorations, and the same lemon slices. People passing by thought he was made in ceramic, but I knew the secret. After all this time I acquired an affection for him and, just now, I thought he looked at me as if saying goodbye. So, I raised my hat to him ...'

LA CASA DE LÚCULO

Dr W. T. Fernie 1911

FISH *not* BRAIN FOOD

One of the last acts of Dr Fernie (on whom see page 185) was
to assemble this crushing demolition of the widely held idea
that eating fish is especially beneficial to the brain.

Respecting what has been stated about Fish as specially feeding the brain, and the nervous system by reason of its furnishing phosphorus in a free soluble form, this supposition is contravened by Doctor Robert Hutchison, of the London Hospital, who explains it away thus:— 'I have made reference to the dictum of Buchner that "without phosphorus thought is impossible." The Swiss naturalist Agassiz, knowing this dictum and being informed by the eminent chemist, Dumas, that Fish contains much phosphorus, put two and two together, and concluded that Fish must be specially good for the brain. But I have shown that the aphorism of Buchner is not altogether true, and there is further no justification at all for the statement that Fish is rich in phosphorus; and thus the belief that as food it is peculiarly adapted for the nourishment of the brain, being founded on a double fallacy, falls to the ground.'

'But as a matter of fact,' says the *Lancet*, 'Fish does not contain more phosphorus than do ordinary meat foods; and it certainly does not contain phosphorus in a free state. The notion that it supplies this element had its origin, without doubt, in the glowing, or phosphorescence of Fish in the dark. Nevertheless this is not a phosphorescence at all, being rather due to micro-organisms. The belief, therefore, that Fish is a brain-feeding food, is just about as reasonable as the idea that because a soup is thick and gelatinous it will therefore "stick to the ribs"; or as sensible as the celebrated advice given to Verdant Green that he should lay in a stock of Reading biscuits when an undergraduate so as to assist his reading. Fish is certainly a nourishing food, partly because of the nourishing character of its constituents, and partly because of its easy digestibility; but it is nohow a specific food for the brain or the nerves.'

Woods Hutchinson votes this delusion about Fish being specially phosphorus-supplying brain food as 'the wildest and most ignorant of all.' 'Fish actually contains no more phosphorus than meat, eggs, or most other proteid foods. How then did it get the reputation of containing it? Simply from the fact that dead Fish allowed to decay upon the decks of fishing-smacks, or upon the sea beach, display very frequently a greenish phosphorescence in the process of decomposition. This phosphorescent light, however, is due not to the Fish at all, but to a group of bacteria which is feeding upon its remains. So the whole fish-phosphorus-brain theory is literally an "ignis fatuus," or "will-of-the-wisp".'

HEALTH TO DATE

Dorothy Hartley   1954

ELVERS

The author was introduced on page 29. In this passage she
deals with a delicacy still known in the West Country of
England – although better known in Portugal, Spain and
Italy, for these infant eels swim up many European rivers after
their transatlantic journey. (See also page 133.)

The discovery of the breeding-place of the eels, in shallow warm water across the
Atlantic Ocean, cleared up the long mystery of the elvers which pour up the
western rivers in spring. From March onwards, the stream of fish begins, and lasts
perhaps a week or more. It happens in most of the western rivers, but very especially in
Somerset. This land used to be half under water, and the shallow entrances and
waterways made it a perfect ground for the eels. Now the land has been drained, but
whether from instinct, or some turn of the sweeping tide, the elvers continue to pour up
the Bristol Channel and turn south down the Rhynes. The Somerset people are divided
into 'farmers' and 'marsh folk'. (The latter live on the reclaimed lands and at present
run a large willow industry.) These marsh people, who live in the lands around Wells
Cathedral, all know elvers.

The elver shoal itself looks like a mass of jelly swimming in the water; it consists of
millions of elvers, and can best be described as transparent spaghetti. The fish are
caught by dipping them out of the Rhynes in scoops made of cloth, or buckets and pans,
as any net would let the fish through. They are washed in running water and then
cooked at once. As soon as the transparent mass touches the hot pan or fat, it turns
opaque (exactly as white of egg becomes opaque and visible). It is stirred and turned till
it is all evenly cooked, and eaten with salt and pepper and bread and butter. It is best
hot, cooked loosely, like whitebait (though never so crisp), but the marsh folk also make
'elver cake', which is the same mass of fish, seasoned with chopped herbs (a suspicion of
onion and butter or bacon-fat added), and the whole turned into a dish, and pressed
down till set and cold. This elver cake then turns out and can be cut in slices. There is no
bone in the fish, it is all pure soft fish, and becomes firm and almost textureless after
cooking. It is especially good for children. (The marsh folk point out the fatness of
young ducklings, which are hatched out in time for the elver feed.) It is certainly good
food and could be the basis of a seasonal canned-food industry. There is no fear of the
fishing of these elvers destroying the future eels, if the main shoal, which sweeps up the
channel, is left untouched, as the Rhynes will be drained, and therefore all the elvers
trampled and destroyed, when the willows are cut a month later.

There is a witchcraft story, vouched for down west, that one old marsh mother having moved up-country to Swindon, her dutiful grandson, a driver on the railway, stopped and left a bucket of elvers at her cottage. The old woman rejoiced loudly in broad Somerset speech, and set the bucket of elvers on to cook, causing an outcry of 'Witchcraft!' For she was 'seen to take a pail of clear water and set it upon the fire, murmuring incantations, and behold! half an hour later *she was enjoying a hot fish dinner*', and her black cat said it was fish too! (The elvers are invisible in clean water.)

FOOD IN ENGLAND

Charles David Badham   1863

EELS *at* NAPLES

*The literary output of Victorian clergymen was formidable. At
its best, their prose, studded with classical allusions, framed in
long and well-balanced sentences, drily spiced with wit, is a
great pleasure to read. The Reverend Badham rates high
marks for his* Prose Halieutics, *the very name of which is a
classical allusion:* Halieutica *was the title of a long poem on
fish and fishing by the classical author Oppian.
Badham's description of eels on sale at Naples is as vivid
as could be; the effect is like that of a church organist pulling
out all the stops. (See also page 113.)*

Eels are as common a luxury at Naples as with us, only not quite so cheap. The following brief notice, extracted from our journal kept on the spot about five years ago, shows this:—

'Christmas Eve. – Nothing can exceed the bustle and noise of the streets today; all the way up the Toledo is one vast scene of excitement: the beggars whine for alms in stronger accents; the cries of itinerant salesmen are perfectly terrific; the vociferation of buyers who will not be sold, and of sellers who will not be bought, rise high above the shrilling of children, the lashing of whips, the yelling of dogs, the chanting of processions, the bursting of petards, the rolling of drums, and the crashing of wheels. The battle of hard bargains is fought with spirit today, and the subject of contention is – eels; every favourite Italian bonbon, frittura, and dolce is on sale as well, but these certainly form the staple commodity, and carry off all the honours of the day, holding the same place in the affections of the lazzaroni, and being as indispensable a standing-dish for his Christmas, as roast beef and plum-pudding are to an Englishman: or hardboiled eggs over Romanized Europe at Easter. Men with their ears bored, and adorned, as well as each greasy hand, with huge gold rings, vociferate fiercely, as they slice, with large long knives, unsightly pastes, called 'rustici e dolci,' — messes composed of flour and rancid grease, into which are stuck a heterogeneous collection of unsavoury sweet and sour confectioneries; fruit-stalls are in great muster: their keepers expecting now to dispose of commodities that have hung some time on hand: not a skewer of baked pears; not an orange on sweet or bitter principles: not a string of rosy tomatas, nor bunch of blushing service-apples, can be spared from the gay gilt booths on this grand occasion. Fish-stalls however everywhere predominate: here giant lobsters expand and flap their fan-like tails, and bound off the board as if they already felt the hot water. Thousands of 'uongli,' piles of 'frutti di mare', and every other species of bivalve, with fish of all shapes and hues, familiar to him who has studied the fresco and mosaic coquillages on the walls and in the floors of the houses of Pompeii, lie in confused heaps upon the street flags; but the predominating delicacy, the fish most in request, is, as we have said, eels. This is indeed 'all-eel day;' not a biped of our race in Naples but hopes to eat them in some fashion or other; the very paupers consider it hard if no friendly Christian furnish them with the means of procuring a taste at least of 'capitoni,' though these expensive luxuries fetch not less than six carlini a rotolo, or about a shilling a pound. The dispensers of the delicacy occupy either side of the Toledo from end to end, and there display the curling, twisting, snake-like forms of their slippery merchandise, in every possible pose, and under every variety of suffering; some, suspended over the booths, wriggle round the poles to which they are attached; others, half flayed to demonstrate the whiteness of the flesh, undulate their slimy coils by thousands in large open hampers; and while some are swimming, but in vain, for their lives in wooden troughs of cold water, others are fizzing and sputtering in the midst of hot grease in huge frying-pans over the fire; customers are incessant in their demands, and every man, woman, and child, carries home eels, cooked or uncooked, for breakfast, dinner, supper, and many an intermediate meal besides. Surely every stranger, though no enemy to eels, must dream of them tonight, and wriggle uneasily in bed for a week to come, after merely passing down the street; while every Scotchman who shall chance to find himself in the midst of such a scene, will learn doubly to hate and recoil from a church which sanctions such an abomination as food.

These eels come principally from Comacchio, the low country below Venice; they are almost as large as the conger, but far more delicate in flavour; when first taken, they are kept in brackish stews, and from thence sent to all parts of Italy, sometimes, as here, alive, but more commonly chopped in pieces, grilled, and preserved in a pickle of salt and vinegar, shrouded in bay-leaves, and served out to customers on the point of a porcupine's quill.

PROSE HALIEUTICS

Astri Riddervold   1987

GRAVLAX

I enjoy reading those few scientist-cooks who succeed in
making themselves clear. Astri Riddervold, a Norwegian, is
one. The currently familiar term 'gravlax' is illuminated in an
unforgettable manner in her essay on the subject. I like the
way she supplements her historical and scientific approach to
the topic with sociological comments on modern Norwegian
eating habits. History is today as well as yesterday.

In modern times *gravlaks* is the name of a much beloved Scandinavian dish which is expensive if purchased from an exclusive shop but less costly if you know how to prepare it yourself. This traditional dish is served for special guests, usually as a first course for lunch or an evening meal with family and friends. The preparation of the salmon is frequently the job of the man of the house, if it is done at home, as is the carving which is looked upon as an art. In Norway, the popularity of buried salmon has been increasing ever since the War. Before the War it was seldom heard of, when smoked salmon was all the rage. Today, both are equally popular, but as buried salmon can be prepared at home, it is likely to prove the more popular in the long run.

The buried salmon of today has not been buried at all during its preparation for the table. However, the process which makes the uncooked fish edible is much the same as the traditional one where the fish really was buried for some time. So when we use the word *gravlaks* today, it is an old term which has survived, applied to a new method. The technique has changed, but the processing of the fish is similar to that of the past.

The word *gravlaks* can be traced back in Scandinavian history to 1348, when a man from Jämtland, called Olafuer Gravlax, is mentioned. In 1509, another man, called Martin Surlax (i.e. Gravlax) is mentioned in the annals of Stockholm. The words *gravlaks* and *surlaks* (buried fish and sour fish) were used as synonyms, buried fish describing the technique, sour fish the result – the fermented stinking fish. In recent times the term *surlaks* has become obsolete and instead we speak of *rakefisk*, meaning fermented fish, often trout, which is the famous rakørret.

The special smell of the sour fish is mentioned very frequently by travellers and professional people, doctors and clergymen, who wrote about different types of buried fish during the 18th and 19th centuries. Two clergymen, living in neighbouring valleys in the east of Norway about the end of the 18th century, seem to have had quite opposite views. Smith, living in Trysil, writes that the stench is such that you would not dare ask a lady for a kiss when you have eaten this wonderful fish. On the contrary, Hjorthøy from Gudbrandsdalen tells how farmers in the area will eat their evil smelling trout every day, adding that, in spite of the stench, it seems to be harmless.

Gravlaks can be eaten by everyone, without any ill effects. So writes Nils Gisler in 1752 when he was a doctor in northern Sweden. He says that it is mostly eaten after three days, though by some after two days and sometimes after five to six hours of preparation. However, the famous botanist Linnaeus, in 1742, says that the fish is put in barrels in spring with very little salt. Then the barrels are stored underground for some months to be eaten during the winter. In another context Linnaeus describes how the fish is laid in holes in the ground which are covered with bark from the silver birch. Bark is also put on top of the fish. The fish, he says, has an unpleasant smell, but is regarded as a delicacy by those who are used to it.

These descriptions make it clear that there were two types of buried fish: the 4 to 6 day procedure which was a preparation of the fish to make it edible uncooked, and the long term procedure the aim of which was to preserve the fish caught in large quantities during the milder part of the year, to be eaten during the winter when ice and snow made fishing difficult.

The two types, however, known nowadays as *gravlaks* and *rakefisks*, are different stages of the same process and there are indications that people may have known it was possible to eat their fish after two to six days as Dr Gisler writes. From Finmark in Norway is reported a tradition where the salmon was eaten after six days in preparation, and what was left was cured in a weak brine to be eaten the following spring. From Numedal in Norway is also reported a tradition of eating the salmon after only two days of preparation. This buried salmon does not smell like mature French cheese, as it does in the preserved stage.

There seem also to be two different methods of burying the fish. It is either put in barrels with salt and then the barrel is buried in the ground for some months, or the fish is put directly into a hole in the ground which is covered with birch bark. Bark is put on top of the fish and stones on top of the bark. It is then left for some time.

Why this peculiar way of preserving fish was so much used in Norway and Sweden for hundreds of years and has survived in Iceland, even with the old technique, has many reasons. Traditions in food habits and taste are among the strongest and most conservative we know of, but this cannot be the only explanation. There must be other additional reasons. A Swedish clergyman, Olof Broman, gives a good practical economic explanation: the fishing lakes, he writes, are usually far from the homestead, in the woods and mountains and also far from one another. The amount of fish you catch in each lake is often substantial. It is impossible to carry the fish back home every night, and impossible as well to transport the catch from one lake to another. Therefore the fish is cleaned and buried in the sand by the lake where it is caught. Transport of salt was problematic for the same reasons. As you never know how much fish you will catch in the next lake, the use of salt must be sparing. Thus buried underground the fish was safe from thieves; those on two, as well as those on four, legs. There was, however, another reason for burying the fish, Broman says, in order to keep it cool, in the ground away from the sun, in order that it should not rot but acquire a certain sour taste, well liked by those who were used to it from childhood but not by everyone.

This food, now a 600 year old tradition, has survived, but not only as a local peculiarity. Its popularity has increased immensely in the decades since the last war, amongst older as well as younger generations, in rural and urban areas. It is popular today to serve *rakefisk* as a main course for an evening party, not to everybody though. There are some who do not eat it. Amongst people who are *rakefisk* fans, friends are classified between rakefisklovers and non-rakefisklovers when the question of who is to be invited to the *rakefisk* party is decided. A *rakefisk* party is relaxed and informal, beer, aquavit and drinking songs are part of the performance.

The reasons for this revitalisation are a fascinating topic of research including several aspects such as national, local and group identity. It also fits well into a modern Norwegian lifestyle due to the practical advantage that there is no need for cooking, save potatoes. To clean and skin the fish is usually the job of the men of the house, and thus the preparations for the party can be shared among the family. The informal party and the traditional dish are also in harmony with typical Scandinavian design using unpolished wood for furniture, wool, linen and cotton textiles, stoneware, copper and pewter instead of silver, crystal and damask on the tables.

There is however a difference between the position of the preserved and fully fermented *rakefisk* with the sour smell and the slightly fermented *gravlaks* which has been prepared for but a few days – to be eaten uncooked with no sour smell. The *gravlaks* emanated from a higher social level in Sweden and started its life in post-war Norway in the same social circles. Salmon was expensive and in this post-war period it was seldom eaten by the local population as it could be sold for money. Today this is changing. All along the coast we find seafarms producing tons of trout and salmon, and the use of *gravlaks* and *graved* trout is increasing throughout all social groups. However, as the taste is mild, and the fish is often served with white wine, this gives the fish a touch of class. It fits in well with silver and crystal as well as cotton, pewter and unpolished pinewood tables.

'Cookery: Science, Lore and Books'
OXFORD SYMPOSIUM DOCUMENTS 1984/5

Elizabeth Watts   *1866*

A SALMON JUMPS *into the* POT

It has been related that at the Falls of Kilmorac, on the Beauly, in Inverness-shire, the Frasers of Lovat, who were lords of the manor, used sometimes to surprise their guests with a voluntarily cooked salmon. A kettle was placed on a flat rock on the south side of the fall, at the water's edge, and kept full and boiling until a salmon fell into it.

FISH AND HOW TO COOK IT

William Woys Weaver   1982

On SHAD *at* PHILADELPHIA

American shad, Alosa sapidissima, *and shad roe are
established delicacies in the region round Philadelphia. The
fish, which are closely related to the two European species of
shad, ascend rivers in the spring to spawn.
The evolution of cookery in Philadelphia, at one time the
culinary capital of the USA, is of particular interest. In the
essay from which this passage comes, Weaver shows that shad
was for a long time a poor man's fish, often prepared in the
Indian style, and that its ascent to the tables of the well-to-do
occurred in the 19th century.*

In Penn's time, even in the second quarter of the 18th century, serving shad had none of the highbrow overtones it has today. To put it simply, it was a poor man's fish.

Mullet, sturgeon, pike, and salmon were fabulously abundant in the Delaware Basin during the 17th and early 18th centuries. Cooks with pretensions for the culinary arts sought out these fish because they could be prepared according to familiar Old World methods. At Philadelphia's leading eateries during this period, such as the Blue Anchor (1682), the State House Tavern (1693), the Penny-Pot, the London Coffee House (1702), and the Pewter Platter (where William Penn, Jr. indulged in a scandalous brawl), it was sturgeon and sea turtle, not shad, that were king.

Those who lived close to the land had no time for fancy tavern cooking. Practical methods of preparation were all that mattered. And if the Indians knew a few culinary shortcuts, then the whites borrowed them accordingly. One of these methods was preserved among the shad fisherman of Bucks County, Pennsylvania. It was recorded by Mrs. J. Ernest Scott and published in her study of early shad cookery in 1917.

The technique was quite simple. Soft mud was rubbed against the scales of the fish, which was then covered with a thick layer of clay. The clay shell was allowed to dry before the fire for fifteen or twenty minutes (depending on the size of the shad), then the whole was buried in hot coals and ashes and baked slowly until the clay hardened. When this shell was broken open, the fish split apart readily. The scales and skin adhered to the clay, the head fell off, and the entrails shrank into a little ball which could be removed with a spoon. Most of the small bones dissolved and the flesh, when properly done, was extremely tender.

This cooking technique is derived from the Delaware Indians, who doubtless used it for many other species of fish as well. It is interesting that a similar Chinese technique for slow baking shad, with the very same results, has recently become voguish in several

East Coast cities. As for the old Indian recipe, some sportsmen still like the nostalgia of the mud, but for the apartment dweller, sturdy luting paste and a hot oven may serve the same purpose.

There are, of course, many other ways to prepare shad. Baked shad can be extremely delicious. This method was more popular with rural cooks, particularly the Pennsylvania Germans, who as a class generally controlled the tavern trade in the state. They carried their preference for baked shad into the Mid-West, where many of their number later settled. One Pennsylvania German recipe, dating from about 1818, called for stuffing the shad with oysters and then baking it in parchment. This was usually served with a rich walnut sauce.

Plain or elaborate, shad was invariably served with asparagus, wild asparagus if at all possible. Wild asparagus has so much more flavor than any of the domesticated varieties that some of our cooks grow quite covetous and tight-lipped when one tries to determine *where* they found their patch. It is valued over friendships and wedding alliances.

There is another school of thought, however, which promotes poke instead of asparagus. In the old days, the common man ate poke with shad. Boiled poke looks a bit like asparagus, but the flavor is not at all similar. It reminds me of very mild rhubarb, but that might be because poke shoots often have a red blush. The plant is poisonous once the stems begin to leaf out.

The subject of poke brings to mind the jabbing which used to occur whenever Philadelphia's reputation for shad was challenged. The culinary imbroglios were sometimes lengthy. Take, for example, the tenacious pot-to-pot combat between Charles Duffy, owner of Philadelphia's Continental Hotel – the city's finest during the 1870s, and Colonel Cake, proprietor of the Willard Hotel in Washington. Duffy always managed to keep his national reputation for the earliest and finest shad intact, but on the other hand, Colonel Cake never conceded defeat. Both of them carried their shad war to Cape May, then a fashionable New Jersey resort, where Cake operated Congress Hall and Duffy the Stockton. It is said that because of shad, the kitchens of these establishments were not on speaking terms.

To attract business, great hotels such as these went out of their way to create huge shad menus each Spring, and at no little expense. The addition of Creole touches became popular in the 1850s and then again in the 1890s, along with a number of garnishes that were more gimmick than improvement. One wonders, for example, what was meant by 'Shad *à la Soyer en bordure*' or 'Shad Pittsburgh *vert pré*'. So much for American menu French. Nothing, however, ever surpassed planked shad in popularity or prestige.

Petits Propos Culinaires (PPC) 11

A LIGHT HAND *with* BLOWFISH

*The zesty approach and breezy style of some American
cookbook writers appeals to me very much, especially when the
author is going on about his or her main enthusiasm and
obviously knows the subject at first hand.* Hook'em and
Cook'em *by Bunny Day is a good example. Low-falutin, one
might say, and fun to read.
The blowfish about which Day writes here is a relation of the
notorious Japanese blowfish,* fugu. *This is prized as a delicacy
but harbours a fatal toxin in some of its organs, so dangerous
that it is illegal for any but specially qualified fugu-chefs to
prepare them. Fortunately, the species caught on the eastern
Atlantic seaboard do not have to be treated with the same
great caution.*

Call them blowfish, bottlefish, sea squab, or chicken of the sea, but don't throw them back into the water when you catch them.

Years ago when we cruised we were bothered when we fished by silly little fish that took our bait. When we took them off the hook we amused the children by tickling the bellies of these fish because they blew themselves up and became funny round balls. When everyone tired of their antics they were thrown back into the sea.

I can't remember who told me they were good to eat or when or how I learned to clean them, but I have been grateful ever since. Cleaned properly, they become a solid chunk of firm white flesh that is easily prepared and delicious to eat. They lend themselves nicely to a variety of seasonings and flavourings. For instance, I had a guest for dinner who declared she'd never eat or like any kind of fish. I cooked blow-fish the way the French cook frogs' legs, called them frogs' legs, and after my guest raved and ate all she could hold I confessed she'd eaten and enjoyed *fish*.

One Sunday we went to my favorite weakfish hole, on Little Peconic Bay, facing Rose's Grove. However, the wind was blowing hard, the weather was threatening, and the weaks were not biting, so we moved behind Holmes Hill, a beautiful high sand cliff facing Robins Island, to catch a few blows.

Blowfish swim in very shallow water. I have felt them around my legs just a few yards from shore. I've caught them in as little as three or four feet of water.

They have a tiny mouth that sucks the bait, so I suggest that you use your lightest tackle and your smallest hooks. Use a 1- or 2-ounce sinker, two of the smallest flounder hooks, one above the other. Slice squid into the tiniest pieces and bait the hooks. The fish are so small and so smart that frequently they will steal your bait without your feeling anything, so check your line often. They are fun to catch, because they keep you alert and the eating will be your reward.

The skin of the blowfish is very tough and prickly, so I heartily recommend that you wear gloves when handling them. I usually like to work without gloves, but I found my hands have a funny itching for a while after handling blowfish.

Place the fish on a board, underside down. With a good knife, cut right through the fish, directly behind the head or eyes to the bottom skin. Grab the skin and peel it off the way you would a glove. The innards will fall out and you will work free a solid piece of fish flesh that does faintly resemble a frog's leg. It will take a little pulling and tugging, but after you get the knack of it, it will become simple, and I guarantee you will love the taste of blowfish.

Hook 'em and Cook 'em

Dorothy Hartley   *1954*

Shrimp Teas

Dorothy Hartley has already appeared on pages 29 and 124,
and needs no more introduction.

There was a little house that said 'Shrimp Teas'. We went through a little wicket gate down a flagged yard (for it was in the grey north). There was a holly-bush growing over a stone wall and a wooden bench went along the wall. There were three strong round wooden tables and against the three tables leant twelve strong square wooden chairs. On the tables were white cloths. You went to the door and told Betsy 'We've come'. Then you sat down and 'drew in'.

Betsy brought out a pot of tea, with a woollen tea-cosy on it, sugar and cream, a cup and saucer each, two big plates of thin bread and butter – brown and white – a big green plate of watercress, and a big pink plate of shrimps. And that was all, except an armoured salt cellar and a robin. Then you 'reached too'.

Presently Betsy Tatterstall came out again, with a big white apron over her black gown, took the teapot in to replenish it, and see if you wanted any more bread and butter (you always did). And you ate, and talked, in desultory fashion (there is something very conversational about a shrimp tea), and the robin hopped about on the table.

Presently you wiped up and sat back, and Betsy carried a bowl of pink-bewhiskered debris to the hens, and you bought some fresh eggs, and a jar of potted shrimps to take away with you. ... Betsy sold that paste in white jars, with whole shrimps embedded in it, and smooth white melted butter on top. It *was* the best in the district, and that, mark you, in a district that was notable for fish paste.

There was always a white jar of potted fish or potted meat on the table for the big Yorkshire high teas. Sometimes, if it was a new jar, they would thoughtfully cut thirty degrees out, and lay neatly across the top, just to encourage you to begin.

FOOD IN ENGLAND

Alexandre Dumas 1873

The HERMIT CRAB

*Alexandre Dumas Père, the great novelist and playwright,
was at the end of his life when he compiled his huge* Grand
Dictionnaire de Cuisine. *Though it is full of flaws and padded
out with 'borrowed' recipes from other authors, it contains
flashes of marvellously good writing. Always gallant, Dumas
expressed the hope that the fingers of 'ladies of light
disposition' would not grow weary turning over the pages of
his dictionary. This translation comes from a selection which
my wife and I prepared from the non-finger-wearing pages.*

A species of crab of which the meat is regarded as a delicious morsel. It is usually grilled in its shell before being eaten.

There is nothing more comical than this little crustacean. Nature has furnished him with armour as far as the waist – cuirass, gauntlets and visor of iron, this half of him has everything. But from the waist to the other end there is nothing, not even a shirt. The result of this is that the hermit crab stuffs this extremity of himself into whatever refuge he can find.

The Creator, who had begun to dress the creature as a lobster, was disturbed or distracted in the middle of the operation and finished him off as a slug.

This part of the hermit crab, so poorly defended and so tempting to an enemy, is his great preoccupation; a preoccupation which can at times make him fierce. If he sees a shell which suits him, he eats the owner of the shell and takes his place while it is still warm – the history of the world in microscopic form. But since, when all is said and done, the house was not made for him, he staggers about like a drunkard instead of having the serious air of a snail; and so far as possible he avoids going out, except in the evening, for fear of being recognized.

DUMAS ON FOOD

William Warner   1976

The Crabs of Chesapeake Bay

When William Warner wrote Beautiful Swimmers *he created a
new genre of book: one about a foodstuff, its nature and its
place in a particular ecological system, how it is caught, how
processed, and by what kind of people. Perhaps Eleanor
Clark's* Oysters of Loqmariaquer *(see page 151) was really
the first, but Warner embraced the entirety of his subject even
more effectively.*

The Atlantic blue crab is known to scientists as *Callinectes sapidus* Rathbun. It is very well named. *Callinectes* is Greek for beautiful swimmer. *Sapidus*, of course, means tasty or savory in Latin. Rathbun is the late Dr. Mary J. Rathbun of the Smithsonian Institution, who first gave the crab its specific name . . .

Those who most appreciate *Callinectes'* beauty, I think, are crabbers and other people who handle crabs professionally. Some years ago in the month of October, I visited a clean and well-managed crab house in Bellhaven, North Carolina, a pleasant town on Pamlico Sound's Pungo River. In the company of the plant owner's wife I watched dock handlers load the cooking crates with good catches of prime sooks. As they should be at that time of year, the sooks were fully hard and fat, although relatively recently moulted. Their abdomens were therefore pure white, with a lustrous alabaster quality. (Later in the intermoult period crab abdomens take on the glazed and slightly stained look of aging horses' teeth; often they are also spotted with 'rust.') The carapaces or top shells were similarly clean. Thus, gazing down at the mass of three thousand or more crabs in each crate, we saw a rich and fragmented palette of olive greens, reds, varying shades of blue and marble white.

'Now, tell me, did ever you see such beautiful crabs?' the owner's wife asked, quite spontaneously.

'Prettiest crabs I seen all year,' a black dockhand volunteered.

I had to agree. Anyone would.

Still, as is often said, beauty is in the eyes of the beholder. We can but little imagine the sheer terror which the sight of a blue crab must inspire in a fat little killifish or a slow-moving annelid worm. The crab's claw arms will be held out at the ready, waving slowly in the manner of a shadow boxer. Walking legs will be slightly doubled, ready for tigerlike springs, and the outer maxillipeds – literally 'jaw feet' or two small limbs in front of the crab's mouth – will flutter distractingly. The effect must be mesmeric, such as the praying mantis is said to possess over its insect victims. Perhaps not quite so hypnotic but of extreme importance to the crab in this situation are its eyes. Like most crustaceans, the blue crab has stalked eyes. When a crab is at peace with the world, they are but two little round beads. On the prowl, they are elevated and look like stubby horns. As with insects, the eyes are compound. This means that they possess thousands of facets – multiple lenses, if you prefer – which catch and register a mosaic of patterns. More importantly, simple laboratory tests seem to indicate that the stalked and compound eyes give the blue crab almost three-hundred-and-sixty-degree vision. Those who with ungloved hand try to seize a crab with raised eyestalks from the rear will have this capability most forcefully impressed on them. If at all, the blue crab may have a forward blind spot at certain ranges in the small space directly between its eyes. Perhaps this accounts for the crab's preference for shifting lateral motion, from which it is easier to correct this deficiency, rather than rigid forward and back movement. Whatever the answer, a blue crab sees very well. Although colors may be blurred, the crab is extremely sensitive to shapes and motions. It has good range, too, at least for a crustacean. I have frequently tried standing still in a boat as far as fifteen feet from cornered individuals and then raising an arm quickly. Instantly the crabs respond, claws flicked up to the combat position.

Beauty, then, to some. Piercing eyes and a fearful symmetry, like William Blake's tiger, to others. But there are no such divided views on *Callinectes'* swimming ability. Specialists and lay observers alike agree that the blue crab has few peers in this respect. Some carcinologists believe that a few larger portunids or members of the swimming crab family – *Portunus pelagicus*, for example, which ranges from the eastern Mediterranean to Tahiti – might be better swimmers. But from what I have seen of the family album, I suspect that these crabs would fare best in distance events in any aquatic olympiad, while the Atlantic blue and some of its close relatives might take the sprints.

*　　*　　*

Most Atlantic blue crabs are caught hard and processed for meat. Although soft-shell crabs are rapidly gaining a new nationwide popularity, the meat of hard crabs – fresh, pasteurized or canned – remains the heart of the industry. First stop for most of the market-bound catch, therefore, is a place where crabmeat is extracted by hand. In the Chesapeake an establishment performing this function is known as a picking plant or more often simply a 'crab house,' as opposed to a 'crab shanty,' which is the shack-like structure used by soft crab pound operators to watch over their shedding floats.

Although Chesapeake crab houses exhibit great variety, all have two essential elements. The first is a device to cook the crabs whole, since the flesh of the blue crab, like that of nearly all other crustaceans, cannot be removed from the shell until it is firmed up by thorough cooking. Large steaming vats or 'cookers' are used for this purpose. Their design has not changed much since the beginning of this century. Some are boxlike chambers into which crates holding almost a ton of crabs fit very snugly. Others are large kettles, the size and shape of which make you think of savages and the parboiling of missionaries, capable of receiving three circular steel baskets each holding about three hundred and fifty pounds of crabs. Both types function in the same manner. Handlers push the crates into the chambers on dollies or let the baskets down into the kettles from overhead rail systems. The steam does the rest, or, more exactly, pressurized steam at 250 degrees Fahrenheit for about twelve minutes. Since so many of the cookers are old, accidents are not uncommon. Crab house proprietors will tell you about them with great relish. Omar Evans, a waterman who at the age of seventy-one runs the only picking plant on Smith Island, vividly remembers the time the door of his ancient Nilsen and White chamber-type cooker let go at the hinges. 'Oh, my heavens, did she blow!' Evans says. 'I wa'nt very popular around here, I tell you that. Crabs was scattered all over town. Found one stuck by his spike in the mast of a buy boat half a mile yonder.'

Barring such problems the crabs emerge from the cooker very much dead and with their top shells and claws almost lobster-red. (The shell of the sternum and abdomen remains obstinately white.) Their muscle tissue is now both free of live bacteria and very firm. They are thus ready for the other crab house essential, or the 'picking room' where they will be split, quartered and dissected for every last gram of meat.

A man enters a picking room at his peril. As many as thirty or forty ladies will be seated around stainless-steel-topped tables, talking loudly and carrying on. Open the screen door and all activity halts. Within seconds the ladies resume their work, but silence, curious stares and a slower production pace remain, much to the annoyance of the manager. You go up to the head lady, traditionally seated nearest the hinged receiving window through which the crabs are shoveled, and try to think of something to say. Her hands fly so fast that it is impossible to see what she is doing. The skill commands immediate respect. You ask her how long it takes to learn.

'Some never do,' she replies tartly, looking at the slower apprentices.

Laughter explodes down the long tables. The ice is mercifully broken. A swell of shrill voices, the clatter of crabs being dumped on steel table tops and the whack of weighted knife handles against stubborn claw shell gradually returns to fill every corner of the room. At full production rhythm the din is overwhelming. You cannot wait for an excuse to leave.

Women who pick crabs are paid either by piecework at fifty to seventy-five cents per pound of meat or by the hour at the federal minimum wage, whichever proves highest. In practice this means that all good pickers are paid by the pound. Only the very slow or idle will fail to pick less than the four pounds per hour necessary to top the minimum wage. Seasoned professionals, in fact, work at over twice that rate. At the crab-picking contest which is part of Crisfield's annual National Hard Crab Derby, experts will regularly pick as much as three or four pounds of meat in an on-your-mark, set, and go race that lasts for fifteen minutes. Since the average blue crab meat yield is .14 of whole crab weight, the three or four pounds mean that the winners swiftly and surely dissect as many as twenty to thirty crabs within the allotted time, or close to two crabs per minute.   BEAUTIFUL SWIMMERS

John Doerper   1984

The GEODUCK

*If any voice is to be heard on the subject of the mysterious
geoduck (pronounced gooey-duck), it has to be a voice from
the Pacific North-West. This piece comes from John Doerper's
interesting study of the foods of the region, which is especially
good on seafood.*

The geoduck is an enormous clam, by far the largest found on the continent. The
shell, which is quite small in proportion to the clam's body, can reach a length of
nine inches. The siphon may stretch to a length of three feet. This allows the geoduck to
live deeper in the substrate (it also likes deeper water), where it is almost beyond the
reach of any but the most energetic clam diggers. But this clam is a prize well worth
seeking out. With the geoduck, the standard rule of bivalve flavor, that large molluscs
have an inferior or coarser taste, does not apply. Of course, the geoducks I have
obtained from seafood markets have weighed out at an average of three to four pounds.
That is quite small for this clam, and perhaps the ones I have sampled still possessed a
juvenile flavor. Full-grown geoducks in the Puget Sound region reach average weights
of eight to twelve pounds; clams weighing more than twenty pounds are found
occasionally, and specimens weighing up to forty pounds have been recorded.

Geoducks have a rather silly scientific name, *Panope generosa*, which translates
into something like 'fat sea nymph.' I have often been amused by biologists who have
felt the need to debunk the highly unscientific spirits of classical mythology by
bestowing their ethereal names on sea slugs and other odd marine creatures. But with
the geoduck they have outdone themselves. There is nothing nymphlike about this
clam. It is, instead, very phallic looking, the subject of many Northwesterners' jests.

Geoducks, like other clams, should always be bought when still alive, preferably a
short time after they have been dug from the ground. Lively geoducks, kept in salt water
until they are sold, can be found regularly at the Hama Hama oyster farm in Shelton,
Washington, and in the fish markets of Vancouver's Chinatown. When clams have been
removed from the water and are displayed on chunks of ice, they can still be fresh. Make
sure they are alive by poking their siphons with a finger. The clam should twitch and
straighten out its neck. (Never buy one that is dead, or you may be in for a quick trip to
the hospital to have your stomach pumped out.) Always make sure the water has been
removed from the clam, first, because you don't want to pay for the extra deadweight
and, second, because you might be in for a wet surprise.

I watched a surprise of this kind a little while back, after I had just bought a
geoduck from a saltwater tank. Both the fishmonger and I were in a hurry and, after a

few perfunctory squeezes, she carried my purchase, upright, toward the cash register. Geoducks are capable of a powerful squirt (their hiding places on the tideflats can often be spotted by these geysers), and this clam, annoyed by being carried, put its heart into the squirt. Its water hit the fishmonger right between the eyes, wetted her hair, and began to run down her face in rivulets. This proved too much for the monger's composure. She angrily grabbed the clam by the neck, held it over the basin, and began to squeeze with a vengeance. I don't think I paid for a single drop of water. It may have been my imagination, but the neck of this geoduck seemed uncommonly tender when I cooked it later that day.

Geoducks (and gapers) have tough outer skins and need to be skinned before they can be prepared. This is a simple process if done properly. Bring a pot of water to a rolling boil and immerse the clam, shell and all. Remove after a few seconds and chill immediately under cold, running water. The skin, shell, and guts should have loosened and be easy to remove. Geoducks have two kinds of meat, the somewhat tough meat of the siphon, which can be beaten into tenderness and fried as a 'steak' or ground for chowder, and the tender belly meat, which includes the mantle and foot muscles. This can be cubed and sautéed lightly in butter, or it can be served raw as sashimi – though I prefer mine cooked. It can also be added to stir-fried vegetables.

Surprisingly few Northwesterners, both natives and newcomers, have actually eaten fresh geoduck. I can understand why. It's difficult to get past this clam's outlandish appearance. A few years back, several commercial processors decided to start the wholesale marketing of geoducks, but they ran into an image problem – not with the way the clam looked, but with its name. After all, what squeamish cook would like to have a 'gooey duck' in the kitchen? So the geoduck was renamed the 'king clam.' And why not? Willapa Bay oyster sales had jumped after the Japanese oysters were sold as 'king' oysters. And demand for the northern spider crab, one of the ugliest creatures in the Pacific seas, a thin, anemic-looking beast with a tiny body and long, spindly legs skyrocketed (to a point where this crustacean is now becoming scarce) after it was renamed 'king crab.' The clam processors were smart enough to disguise the shape of the geoduck by selling its meat chopped up or flattened into fillets (I sometimes think you can sell anything to the American consumer, as long as it is ground up like hamburger or sliced and sold as 'steak').

Today, if you look hard enough, you can find processed geoduck in many supermarket freezer bins. On the other extreme, you can find sliced, raw geoduck sold as sashimi in Japanese markets. I still prefer to buy my geoduck live and fresh, do the cleaning myself, and thus enjoy its flavor at its best. There are several delectable ways of fixing this clam. And don't worry about taking this odd-looking creature home: fishmongers will wrap it in newspaper, and you should be able to get it to the privacy of your kitchen without exposing yourself to the stares and giggles of less enlightened gastronomes.

EATING WELL

Sheila Hutchins   *1980*

COCKLES *and* WHELKS

There are rather few good books on the food and cookery of
particular regions of England. One is Sheila Hutchins'
Grannie's Kitchen, *which deals with East Anglia: a rich mine*
of information gathered on the spot. The chapter on seafood
has the number one spot at the beginning of the book and
includes these items.

COCKLES

Leigh-on-Sea in Essex faces the Thames estuary and is part of the real old Cockney seaside where people used to come on day trips in the old charabancs (before they all went to the Costa Brava instead). There were works' outings and washerwomen's picnics and it was the superb cockles that pleased them – 'the poor man's oyster', now almost forgotten. This is a real regional delicacy. The shore at Leigh is not sand at all, just millions and millions of cockle shells going back for centuries. One of my readers in Ahrensburg, Germany, once wrote to me that the best cockles he had ever eaten in his life were outside a shed in Leigh-on-Sea 'not five feet away from the boat that brought them'.

'You get a helping there which is double the size you get in London,' he wrote to me. 'Sitting there on the wooden benches at a small table with vinegar bottles, eating cockles is a pleasure which epitomizes the joy of spending my holidays in England. If you like cockles – go to Leigh in September and you will know what I mean.'

'People come here because they're fresh,' Mr Meddle told me in Osborne's famous Cockle Shed. 'A few years ago we got down with hand rakes for 'em, had to get out of the boat. Now it's all changed, we've got suckers aboard. They're something like a vast vacuum cleaner for getting the cockles up from the sand. They go out on the flood tide nowadays and come in on the ebb, the boats have got to be afloat to work.'

'Osborne's have given their life to it, cockles,' said one of the customers who later told me he had a jellied eel business near Southend pier. 'Dedicated, they are, dedicated!' Some Sundays there are queues everywhere for tea, rolls and butter or beer, to go with the shellfish.

'The cockles were cooked at three this morning, and all finished by eight a.m. – *steamed*, not boiled, luv!'

This is the great Leigh speciality. In other places they boil, instead of steaming the cockles, and a lot of the flavour no doubt is wasted in the cooking liquor. After that they're put in a good mild vinegar for people to eat on those nice little white cockle and whelk saucers. They are delicious but you can't use them for cooking in a cockle recipe;

the vinegar kills the flavour, which is a pity because fresh cockles bought in the shell, washed free of sand and cooked briefly like mussels, are superb. You can cook them according to any good mussel recipe. Try a fresh cockle risotto for instance. They also make a mouth-watering omelette filling. The freshly cooked hot cockles should be folded in at the last moment, just before it sets and is slid out of the pan.

'Sorry, luv! Can't sell cockles raw, it's against the law,' said Bill Meddle as we sat eating them in the sunshine and drinking whiskies and soda. 'A bye law really from some time in the 1880s about them having to be cooked. It'd be something like a £150 fine and six months prison if I let you have them raw.' It seems awfully unfair, for one can buy raw cockles in the shell in other parts of the country. There is also a lot of talk of doing away with the whole thing, the cockle sheds, the boats drawn up in cottage yards and the notices saying 'fresh bait' in the front windows.

This would be tragic, so go down there now while you can still sit by the sea-wall next to the Old Peter Boat pub and eat cockles, drink beer and whisky and stare at the fishing boats.

'It's all one big family down here,' the barman said. 'For cockles you must be an Osborne or a Harvey, or you marry into cockles or shrimps. That's all there is to it.'

Mrs Ivy Osborne's blue painted shellfish stall outside the Old Peter Boat pub has been in her family for generations.

'I'm related to the number three shed,' she told me, 'not those Osbornes down the road. I'm 66, have six grandchildren and I love it all! You can live for ever in God's fresh air! My dear old Nan used to cook and hand sieve the cockles by candlelight. The old barges used to come in here then. And people walked to Southend with yokes on their shoulders. My Mum had the stall too. Lovely in her ways she was. She gathered her own. Water working is very nice, she used to say, but you must wait for the tide.'

We were both munching the local shrimps, though Mrs Osborne says she likes a nice hen crab better than anything: 'You can eat the whole thing. But always take out those grey banana-shaped things, they won't hurt you but they make it taste bitter. The hen crab's got smaller claws and lighter flesh than the cock.'

Hot buttered cockles are delicious with brown bread and butter. Serve them heaped up in a hot soup plate, with a jug of melted butter, a jar for the empty shells, and a bottle of white wine to go with them. Pour the melted butter on a tilted side plate and dip the cockles in it as you eat them.

Fresh cockles in their shells are very sandy, so rinse them several times in cold water, then, to get rid of the sand inside the shells, leave them overnight in a bucket of cold water by which time they should have cleaned themselves.

Like mussels or oysters, long cooking makes them tough. Put at least two tablespoons of butter in a wide pan. When hot, tip in the drained cockles and stir. Wring out a tea towel in hot water and lay it on top.

Cook the cockles for only five minutes – like mussels – until all the shells are open, stir them once or twice so the cockles on top fall closer to the heat and open.

WHELKS

'You're never going to eat that,' a little boy exclaimed as I stood in front of the fish stall on the quay at Blakeney, Norfolk, with a carton of whelks. They were freshly cooked, fresh out of the sea, and tasted delicious. I think some whelks you get in other parts of the country are often dried up or over-cooked. 'But you have to cook them fairly well,' said the fish stall girl, 'or we can't wind them out of the shells.' This is done with a skewer in some circles. We were, of course, within four miles of Wells-next-the-Sea, the whelk centre of all England which is where virtually all the whelks on all the shell-fish stalls in the country are caught. It's a little old fashioned fishing port and the whelks have to come in across the bar, a breath-taking business in stormy weather when the small town's six-boat fleet returns loaded with whelks. These are caught about 20 miles out at sea in pots similar to those used for lobsters. Because there is no other shelter the boats must ride in over the bar. It is a busy little port with a fishing fleet that also catches shrimps, sprats and whitebait and you see boats from Germany and Holland unloading cargoes of fertilizer and filling up with barley and sugar beet.

The whelks are boiled in sheds at the other end of the quay past the Shipwright's Arms and sent off by motor lorry to London and elsewhere.

In Norfolk pubs some of the fishermen are very fond of eating them hot, and as a matter of fact, they are gorgeous as an appetizer or what the French call an 'amuse-gueule' with drinks. I like them with gin and tonic, though some people maintain fiercely that this doesn't go with shellfish. My impression, however, is that the average English person couldn't care less about whelks and thinks they are rather common. Some of them look, well, what you might describe as rather rude. It's a kind of sea snail really and the top is the best part with a strong seaside flavour like oysters, but much cheaper. The other end is sometimes a bit chewey.

The little boy was still standing there with his mouth open. 'Have an introductory whelk,' I said. He took it and disappeared up a side street, no doubt torn between good manners and what his mother had said about never accepting whelks from strangers. I do hope he wasn't sick.

At Brancaster Staithe we produce several tons of whelks daily, more than Wells. I think if you contact the shellfish buyer at Boston he will tell you we produce the most in Britain. By the way, whelks are best small and more tasty if they have been fished two days later than the pots being baited, they have then digested and passed the decomposed bait used in the pots. This only happens if the sea is too rough to get out the following day ...

Nelson Wolsey, Brancaster Staithe, Kings Lynn

When I met him, Mr Alf Burder, the whelk specialist of Leigh-on-Sea, had a bucket of hot whelks between his knees and was busy extracting them from their shells with a packing needle. 'They're cooked first and I put them in a bucket of hot water so as to get them out easier,' he explained. 'The tail is the best part.' I tasted some and it was, more flavour and less chewey.

'These are all right-hand ones,' he said picking on a few more and passing them to me. 'They're not local, they come from Wells. That's in Norfolk. You can wait a long time till you get a left-hand one – very rare – I had 3 or 4 last year though. They're worth a lot, showing them to blokes in pubs.' Whelks are delicious when all fresh and moist like these were, but some of the South coast seaside ones are a bit chewey and all dried up. 'Well, yes. You could call me the Whelk King of Leigh, for nobody else wants the job,' he said diving down into the bucket for an enormous green and glistening specimen which I ate.

'Only way of keeping the missis quiet too,' he added, with what I believe is known as an old-fashioned look, 'is to buy her a plate of whelks and get them in her mouth so she can't speak.'   GRANNIE'S KITCHEN: RECIPES FROM EAST ANGLIA

J. George Frederick and Jean Joyce   1939

WHICH CHOWDER?

*A matter for hot debate, not quiet rumination. But author
Frederick (from whose part of the jointly authored book this
piece comes) managed to produce a dispassionate survey of the
matter. He believed, by the way, that our special feelings about
seafood reflect the fact that primordial life began in the waters.*

If anybody tells you that the American people are 'regimented' or 'standardized', just ask quietly. '*What about clam chowder?*' Your cocksure informer will get very red in the face, for nothing is more notorious than that various sections of Eastern America come to blows over chowder. Tomatoes or milk is the crucial question, also caraway seeds and salt pork. New England is rent and torn over these dissenting practices, but Boston, Maine, and Connecticut are allied against Manhattan or Long Island chowders, while Rhode Island teeters in between.

Where did this disputatious chowder family come from? Chowder has a much more fascinating origin than most of us realize; in fact it is so 'communistic' in origin that the Dies Committee at Washington is likely to get excited about it as a red invasion! It originated in the fishing villages of Brittany, France, where *faire la chaudière* (prepare the caldron) was a community enterprise of the fishermen for common use, each one contributing something to the pot, whether fish, vegetable or spices, and each receiving a proportionate quantity of the finished hodge-podge, made with fish and ship biscuits, vegetables and savory ingredients. Nothing is said of milk in these early origins in

France, nor, it must be admitted, anything about tomatoes! The French fishermen, settling in Newfoundland, brought along their *faire la chaudière* habit, using the rich abundance of seafood in their new home. This name traveled to the Maritime Provinces and then into New England a very long time ago; and of course quickly also traveled across the narrow inlets of Long Island Sound to the eastern end of Long Island, thence to Manhattan. On the way *'chaudière'* naturally became anglicized to *chowder*.

In those early days, before the American Revolution, admittedly nearly all chowders were milk chowders. Some chowders, like the original one, never had either milk or tomato. The tomato, it must be recorded, had few friends in any dish made to eat in those days, being called a 'love apple' by the romantic, and designated by an encyclopedia of the period as a 'straggling, clammy, ill-smelling, grayish-green plant.' The fruit of this plant, the tomato, was regarded as possibly poisonous, certainly objectionable, and in any event disgusting!

Since Long Island has all this time been the place where New York and New England merge (at the eastern tip) it is not surprising that the chowder controversy rages even today on Long Island, despite the fact that a majority opinion certainly sides with tomato. But a few old, gnarled eastern island baymen, and hardy old ladies, who learned the cookery arts somewhere around the Civil War period when the tomato was still an outlaw, today continue to cling to the milk basis for chowder, and will not surrender. Canceling this out is the fact that many New Englanders, even up into Maine, and particularly in Rhode Island, have acquired the tomato chowder idea and uphold it against their scandalized neighbors . . .

What is the actual merit of this violent chowder controversy? What started it? It is admitted to be the most famous gastronomic controversy in American history, exceeding easily the strawberry shortcake controversy. In February, 1939 Assemblyman Seeder introduced into the Maine legislature a bill to make tomato in clam chowder illegal!

Long Island's tomato clam chowder first captured New York City, where it was adopted and dubbed Manhattan clam chowder, and has since spread its conquering way throughout the rest of the country. Clam chowder, to most of America, means tomato clam chowder, even in the canned varieties of it sold nationally. Long Island came very naturally by the tomato base for clam chowder because it is great truck farm region and tomatoes are very plentifully grown there; whereas in New England with its colder climate, tomatoes are not so readily grown, and therefore not so inexpensive as on Long Island and in New York.

There are definite things to be said for tomato clam chowder which are lost sight of in the mere argumentative heat of battle. The New England clam chowder appears to have been used widely, like the New England fish chowder, as a whole meal by itself. Thus it could be, and was desired to be, particularly substantial. In New York and on Long Island, clam chowder was developed more as a soup course, which therefore was *not* desired to be so substantial as to clog the appetite for the other courses. The restaurants of New York, in particular, were not patronized in earlier days by those who wanted to dine only on clam chowder. They wanted a soup which would fulfill what French masters of cookery have always allotted to soup as its proper function, namely to *whet*, rather than to completely satisfy the desire for food.

So clam chowder (Long Island or Manhattan) was made with tomato instead of milk, and thus it performed its function admirably – even though the old New Englander finds it too insubstantial, and thinks he can logically scorn it for this reason. He does not stop to consider the point that a milk clam chowder is too filling – which was a merit in the old frugal days of New England, but not now when the diner wishes to go on eagerly to several other courses. Admitting quite readily that clams, like oysters, have a nice affinity for milk and cream, the Long Islander contends that the clam's affinity for tomato is also well demonstrated. I like a milk clam chowder for the same purpose that I like a milk fish chowder – because it does so well for a whole meal! But it would be rather ill-advised and even absurd, speaking from the gourmet or the nutritive standpoint, to serve a milk clam chowder, New England style, on a five or seven course dinner menu, with hors d'oeuvres before it, and fish and meat, salad and dessert courses to come after! Manhattanites and others have come to like a rather thin tomato clam chowder, for precisely this reason. The same principle can be seen at work in gumbos. A gumbo as served in New Orleans is a meal in itself, and used as such; and therefore the thin chicken gumbo soup usually served elsewhere elicits the contempt of such New Orleans folk who are in the habit of dining on heavy gumbos and little else. But the tendency is perfectly understandable in a day of more ample provision and fuller menus. At an ample dinner menu served at Antoine's, New Orleans, the soup course is never a thick gumbo. Antoine's knows better, just as the New Englander should.

The New Englander also may use the soft shell clam for his clam chowder, largely (we Long Islanders suspect) because New England's soft shell clams are likely to be more succulent than their quahogs (hard shell clams). On Long Island, however, the hard shell clams come in smaller and more succulent size ('cherrystones', for example) and thus make better chowder. The soft shell clam is more perishable, losing its freshness more easily, and is harder and less sanitary to handle.

Long Islanders and New Yorkers, in their opinion, reserve for the soft shell clam its true place – for steaming and eating with melted butter. Certainly no one can deny its extra deliciousness in this form, or the succulence of clam chowder made from the smaller quahogs. Long Islanders also occasionally make clam chowder out of soft shell clams, but they prefer the others, and New Yorkers are better served with fresher clams when their chowder is made from quahogs. Thus another difference between Long Island and New England seafood is explained, not as a mere cockfight of intransigent opinion, but as fact. That the rest of the United States tends strongly, I think, to agree with Long Island and New York City, rather than New England, seems to point to the solid basis of fact behind Long Island's practice.

LONG ISLAND SEAFOOD COOK BOOK

PROVINCETOWN SQUID STEW

Seafood cookery in Provincetown, Cape Cod, is of special
interest because of the long-standing Portuguese influence
there. Like Bunny Day (page 132), Howard Mitcham writes
with a breezy tang and infectious enthusiasm.

This is the story of a small restaurant and a big stew. The restaurant is Cookie's Tap
in Provincetown, and the stew is squid stew. Cookie's is one of the few restaurants
in New England that still makes a good Portuguese squid stew; it's becoming a lost art.
The wives of Provincetown fishermen sometimes make it at home, but not very often:
they don't like the muss and fuss of cleaning squids. But the Portuguese are so fond of
squid stew that they attach an almost mystical significance to it. A good Portygee would
walk two miles through a howling nor'east gale just to wrap himself around a hot bowl of
squid stew.

Squid stew is definitely not a dish for an impatient landlubber. The first dish
shocks you; it tastes like chopped up tennis shoes to many people. The second dish
numbs you. Somewhere along about the sixth bowl you begin to realize that the dish
does have a unique and distinctive flavor and from then on, brother, you are hooked.

The Lord took away a great *bon vivant* and gourmet back in 1946 when he laid a
heart attack on Friday Cook in the prime of his life, only forty-eight years old. His
grandfather had come here as cabin boy and cook on Captain Kibby Cook's whaling
vessel, and the family adopted the name both of the vocation and the benefactor. Friday
ran one of the most amazing bars and restaurants in America. All the fishermen hung
out at Cookie's and they would bring in their 'trash' for which there was no ready
market: crabs, giant lobsters, squids, butterfish, catfish, wolffish, pollocks, blinkers,
conches, tinkers, quahaugs and Lord knows what else. Friday and his wife, Clara (and
later, sons Wilbur and Joe) would cook this stuff in all sorts of tantalizing ways, and
they'd pile it on the counter. Anybody who didn't look TOO greedy and hungry was
invited to help himself. I remember that in my first summer here I didn't spend a nickel
on food; I spent my dimes on beer at Cookie's, and the food was on the house. The late
John Gaspie, the clamdigging *bon vivant*, would sit with me all afternoon, spinning
fabulous yarns as we devoured galvanized tinkers and squid stew, and sipped the foamy.
Halcyon days they were.

Friday is gone, but Clara and Wilbur and Joe are still carrying on. As is typical in
the strongly matriarchal society of the Portuguese, the mother is the backbone of the
business; she works discreetly in the background, but does she produce! Clara Cook is a
walking encyclopedia of the tricks and twists of Portuguese cookery. But darn it, not

even her own children can get her to write down any of her recipes. In fact she does not have any; she plays by ear, straight from the heart, guided by intuition and her taste buds. *That* is Fine Art. I could never hope to duplicate Clara's squid stew, but here's a formula that will do for a starter.

Squid Stew

3 dozen squids and their tentacles
diced potatoes equal in volume to the squids
1 quart red wine
1 quart water or fish stock (more if necessary)
1 can tomatoes, squeezed up
1 small can tomato paste
1 onion, chopped
6 cloves garlic, minced
3 tbsps. olive oil
2 tbsps. Worcestershire sauce
pinch of ground allspice
pinch of ground cominos
salt to taste
enough powdered cayenne or Tabasco to make it hot as hell

Saute the onions and garlic in the olive oil until they are soft and dump them into the stew pot. Put all the vegetables, liquids and condiments into the pot, bring to a boil, then lower the heat and simmer for 1 hour. Then add the squid meats and tentacles; raise the heat to a boil, then lower to the simmer and cook for 1, 2, 3, 4 or 5 hours, according to the amount of time you have on your hands. Stir it now and then, and if necessary add more liquids. Serve in large bowls with hot Portuguese bread.

On a cold winter night a bellyful of squid stew will make you sleep well.

PROVINCETOWN SEAFOOD COOKBOOK

On COOKING YABBIES

Crayfish are acclaimed as a delicacy in the Scandinavian
countries and in the State of Louisiana; but few people realise
that there are only 7 species in Europe, compared with over 250
in North America; and that a great abundance of species (over
100), and the largest crayfish, are found in Australasia. The
'marron' of Western Australia and the giant black crayfish of
Tasmania (a real giant, measuring up to 2' 6" from tip of
claw to tip of tail!) are famous, but the best known species is
the 'humble yabby', Cherax destructor, *in whose honour*
Olszewski writes, and about which he has many amusing
anecdotes.

Beer is inextricably bound up with the yabby boiling ritual in the bush. Dave Kimbo, of Loxton, South Australia, describes how his friends go about the business, and relates how a chap called Zeke, of Loxton, an ace yabby catcher, and his mates have a definite yabby cooking ritual. Many stubbies of beer are required to put the yabby eater into the correct frame of mind. An old style copper is stoked (lately they've changed to gas) to boiling point. About 1 kg (2 lb) of salt is thrown in, the water being eyed critically from behind the ever-present stubbies. The yabbies are transferred from a mesh holding basket kept in the river, and rapidly tipped into the copper when the water is boiling merrily. Watches are checked. More stubbies are consumed and after precisely 12 minutes of cooking (although others cook 'em for as little as 5 or 7 minutes) the yabbies are removed to a nearby table, empty stubbies are replenished, and the eaters tuck in.

The performance involves nothing fancy. No washing bowl. Eat the 'mustard' and all. Fresh bread for the really fussy. Zeke, following his philosophy of 'waste not, want not', will willingly demonstrate how you even find sustenance in the body: 'Ya grab the body like this, rip the under-belly away, and suck the guts like this', says he, doing just that – jamming the body to his mouth, sucking viciously at the same time.

Most Australians eat only the yabby tail and, if large enough, the claws. Eating the inside of the head, chest, or thorax (the guts) is rare, but European and American crayfish connoisseurs regard this part of the crayfish as a supreme delicacy, and it's usually served as an adjunct to the meat.

Australian Aborigines also eat the yabby's head. Steve Buck, a professional shooter, supplements his income by catching yabbies. While fishing the Darling River at Wilcannia, he observed how Aborigines ate yabbies:

After a day on the river I used to pull in and there was always a crowd of Aborigines and their kids waiting for me. I always gave them a few kilos to split up between them. An interesting point is that one day I really got a sermon from an old woman for throwing the heads away. The Aborigines regard this as the best part of the yabby. After removing the tails and claws, they scoop out a hole in the ground and pour in the heads, covering them with hot ashes. Sometimes they dip the heads in a mixture of flour and water before putting them in the hole. After 5 minutes the heads are taken out of the hole, and a small forked stick is pushed up into the carcass and then withdrawn, together with the entrails, which are then of course eaten.

A SALUTE TO THE HUMBLE YABBY

Cassell's Dictionary of Cookery   *late 19th century*
Julio Camba   *1937*

HUNTING *the* RAZOR-CLAM

The idea that one can entice razor-clams up to the surface of
the sand by using salt bobs up all over the place. Here are two
examples, from 19th century England and 20th century Spain.

'Another bivalve,' says Dr. Lancaster, 'sometimes eaten by the inhabitants of our coasts is the Razor-Fish (*Solen maximus*). This creature would be interesting enough to us if it were not eaten, on account of its long, slightly-curved, and truncated shells, which resemble the blade of a razor. It is not uncommon on our sandy shores, where it lives buried in the sand. It is not difficult to find, as above the spot into which it has retired it leaves an impression of two holes united, something like a keyhole. It is, however, almost useless to attempt to dig them up, they back away from you so skillfully. After many vain efforts to secure one of these creatures alive, I mentioned my failures to the late Professor Edward Forbes. "Oh," he said, with a waggish smile, "all you have to do is to put a little salt over their holes, and they will come out." I remembered the story of putting salt on birds' tails; and although I resolved secretly to follow my friend's plan, it was so simple I had not the courage to tell him that I would. I had, however, no sooner got to the seaside than I quietly stole to the pantry, and pocketed some salt, and then went alone at low tide to the sandy shore. As soon as I espied a hole I looked round, for I almost fancied I heard my friend chuckle over my shoulder; however, nobody was there, and down went a pinch of salt over the hole. What I now beheld almost staggered me. Was it the ghost of some razor-fish whose head I had chopped off in digging that now rose before me to arraign me for my malice, or was it a real live razor-fish that now raised its long shell at least half out of the sand? I grasped it, fully expecting it would vanish, but I found I had won my prize. It was a real solid specimen of the species *Solen maximus* that I had in my hand. I soon had a number of others, which were all carried home in triumph. Of course, there were more than were required for the purposes of science, and at the suggestion of a Scotch friend the animals not wanted were made into soup. When the soup was brought to table, our Scotch friend vowed it particularly fine, and ate a basinful with at least twenty razor-fish in it. One tablespoonful satisfied the ladies, whilst I and an English friend declared – against our consciences, I do verily believe – that we had never eaten anything so excellent. I counted the number of the creatures I was able to swallow; it amounted to exactly three. After a tumbler of whisky and water – taken, of course, medicinally – arrangements were made for a dredge in the morning. The Scotchman was up at five, but I and my English friend could not make our appearance. Nightmare and other symptoms of indigestion had fairly upset us, and unfitted us for anything so ticklish as a dredging excursion. Now, I do not wish to say anything against razor-fish as an article of diet, but, from what I have told, they would seem to possess an amount of resistance to the ordinary digestive activity of the stomach that would make it highly desirable to ensure before taking them, such a digestion as a Highlander fresh from his mountain-wilds is known to possess.'

CASSELL'S DICTIONARY OF COOKERY

I must tell you about one of my favourite sports, which is fishing for the *lingueiron* [razor-clam], also called *cuchillo* [table knife] or *navaja* [dagger].

When the tide is out, these cautious molluscs hide in the sand at a depth of 15 to 20 centimetres, and wait tranquilly for the tide to come in. Just a tiny hole in the sand indicates each hiding place. Even if it were possible to scoop away the sand with one's hand in order to reach the creature, it is better to wait for him to come out of his own accord. All you have to do is to convince him that the tide has finally come in. But he is very suspicious! How to convince him?

I must say at once that I am not the inventor of the ruse which does the trick. I make this disclaimer, not because I fear revenge on the part of the *lingueiron*, but because I would not wish to take credit for somebody else's invention.

All you have to do is put a little coarse salt on the little hole in the sand. 'Caramba, caramba!' says the *lingueiron* when he detects the emanations from the salt: 'I could have sworn that it was not yet due, but here is the tide coming in. I'll go up and join my friends and start looking for the day's food.'

When he comes out, you grab him, either to eat him right away or to let him go so that you can catch him again the next day.

LA CASA DE LUCÚLO

Eleanor Clark   *1965*

The OYSTERS *of* LOCMARIAQUER

*If one wants the full story about oysters and the people who
start them on their journey to the table, this is the book to
read. The extracts are about tasting oysters and about how
they are trained to withstand the journeys they must make.*

The outcome is a little luxury item, of rather large economic consequence but no great importance to the world's nourishment. It should be. The oyster is very high in nutrition value, at least as much so as milk, but that is scarcely relevant as things stand because not enough people can afford it. So the whole point is flavor, and sociologically speaking, how can you justify that? Is it worth all the pain and trouble? Should it even be allowed?

You can't define it. Music or the color of the sea are easier to describe than the taste of one of these Armoricaines, which has been lifted, turned, redbedded, taught to close its mouth while traveling, culled, sorted, kept a while in a rest home or 'basin' between each change of domicile, raked, protected from its enemies and shifting sands etc. for four or five years before it gets into your mouth. It has no relation at all to the taste, if there is one, of the usual U.S. restaurant oyster, not to mention the canned or frozen one. (No Armoricaines are canned, or frozen; there is no such business.) Or rather yes, it has the relation of love to tedium, delight to the death of the soul, the best to the tolerable if tolerable, in anything. Or say of French bread, the kind anybody eats in France, to ... well, never mind. It is briny first of all, and not in the sense of brine in a barrel, for the preservation of something; there is a shock of freshness to it. Intimations of the ages of man, some piercing intuition of the sea and all its weeds and breezes shiver you a split second from that little stimulus on the palate. You are eating the sea, that's it, only the sensation of a gulp of sea water has been wafted out of it by some sorcery, and are on the verge of remembering you don't know what, mermaids or the sudden smell of kelp on the ebb tide or a poem you read once, something connected with the flavor of life itself ...

You can eat them in the fancy restaurants of Nantes or Paris, or right out of the yard if you are lucky, or at almost any village café in the coast region. There, you can eat them at any time of year; in late June and July, the reproductive season, some are 'milky' and horrid-tasting, but those are spotted when they are opened. The sign says BAR – CRÊPERIE – DÉGUSTATION D'HUÎTRES, and the word dégustation means what it says: not 'consumption of' but 'tasting,' 'savoring.' It does not mean having a snack, with no suggestion beyond feeding your face. You are in the country of the art of good food, and this dégustation is very like what you do in an art gallery, unless your soul is lost; it is essential to be hungry but impermissible to be merely that; you have to take your time, the imagination must work; the first rule is to pay attention to what you are doing.

There is a certain expression that comes on a middle-to-upper income bracket Frenchman's face when he is about to déguster something really good, cheese, wine, any sort of culinary specialty, that starts out as a sudden interior break in the train of conversation. Silence; he is about to have a gastronomic experience. Then as the fork or glass nears his mouth, his eyes and ears seem to have blanked out; all is concentrated in the power of taste. There follows a stage when the critical faculties are gathering, the head is bent, eyes wander, lips and tongue are working over the evidence. At last comes the climactic moment of judgment, upon which may hang the mood of the meal and with it who knows what devious changes in the course of love, commerce or the body politic. The thing was poor or indifferent; the man shrugs, applies his napkin as though wiping out the whole experience, and goes on with what was interrupted, not quite relaxed; some sense of letdown, a slight disgruntlement lurks in the conversation. It was good, excellent, perfect, and oh what an expansion of frame and spirit; the chair will hardly hold him; he is not smiling, not just yet, but life is as he sits back gravely nodding, eager to look his companion and all the world in the eyes, and this time the napkin touches his lips like a chaste kiss, or a cleaning rag on an objet d'art.

*   *   *

There had been abnormal cold and storms as early as November. Still, until Christmas the chantiers had all been bustling as usual. That really isn't the word for it. Inside the chantier buildings, most of them very small, there is a subdued racket of chatter and shells and wooden sabots on cement as the women go about the business of sorting *le triage*, plus the noise of the sorting machine when the establishment is fancy enough to have one. But most of the work on the parks has a slow and lonely look. It is nothing like May and June. The work is of a different kind, and there is no whiteness around; the tiles with their wonderful accretion will mostly stay where they are until February. This is the time for moving the older crops, whether for shipment or relocation farther out from shore, and for the general work to be done off and on through the winter.

There are basins to scrub, crabs to kill, fences to mend, that is the park fences, fifty or more yards to a side and about eight inches high, with or without the out-thrust ledge and wire at the top, depending on the oysters' age and vulnerability. One of the few operations the oyster spares its keeper is feeding it, but he has to guard it from being fed on, and the wood too. Some oystermen import sacks of little snails from Ireland to eat algae. The parks have to be cleaned, and in some places spread with gravel to make the bottom firm and lessen the chance of smothering, which is most crucial for the yearlings and eighteen-months; for the older ones the danger is not so great. There is some piling up of silt at best and all the oysters have to be raked now and then, especially after a storm, either with hand rakes or at high tide with a harrow, about the width of a drag and pulled behind a boat in the same way. But the big event this time of year is change of domicile. Nearly all the millions of oysters are being moved, here and there by mechanical dragging and dumping but in great part by hand, and unless they are to be rebedded immediately, this involves a procedure called 'fooling the oysters' – *tromper l'huître*.

It is actually a double procedure, to make the animal (1) clean itself out, and (2) learn to stay shut during transportation. Anthropologists would call this a rite of passage, and very solemn it is, not only as marking advancement to another stage of life, which the oyster may not appreciate, but because neglect of it can have, has had in the past, tragic consequences all round. The principals in the ceremony – youths, maidens and in-betweens but it goes for all later initiations too, through the last and most solemn, on the way to the table – go for three or four days into the stone or cement basins you have been seeing, called *dégorgeoirs*, where a judicious withholding of water and food at certain intervals causes them to disgorge their impurities. The educational part comes about as a result of the oyster's habit of 'yawning' when exposed to air. The trickery, which must create some nervous breakdowns but leads to an extraordinary degree of self-control in the majority, lies in depriving it of water not just once but over and over when it is least expecting it. At the end of this trial it is conditioned not to yawn and thereby lose its liquid, and can travel for quite a long time without risk of suffocation.

It is an ancient practice, followed from way back in Brittany and the other great oyster regions. In the days before trucking and railroads, or when railroads were flourishing inland but didn't extend to many points on the coast, and the time of shipment by sailing vessels might be doubled by bad weather, few oysters would have lasted out a trip if they had not been cleansed and had their characters fortified this way.

THE OYSTERS OF LOCMARIAQUER

On Hoof *or* Wing

*If looking for paeans about the glories of roast
beef etcetera, try another book. Read here
about the butcher in far away Tibet who decided
that he couldn't be a butcher any more. Relive
with Flora Thompson her childhood experience of
the killing of a pig. Marvel at the place of
honour given to fat in the Middle East. And
don't miss the description of the beautiful Lisa
presiding over her charcuterie stall – 'her
pink cheeks echoing the gentle flesh tones of the hams'.
But, first, open your ears to a message from
Scandinavia about blood.*

Birgit Siesby   *1980*

BLOOD *is* FOOD

*Yes, blood is food, and most people know what's in black
pudding. But I don't think that anyone else has developed the
theme as fully as Birgit Siesby, in the essay of which this is
part. Among Danish writers on food she is distinguished by
her combination of special interests: history and nutrition.*

Our ancestors knew the value of blood. They used the blood as food and as an offering to the gods.

Why have we given up the traditional blood dishes? Why are enormous quantities of slaughter blood wasted in many industrial countries? Considering the great nutritional value of blood, such waste seems an absurdity at a time characterized by growing concern about food resources.

Blood has been conceived by many peoples as the very soul of the animal. This basic idea has, however, led to opposite attitudes. The ancient Jews banned the eating of blood (Genesis, Ch. 9, verse 4) and so did the early Christianity and Islam. The Nordic peoples on the other hand did not find it proper to waste the souls of animals. On the contrary they thought that by drinking the blood they might partake of the strength and qualities of the slain beasts. Thus Saxo Grammaticus in his *Gesta Danorum* from the 12th century tells the story about the great warrior Bjarke who slew the giant bear and let his young follower Hjalte drink its blood in order to acquire the bear's strength and fighting spirit. Judging from Hjalte's later deeds the blood had the desired effect.

The introduction of Christianity did not make the Nordic peoples give up their traditional blood dishes such as black soup, black pudding and paltbread; neither did the French give up their boudin noir and the civets, nor the Irish their drisheen (presumably a recipe inherited from the Norse people who founded Cork and Dublin).

Industrialisation and the disappearance of home slaughtering, however, meant that blood dishes fell into disuse in Denmark – only about 1% of the available blood is being used for traditional blood dishes today, whereas in the other Scandinavian countries the tradition of eating blood dishes once a week is still upheld.

It ought to be easy to introduce new ways of utilizing blood in the countries mentioned above where the traditional blood dishes have survived. In the Western countries where the traditional dishes have fallen into disuse the public may be prejudiced against blood, although hardly for religious reasons.

The taste and flavour of blood is very mild, almost neutral, with a faint liverlike touch. The main problem is the colour. When blood is heated the colour turns from bright red to brown so that dishes with blood added get a darker colouring. In some cases the colour may be an advantage because it may make artificial colouring unnecessary. But it is generally regarded as a disadvantage.

In order to solve the colour problem food industries have removed the red fraction (the hemoglobine fraction) by centrifugalizing. The rest, the colourless plasma fraction, has for some years been used as a cheap protein enrichment in meat products. But discarding the red fraction results in the removal of all the important heme iron together with the major part of the protein. My concern, therefore, has been to find uses for full blood; and the Danish experiences have shown that this can indeed be utilized in the food industry without complications ...

A feature common to several nomad peoples is the utilization of blood obtained by bleeding. It is well known that the tall proud Massai herdsmen, while travelling with the herds, live mainly on a mixture of blood and milk. They tap approximately 2–4 litres of blood by piercing the jugular vein with an arrow wrapped in string. A thong is tied around the animal's neck, causing the vein to swell and the bleeding simply stops when the thong is loosened. The Massai are reluctant to slaughter their animals as the wealth of the owner depends entirely upon the number of cattle. Besides being a practical solution to the storage problem in a tropical climate the bleeding may also be a way to increase the production of animal protein. By bleeding a well nourished European cow 4 litres every second week over a period of $2\frac{1}{2}$ years it is possible to obtain an amount of protein roughly equal to the amount obtained by slaughtering the cow. Furthermore, in order to overcome certain religious scruples, due to the conception of blood as the animal's soul, bleeding may be preferable to slaughter blood for the simple reason that the animal continues to live happily after bleeding.

Marco Polo describes in detail how the Mongol armies in the 13th century lived on bleeding their horses. Each man had a string of 18 horses and they travelled 'without provisions and without making a fire, living only on the blood of their horses; for every rider pierces a vein of his horse and drinks the blood'. A very easy and cheap way of getting food without having to prepare it. Fuel was not easy to find on the steppes of Central Asia and to light a fire might be fatal because the enemies could see the fire for many miles around. The blood was drunk hot and the souls of the horses remained safe and sound.

As a curiosity it may be mentioned that the Lapplanders occasionally bleed the growing antlers of the reindeer.

The Scandinavian and Irish peoples have also made use of the bleeding method, especially during the hunger periods. A French traveller (M. Henri Misson de Valbourg) noted in the seventeenth century that the peasants in Ireland 'bleed their cows and boil the blood with some of the milk and butter that come from the same beast; and this with a mixture of savoury herbs is one of their most delicious dishes'. He refers to the national Irish dish drisheen which has become fashionable – today it is served even at the fine restaurants in Ireland.

PETITS PROPOS CULINAIRES (PPC) 4

Émile Zola   1873

LISA, *the* CHARCUTIÈRE

To match Zola's description of the vegetable and fish markets
(see pages 84 and 120), here is his portrait of a market person:
la belle Lisa, who presided over the charcuterie.

Lisa stood behind the counter, her head turned slightly towards the Halles, and Florent observed her in silence, surprised to find her so beautiful. He had never really seen her properly before that moment, not knowing how to look at a woman, and there she stood behind the meat on her counter. In front of her, displayed on white porcelain plates, were sausages from Arles and Lyon from which slices had been cut, tongues and chunks of boiled ham, a pig's head drowned in jelly, an open jar of rillettes and a tin of sardines whose punctured metal revealed a lake of oil. To the left and right, on the floor, were cheeses from Italy, brawn, a local pale pink ham, a red-fleshed York ham, covered in a thick layer of fat. There were more round and oval plates, plates of stuffed tongue, truffled galantine, brawn with pistachio nuts, while next to her, within reach, were larded veal, liver and hare pâté in yellow terrines. As Gavard wasn't coming, she placed the brisket fat on the small marble shelf at the end of the counter, and placed the jar of lard and the jar of dripping next to it, wiped the nickel silver trays on the scales, and felt the stove, which was going out. Then she silently turned her gaze once more to the far end of the market. The heavy scent of the meat rose, and she became almost tipsy in the rich bouquet of the truffles.

That day she looked superbly fresh, the whiteness of her apron and sleeves reflecting that of the plates, her stout neck and pink cheeks echoing the gentle flesh tones of the hams and the pallor of the transparent fat. The more he looked at her, the more intimidated Florent became, unsettled by the four-square frankness of her bearing, resorting to surreptitious glances in the mirrors dotted around the shop. He saw reflections of her back, her front, her sides; he even found her on the ceiling, her head bowed, exposing her tight bun and her fine hair smoothed back at the temples. There was a whole crowd of Lisas, broad-shouldered, their arms powerfully jointed, the curvature of their breasts so taut and silent that they aroused no carnal thoughts in him, so much did they remind him of a paunch. He stopped to admire one particular profile, there in the mirror next to him between two sides of pork. Pork and lumps of lard, hooked over the notches of a metal rail, hung from end to end of the length of the marbled, mirrored shop. And Lisa's profile, with its solid throat, its rounded lines and protruding bust was a well-fleshed queen in effigy amid all that fat and meat. Then the beautiful butcher's wife leant over the aquarium which formed part of the display and gave a friendly smile to the two goldfish swimming there, endlessly.

LE VENTRE DE PARIS

Flora Thompson   *1939*

KILLING *the* PIG

There are fine descriptions of killing a pig in the literature of
many countries. Flora Thompson's account of it, as it used to
occur in an English hamlet, is among the best.

The killing was a noisy, bloody business, in the course of which the animal was hoisted to a rough bench that it might bleed thoroughly and so preserve the quality of the meat. The job was often bungled, the pig sometimes getting away and having to be chased; but country people of that day had little sympathy for the sufferings of animals, and men, women, and children would gather round to see the sight.

After the carcass had been singed, the pig-sticker would pull off the detachable, gristly, outer coverings of the toes, known locally as 'the shoes', and fling them among the children, who scrambled for, then sucked and gnawed them, straight from the filth of the sty and blackened by fire as they were.

The whole scene, with its mud and blood, flaring lights and dark shadows, was as savage as anything to be seen in an African jungle. The children at the end house would steal out of bed to the window. 'Look! Look! It's hell, and those are the devils,' Edmund would whisper, pointing to the men tossing the burning straw with their pitchforks; but Laura felt sick and would creep back into bed and cry: she was sorry for the pig.

But, hidden from the children, there was another aspect of the pig-killing. Months of hard work and self-denial were brought on that night to a successful conclusion. It was a time to rejoice, and rejoice they did, with beer flowing freely and the first delicious dish of pig's fry sizzling in the frying-pan.

The next day, when the carcass had been cut up, joints of pork were distributed to those neighbours who had sent similar ones at their own pig-killing. Small plates of fry and other oddments were sent to others as a pure compliment, and no one who happened to be ill or down on his luck at these occasions was ever forgotten.

Then the housewife 'got down to it', as she said. Hams and sides of bacon were salted, to be taken out of the brine later and hung on the wall near the fireplace to dry. Lard was dried out, hog's puddings were made, and the chitterlings were cleaned and turned three days in succession under running water, according to ancient ritual. It was a busy time, but a happy one, with the larder full and something over to give away, and all the pride and importance of owning such riches.

On the following Sunday came the official 'pig feast', when fathers and mothers, sisters and brothers, married children and grandchildren who lived within walking distance arrived to dinner.

If the house had no oven, permission was obtained from an old couple in one of the thatched cottages to heat up the big bread-baking oven in their wash-house. This was like a large cupboard with an iron door, lined with brick and going far back into the wall. Faggots of wood were lighted inside and the door was closed upon them until the oven was well heated. Then the ashes were swept out and baking tins with joints of pork, potatoes, batter puddings, pork pies, and sometimes a cake or two, were popped inside and left to bake without further attention.

Meanwhile, at home, three or four different kinds of vegetables would be cooked, and always a meat pudding, made in a basin. No feast and few Sunday dinners were considered complete without that item, which was eaten alone, without vegetables, when a joint was to follow. On ordinary days the pudding would be a roly-poly containing fruit, currants, or jam; but it still appeared as a first course, the idea being that it took the edge off the appetite. At the pig feast there would be no sweet pudding, for that could be had any day, and who wanted sweet things when there was plenty of meat to be had!

LARK RISE

Rinjing Dorje 1985

The BUTCHER *and the* LAMB

*Rinjing Dorje, a Tibetan living in the USA, was cook in a
Tibetan monastery in his youth. He wrote* Food in Tibetan
Life *in order to place on record the foodways and recipes of his
native country; and was honoured when the book received the
imprimatur of the Office of the Dalai Lama. His prose breathes
love of his country and touching enthusiasm for the way of
life which he and the numerous other refugees from Tibet
should rightfully have inherited. (See also page 278.)*

Among the families of the ordinary people the women are the cooks. But, of course, in monasteries the cooks are men, and the professional cooks are also men. Noble or rich families would probably have a man to cook for them. These cooks are called *gyal se machem* or the master cooks. They acquire their mastery with food by working with other masters at first. It takes years of training and work as an assistant cook before they can qualify as master cooks. These master cooks are normally found in the larger towns and Lhasa, not in the villages. A master cook is hired for wedding parties, special ceremonies that can last for days, or any large banquet. In Tibet this is considered a good skill to acquire, and anyone who wants to do so can join a master cook as his assistant and learn it.

Occupations in Tibet may be determined either by personal choice or by what profession your parents and grandparents practised. Trades and skills are passed on within a family from parents to children. Blacksmiths, butchers, shoemakers, and beggars are considered low class, and a person belonging to one of these categories usually only marries someone else from the same class. But in Tibet this is not a rule that would lead to punishment if someone broke it. Even people from a low class seem to be quite as happy as everyone else. After all, they are very important for the daily lives of everyone in the villages and towns. They know how much they are needed.

There is an old legend about how one particular butcher clan named *Shempa Marutsepa* came into being. Marutsepa lived a long time ago, and was a butcher by trade. He did not particularly like to slaughter animals, but that was how he made his living and supported his family.

One day he took a herd of lambs up into the mountains to butcher them. It was the custom to take the animals away from the village before slaughtering them. It was also the custom to bind the animals' feet before cutting their throats. While Marutsepa was busy going around doing this, one lamb picked up Marutsepa's butchering knife and hid it clumsily in the dirt. Then the lamb lay down on top of the knife and started to weep.

Marutsepa saw the lamb crying, which was a very unusual thing for an animal to do. He went over and took the lamb in his arms. Then he saw the knife handle sticking out of the dirt. In a shock he recognized that the animal was like a human being and did not want to die. But it had no voice to speak with.

Marutsepa felt such a sharp regret that he decided he could no longer live by killing. He freed all the animals and then jumped from a high cliff. His family found his body and brought it home.

It is the custom in Tibet to place the body in a sitting position in the house, near the family altar while they call in a lama to perform religious rites. It is kept there for either twenty-one or forty-nine days while the family performs all the proper funeral ceremonies. The body is disposed of when these rites are completed; they will take anything from a few to forty-nine days depending on the family astrologer's computations.

The next day, as Marutsepa's family was performing the ceremonies, his body miraculously came to life again. He had discovered the wisdom of the Buddha's compassion and become enlightened. Since that time, it is said that any animal butchered by one of Marutsepa's clan is always transferred to a better existence in its next life.

FOOD IN TIBETAN LIFE

Sami Zubaida *1986*

FAT *in the* NEAR EAST

Here is the greater part of a penetrating essay on how animal
fat has been viewed in the Near East. Sami Zubaida, a fine
cook and an eminent scholar of food in that part of the world,
contributed the essay to a congress of food historians at Konya
in Turkey. As befits a sociologist, he displays a conspicuous
urge to unravel the truth about what people did or do, rather
than to play with stereotypes, and an ability to marshal with
elegance the evidence which is relevant to his subject.

There are individual differences in taste, including taste for fat, everywhere. As the English nursery rhyme goes:

Jack Spratt could eat no fat, his wife could eat no lean
And so between them both, you see, they licked the platter clean.

But these individual differences occur within cultural systems which present the choices to individuals. In north European cultures, the choices relate primarily to the amount of fat or oil used in the cooking, and to the amount of fat eaten attached to the meat, this latter varying from no visible fat at all to a small amount relative to the meat. Within these cultures, the idea of actually fatty meat is almost universally detested. The idea of eating fat by itself is unthinkable. In the context of Middle Eastern cultures, these fatty indulgences are not only thinkable, but positively welcomed by many. The clash between these two tastes is recorded in the accounts of English travellers and residents in Arab lands. Let us consider some relevant passages.

Sir Richard Burton, British nineteenth century orientalist and traveller, translator of *The Thousand and One Nights*, undertook a pilgrimage to the Islamic holy places, disguised as a Persian *darweesh* and doctor. The memoirs of these travels were later published under the title *Personal Narrative of a Pilgrimage to Al-Madinah and Meccah*. The work includes many detailed observations of people and manners, but very little on food and its preparation. Here is one of the few passages on the subject:

> ... the citizens [of al-Medinah], despite their being generally in debt, manage to live well. Their cookery, like that of Meccah, has borrowed something from Egypt, Turkey, Syria, Persia, and India: as all Orientals, they are exceedingly fond of clarified butter. I have seen the boy Mohammad drink off nearly a tumbler-full, although his friends warned him that it would make him as fat as an elephant. When a man cannot enjoy clarified butter in

these countries, it is considered a sign that his stomach is out of order, and all my excuses of a melancholic temperament were required to be in full play to prevent the infliction of fried meat swimming in grease, or that guest-dish, rice saturated with melted – perhaps I should say – rancid butter. The 'Samn' of Al-Hijaz, however, is often fresh, being brought in by the Badawin; it has not therefore the foul flavour derived from the old and impregnated skin-bag which distinguishes the 'ghi' of India.

A footnote adds:

Physiologists have remarked that fat and greasy food, containing a quantity of carbon, is peculiar to cold countries: whereas the inhabitants of the tropics delight in fruits, vegetables, and articles of diet which do not increase caloric. This must be taken *cum grano*. In Italy, Spain, and Greece, the general use of olive oil begins. In Africa and Asia – especially in the hottest parts – the people habitually eat enough clarified butter to satisfy an Esquimaux.

Note the inclusion of olive oil in the same category as other fats. To the nineteenth century Englishman, as to many of his more recent compatriots, these are manifestations of foreignness, 'greasy' foods, whether saturated in olive oil or clarified butter. His own consumption of fat, whether lard for frying, meat fat and dripping, or butter on bread, are not, in his eyes, visible or identifiable as 'grease'. But relative perceptions apart, there is obviously a cultural threshold of toleration of fat, especially when it is not absorbed or incorporated in another material.

T. E. Lawrence (renowned as 'Lawrence of Arabia') describes a Bedouin banquet. The scene is the tent of a tribal chief, and the assembled guests, all Arabs apart from Lawrence, are being served:

The bowl was now brim-full, ringed round its edge by white rice in an embankment a foot wide and six inches deep, filled with legs and ribs of mutton till they toppled over. It needed two or three victims to make in the centre a dressed pyramid of meat such as honour prescribed. The centre-pieces were the boiled, upturned heads, propped on their severed stumps of necks, so that the ears, brown like old leaves, flapped out on the rice surface. The jaws gaped emptily upward, pulled open to show the hollow throat with the tongue, still pink, clinging to the lower teeth; and the long incisors whitely crowned the pile, very prominent above the nostrils' pricking hair and the lips which sneered away blackly from them.

This load was set down on the soil of the cleared space between us, where it steamed hotly, while a procession of minor helpers bore small cauldrons and copper vats in which the cooking had been done. From them, with much-bruised bowls of enamelled iron, they ladled out over the main dish all the inside and outside of the sheep; little bits of yellow intestine, the white tail-cushion of fat, brown muscles and meat and bristly skin, all swimming in the liquid of butter and grease of the seething. The by-standers watched anxiously, muttering satisfactions when a very juicy scrap plopped out.

The fat was scalding. Every now and then a man would drop his baler with an exclamation, and plunge his burnt fingers, not reluctantly, in his mouth to cool them: but they persevered till at last their scooping rang loudly on the bottoms of the pots; and, with a gesture of triumph, they fished out the intact livers from their hiding places in the gravy and topped the yawning jaws with them.

Two raised each smaller cauldron and tilted it, letting the liquid splash down upon the meat till the rice-crater was full, and the loose grains at the edge swam in the abundance: and yet they poured, till amid cries of astonishment from us, it was running over, and a little pool congealing in the dust. That was the final touch of splendour, and the host called us to come and eat ...

Lawrence relates this episode with the same mixture of amused irony and understanding indulgence with which he treated other peculiar customs and foibles of his hosts. He makes the banquet sound like an ordeal, which he endures with the same forebearance and good humour with which he endures all other desert hardships. He dwells upon, what to him and his presumed English reader, are grisly details of heads, jaws, pink tongues still attached, hideous bits of intestines and innards, and lots and lots of fat. It is clear that the cooks are not content with the mutton fat itself, but add copious quantities of butter.

This delight in flesh and fat, it may be objected, are but the cravings of the otherwise deprived desert people, whose normal diet is meagre and lacking meat proteins. It is a rare indulgence and not a regular eating habit. This is, of course, true. But the taste for flesh and fat is also shown by many more prosperous Arabs, as we learnt about the good-living inhabitants of Medina (from Burton's account above). In particular, the taste for the 'white tail-cushion of fat' (the Arabic *liyya*, Persian *dumba*), is widespread throughout the Middle East and parts of North Africa, especially among the prosperous classes who have regular access. It is sliced into stews of meat and vegetables, cubes of the fat are skewered with cubes of meat in kebabs, and it is minced with the meat for kofte kebabs. However, the Middle East is an area of great cultural diversity. The diversity of culinary cultures do not necessarily follow national or linguistic boundaries. The greatest differences are those between desert, mountain and city (with its rural hinterlands), and within this latter, there are great differences by class and by ethnic or religious community. By the nineteenth century, the prosperous classes of the urban centres were more or less strongly influenced by Ottoman culture. The Ottomans developed a highly sophisticated food culture, and part of what we mean by sophistication is balance, and the careful use of different ingredients to produce varieties of flavour. The gross excesses of rude desert culture as recounted by Lawrence are avoided.

'The Taste for Fat'
PROCEEDINGS OF THE KONYA CONFERENCE ON FOOD HISTORY 1986

Monica Sheridan   *1965*

IRISH SAUSAGES

There has always been a great tradition of sausage-making in Ireland, and many of the emigrant Irish now living in England place regular orders with pork-butchers in Dublin for a weekly supply of their favourite brand. Among the most celebrated are the Hafners sausages of Dublin and the Hick sausages of Dalkey and Dun Laoghaire. Indeed, no compatriot ever went to see James Joyce in Paris without bringing him 2 lb. of Hafners sausages and a bottle of Powers whiskey.

When Bertie Smyllie, then an excitable young reporter on the *Irish Times*, learned from the news-tape that W. B. Yeats had won the Nobel Prize for Poetry in 1923, he 'phoned the poet to tell him the good news.

'Let me be the first to congratulate you, Mr. Yeats,' said Smyllie, bubbling into the 'phone. 'You have won the Nobel Prize.'

'How much is it?' asked Yeats.

'Over seven thousand pounds, sir.'

'Splendid, my good man. You must come round and celebrate with us. We are having sausages for tea.'

In Ireland sausages are eaten for breakfast, for lunch, for tea, for cocktails, for picnics.

MY IRISH COOK BOOK

Louis Szathmary *1983*

GOULASH *not what you* THINK *it is*

*Louis Szathmary, a larger-than-life figure who runs a famous
restaurant in Chicago, has a magnificent library of cookbooks
which have provided the basis for a number of lively historical
studies from his pen. The one quoted here served to remove
from my mind long-held misconceptions about 'Hungarian
goulash'.*

In Hungary, the word 'goulash' today refers to the cattle driver, the 'cowboy'. The only place on a Hungarian menu where you would find goulash ('gulyás', as it is written in Hungarian) would be among the soups, and it would be called 'gulyás leves', meaning 'the soup of the cowboy'. What is known all over the world as 'Hungarian goulash' is called in Hungary 'pörkölt' or 'paprikás'. 'Pörkölt' contains no sour cream. It is called 'paprikás' if sour cream has been added to the 'pörkölt'.

For a country that has a history of 1,100 years in one geographical location, the Carpathian Basin, the dish of goulash is relatively new under either of its names. Hungarian cattlemen, shepherds and pigherders cooked cubed meat with onion and spices (with a 'short sauce', meaning a very small amount of liquid) for at least 300–500 years. But the dish could not be called 'pörkölt' or 'paprikás', because this spice, the paprika, today considered the most Hungarian of all spices, is relatively new to the Hungarian cuisine. It was not known in Hungary until the 1820s when it became extremely popular and practically eliminated black pepper and ginger from the average Hungarian kitchen.

Black pepper from southern Asia was introduced to Europe through the Levant during the time of the Pharaohs, and it was the principal spice and preservative during the time of Christ. The suppliers of pepper had been merchants, who, whatever their nationality or religion, were predominantly citizens of the Ottoman or Turkish Empire. When red pepper was introduced to Europe by early explorers of the New World, the seed and fruit of the capsicum plant were distributed throughout the Mediterranean area, again by merchants from the Levant and from Venice.

Spain and Hungary became the two strongest producers of this relatively new spice, because of their favorable soil and climate.

Black pepper was used not only to give flavor and aroma to the food, but also as a preservative. Raw meat was rubbed and practically covered with ground pepper to keep it fresh longer. The pepper was used with salt, with sugar, or alone. People attempted to use paprika as a preservative and rubbed it on the raw meat. When this raw meat rubbed with paprika came in contact with the heat from the frying kettle, the paprika-covered meat formed a brown crusty surface with a pleasantly different taste resembling that of meat roasted over an open fire to the point of almost burning.

To get a piece of meat to this point is described by the Hungarian verb 'pörköl', which means to slightly burn the surface. The meat treated with paprika reaches this taste without the actual burning. That's why the new dish – the meat fried in small cubes with fat and onion – was called 'pörkölt'. After beef, the same process was applied to pork, rabbit, veal and poultry. Each one of these dishes can be called pörkölt. If sour cream is folded into the meat or poultry or fish after it is cooked, it is called paprikás.

The characteristic behavior of the ground, dried red pepper (called paprika) during heating in high smoke-point fats (such as lard or rendered bacon fat) provided a new taste and required a new technology. Meat cubes and strips have been cooked with onions over high heat over open fires for ages all over the world, from Chinese woks to Gaelic clay pots. But the addition of paprika at the beginning of the searing of the meat, and a second time just before the dish was finished, gave an extremely appealing fragrance, a desirable deep red color, and a taste which was pleasing to most.

The price of black pepper went up during the decline of the Ottoman Empire, and the demand increased, so paprika came at the right time to replace it.

Because paprika was not as compatible with ginger as black pepper, ginger faded from the Hungarian cuisine.

In the middle of the nineteenth century, the new dish, pörkölt, became as popular as chicken, veal or pork similarly prepared with paprika. Because these had been holiday dishes served on special occasions to guests, they spread much faster than more commonplace dishes. Because visitors from Austria, Bohemia, Poland and Switzerland were treated as honored guests and had been fêted with pörkölt or paprikás, those dishes found their way quickly into the cookbooks and the restaurants of the neighboring countries.

What does all this have to do with 'goulash'? The difference between the Hungarian pörkölt, known all over the world except in Hungary as 'goulash', and goulash soup, is in the amount of liquid added to the meat, and whether potatoes and pasta are included. In the real Hungarian pörkölt or paprikás (in English 'goulash') there are no other ingredients except the beef, pork, veal or chicken, shortening (almost always from pork), paprika, onions, and once in a while, herbs, spices, condiments such as fresh green or red peppers, an occasional clove of garlic, and small amount of tomato, caraway seed or dried marjoram.

'Food in Motion'
OXFORD SYMPOSIUM DOCUMENTS 1983

Ramon J. Adams   1952

SONOFABITCH STEW

The book Come an' Get It *is 'the story of the old cowboy cook'.*
Praise to the University Press of Oklahoma for publishing a
book with such an arresting title and such a lively content.

It seems this barber had tired of his profession and decided he wanted to be a cowboy. When he arrived at the wagon to seek a job the cook was cooking a stew.

'What's that cookin'?' he asked.

'That's a sonofabitch. Did y'u ever eat one?' answered the cook.

'No,' replied the barber, 'I never et one, but I've shaved a helluva lot of 'em.'

This stew was called by many other names, according to the locale or the enemy of the group, but always its implication was obvious. When the law began its westward march and started to clamp down on the government of the cowman's happy, carefree days, the blame for this cramping of liberties was placed upon lawyers. This caused the offended cowmen to feel resentful toward the law, and they soon began calling this dish 'District Attorney' as an outlet to their indignation. After the Taylor Grazing Act was passed, the cattlemen and the Forest Service had so many misunderstandings that this stew often took the name of 'Forest Ranger.'

A cowhand at the wagon might become offended at the congressman from his district over some action or lack of it. When he said, 'I believe I'll have another dish of Congressman Blank,' the others nodded approval, and the stew was called by that name for a few weeks, or for the season. It has been called 'Cleveland' because this president ran the cattlemen out of the Cherokee Strip, and, in later years, 'Hoover,' on account of the depression which occurred during President Hoover's term of office.

The feuding of rival towns also furnished names at various times. A man from a near-by envious town might call it 'The Gentleman from Odessa,' 'The Gentleman from Cheyenne,' 'The Gentleman from Roswell,' or any other. In some sections it frequently went by the name of 'Rascal'; others called it by the abbreviated 'SOB'.

Occasionally the wagon cook named his first stew of the season after some one against whom he had a pet peeve and it retained that name for the rest of the roundup. Cooks have been fired for calling this dish by the boss' name.

Many arguments have developed about the proper way to make this famous stew. Though perhaps no two cooks would make it exactly alike, each might think his way the best. Some made it the easier, safer way by cooking in water, while others claimed that by using only the juices of the meat, a finer flavor would be obtained. Some might add an onion to the mixture; others claimed this merely made a hash of it; some wanted to use chili powder, this ruined it for others. But all agreed that no vegetables, such as corn, peas, or tomatoes, were to spoil the dish. Some liked it thick, some thin, but whatever its consistency, it must be served hot. Also some claimed it was good only when served fresh, others that a warming up the next day made it better, but rarely was there any left to prove this theory.

Aside from the mystery of the title itself, the one thing, as we have said before, which gave this stew a bad name among the uninitiated was the word 'marrow gut'. Yet, as all cowmen know, this marrow gut was a most necessary ingredient, though only a small portion was used in comparison with the other solids. It gave the stew its distinctive flavor. Another ingredient or two might be omitted, but as one cowman said, 'A sonofabitch might not have any brains and no heart, but if he don't have guts, he's not a sonofabitch.' Marrow gut is not a gut at all, but a tube connecting the two stomachs of cud-chewing animals. It is good only when the calf is young and living upon milk, as it is then filled with a substance resembling marrow through which the partially digested milk passes. This is why only young calves were selected for a good stew. The marrow-like contents were left in, and they were what gave the stew such a delicious flavor.

To make this stew, a fat calf was killed. While the meat was still warm, the heart, liver, tongue, marrow gut, some pieces of tenderloin, sweetbreads, and the brains were taken to be prepared. First the cook cut the fat into small pieces and put them into a pot. While the fat was being rendered he cut the heart into small cubes, adding it first because it was tougher than the other ingredients. The tongue was skinned and cubed likewise, then added. This gave the two toughest ingredients longer cooking time. While these were cooking, the cook proceeded to cut the tenderloin, sweetbreads, and liver into similar pieces. The liver was used sparingly, or the stew would become bitter. The marrow gut was cut into small rings and added to the whole. If water was used, it must be warm, the ingredients well covered with it, and more added from time to time. The various ingredients were added a handful at a time, the contents being slowly stirred after each addition. Between stirrings, the cook proceeded to clean the brains of blood and membrane. The brains were cooked separately, some cooks adding a little flour to make them thick. When cooked until they became beady, these were added to the stew. This was the last ingredient added, and it gave the stew a medium of thickening. Salt and pepper were then added to taste, and some cooks put in an onion, or 'skunk egg' as the cowboy sometimes called this vegetable.

It took several hours to cook the stew, and about the only way you could ruin a good one was to let it scorch. If a cook committed this blunder, he had better be prepared to receive some titles less complimentary than the one given the stew. When it was done, you had something sweet and delicious, and after eating it you would no longer be a skeptic.

While range men have seemed to keep this dish mysterious to the outlander, to an old cowman the only mystery about it was whose calf went into its making.

COME AN' GET IT

SOMERSAULTS *in* MEAT COOKERY THEORY

One of the great themes of 19th century books on food and cookery was that of 'sealing in the juices' of meat (or not doing so if the meat was being used to produce broth). The accepted wisdom on the subject was turned upside down by the famous German chemist, Baron Liebig, in mid century. Over a century passed before Harold McGee, exploring and expounding the scientific aspects of cookery in his superbly lucid book On Food and Cooking, *and in an address at Oxford, set this convulsion in its content and explained the truth of the matter, as it is perceived in the 1980s.*

I would like to describe in some detail the most spectacular example I know of a scientific idea overturning a culinary tradition. The idea turned out to be wrong, and the story gives us some feeling of the plasticity of tradition, and for the powerful attractions of scientific and pseudoscientific thinking, and for the pitfalls of applying scientific findings to culinary practice.

The issue is the fundamental one of how best to roast a large piece of meat. Not much is said about techniques in the oldest cookbooks we have, but certainly by the 18th century the standard method in Britain, France, and America was to begin with the meat well away from the fire, and move it closer to brown it at the end of the process.

The turning point in Britain and America comes in the middle of the 19th century, and a single man was responsible: the eminent German chemist Justus Liebig. Liebig was a remarkable man. He was a pioneer in organic chemistry, to which he brought great rigour of analysis and reasoning. He founded the first institute devoted to scientific education through research, the prototype of the modern graduate schools. And he edited one of the most important research journals of the day.

During the 1840s in the middle of his long career, Liebig became interested in the application of organic chemistry to agriculture, and then to animal physiology. His books on these subjects gave great impetus to the as yet uncommon idea that living processes are amenable to chemical analysis. However, because physiology is even more complex than organic chemistry, and at that time was still poorly understood, Liebig's inclination to theorise was held less in check by solid information, and he made quite a few errors.

In 1847, after spending a mere six months on the subject, Liebig published a monograph which was immediately translated into English under the title *Researches on the Chemistry of Food*; an American edition appeared a year later. On the basis of recent research in muscle chemistry, Liebig proposed in this book that the essential nutrients in meat are found not in the so-called fibrous material, but in the muscle fluids, which are easily lost during cooking. So it would be best to minimise fluid loss in order to maintain the nutritional value of the meat.

This could be done, Liebig said, by initially heating the surface of the meat quickly enough that the juices would be sealed inside. He describes what he thought would happen when a piece of meat is plunged into already boiling water, and then the temperature reduced to a simmer: 'When [the meat] is introduced into the boiling water, the albumen [what we would call the protein] immediately coagulates from the surface inwards, and in this state forms a crust, or shell, which no longer permits the external water to penetrate into the interior of the mass of flesh. But the temperature is gradually transmitted to the interior, and there effects the conversion of raw flesh into the state of boiled or roasted meat. The flesh retains its juiciness, and is quite as agreeable to the taste as it can be made by roasting'.

And if the crust can keep the water out during boiling, it seems reasonable that it would keep the juices in during roasting. So, although Liebig himself does not address this point directly, it would be consistent with his description of boiling to sear a roast near the fire at the outset, and then continue with the meat further away from the fire to finish the insides.

Despite the fact that it turned at least a century of tradition on its head, Liebig's account seems to answer an unspoken hunger for a rationalised, systematic approach to cookery. Its influence was swift, and in England and America, inescapable. The revolution was most obvious in Eliza Acton's *Modern Cookery for Private Families*, which in its second edition of 1845 gives traditional directions for boiling meat – that is, being with cold water rather than hot – and for roasting – that is, sear last, not first. In the next edition, published post-Liebig in 1855, the subtitle has become, 'In which the principles of Baron Liebig and other eminent writers have been as much as possible applied and explained'. The directions for boiling meat are now pure Liebig, and roasts are to be seared at the outset.

If you didn't follow Liebig's advice, you at least had to argue openly with him. In 1860, 'Tabitha Tickletooth' argued that the Liebig technique 'set the osmazome' too quickly and results in unpleasant flavours and tough meat. And Ann Bowman, in her 1867 *New Cookery Book: A complete manual of English and foreign cookery on sound principles of taste and science*, argues with what she calls 'the modern professors', saying 'We are not converted to the belief that the hardened surface gives us the best roast beef'. But such voices were a distinct minority. Although France was slow to jump on the bandwagon, in a few decades even Escoffier was expounding 'the process well-known in physics under the name of Capillarity', a process that drives the fluids toward the centre of the meat during searing.

And the name Liebig was soon a household word. The Liebig Extract of Meat Company was formed in the 1860s to take advantage of cheap South American cattle, and was probably one of the first multinational food corporations.

Today, however, we know that Liebig's analysis was faulty in several respects. The water-soluble components on whose retention he places such stress are minor products of muscle metabolism and nutritionally negligible. Any crust that forms during searing is hardly a barrier to the passage of water. And when controlled experiments were done at the University of Missouri in 1930, it was found that seared roasts actually lose somewhat more liquid than roasts cooked at relatively low constant temperature. In fact, a similar result had already been obtained decades before Liebig, when Count Rumford took identical legs of lamb, and roasted one at a relatively low temperature in his roaster, and the other in the conventional way over a fire. Both were browned at the end. The former ended up six per cent heavier than the latter, was juicier, and devoured more completely by his test subjects.

Still, despite many books that have promulgated the modern view, the searing idea lives vigorously on. My guess is that it thrives because the image it conjures up is so vivid, apparently commonsensical, and appealing.

'Cookery: Science, Lore and Books'
OXFORD SYMPOSIUM DOCUMENTS 1984/5

Nathan d'Aulnay [Richard Olney] 1980

A MATTER *of* FORM

Richard Olney* is both painter and writer on food. This
passage shows also a feeling for sculptural quality.

The mechanics of cookery are often imposed by the form of the raw material; and so it is with a boned and stuffed shoulder. Laid out skin-side down, but with the skin previously removed, the shoulder forms an irregular star shape with uneven mounds of flesh; the whole object being almost amorphous. The only sensible manner of creating a compact shape which will lend itself to uniform cooking is, after having trimmed the meat, to gather the points of the star together, tacking them with kitchen string, and then to tie the meat into the semblance of a football.

This kind of package, if one may so call it, cannot support an abundant stuffing; but both a preliminary sojourn in a simple marinade (herbs, white wine, a dash of olive oil, two crushed cloves of garlic, a few bruised juniper berries) and, smeared over the surface of the meat before it is tied up, a slight stuffing (garlic compounded to a purée with salt and pepper, the chopped trimmings, chopped parsley and a choice of fresh or dried – thyme, oregano, marjoram savory, hyssop ..., a small handful of fresh breadcrumbs, possibly an egg yolk, or simply a dash of olive oil to pull together the mixture) will enhance the flavour of the preparation.

Whereas a flat piece of meat, having the shape of a thick steak, is best seared on top of the stove as a preliminary to being braised, this approximately spherical shape, first rubbed with a little oil to encourage it to take colour, lends itself best to being seared in the oven with dry heat radiating upon it from all sides – a procedure which may take up to 45 minutes.

The remainder of the braising process is standard. The pot in which the meat is enclosed should be of a size just to contain it so that it may be partially immersed in a minimum of liquid – the bones may be tucked around here and there if the space permits. The roasting pan is first drained free of fat, then deglazed with the strained marinade (a little more wine being added if necessary), and this is poured over the meat with enough boiling stock to immerse it to the extent of between one half and two thirds. It should be braised gently, the pot covered, in a slow oven for about an hour and a half, with occasional basting. The lid may be removed and the heat increased during the last half hour of cooking, while the meat is repeatedly basted to form a glaze. Finally, the cooking liquid is strained into a small saucepan to be cleansed and reduced, while the meat is kept warm, covered, in its pot. The strings are removed, the meat carved either into slices or into wedges resembling those of a pie, as your fancy dictates, and the sauce is served apart. A generously buttered white purée composed of potatoes, celeriac, turnips, onions and garlic constitutes an accompaniment which deserves to be called sublime.

PETITS PROPOS CULINAIRES (PPC) 2

---

*He wrote this and some other pieces under a pseudonym for an odd reason, and one which affected my life considerably. He was masterminding for Time/Life Books their extensive 'Good Cook' series of books and found himself hampered by the bureaucratic rules they had invented for the series, e.g. that no recipe could go in the books unless it came from a published source. He was determined to include certain recipes of which there were no satisfactory published versions; but the bureaucracy would not yield an inch.

On one occasion when he was fulminating about this problem I asked: 'What would happen if a new journal on food history were to be published – perhaps one issue only – in which some of these 'missing' recipes were published, just the way you want them, in fact written by you under a pseudonym?' He pondered. 'Well, I guess that would solve the problem.' Within months the first issue of *Petits Propos Culinaires (PPC)* had appeared. The Time/Life bureaucrats, unknowingly outwitted, duly paid a reproduction fee for using Nathan d'Aulnay's recipes (thus helping the Royal National Lifeboat Institution, in aid of which the first issue was published). Triumph!

But my wife and I now had a cuckoo in our nest. *PPC*, a lusty infant whose birth was celebrated in the *New York Times*, clung stubbornly to life. Its 30th issue will soon [1988] be out. Richard Olney has long since gone back to his studio in Provence. Time/Life Books have long since been busy on other projects. But the Davidsons are doomed to go on for ever, it seems, nourishing the accidental cuckoo.

Food *from the* Dairy

Delight in dairy products is a privilege which only about half the world's inhabitants enjoy; see Françoise Sabban. But for those of us thus blessed the subject provides a rich diet of eloquent writing. Start by taking a fresh look at cheeses through the eyes of Mr Palomar. Or, since the dairy is where it all begins, enjoy first Thomas Hardy's description of Tess therein.

Italo Calvino   *1983*

The CHEESE MUSEUM

Italo Calvino, who was probably Italy's leading novelist
before he died, created Mr Palomar, a nervous hero in whom
everyday events provoke bewilderment and through whose eyes
we see commonplace things in a disturbing aura of
supercharged reality. There is something of
Charlie Chaplin here ...

Mr Palomar is standing in line in a cheese shop, in Paris. He wants to buy certain goat cheeses that are preserved in oil in little transparent containers and spiced with various herbs and condiments. The line of customers moves along a counter where samples of the most unusual and disparate specialties are displayed. This is a shop whose range seems meant to document every conceivable form of dairy product; the very sign, '*Spécialités froumagères,*' with that rare archaic or vernacular adjective, advises that here is guarded the legacy of a knowledge accumulated by a civilization through all its history and geography.

Three or four girls in pink smocks wait on the customers. The moment one of the girls is free she deals with the first in line and asks him to express his wishes; the customer names or, more often, points, moving about the shop towards the object of his specific and expert appetites.

At that moment the whole line moves forward one place; and the person who till then had been standing beside the 'Bleu d'Auvergne' veined with green now finds himself at the level of the 'Brin d'amour', whose whiteness holds strands of dried straw stuck to it; the customer contemplating a ball wrapped in leaves can now concentrate on a cube dusted with ash. At each move forward, some customers are inspired by new stimuli and new desires: they may change their minds about what they were about to ask for or may add a new item to the list; and there are also those who never allow themselves to be distracted even for a moment from the objective they are pursuing – every different, fortuitous suggestion serves only to limit, through exclusion, the field of what they stubbornly want.

Palomar's spirit vacillates between contrasting urges: the one that aims at complete, exhaustive knowledge and could be satisfied only by tasting all the varieties; and the one that tends towards an absolute choice, the identification of the cheese that is his alone, a cheese that certainly exists even if he cannot recognize it (cannot recognize himself in it).

Or else, or else: it is not a matter of choosing the right cheese, but of being chosen. There is a reciprocal relationship between cheese and customer: each cheese awaits its customer, poses so as to attract him, with a firmness or a somewhat haughty graininess, or on the contrary, by melting in submissive abandon.

There is a hint of complicity hovering in the air: the refinement of the taste buds, and especially of the olfactory organs, has its moments of weakness, of loss of class, when the cheeses on their platters seem to proffer themselves as if on the divans of a brothel. A perverse grin flickers in the satisfaction of debasing the object of one's own gluttony with lowering nicknames: *crottin, boule de moine, bouton de culotte*.

This is not the kind of acquaintance that Mr Palomar is most inclined to pursue: he would be content to establish the simplicity of a direct physical relationship between man and cheese. But as in place of the cheese he sees names of cheeses, concepts of cheeses, meanings of cheeses, histories of cheeses, contexts of cheeses, psychologies of cheeses, when he does not so much know as sense that behind each of these cheeses there is all that, then his relationship becomes very complicated.

The cheese shop appears to Palomar the way an encyclopedia looks to an autodidact; he could memorize all the names, venture a classification according to the forms – cake of soap, cylinder, dome, ball – according to the consistency – dry, buttery, creamy, veined, firm – according to the alien materials involved in the crust or in the heart – raisins, pepper, walnuts, sesame seeds, herbs, molds – but this would not bring him a step closer to true knowledge, which lies in the experience of the flavors, composed of memory and imagination at once. Only on the basis of that could he establish a scale of preferences and tastes and curiosities and exclusions.

Behind every cheese there is a pasture of a different green under a different sky: meadows caked with salt that the tides of Normandy deposit every evening; meadows scented with aromas in the windy sunlight of Provence; there are different flocks with their stablings and their transhumances; there are secret processes handed down over the centuries. This shop is a museum: Mr Palomar, visiting it, feels, as he does in the Louvre, behind every displayed object the presence of the civilization that has given it form and takes form from it.

This shop is a dictionary; the language is the system of cheeses as a whole: a language whose morphology records declensions and conjugations in countless variants, and whose lexicon presents an inexhaustible richness of synonyms, idiomatic usages, connotations and nuances of meaning, as in all languages nourished by the contribution of a hundred dialects. It is a language made up of things; its nomenclature is only an external aspect, instrumental; but, for Mr Palomar, learning a bit of nomenclature remains still the first measure to be taken if he wants to stop for a moment the things that are flowing before his eyes.

From his pocket he takes a notebook, a pen, begins to write down some names, marking beside each name some feature that will enable him to recall the image to his memory; he tries also to make a synthetic sketch of the shape. He writes 'Pavé d'Airvault' and notes 'green mold', draws a flat parallelopiped and to one side notes '4 cm circa'; he writes 'St-Maure', notes 'gray granular cylinder with a little shaft inside' and draws it, measuring it at a glance as about '20 cm.'; then he writes 'Chabicholi' and draws another little cylinder.

'*Monsieur! Hoo there! Monsieur!*' A young cheese-girl, dressed in pink, is standing in front of him, as he is occupied with his notebook. It is his turn, he is next; in the line behind him everyone is observing his incongruous behavior, heads are being shaken with those half-ironic, half-exasperated looks with which the inhabitants of the big cities consider the ever-increasing number of the mentally retarded wandering about the streets.

The elaborate and greedy order that he intended to make momentarily slips his mind; he stammers; he falls back on the most obvious, the most banal, the most advertised, as if the automatons of mass civilization were waiting only for this moment of uncertainty on his part in order to seize him again and have him at their mercy.

MR PALOMAR

Jacques Montandon   *1980*

An AERIAL DESCENT *of* CHEESES

*A comprehensive book on Swiss cheeses, such as that of
Montandon, is of course bound to dwell on the famous ones,
and he does; but I enjoyed reading what he has to say here
about the people who make the less famous cheeses of Tessin.*

Along their southern flank the Alps fall away abruptly down to the lakes and the Lombardy plain. The valleys of Ticino are gauged so deep, enclosed by mountain sides so steep that you ask yourself how on earth the forests which cover them ever managed to take root. Nowhere does the ground level out on these wooded slopes. You have to climb to an altitude of four and a half thousand feet before you find the first grassy patches and the start of abrupt stoney pastures. It isn't until you have virtually reached the tree line that you come across sparsely covered, close cropped meadows, delicately scented by the flora scattered hereabouts.

Driving a herd of cattle up these mountains is an extremely delicate operation. An entire village, or at least all the able bodied men of the village, marches some ten to fifteen hours with the herd along narrow mountain paths, goading them upwards, shouting and waving their arms if not actually manhandling them, towards the summer pastures. The cattle, whose only preparation for this climb has been the occasional springtime jaunt among the meadows of the valley, arrive at the top of the mountain harassed, exhausted, scarcely able to stand up. Several days of decent feeding in the immediate vicinity of the alpine chalet are needed to restore the cattle to an acceptable physical condition. From this point on the job of the herdsman is to see to it that his cows do not wander off onto dangerous terrain, slopes too steep for them, overhanging sheer rock faces which would be lethal. Virtually no summer passes without a certain number of cows meeting their end at the foot of the rocky cliffs. Unfortunately, the barren landscape also claims its human victims. Practically every peasant family from the valleys of northern Ticino mourns a death, or, at the very least, nurses a permanent injury due to a serious fall during the summer grazing.

The goats, which more often than not accompany the herds of cattle, are much better adapted to this kind of terrain. Their agile feet, like those of the chamois, pick their way among the rocks, and they often venture into places where no man would set foot. Blowing small, shrill horns at early evening, the herdsmen attempt to summon them to the stalls to be milked.

Such conditions mean that Ticino is one of the rare parts of Switzerland where herds of goats in significant numbers move up the mountains in summer to graze the uplands.

Cheeses made from cow's milk, or a mixture of cow's and goat's milk, produced, as they are, in such places, pose no particular problem. They are made on the spot by a *fromager* who accompanies the herd, and they are brought down into the valley on the backs of donkeys at the end of the summer grazing season, which only rarely exceeds eighty days, given the altitude of the pastures. For cheeses made from pure goat's milk it is quite a different matter. Here it is necessary to find a way of transporting the soft cheeses down to the valley on a regular basis.

The inhabitants of Ticino are particularly fond of the little soft cheeses known as 'formaggini', or, when they are smaller, 'buscion'. A herdsman from Mergosica, in the Verzasca valley, has even found a most original solution to the problem. He has managed to set up a makeshift cable system which links his pasture with one of the houses in the village. To drive the motor which keeps a primitive basket running up and down the wire, he has constructed a little hydro-electric plant powered by the stream which flows close to his house.

At the end of the day he collects the milk in a brass container and adds rennet to it. He leaves it to stand for twenty four hours at room temperature during which time the milk curdles. He then drains off the liquid, but does not slice the curds. The whey is used to feed the kids: as for the curds, this is sent down to the valley courtesy of the basket and cable system. Here the women season, knead and shape it, putting it into an old sausage machine which will turn out the 'buscion' carefully wrapped and packaged, standing shoulder to shoulder in their box like 'petits-suisses'. The evening post bus takes them to Locarno where they go straight on sale in the shops as fresh as can be.

LES FROMAGES DE SUISSE

Some AMERICAN CHEESES

*In the 1930s and 1940s the Brown family, Cora, Bob and
Rose, were among the most prolific cookery writers in the USA.
Cora was the mother, Bob her son, and Rose his wife. As a
team, they covered most cookery subjects. Their magnum opus
was not* 10,000 Snacks, *formidable volume though that is, but
a book of regional American recipes,* America Cooks, *which is
still sought after. Between them they had experience of
cooking in many parts of the world, and what they wrote
should not be under-rated because of the chatty style. When
Bob's book on cheese came out in 1955, it bore his name alone,
so perhaps Cora and Rose were no more by then. The style and
the merit of the content were unchanged.*

We come now to our own land, with which from the cheese-lover's viewpoint we may merge our good neighbor Canada. A Rembrandtesque picture presents itself, a dramatic mingling of light and shade.

The blanket shadow, of course, is cast by processed 'cheese.' The word should always, like Soviet 'democracy,' be framed in quotes, for no matter what the law may say, I refuse to call this cheese. For me (though it is only fair to state that millions of us seem to like the stuff) processed 'cheese' belongs to the same Kallikak family as ordinary commercial white bread, powdered coffee, cellophaned cake and our more popular carbonated beverages. The best I can say for it is that it is nonpoisonous; the worst, that is represents the triumph of technology over conscience.

In the preparation of this solidified floor wax – often the product of emulsification with sodium citrate, sodium phosphate or rochelle salts; of steaming and frequently blending odd lots of cheese; of paralyzing whatever germs might result either in loss of profit or gain of flavor – every problem but one is solved: packaging, keeping, distribution, slicing, cost. One problem alone is not solved: that of making cheese.

Bernard Shaw once warned us (he was speaking of mass entertainment) to be sure to get what we liked; otherwise we might begin to like what we got. There is the point – not that processed 'cheese' is so bad in itself (though it is) but that its convenience, neatness and cheapness give it so many advantages that it may elbow real cheese aside and in the end compass the death of our cheese-palates. Let us not be fooled. My guinea-pig son aged one year and seven months, was not: fed a 'cheese spread,' he spat it out; fed a tiny bit of Stilton he took to it like an angel. Give our American children the processed corpse of milk and they will grow (I dare not say mature) into processed men, all package and no character.

I can call to mind one exception to these strictures. But even that is not a native product. It is a Danish import called, horribly enough, Littlefellow, a processed cheese spread, mild, creamy, with an interesting tang. As for other processed plastics, remember only that the wrappings of foil are the cerements of death.

But enough of bitterness. It is sad work and I take little pleasure in it. Processed 'cheese,' 'cheese spreads' and 'cheese foods' (often hypoed with onions, garlic and similar horrors in order to mask the taste of the corpse) represent only the baser element in what is on the whole an honorable and progressive industry. Let us joyfully aver that we have a God's plenty of sound, decent domestic cheeses, most of it Cheddarish in nature, some of it an excellent aping of greater European originals, such as Gruyère or Roquefort.

Our basic trouble is that we are in a hurry and cheese is not. Honest, edible Cheddar is easily found, but really mature, shelf-cured Cheddar, dry and on the point of crumble, is rare. Still I have eaten good Cheddar from Canada, Vermont, New York and Wisconsin; and I once tasted an Oregon Tillamook filled with both the goodness and severity of God. Sage Cheddar, Vermont's pride, can be a wondrous thing. It eats supremely well on a hot summer afternoon in the country (circumstances alter cheeses), especially if you mate it incestuously with its mother, milk, and support it on cracker-barrel crackers – even though for the most part crackers are the enemy of cheese, just as bread is its friend. I mean real bread – pumpernickel, dark rye, stone-ground whole-grain bread, or crusty French loaf, not the pre-sliced leprous 'bread' of large-scale commerce.

LIMBURGER

Limburger has always been popular in America, ever since it was brought over by German-American immigrants; but England never took to it. This is eloquently expressed in the following entry of the English *Encyclopedia of Practical Cookery:*

> Limburger cheese is chiefly famous for its pungently offensive odor. It is made from skimmed milk, and allowed to partially decompose before pressing. It is very little known in this country, and might be less so with advantage to consumers.

But this is libel. Butter-soft and sapid, Limburger has brought gustatory pleasure to millions of hardy gastronomes since it came to light in the province of Lüttich in Belgium. It has been Americanized for almost a century and is by now one of the very few cheeses successfully imitated here, chiefly in New York and Wisconsin.

Early Wisconsiners will never forget the Limburger Rebellion in Green County, when the people rose in protest against the Limburger caravan that was accustomed to park in the little town of Monroe where it was marketed. They threatened to stage a modern Boston Tea Party and dump the odoriferous bricks in the river, when five or six wagonloads were left ripening in the sun in front of the town bank. The Limburger was finally stored safely underground.

LIVAROT

Livarot has been described as decadent, 'The very Verlaine of them all,' and Victor Meusy personifies it in a poem dedicated to all the great French cheeses, of which we give a free translation:

> In the dog days
> In its overflowing dish
> Livarot gesticulates
> Or weeps like a child.

THE COMPLETE BOOK OF CHEESE

Henri Pourrat   *1956*

The BIRTH *of* ROQUEFORT

> *There is a strong tradition in France of lyrical and romantic writing about food and its history. At its worst, this can be an irritation, devoid of either fact or inspiration. At its best, as in this extract from Henri Pourrat's book about Roquefort, it has charm, and provides amusement.*

There is a kind of history that speaks louder than history itself: legend, in which popular imagination has put into pictures all events of real interest, the true saga of the countryside.

It was on a spring morning, at the time when lambs were weaned, and curds were being made of the mothers' milk. A shepherd was grazing his flock on the Combalou. Even on the north slope of the mountain, the air was soft as a breath of kindness. Buds shone on the bare cherry branches, stirred gently by passing breezes. Violets were everywhere, half-hidden among dead oak-leaves; they had almost no stem, but they gave out a fragrance, and he breathed it in deeply, as though he were ready to run a race.

The shepherd watched his flock, as he sat by a cave to eat his lunch. From his scrip he took a loaf of rye bread and curds of ewes' milk.

Suddenly he stood up. At the foot of the Combalou there was a stream. Coming down the pasture on the other side, he saw the daughter of his master, a young and lovely girl, with cheeks the color of the morning-glory and hair like a blackbird's wing. Yesterday he had met her under an oak; she had looked up at him from the depth of her black eyes and had then drawn back, like a fleeing doe. And the blood inside him had gone round like a wheel.

On the spur of the moment, without thinking what he was doing, he set down his bread and cheese upon a jutting stone, and left, taking his flock with him. He went down toward the valley, toward the girl with the black eyes. There she was, her body slim and straight as a hazel-shoot, going to the brook to gather green herbs, lambs-lettuce, sorrel and dandelion, that she would cook with cream and salt. She stooped, and rose again, pushing back her hair. Ah, the brown doe, the hazel-spray by a fountain, the wild iris opening to the sun – how could he look on her without giving her his heart?

He left, and he did not come back that day.

Three months later he came back. On the rock in the grotto he found his cheese, with a mouthful of stale bread on it. And the blue mould of the bread had turned the curd blue, as though blue-green twigs were hidden in it, twigs of thyme or wild verbena.

And it all came back to him: that morning of early spring, the noon hour, and how they had met each other beside the running water. He laughed, and stretched out his hand for the curd; what did he care if it was mouldy, veined with blue? It was memory, it was hunger, both of them strong within him.

And then, a wonder befell! The curd was no longer curd; it was something else, with a flavor that blessed and fortified the heart.

This was not the first time that he had eaten old curd, forgotten and found again, become hard and bitter. A shepherd could not be too particular when his teeth were sharpened by hunger. But this! There must be some secret about it, he thought: the cold damp air, rising from the entrails of the grotto: the spirit of the Combalou.

Right then, he understood: there before him was a gift of the good spirits, a food of joy and exaltation, like the cluster of strawberries in red, red drops on the forest bed of moss and shadow. But this was rarer and more vigorous. A food that nourished and reawakened hunger, that made a man over. And he could feel it now: he was made for a life that was there for him to discover, on the side of the sun.

The story is true; there was once this shepherd, his curd, and his adventure. Moreover, that is how discoveries are made: cold fried potatoes put back in the pan become *pommes soufflées*; burnt sugared almonds become pralines. As if Nature, in a spirit of malice, gave man to understand that her resources went far beyond his researches. And so the failure becomes a success; the botched job, a wonder.

THE ROQUEFORT ADVENTURE

Thomas Hardy   1891

TESS ARRIVES *at the* DAIRY

Tess of the d'Urbervilles is a great novel; Hardy's greatest
according to some critics, who are no doubt thinking of the
great themes which it treats – love, seduction, betrayal, etc.
Here I have plucked out two passages about the dairy, the
workplace of Tess and the setting in which these major themes
developed.

Not quite sure of her direction Tess stood still upon the hemmed expanse of verdant flatness, like a fly on a billiard-table of indefinite length, and of no more consequence to the surroundings than that fly. The sole effect of her presence upon the placid valley so far has been to excite the mind of a solitary heron, which, after descending to the ground not far from her path, stood with neck erect, looking at her.

Suddenly there arose from all parts of the lowland a prolonged and repeated call – 'Waow! waow! waow!'

From the furthest east to the furthest west the cries spread as if by contagion, accompanied in some cases by the barking of a dog. It was not the expression of the valley's consciousness that beautiful Tess had arrived, but the ordinary announcement of milking-time – half-past four o'clock, when the dairymen set about getting in the cows.

The red and white herd nearest at hand, which had been phlegmatically waiting for the call, now trooped towards the steading in the background, their great bags of milk swinging under them as they walked. Tess followed slowly in their rear, and entered the barton by the open gate through which they had entered before her. Long thatched sheds stretched round the enclosure, their slopes encrusted with vivid green moss, and their eaves supported by wooden posts rubbed to a glossy smoothness by the flanks of infinite cows and calves of bygone years, now passed to an oblivion almost inconceivable in its profundity. Between the posts were ranged the milchers, each exhibiting herself at the present moment to a whimsical eye in the rear as a circle on two stalks, down the centre of which a switch moved pendulum-wise; while the sun, lowering itself behind this patient row, threw their shadows accurately inwards upon the wall. Thus it threw shadows of these obscure and homely figures every evening with as much care over each contour as if it had been the profile of a Court beauty on a palace wall; copied them as diligently as it had copied Olympian shapes on marble *façades* long ago, or the outline of Alexander, Cæsar, and the Pharaohs.

They were the less restful cows that were stalled. Those that would stand still of their own will were milked in the middle of the yard, where many of such better behaved ones stood waiting now – all prime milchers, such as were seldom seen out of this valley, and not always within it; nourished by the succulent feed which the water-meads supplied at this prime season of the year. Those of them that were spotted with white reflected the sunshine in dazzling brilliancy, and the polished brass knobs on their horns glittered with something of military display. Their large-veined udders hung ponderous as sandbags, the teats sticking out like the legs of a gipsy's crock; and as each animal lingered for her turn to arrive the milk oozed forth and fell in drops to the ground.

The dairymaids and men had flocked down from their cottages and out of the dairy-house with the arrival of the cows from the meads; the maids walking in pattens, not on account of the weather, but to keep their shoes above the mulch of the barton. Each girl sat down on her three-legged stool, her face sideways, her right cheek resting against the cow; and looked musingly along the animal's flank at Tess as she approached. The male milkers, with hat-brims turned down, resting flat on their foreheads and gazing on the ground, did not observe her …

TESS OF THE D'URBERVILLES

Dr W. T. Fernie   *1911*

MILK *and* BLOOD

*Dr Fernie completed his series of works (*Meals Medicinal,
Kitchen Physick, *etc) on food and health at an advanced age.
He strove hard to be up-to-date. So, writing* Health to Date *in
1911, he inevitably had much to say about the current fad for
Lactic Milk, soured in the Bulgarian fashion and strongly
recommended by Metchnikoff. In this passage he draws on the
teaching of another guru of the time, Dr Harlow Davis, whose
observations on milk incorporate a weird glimpse of what went
on in the abattoirs of New York. (See also page 123.)*

Doctor Harlow Davis has pronounced in forcible terms respecting the physiological endowments of the mother's Milk as a living ferment, which is best calculated to play an important part in the mental, as well as in the physical, development of the child. 'It is,' says he, 'the presence of this occult influence in the mother's Milk which makes any adequate substitute for it impossible.' Similarly he pays a tribute to the inestimable value of new Milk, fresh from the cow, for benefiting consumptive or bloodless patients, the said Milk being drunk 'before the magnetic warmth of the cow has left it.' In other words, the patient should be present at the milking of the cow, or should drink the Milk within a few minutes afterwards. 'Herein lies the great secret which, strange to say, has been overlooked, not only by the laity, but also by most medical men. Every glass of Milk which is drunk by the patient while it is yet warm from the cow, is equivalent in nourishing and stimulating qualities to a glass of blood.'

'Any morning in New York one may witness numbers of patients in the abattoirs, who have been sent there by their respective physicians for the purpose of drinking the blood of the oxen as soon as these animals are killed. There is no doubt as to its efficacy in imparting strength and vigour to the patient. I have witnessed several human wrecks in various stages of consumption holding their glasses to the severed throat of the ox, and drinking the life-blood with evident relish. It is a common sight at the great pork-packing factories of Chicago to witness the pig-stickers regaling themselves on the blood of their victims; and I venture to say they are as fine and healthy a body of men as one could find anywhere. To those persons who may think that the taste of the blood must be nauseating, I may add that with eyes closed it is practically impossible to tell the difference between the blood, and milk warm from the cow. Not only are they similar in taste, but likewise in physiological effects. Once more I will emphasize the fact that there is a vast difference between the Milk warm from the cow and Milk when artificially heated. One glass of the naturally warm Milk will give more vitality than a quart or more of milk which has lost its natural warmth. This is owing to Milk straight from the udder teeming with electricity, or animal magnetism, which is in reality a form of liquid life; and all of such life-element is lost by evaporation after the milk has cooled.'

HEALTH TO DATE

Richard Bradley 1727

On CHEESE

We met Bradley on page 61. Here is a passage typical of his
agreeable ruminations about agricultural matters and the
annual round of countryside events. It comes from a chapter on
May, the 'busy month for the Dairy'.

It is to be obferv'd, that if in any fort of Cheefe, which is here mentioned, there is not a ftrength of brisknefs of tafte agreeable to every Palate, it may be ftrengthned, by putting either Spice into the Rennet Bag, as Pepper, or Mace, or Cloves, which will make the Rennet very ftrong, and the Cheefe of confequence more fharp to the Palate; or elfe add the Juices of ftrong fweet Herbs to the Milk, when the Rennet is put in: the

Juice of Marygolds efpecially helps the richnefs of the Milk, or Cheefe. The Mace in good quantity put into the Rennet will give the Cheefe a moft agreeable warmth.

As for the Antipathy which fome People bear to Cheefe, I judge that it muft proceed from the firft impreffion made from the Nurfe that fuckles Children, or from the firft Cow's Milk that is given them: for as the Stomach is the firft part which the Nourifhment is received into; fo, as that Nourifhment is at firft favourably receiv'd into the Stomach, fo the Tone of the Stomach will ever remain afterwards, unlefs it could be fo clear'd from the firft Impreffion by fuch a Tryal as Human Nature can hardly bear. I guefs too, that from this Prejudice in the Stomach proceeds the Averfion which fome People have to the Smell of Cheefe; and if I may go a little farther this way, I fuppofe that the Diflike to Cats, and the Antipathy fome People bear to them, is from Frights which the Mothers have receiv'd from them during their Pregnancy: concerning which laft Particular, I have offer'd my Sentiments in the Article of the Longing of Women, in my *Philofophical Account of the Works of Nature*. But as for the other things, which fome People bear an Averfion to, as the Mutton of black Sheep, or a Breaft of Mutton, *etc.* they depend upon the loathing of the Stomach, from the firft Impreffion. What I have remark'd here, concerning the preparing and foftning of the quality of the Rennet Bag, is in part a reafon for the firft good or bad Impreffion that may be made upon Mankind with regard to Cheefe; and I think the following relation, which I had from a noble Peer, from whom I have learnt many curious and ufeful things, tending to the good of my Country, will be acceptable to the World.

Some Gentlemen that had been hunting, and were led by their Sport to a retir'd part of the Country, where they found only a Cottage to refrefh themfelves in, were forc'd to take up with Bread and Cheefe; there was nothing elfe to be had, and they had craving Stomachs: but one of the Company was fo unfortunate as to have an averfion to Cheefe, and could never bear either the tafte or fmell of it; however, at this time feeing how heartily it was eaten by his Companions, and being very hungry, he refolved to venture upon it, and eat heartily of it; but about an hour after was taken fo very ill with Purging and Vomiting, that in a fhort time his Life was defpair'd of. He had the Advice of the beft Phyficians, but no Medicine took place, and he was given over, after he had lain in that condition a Week; however, at length the Diftemper went off, and by degrees he got ftrength enough to go homeward, and in his way happening to ftop at an Inn, where there ftood a Waggon Load of *Chefhire* Cheefes, he found that he had a ftrong Appetite to eat fome of that fort, and had one cut on purpofe, and eat heartily of it, without fuffering the leaft inconvenience, and has ever fince been a great lover of Cheefe. So that there is an Example of getting over this Averfion; but confidering the difficulty he went thro', it fhews the danger of fuch an Attempt: Nothing lefs than the violent Scouring he underwent could have chang'd the firft Impreffion made in his Stomach. But thus far of Cheefe.

THE COUNTRY HOUSEWIFE AND LADY'S DIRECTOR

Sigridur Thorlacius 1980

Do You Know Skyr?

Any visitor to Iceland is bound to meet and enjoy a special
fermented milk product, of the yoghurt family, called skyr. So
far as I know, the essay by Mrs Thorlacius (here abridged) is
the only proper account of it in English. It was very daring of
her to mention the apparent equivalence between skyr and the
Indian shrikhand, *and the successful making of skyr in*
Denmark, since it is an article of faith for most Icelanders that
skyr is exclusive to them (and they will tell you gleefully
about the unsuccessful efforts made by people elsewhere to
produce it – 'of course it didn't work').

A visitor to Iceland will soon be offered a dish of skyr for dessert. He will be given a bowl of a soft, white substance, offered sugar and cream to pour over it, and if he is very fortunate, some blueberries to go with it.

What is this, the visitor will ask, and his hosts will give a rambling explanation about the story and making of skyr. For ages this has been a favourite dish and valuable ingredient of the nutrition of the Icelandic people, formerly made on every farm, now produced in huge machines in the dairies.

Skyr is made out of milk, the culture of certain bacteria, and rennet. When asked about the origin of the dish, we have to admit that we only know from our ancient literature, the Sagas (written in the 11th to 14th centuries), that skyr has been made in Iceland since the first settlers landed there in the 9th century. When archeologists dug up the site where, according to the Saga of Burnt Njall, the farm of Njall should have been, they found remnants of buildings destroyed by fire and among them traces of skyr. This was in 1870–80. The reason why they could find these traces was that, up to modern times, the skyr was stored in big barrels.

We also learn from the Sagas that skyr was not commonly known in Scandinavian countries at that time; whereas a modern expert of nutrition states that certainly skyr was made in Scandinavia and the British Isles in ancient times, but probably disappeared when the growing of grains increased.

Be that as it may, in modern times skyr was not made anywhere in these countries, until a Dane, who had worked in a dairy in Iceland, brought the formula with him to Denmark and started making skyr in a dairy in Jutland with great success.

A personal experience made me wonder about the origins of skyr, but brought me no nearer to a conclusion. Many years ago my husband attended a dinner party in New

Delhi, given by the late Prime Minister Nehru. The last item on the menu was something called Shrikhand. Great was his surprise when this turned out to be skyr, made and served in exactly the same way as in Iceland. He was told it was a very popular dish in Northern India.

I have since been told that it is also made in the Caucasus and other eastern countries. It is difficult to find facts about the eating habits of people in such far away places. But in the Sagas we have many accounts of Icelanders travelling to the east, to Novgorod and Constantinople, so they might have learned the method there.

The people in Iceland went through great hardships in times past. Famine was more than once brought on by pestilence; volcanic eruptions destroyed animals and spoiled the grazing; a deteriorating climate and many other things led to abject poverty. To mention just one example, one third of the population died of smallpox in 1707–9.

The people had to learn to use all possible resources of nourishment to stay alive. Perhaps the skyr and the whey extracted from it played an important role, not only as food, but also as a means to preserve food.

Skyr is made of skimmed milk. Before separators came into use, every farm had several wooden bowls or troughs made with holes near the bottom, stopped by plugs. After sieving the milk it was poured into these vessels to set and at the right time the plug was removed and the milk poured through the holes, leaving the cream in the vessel. The skimmed milk was then poured into a pot and boiled to kill the undesirable bacteria. Big wooden bowls, carefully scrubbed and dried in the fresh air, were filled from the pot and the milk cooled down to 37°C. There were no thermometers at the farms, so the heat was simply tested with the tip of a finger. For each ten litres of milk a good spoonful of skyr or curdled milk was needed, and only two drops of rennet.

I remember it as a very serious moment when my mother taught me how to make skyr. It was considered something of an art to make a really good skyr and anyone who was so unlucky as to make a batch that was not perfectly bland, and even, felt degraded.

After 1½–2 hours the milk had curdled. A wooden frame to which was tacked a sieve of cotton cloth was put over a barrel, the skyr carefully spooned into the sieve, so that the whey could run out of it into the barrel. After a couple of hours the skyr was ready for eating. In a cool place it kept its freshness for some days and then started getting sour. Some preferred it that way.

To our own day, plain skyr or skyr mixed with porridge, served with a slice of liver- or blood-sausage and milk, is found by many to be a very satisfying meal and much recommended by nutrition experts.

Today skyr is one of the most popular products of the Icelandic dairies. It is easy to serve, tastes good and is rich in nutritional value. It can be varied by whipping a raw egg into it or mixing it with fruit. Weight watchers mix it with honey and eat it with skimmed milk. But to get the full enjoyment out of your first taste of skyr, just sprinkle it with sugar and pour some cream over it and forget about the calories.

PETITS PROPOS CULINAIRES (PPC) 4

Françoise Sabban   1986

LACTOSE INTOLERANCE *in* CHINA

For those of us who unquestioningly regard milk (and milk
products) as 'ideal' or at least 'very health-giving' foods, it
comes as a surprise to learn that a high proportion of the
inhabitants of the world cannot, when adult, take milk. The
phenomenon, known as 'lactose intolerance', has been the
subject of many learned papers through which I have ploughed
my way, but they tend to be narrowly focused and extremely
technical; very few even try to address the subject in a synoptic
and intelligible manner.
It was in a French paper about food practices in ancient China
that I came across this illuminating statement.

The author of a recent study of attitudes to dairy products shows that there are degrees of acceptance and rejection of dairy foodstuffs, the ultimate refusal being that of those who see milk as just an animal secretion no more valuable than urine, and who have never even imagined it being consumed by a human being! He concludes the article with a brief note on China in which he accords less significance to the influence of India in the matter, via *Buddhism*, than he does to the influence of the Tibetans, Mongols and other neighbouring peoples who pursued a pastoral way of life. However, despite this, 'the non-milking attitude has persisted and is widespread among Chinese today'.

To explain this rejection of milk on the part of the Chinese, commentators have occasionally invoked an intolerance to lactose which is generally found among Asian peoples. Like the majority of Asian peoples, the Chinese, it is claimed, exhibit a deficiency in lactase, the enzyme which is indispensable for the digestion of lactose, and which enables the feeding baby to drink its mother's milk to beneficial effect. In certain individuals it is preserved and maintained into adulthood, whereas in others it disappears during childhood, inducing at times severe digestive problems following the ingestion of foodstuffs containing lactose. This deficiency should not astonish us unduly, since if milk seems to be a beneficial source of nourishment to man, we have seen that this belief is not universally shared. The consumption of milk by an adult is in fact a form of perversion which, throughout the entire animal kingdom, is practised only by man and his domestic pets.

Several American researchers have stressed the correlation which they claim exists between intolerance to lactose and an 'instinctive' aversion to dairy products. They have in fact established that the majority of so called 'pastoral' communities have a high degree of tolerance to lactose whereas the lowest levels of tolerance are to be found among peoples who do not rear cattle and do not practise dairy farming. However, they point out that several groups appear to contradict this rule; certain people of Asian origin for example who exhibit a lactase deficiency which has been duly registered, nonetheless continue to consume dairy produce, and other individuals belonging to societies which traditionally practise dairy farming exhibit, nonetheless, a lactase deficiency

Such facts invite mature reflection as to their significance and caution is called for when judgements are being made about certain attitudes in the China of the past. The current debate is in our opinion centred on three points:

1 Milk-based foodstuffs have different concentrations of lactose which vary according to the way in which they are produced. During the fermentation process lactose is transformed into lactic acid which is readily digestible. Thus the lactose level of certain cheeses, of butter and fermented products, tends to diminish; hence, for example, a three week-old koumis contains no more than 0.23% lactose. A person therefore suffering from a lactase deficiency might consume certain dairy products without ill effects while a glass of milk would procure a negative reaction. The American researchers are particularly sensitive to the problem posed by the indigestibility as they see it of fresh milk since, a highly valued source of nourishment in their society, fresh milk occupies an important position in their own diet. Might not this slight ethnocentricity blind them to the fact that a certain number of countries where dairy farming was traditionally practised converted the bulk of their milk production into, for example, cheese, not to mention countries outside Europe whose practices are less well-known to us?

2 Digestion is not simply a mechanical process in which enzymes join battle with foodstuffs. An individual's likes and dislikes have a major part to play in his ability to digest his food. It is clearly one thing to swallow the smooth and creamy contents of an industrially processed tin of condensed milk, and quite another to swallow the warm milky liquid whose animal origins one is only too well aware of. This is why we should not be surprised that the Vietnamese questioned by P. Gourou in 1945 grimaced at the thought of drinking the milk of their buffalo, while gorging themselves on imported condensed milk. How many people, after all, whose mouth waters at the thought of gulping down a carton of cool milk perfectly preserved in the refrigerator, would be genuinely enthusiastic about drinking from a ladle, still steaming with the cow's heat, as it is lifted from the bucket into which the beast has just been milked?

3 As for the Chinese, an analysis of their aversion to dairy products has yet to be carried out which takes account of their surprising tendency to consume human milk in adulthood. Human milk, as well as a range of other substances of human origin, is one of the elements used in traditional Chinese medicine. It is prized for its fortifying and rejuvenating qualities and is particularly recommended to the elderly. Such therapeutic uses are more than mere theory since we have records of the public and private sale of

breast milk in certain towns, and evidence that wet-nurses hired out their services towards the end of the 19th century. In this respect a story is cited of a young mother who, moved by a strong sense of filial affection, proclaims that she would sooner give suck to her toothless mother-in-law than to her child. Even if situations have arisen in our society where women have breast-fed fully grown adults, such situations are clearly the exception rather than the rule. Bearing in mind that the lactose content of human milk is virtually twice that of Chinese buffalo milk, it can be seen that care must be exercised when we speak of the Chinese aversion to dairy produce and link it to their intolerance to lactose.

UN SAVOIR-FAIRE OUBLIÉ: LE TRAVAIL DU LAIT EN CHINE ANCIENNE

Furugh Hourani   *1984*

LABAN, LABAN

*Reflecting on the way in which yoghurt has been moving
steadily westwards from its area of origin, and on the extent
of the new territories which it has conquered, I am surprised
that it has inspired little writing except of a routine kind.
Here, however, is one highly evocative piece.*

'*Laban, laban*' is a cry that brings back to me memories of my childhood in Baghdad. It was the Beduin woman announcing her arrival. She would come at dawn on hot summer days balancing on her head a stack of trays made of mulberry-wood filled with yoghurt, topped with a thick layer of cream, all made from buffalo milk. Our Assyrian cook Anna would gently remove some of this cream, sprinkle it with sugar and honey, and give it to us for breakfast.

Anna came to us as a refugee from the area of Lake Urmia in northern Iran: she remembered vividly the lush valleys and mountains of her childhood, and would describe to me that lost paradise of fruit trees and running water. When nostalgia overtook her she would make us an Assyrian yoghurt soup, which I think was the only recipe she brought with her.

She would buy very thick strained yoghurt, thin it out again with a little water to bring it to the consistency of a thick cream: to this she would add a dessert spoon of cornflour to stabilize the yoghurt while cooking, and two or three whole green peppers (capsicums) would be floated on its surface. The pot would be placed on the fire, and I was often allowed to stand on a high stool to stir it with a long wooden spoon while she repeated '*yavaş, yavaş*' – 'slowly, slowly', and told me to stir always in the same direction clockwise. While she was giving me these instructions she chopped up onions and celery into thick chunks and boiled them. Once cooked she added them and the water in which they had been boiled to the yoghurt, with a little rice, salt, and a few sprigs of parsley and fresh or dried dill: and when the peppers and the rice were cooked, the soup was ready to serve, and was equally delicious hot in winter and cool in summer.

Many years later when I was first married I went to Lebanon and then to my husband's home town of Marjeyoun which overlooks the western slopes of Mount Hermon, with views of the Jaulan Heights and even the Ajlun hills in Jordan on a clear day. On my first day in the town I was startled at early dawn by '*laban, laban*' the same cry of my childhood. It was once more a Beduin woman whose people kept their cows and sheep and goats in a not-distant area which lay on the borders of Lebanon, Syria and Palestine, today between Lebanon and Israel. She came almost every day in spring and summer when milk is plentiful, to sell her yoghurt to the people of Marjeyoun who did not care to keep livestock themselves but preferred to purchase their products from others. One such supplier of yoghurt and cheese was a man from Shib'a high up on Mount Hermon: in the spring he brought his fresh *lebne* which was eagerly and rapidly eaten up by his clients who all winter had only their preserved *lebne* balls at hand. In the summer he would take orders for the autumn and winter. Some day in late September or October he would arrive with his donkey carrying on both its sides heavy white cloth bags tied up with string or bits of old rags. Our neighbours all consumed vast quantities of yoghurt transformed into *lebne* by straining and the addition of salt. Three or four hundred kilos a year was not an exceptional intake for one family.

One of these neighbours, a man who always enjoyed the privilege of negotiating and taking delivery of the *lebne*, would first of all prod the bags to find out if they were solid or still liquid with unstrained water; the bags would then be opened and inspected to make sure the *lebne* was sufficiently firm, and tasted to make sure it was not sour or rancid, and not diluted with cow's milk – for it is only goat's milk which preserves its consistency and taste throughout many months, and does not turn bitter and disintegrate as cow's milk will quickly do. Almost every year we would hear shouting and protestations as mutual accusations were exchanged about the quality of the *lebne*, its weight and its price.

Once the matter had been concluded the women and girls of the family would gather around the table which had been scrubbed like their hands and arms to remove any dirt or dust which would cause the *lebne* to turn bitter and disintegrate; each one would cut off a small portion from the large and solid mountain of *lebne* and roll it in the palm of the hands into small balls the size of a quail's egg, though some families preferred a larger ball the size of a ping pong ball. The balls would then be placed in rows on large trays, covered with a clean cloth, and placed in a cool spot to dry for about two more days. Finally they would be put into large jars and covered with olive oil. Preserved like this, *lebne* lasts until the following spring or even longer if kept in the refrigerator.   PETITS PROPOS CULINAIRES (PPC) *26*

FASTING *and* FEASTING

*Both involuntary and deliberate fasting
are represented here, at one end of the
spectrum. At the other are items on what
are indisputably feasts. Hovering in
between are pieces such as 'Hebridean
Hospitality' and that by Virginia Woolf:
food for thought. What is a 'feast'?*

HUNGER

*This section would not be complete without, and indeed must
begin with, a passage on hunger: real hunger as opposed to
routine, casual hunger. The book whose title is just that,*
Hunger, *by Knut Hamsun, the Norwegian author who is
widely regarded as father of the modern novel, contains more
than one such passage. His description of the incident of the
'gorgeous little bone' is one of the most powerful of these.*

When it was dark, I shuffled over to the city jail – God knows how I got there – and
sat down on the edge of the balustrade. I ripped one of my coat pockets out and
started chewing on it, not for any purpose particularly, and in a hopeless mood, my eyes
staring straight in front of me without seeing. I heard some small children who were
playing around me, and I instinctively became alert whenever someone walked past me;
otherwise, I was oblivious to the world.

All at once I got the idea of walking down to one of the open-air booths underneath
and getting a piece of raw meat. I stood up, crossed the balustrade, over towards the far
end of the booths, and walked down the stairs. When I was nearly down to the butcher
stalls, I shouted up through the stair arch and motioned angrily backwards as if talking
to a dog up there, and then spoke boldly to the first butcher I met.

'Would you be so good as to give me a bone for my dog?' I said. 'Just a bone – it
doesn't have to have any meat on it, just something he can carry around in his mouth.'

I got a bone, a gorgeous little bone with some meat still on it, and put it under my
coat. I thanked the man so warmly that he looked at me astonished.

'Nothing to thank me for,' he said.

'Oh yes, there is,' I said. 'This was very good of you.'

I walked back up. My heart thumped inside.

I sneaked into a blacksmith's yard, as far in as I could go, and stopped in front of a
fallen-down gate in the back. There was not a light visible anywhere, the darkness was
sweet and thick all around me; I started chewing on my bone.

It had no taste at all; a nauseating odour of dried blood rose from the bone, and I
started throwing up immediately, I couldn't help it. I tried again – if I could only keep it
down, it would do some good; the problem was to get it to stay down there. But I
vomited again. I grew angry, bit fiercely into the meat, ripped off a small piece, and
swallowed it by force. That did no good either – as soon as the small pieces became
warm in the stomach, up they came again. I clenched my fists madly, started crying
from sheer helplessness, and gnawed like a man possessed. I cried so much that the

bone became wet and messy with tears. I vomited, swore, and chewed again, cried as if my heart would break, and threw up again. Then I swore aloud and consigned all the powers of the universe to hell.

Silence. Not a person around, no lights, not a sound. I was in a wild state, I breathed heavily and audibly, and sobbed, gnashing my teeth, every time I had to abandon these bits of meat which might have satisfied my hunger. When nothing helped, no matter how hard I tried, I threw the bone against the gate, maddened by the most impotent hatred. Carried away by rage, I shouted and roared threats up to the sky, shrieked God's name hoarsely and savagely, and curled my fingers like claws ...

HUNGER

George Lang 1971

THOUGHTS _on_ POVERTY _in_ HUNGARY

_A thoughtful piece of writing, on the relative nature of
poverty, from the most eloquent writer on Hungarian food and
cookery. See page 220 for more of Lang._

Some individuals go to pieces in poverty. There are others who take deprivation as a challenge and use their energy and ability to get out of this degrading state. Hungarians see no virtue in poverty and try to make the best of a temporary or permanent indigence. They feel that God supports only the rich man with a stake; the poor man must carve his own.

Amerigo Tot, the great Hungarian sculptor presently living in Rome, comes from a small village. When he was a child, his whole family would sometimes sit under a big tree in the yard where the neighbours could observe them, but could not see that they were ladling nothing into their soup plates from a tureen, so no one would think that they were starving. This sort of pride and vanity, combined with a peculiarly ingenious thinking process, produced some very interesting foods and drinks. Toward the end of the eighteenth century, Parmentier won a competition 'to find a plant that can replace cereals in time of famine. Poor Hungarian households should have his image right next to Christ's since potatoes have saved many families from starvation in the past two centuries.

The frying of onion in bacon or lard, adding paprika to it, is about as simple a culinary process as one will find anywhere. However, many a poor Hungarian farmer's wife is able to control the subtle differences in this process so that the various plain dishes using this as a foundation will taste like anything from fish to meat with many variations in between. Thus, a plain paprika potato can taste like a meat and vegetable casserole, and a millet porridge (*Köleskása*) like a fish specialty.

A Hungarian housewife would be angered at a French or Western European cookbook's direction on stock, basic to making a soup. She might feel like a Scotsman toward the American system of conspicuous consumption. Fresh, pure water is what she uses, never any meat and rarely even bones, and yet she is able to make an onion broth with garlic toast that tastes better than most fancy soups in expensive restaurants. Offals are used as substitutes for meat in some kitchens, but a Hungarian lung stew in a lemon sauce became a national favorite. Pork crackling or the nose and ears of the pigs all became delicacies when the simple Hungarian household got through with them.

Poverty, of course, is a very relative term, and entire provinces in Hungary probably would object to the notion that eating potatoes without meat is a sign of poverty. The people of the Nyírség (and some other counties) had to catch, cook and live on sparrows, crows and gophers. They had to grind tree barks into a kind of flour and bake bread with it, and on very special 'red letter days' make a 'chestnut' purée out of mashed beans to celebrate an important event. Not only did they have to rub chicory beans against coffee beans, dropping the chicory beans into the water to make coffee, but at times even the substitute became scarce and they had to rub the chicory beans against some kind of wild plant and use the latter to make coffee. (During World War II, I tried everything to quiet my demanding stomach, but I did not find a pancake made of dried corncob flour very satisfactory.)

There is a craving for sweets after a while, not only by children, but by grownups, too. In Hungary, there are, unfortunately, no maple trees, but there is a kind of white birch (*nyírfa*) which gives out a sweet sap, and the poor people learned to boil this down and make a few desserts from it. (This tree gave its name to the province.) Fortunately apples in the county of Szabolcs and plums in the Szatmár area are the finest in the country and plentiful. The latter are made into the powerful and famous Szatmári plum brandy.

Flowers were another food source for the poor, particularly the buds and even the sprouts. (The most unlikely bedfellows: Hungarian poor people's food and the recherché esoterica of flower-cookery. . . .)

THE CUISINE OF HUNGARY

Léo Moulin 1978

MONKS FASTED *but were* PLUMP

*Léo Moulin here explains by reference to their dietary
habits the characteristic appearance of medieval monks,
which was not as lean and ascetic as one might
have expected.*

Yes, but just look at those rotund, ruddy faced monks, some will say (and there was no shortage of such comments in the Middle Ages): aren't they little more than a sanctimonious bunch of self-indulgent lushes, gorging and guzzling, away from the public gaze? After all, if they adhered strictly to their vows, how could they be so fat?

A curious and soundly researched article by Michel Rouche makes it possible for us to consider the issues with a little more understanding. He has made a study of the daily rations in monasteries and trappist convents, and has shown the following: the bread ration varies from 1.5 to 2 kilograms (nothing exceptional for the period, as has been observed); the cheese ration from 70 to 110 grams; that of dry vegetables from 135 to 230 grams; honey, 0.60 to 1.10 grams. The fat ration (where permitted) was about 35 grams, and salt 20 or so grams. The wine (or beer) ration was on average one and a half litres. Converted into calories, these rations total more than 4,700 calories a day, the maximum being at St-Germain-des-Prés with 6,882 calories. Notice that the total does not include additional herbs, roots and fruit with which the monks might have supplemented their diet. If, taking account of miscalculations always possible in this kind of work, we reduce Rouche's estimates by one third, we still arrive at some startling calorific values, even if we are basing our estimates on normal days alone, leaving aside the church calendar with its high and holy days.

How is such gluttony to be explained? One explanation might be the constant battle against the cold, which would ravage the entire monastery, with the exception of the heated day room, throughout the winter months. This was not the case during the warmer months, however. Was it that a monk was a 'solidly built colossus, overcoming a ferocious struggle for survival', with an appetite to match? There is no reason to believe that medieval man was colossal in stature – armour from the period suggests the opposite. And even if they had been, the rations are still enormous. In fact, it is socio-cultural conditioning, our eating habits, which throughout history, and still today, determine what and how much we consume. Certain nations eat a lot, others eat less, and neither climate nor physiology can account for such differences. Hunger is in many respects a psychological phenomenon. Medieval man, living with the constant fear of want, a fear largely founded, would react by eating at every opportunity. And as much as possible.

The English national appetite is legendary: 'Heavy drinking, heavy feeding', writes Knowles. 'Eat your fill as the English do', states one text. The Flemish appetite was equally renowned.

As for our monks, they stuffed themselves with carbohydrates, starch and vegetables. Their diet was unbalanced due to a lack of protein and the scarcity of vitamins. And it is for this reason that they were thought to sport a pot belly and a ruddy complexion. In reality they were enveloped in fat, riddled with tooth decay – teeth they were soon to lose because of vitamin deficiency and because such was the common lot – they were slow to digest and full of gas. The result of this, according to Michel Rouche, was 'a marked tendency towards splenetic temperament, moody pessimism and outbursts of loathing for a body which was constantly clamouring for attention'.

I am not sure that I would go along with this entirely. The point is, for our purposes, that apart from days of fasting, monks tended to eat in a way that was both irrational and immoderate. These practices promoted an obsession with food, and on the other hand, led to a sense of suffering (which has its merits) when they mortified the flesh by fasting. Leaving the table without having wholly satisfied one's hunger, not eating between meals, abstaining from meat – the most beneficial thing they could have done – these things were in fact a challenge which was no doubt more keenly felt than the twin burdens of chastity and obedience.

An outraged Cistercian novice gives us an idea of what it was like when, reporting to the infirmary for no apparent reason, he began to argue vociferously for his meat and wine ration to be restored. The friars claimed that they were unable to chant, the new converts unable to work, unless they were full and belching (*pleni et ructuantes*).

It is beyond any doubt that members of religious orders, subjected to a diet which veered between indigestible food and searing fasts, more than once sought solace in eating well. And 'eating well' in the language which prevailed up until the dawning of the present century really means 'eating a lot'. Here is, for instance, what featured at a meagre banquet bringing together Benedictines from Saint-Benigne and Carthusians from Dijon: pike, carp, white herrings and *soretz*, butter, olive oil, spices, saffron, *bledz* (a kind of green wheat used to season the salad), cress and pimpernel, sugar, white bread, canary bread, *taltre*, eggs, pears, apples, chestnuts, not forgetting the white wine for cooking the fish. True, this was in the fifteenth century when the rigours of earlier times had somewhat been relaxed.

It is easily understood why indigestion was a common complaint. *Secretum Secretorum* (The secret of secrets), quoted by Langlois, suggests two so-called medicines for dealing with 'pains of the stomach'. The first is to take a pretty and innocent young woman in your arms (*puellam candidam et speciosam*) – a remedy which is nothing if not intriguing, given the fact that the suggestion is made to monks. The second, which is infinitely wiser and more effective, is to place a warm, heavy shirt over the abdomen.

La Vie Quotidienne des Religieux au Moyen Age

Dr Doran *1854*

Frugal Habit *of* Sir J. Cutler

Sir John Cutler was ingenious in his thrift. This rich miser ordinarily travelled on horseback and alone, in order to avoid expense. On reaching his inn at night, he feigned indisposition, as an excuse for not taking supper. He would simply order the hostler to bring a little straw to his room, to put in his boots. He then had his bed warmed, and got into it, but only to get out of it again as soon as the servant had left the room. Then, with the straw in his boots and the candle at his bed-side, he kindled a little fire, at which he toasted a herring which he drew from his pocket. This, with a bit of bread which he carried with him, and a little water from the jug, enabled the lord of countless thousands to sup at a very moderate cost.

TABLE TRAITS

Sophie Coe *1985*

Aztec Food

The twin themes of fasting and feasting are neatly married in this extract from Sophie Coe's major essay on Aztec cuisine.

Another source says that when the messengers returned to Motecuhzoma, the Spaniards sent with them some ship's biscuits, a pot of preserves, and some wine, which the emperor tasted.

Once the Spaniards landed and were marching towards Tenochtitlan, they lived off the country. Bernal Díaz records the food brought to them by the inhabitants of various towns and cities on the way: fowls and honey; fowls, roasted fish, and maize; fowls, maize bread, and 'plums'; fowls, fruit, and roasted fish; 'plums' and maize bread; fowls, maize bread, and fruit; and so on. Fowls in this case means birds, not chickens, and most probably turkeys, and 'plums' are *Spondias* fruit. This should not be taken word for word, having been written, as I said, many years later, but it gives the flavor. Finally Cortés and his men reached Tenochtitlan, which Bernal Díaz in a famous passage in his narrative compares to an enchantment from the legend of Amadis. Once in Tenochtitlan Bernal Díaz gives us an even more famous description, from a culinary point of view, that of Motecuhzoma's so-called banquet. Actually banquet is a misnomer; Motecuhzoma did hold banquets, but what Bernal Díaz saw and described was an ordinary daily meal:

For each meal, over thirty different dishes were prepared by his cooks according to their ways and usage, and they placed small pottery brasiers beneath the dishes so that they should not get cold. They prepared more than three hundred plates of food that Montezuma was going to eat, and more than a thousand for the guard. When he was going to eat, Montezuma would sometimes go out with his chiefs and stewards, and they would point out to him which dish was best, and of what birds and other things it was composed, and as they advised him, so he would eat, but it was not often that he would go out to see the food, and then merely as a pastime.

I have heard it said that they were wont to cook for him the flesh of young boys, but as he had such a variety of dishes, made of so many things, we could not succeed in seeing if they were of human flesh or of other things, for their daily cooked fowls, turkeys, pheasants, native partridges, quail tame and wild ducks, venison, wild boar, reed birds, pigeons, hares and rabbits, and many sorts of birds and other things which are bred in this country, and they are so numerous that I cannot finish naming them in a hurry; so we had no insight into it, but I know for certain that after our Captain censured the sacrifice of human beings, and the eating of their flesh, he ordered that such food should not be prepared for him thenceforth ... They brought Montezuma fruit of all the different kinds that the land produced, but he ate very little of it. From time to time they brought him, in cup-shaped vessels of pure gold, a certain drink made from cacao which they said he took when he was going to visit his wives, and at the time he took no heed of it, but what I did see was that they brought over fifty great jugs of good cacao frothed up, and he drank of that, and the women served this drink to him with great reverence ... As soon as the Great Montezuma had dined, all the men of the Guard had their meal and as many more of the other house servants, and it seems to me that they brought out over a thousand dishes of the food of which I have spoken, and then over two thousand jugs of cacao all frothed up, as they make it in Mexico, and a limitless quantity of fruit, so that with his women and female servants and bread makers and cacao makers his expenses must have been very great ... while Montezuma was at table eating as I have described, there were waiting on him two other graceful women to bring him tortillas, kneaded with eggs and other sustaining ingredients, and these tortillas were very white, and they were brought on plates covered with clean napkins, and they also brought him another kind of bread, like long balls kneaded with other kinds of sustaining food, and 'pan pachol' for so they call it in this country, which is a sort of wafer. There were also placed on the table three tubes much painted and gilded, which held *liquidambar* mixed with certain herbs which they call *tabaco*, and when he had finished eating, after they had danced before him and sung and the table was removed, he inhaled the smoke from one of these tubes, but he took very little of it and with that he fell asleep.

While Motecuhzoma's state impressed the Spaniards they were also struck by the voluntary austerity of the Aztecs. They express amazement that the people could survive on so little. Motolinia goes so far as to say that the Indians do not sing well because they eat so scantily. There is indeed a strong strain of puritanism in the culture. The Codex Mendoza gives the tortilla (a thin round cake made of ground, limesoaked corn) ration for children: one tortilla per meal per child when they are five, one and a half per child when they are eleven, to teach them not to be greedy, two tortillas per meal when they are fourteen and doing the work of adults.

These rations are hard to understand because we are not sure how many meals a day the Aztecs had. Most sources say two, one in the morning and one in the afternoon; but Tezozomoc, in describing the moving of a great stone statue to Tenochtitlan – a statue which at times refused to move, and which spoke (another in the series of prodigies) – said the workmen coping with it were fed three times a day: at dawn, at nine in the morning, and at three in the afternoon.

The children were also given length homilies about food and eating. Moral lectures of this sort were a common literary form among the Aztecs, and many of them have survived.

Eighth: Listen! Above all you are to be prudent in drink, in food, for many things pertain to it. You are not to eat excessively of the required food. And when you do something, when you perspire, when you work, it is necessary that you are to break your fast. Furthermore, the courtesy, the prudence [you should show] are in this way: when you are eating, you are not to be hasty, not to be impetuous; you are not to take excessively nor to break up your tortillas. You are not to put a large amount in your mouth; you are not to swallow it unchewed. You are not to gulp like a dog, when eating food . . .

And when you are about to eat, you are to wash your hands, to wash your face, to wash your mouth. And if somewhere you are eating with others, do not quickly seat yourself at the eating place with others. Quickly you will seize the wash water, the washbowl; you will wash another's hands. And when the eating is over, you are quickly to seize the washbowl, the wash water; you are to wash another's mouth, another's hands. And you are to pick up [fallen scraps], you are to sweep the place where there has been eating. And you, when you have eaten, once again you are to wash your hands, to wash your mouth, to clean your teeth.

PETITS PROPOS CULINAIRES (PPC) *19, 20 21*

Virginia Woolf   *1929*

A CONTRAST *in* COLLEGE MEALS

The passages juxtaposed here are separated by several pages in
A Room of One's Own, no doubt so that the contrast would
thus be heightened. Both the ideal luncheon in private rooms
in a men's college and the deplorable college dinner in a
women's college are set in 'Oxbridge'.
Virginia Woolf makes her point, but perhaps exaggerates the
dependence of good talk on good food. What strikes me is that
the second of her two descriptions is what corresponds to the
sort of meal I was used to at my men's college, and that
unexciting food didn't seem to entail uninspired talk. And we
kept on talking through the evening on a simple diet of
Nescafé – no 'squat bottle and little glasses' for us.

It is a curious fact that novelists have a way of making us believe that luncheon parties are invariably memorable for something very witty that was said, or for something very wise that was done. But they seldom spare a word for what was eaten. It is part of the novelist's convention not to mention soup and salmon and ducklings, as if soup and salmon and ducklings were of no importance whatsoever, as if nobody ever smoked a cigar or drank a glass of wine. Here, however, I shall take the liberty to defy that convention and to tell you that the lunch on this occasion began with soles, sunk in a deep dish, over which the college cook had spread a counterpane of the whitest cream, save that it was branded here and there with brown spots like the spots on the flanks of a doe. After that came the partridges, but if this suggests a couple of bald, brown birds on a plate you are mistaken. The partridges, many and various, came with all their retinue of sauces and salads, the sharp and the sweet, each in its order; their potatoes, thin as coins but not so hard; their sprouts, foliated as rosebuds but more succulent. And no sooner had the roast and its retinue been done with than the silent serving-man, the Beadle himself perhaps in a milder manifestation, set before us, wreathed in napkins, a confection which rose all sugar from the waves. To call it pudding and so relate it to rice and tapioca would be an insult. Meanwhile the wineglasses had flushed yellow and flushed crimson; had been emptied; had been filled. And thus by degrees was lit, half-way down the spine, which is the seat of the soul, not that hard little electric light which we call brilliance, as it pops in and out upon our lips, but the more profound, subtle and subterranean glow which is the rich yellow flame of rational intercourse. No need to hurry. No need to sparkle. No need to be anybody but oneself. We are all going to heaven and Vandyck is of the company – in other words, how good life seemed, how sweet its rewards, how trivial this grudge or that grievance, how admirable friendship and society of one's kind, as, lighting a good cigarette, one sunk among the cushions in the window-seat . . .

Here was my soup. Dinner was being served in the great dining-hall. Far from being spring it was in fact an evening in October. Everybody was assembled in the big dining-room. Dinner was ready. Here was the soup. It was a plain gravy soup. There was nothing to stir the fancy in that. One could have seen through the transparent liquid any pattern that there might have been on the plate itself. But there was no pattern. The plate was plain. Next came beef with its attendant greens and potatoes – a homely trinity, suggesting the rumps of cattle in a muddy market, and sprouts curled and yellowed at the edge, and bargaining and cheapening and women with string bags on Monday morning. There was no reason to complain of human nature's daily food, seeing that the supply was sufficient and coal-miners doubtless were sitting down to less. Prunes and custard followed. And if anyone complains that prunes, even when mitigated by custard, are an uncharitable vegetable (fruit they are not), stringy as a miser's heart and exuding a fluid such as might run in misers' veins who have denied themselves wine and warmth for eighty years and yet not given to the poor, he should reflect that there are people whose charity embraces even the prune. Biscuits and cheese came next, and here the water-jug was liberally passed round, for it is the nature of biscuits to be dry, and these were biscuits to the core. That was all. The meal was over. Everybody scraped their chairs back; the swing-doors swung violently to and fro; soon the hall was emptied of every sign of food and made ready no doubt for breakfast next morning. Down corridors and up staircases the youth of England went banging and singing. And was it for a guest, a stranger (for I had no more right here in Fernham than in Trinity or Somerville or Girton or Newnham or Christchurch), to say, 'The dinner was not good,' or to say (we were now, Mary Seton and I, in her sitting-room), 'Could we not have dined up here alone?' for if I had said anything of the kind I should have been prying and searching into the secret economies of a house which to the stranger wears so fine a front of gaiety and courage. No, one could say nothing of the sort. Indeed, conversation for a moment flagged. The human frame being what it is, heart, body and brain all mixed together, and not contained in separate compartments as they will be no doubt in another million years, a good dinner is of great importance to good talk. One cannot think well, love well, sleep well, if one has not dined well. The lamp in the spine does not light on beef and prunes. We are all *probably* going to heaven, and Vandyck is, we *hope*, to meet us round the next corner – that is the dubious and qualifying state of mind that beef and prunes at the end of the day's work breed between them. Happily my friend, who taught science, had a cupboard where there was a squat bottle and little glasses – (but there should have been sole and partridge to begin with) – so that we were able to draw up to the fire and repair some of the damages of the day's living.

A ROOM OF MY OWN

Bridget Ann Henisch

1976

ASPECTS *of* MEDIEVAL DINNERS

This survey of the more startling aspects of medieval dinners is
mapped out for us with the wit which we have learned to
expect from Bridget Ann Henisch (see also
pages 18 and 314).

Music, song, and dance lent their charms to a dinner and heightened its excitement. Other ingredients added their own touches of drama and beauty. For even the humblest and the hungriest spectator, squashed disregarded in a drafty corner, there was always something to delight the eye and excite the imagination as courses were brought in, dishes presented, carved, accepted, waved aside. Ceremony transformed the simple, daily acts of eating and drinking into high theater. Everyone shared an ingrained sense of occasion, and the great and powerful could be relied on to satisfy it. When about to eat his supper alone, without guests, Gaston de Foix still made his formal entrance into the hall each night as 'twelve lighted torches were carried before him by twelve serving-men, and these twelve torches were held up in front of his table, giving a bright light in the hall, which was full of knights and squires.'

Whether glimmering by torchlight or shining in the mid-day sun, displays of the best tableware enriched the splendor of the scene, while the liveliness of design and the lavish use of motto and rebus added to the fun and interest. For special occasions flowers and leaves were brought in to decorate the tables and the lucky guests. In his list of details to be attended to for a May wedding, the Goodman of Paris notes that 'branches, greenery, violets, chaplets' must be bought in good time 'at the Porte-de-Paris.' To supplement these there would be needed the services of 'a woman chaplet maker who shall deliver garlands on the wedding eve and on the wedding day.' Just such a chaplet is being used to put a guest in the right mood in a thirteenth-century stained-glass window at Bourges Cathedral. The Prodigal Son, an innocent abroad with his pockets full of money, has been coaxed to sit down to dinner with two prostitutes. By the end of the evening they will have taken every penny from him, but at this stage in the rake's progress he is still enjoying his night on the town. A roast chicken has been brought in and the women are charming their victim out of his senses: one caresses him while the other is about to crown him king of the feast with a garland of flowers.

If all this were not enough to amuse the most jaded diner there was always the possibility of jolting him out of his indifference with a well-planned surprise. The medieval public would have dearly loved the detachable jam stain and the plastic spider that do duty today at countless family dinner tables throughout the Western world when children reach a certain age. Lacking these, they made do with whatever came to mind and hand. Even the Goodman of Paris, that model of sober common sense, had his own recipe for making a glass of white wine turn red before the astonished drinker: '*To Make White Wine Red at Table*: Take in summer the red flowers that grow in the corn ... and let them dry until they can be made into powder, and cast it privily into the glass with the wine and the wine will become red.'

A more ambitious, or more desperate host might consider the use of a jumping chicken to liven up a tedious party. In one of the great medieval bestsellers, the late thirteenth-century *Book of Secrets of Albertus Magnus*, there are helpful instructions under the heading 'If thou wilt that a Chicken or other thing leap in the dish.' Mercury, or quicksilver, is to be put inside the cooked bird, 'for seeing Quicksilver is hot, it moveth itself, and maketh it [the chicken] to leap or dance.' The mechanical principles involved were not revealed.

Rather than ruin a perfectly good chicken, the economical might prefer to baffle guests with a re-usable puzzle jug. A handsome and elaborate example was dug up in Exeter in 1899. It was made in the sophisticated potteries of Saintonge in southwest France in the late thirteenth century, and must have been imported for a very prosperous customer. Liquid poured into its mouth passes down the hollow handle, across the base, and out again through the spout. The main body of the jug is made to look like a three-storied building, its walls pierced with windows. Bishops or abbots can be glimpsed through these openings, standing just inside on the first and third floors, while from the middle one women lean out of windows to listen to fiddlers playing below. The jug is so fretted with holes that its ability to retain the contents is a baffling mystery until the inner structure is explained.

Just as mystifying to the uninitiated was the Tantalus cup. In this, by means of concealed hollows and tubes, the level of wine sinks as the drinker tilts the cup, and he is left either frustrated and dry or frustrated and soaking wet as the liquid pours out from the base all over his lap. Horace Walpole in the eighteenth century loftily dismissed such 'tricks of waterworks to wet the unwary' as both tedious and offensive, but in the medieval period they were considered to be enchantingly ingenious, and sharp eyes were always on the lookout for new examples. Villard de Honnecourt, the thirteenth-century architect who worked for the Cistercian order and traveled even as far as Hungary on its behalf, kept a notebook filled with sketches of architectural details, ornamental motifs, and oddities which had caught his attention as he moved from place to place. On one page he found space to draw his own design for a particularly infuriating cup in which, while the drinker's lips never manage to touch the wine, a bird perched at the brim seems able to sip to its heart's content.

FAST AND FEAST

Barbara Ketcham Wheaton   1983

SUBTLETIES EXPLAINED

*For an American writer about French gastronomy to have her
work translated into French and awarded a French prize is no
mean achievement. It seems safe to say that Barbara Ketcham
Wheaton is the only author to whom this has happened. The
hypothesis, or analogy, in the last paragraph of this extract
seems highly plausible to me and goes a long way to explain
phenomena which would otherwise seem just plain weird.*

The mechanics of dining were fairly simple. A typical main dish consisted of several kinds of meat tumbled together on a platter – a form of presentation later called *service en confusion*. The diner cut off slices of moderate size, taking them with thumb and two fingers, not with a greasy fist. One was not supposed to return unwanted pieces to the common dish or to dip meat directly into the salt cellar. Sauces were pungent and thick, mustards were used heavily. The diner put a spoonful of sauce on his trencher and then dabbed the meat in it. Pies were an important part of the meal, with the crust serving more as a container than as a food. As any baker of freestanding pies knows, tenderness must often be sacrificed for structural strength. For venison pies, which were expected to make repeated trips to the table over several weeks, a rye pastry was used. In serving a pie, the carver cut straight down around the top crust, just inside the pie's vertical wall. Either the entire lid was removed or sections of it were cut or broken away. The diners could then reach in with hand, spoon, or knife, depending upon the consistency of the filling. Rummaging with the hand would have helped distinguish meat from bone, which was commonly not removed from meat, poultry, or even fish. The more liquid foods, such as soups and hashes, went into the bowl to be eaten with a spoon. The sources do not tell how a pair of diners decided what to put into the bowl or how they shared it.

While the diners ate, they observed the spectacle that was performed between courses. The course was called a *met*; the activities between courses were therefore the entremets. The contemporary English term was 'soteltie.' The subjects, however, were not always subtle as when a woman in childbirth was depicted as a soteltie for a wedding. There were two basic types: the plainer was a set piece, made of anything from pastry or butter to wood and canvas; the more elaborate ones (the entremets *mouvants*) included automatons or live participants. They were amalgams of song, theater, mechanics, and carpentry, combined to convey an allegorical fantasy or even a political message. The execution of a series of entremets for important festivities occupied large numbers of people. The preparations for the entertainments at the wedding of Charles the Bold brought craftsmen to Bruges for weeks at a time – painters, sculptors, carpenters, and wax modelers by the dozens. The banquet entremets displayed the ducal wealth; their imaginativeness revealed the mentality of a culture. At the Feast of the Pheasant, for example, Philip the Fair was trying, at least ostensibly, to induce his guests to join him on a crusade to rescue Constantinople from the infidel. Assuming leadership of a crusade, traditionally the role of the Holy Roman emperor, would have enhanced Burgundy's claims to higher political status. A programmatic entremet was enacted to stimulate enthusiasm. A giant Saracen entered, leading an elephant (the chronicle unfortunately does not tell how it was contrived). Seated on the elephant was that excellent knight, co-organizer, and later chronicler of the feast, Olivier de La Marche, playing the role of the captive Eastern church. He wore a long white gown and sang, in a falsetto voice, a moving plea to Duke Philip.

The line between entremets made to be eaten and for allegorical purposes was not strictly observed. At Charles the Bold's festivities a course at one meal consisted of some thirty pies, each enclosed in a silk pavilion and each bearing the name of a walled town under Charles's rule. The visual effect was that of a military encampment; the message was clearly a statement of Charles's military strength. A more pastoral, poetic conception appeared at the last of these wedding feasts. Thirty platters were made up to look like gardens, each with a golden hedge surrounding a different kind of fruit tree; each tree bore the name of a ducal abbey. Around the trees were figures of peasants harvesting the fruit while others held baskets with candied spices and fruit for the guests to eat. Other entremets at these festivities were more fantastic: a court dwarf rode in on the back of a lion and was given to the bride, Margaret of York, to whom it sang a song and presented a daisy (in French, *marguerite*); they were followed by a dromedary ridden by Indians who released live birds to fly around the hall. There were also automatons and a whale containing musicians.

How are we to understand these festivities? Johann Huizinga, usually sensitive to the nuances of late medieval expression, wrote that it is 'difficult to regard these entertainments as something more than exhibitions of almost incredible bad taste,' and he describes the feast as a 'barbarous manifestation.' I would suggest instead that the medieval banquet be regarded as would an illuminated manuscript page of the same period. The manuscript page is composed of several elements. The written text, the content of which gives rise to the illuminations, is likely to be plain or only moderately embellished; an elaborate initial letter is followed by legible, uniform script. The framed illustration puts the significance vividly before the reader, who, in the fourteenth century, may well have given more attention to the picture than to the written word. Smaller images elsewhere on the page may represent other ideas associated more or less appropriately with the principal subject. Further fantastic ornaments and drolleries seem to reflect free – often very free – associations in the illuminator's mind.

The medieval feast contains similar components. Food is analogous to the manuscript text: eating the meal was the occasion for the events that went on around it.

As the lettering of the text was of subsidiary importance on the page to the beholder, so the dishes on the tables were only a modest part of the elaborate spectacle. The major entremets *mouvants*, such as the allegorical conquest of Jerusalem, are comparable to the formal framed scene on the vellum page. The lesser entremets – the fantastic creatures, the singing lions, the griffons spewing forth live birds – are similar to the more loosely related ornaments on the manuscript page. The plausibility of this analogy is supported by the fact that the same artists who were called upon to produce paintings and manuscripts also worked on the feasts. Among the artists who helped create the spectacles for Charles the Bold's wedding were Jacques Daret, who had been a student of Robert Campin, and Hugo van der Goes. Medieval manuscripts are a feast for the eye; medieval banquets addressed the other senses as well.

SAVORING THE PAST

Tabitha Tickletooth   *1860*

DINNERS *for* SNOBS

Tabitha Tickletooth (see page 93) here shows her claws.

'Sir, – Since sending to the *Times* my letter, of a column and a half in length, in which I laid down the true principles on which dinners should be given (or rather exchanged, for I need not say that a dinner creates a debt, due from those we invite, except where a writer, buffoon, traveller, or other attraction is introduced as part of the *menu*, and, indeed, he ought to be written down in it), I have been reminded that there are a good many persons in this country who, though neither millionaires, nor even possessing a decent income of three or four thousand a year, arrogate to themselves, in this levelling age, the right to know what they are eating and drinking, and who complain of the present system of dinner-giving. I allude to those whom, without my being unnecessarily offensive, I may call Snobs, with perhaps six, seven, or eight hundred a year. I have been asked to give, for the benefit of such persons, a few hints in the spirit of the letter which I addressed to their betters. It is, I fear, almost insulting their wretchedness to advise them on such a subject, but it is our duty to help our inferiors, and endeavour to make them feel that the state of life in which Providence has placed them, to labour, and look up to us for direction, is as comfortable as they deserve it should be.

'Of course, I do not speak to them of "dinner at 8," when, if they have worked as they ought to do, they are yawning for bed; of chairs with "spring seats and spring backs;" of "Sèvres china," "abundance of flowers," "child with *corbeille* full of grapes," "French painted moss," "a rose or bunch of violets by the napkin," "ortolans and beccaficos," or the other necessaries of civilized life. To mock the needy is the basest vulgarity. I will merely give the Snobs I have referred to a little counsel, derived from practical knowledge of their habits and wants.

'Addressing such persons, I would say, –

'You had better give no dinners at all. It is for your betters to dine; you have only to eat. Tea, at five o'clock, with plenty of muffins, Sarah Lunnes, and toast, is a more befitting repast for you to offer to your friends: and perhaps some bread and cheese, spring onions, or even a salad, afterwards, may not be regarded as extravagance. Beer is not an unwholesome drink for the inferior classes. I suppose that your females tolerate tobacco. Why not be content with the enjoyments natural to your order?

'But, if you *will* imitate your superiors, and ask persons to dinner, attend to the following hints: –

'Always invite the wives of your male friends. These women will much abridge the evening, being desirous to get home to their children (for whom, of course, they have no nursery governesses and nurses), and they will in some measure check intemperate habits.

'Give your meal at 6, as persons of your class are unaccustomed to wait so long, and will have lunched, whereby you will save.

'Make your table pretty, by all means. A plaster cast of the Emperor Napoleon, or a Church with coloured windows, for illumination, can be bought for a few pence; and will lead the conversation to politics, or to religion, and kindred subjects on which your class imagines itself to have a right to speak.

'To have a *menu* would be a mockery, but as you, as well as we, have "stupid or silent guests," let your little boys write out on copy-book paper a few maxims, and lay a copy by each person. "Gluttony leads to want," "Temperance profiteth much," "Let not your Eye be bigger than your bell-Eye," and similar morals, may do good, besides improving your brats' writing. Instead of a rose or violet, place by each male person a cold saveloy, and by each female a piece of gingerbread, to be "munched" instead of bread (as in high life) during the pauses.

'Never put tallow candles on the table. A lamp is cheap, and if the mistress of the house cleans it herself, will long keep in order.

'No soup that you can make is fit to eat. But oysters may begin your dinners as well as ours, only instead of "four or six," let each person have a couple of dozen, with roll, butter, and beer. This will materially help you with the rest of the dinner.

'There is no objection to cheap fish, and I have seen apparently good fish cried in the streets in which you reside. But a few fresh herrings, or sprats, will be the safest. Remember that fish should be eaten with the fork, even though made of steel. But albata is not dear, and looks nice, if the mistress herself rubs it with wash-leather.

'Instead of the huge, tough, gory joints in which you delight, try hashed mutton, Irish stew, or harico. Fried potatoes are a delicacy easily attainable. The mashed potato, with small sausage on the top, will wean many a husband – not from his club, for you have, happily for you, no such temptations – but from the chop-house. Marrowbones, when you wish to be particularly "genteel" (as you call it), may be introduced.

'Why have a pudding course? Ugly, sloppy, or hard, unwholesome things are your puddings. Go to a respectable grocer's, and ask him for an article called macaroni. He will tell you how to cook it. With a little grated cheese, you will find it a novel luxury. Treacle on toast will please the juveniles.

'Then your slatternly servant (by the way, insist on her washing her face, and wearing a cap – never let her come in with her bonnet on) will heave on to the groaning table a hemicycle of cheese like half a millstone. Keep this away, and have some slices handed round. Do not, from a foolish feeling of "gentility," deny yourselves onions, which you like. You will not be a bit more like us if you never touch another onion to your lives' end.

'By all means have what you consider dessert. Apples, oranges, and biscuits you have in your gallery at the theatre, why not on table? A drum of figs, covered by one of your girls with coloured paper, or stuck over with red wafers, will be a tasteful centre ornament, and to the sweet fig you may charge the bad taste of your wine. For I suppose you will give three-and-sixpence, or even four shillings, for this nastiness, though I advise (and your females prefer) brandy and water.

'I tell you frankly not to be ashamed of tobacco-pipes. We take a cigarette, and what is that but a tobacco-pipe of paper?

'Your best *chasse* is being driven up-stairs to tea. The sooner this is announced the better for the temper of your females, and for your own heads when you go to your work next morning.

'Keep your children up. If they are tired and cross, it is only once in a way. They materially help to break up a party, and my object has been to show you how, with your narrow means, you may in a humble and cheerful way, imitate your superiors, while exercising a wise economy. Let me add, never hesitate, if it be a wet night, to send your maid for cabs, instead of asking your guests to delay their departure. But give the poor girl one glass of spirits; remember what you save by dismissing your friends.

'If these hints are of any use to persons with not more than eight hundred a year, I shall have done my duty to the poor, and remain,

Your obedient servant,

Berkeley-street.

G.H.M.

THE DINNER QUESTION

F. Marian McNeill   1929

HEBRIDEAN HOSPITALITY

Marian McNeill devotes a whole chapter in her classic work
The Scots Kitchen *to memorable descriptions of meals in the
past. Here is the experience which befell Alexander
Carmichael in the Outer Hebrides, when he was gathering
material for a book. Simple hospitality at its best, with a
biblical aura to the description.*

Alexander Carmichael describes an experience when collecting material for his *Carmina Gadelica* (published in 1900) in the Outer Hebrides:

'The house was clean and comfortable, if plain and unpretending, most things in it being home made. There were three girls in the house, young, comely, and shy, and four women, middle-aged, handsome, and picturesque in their home spun gowns and high-crowned mutches. Three of the women had been to the moorland pastures with their cattle, and had turned in here to rest on their way home.

' "Hail to the house and household," said I, greeting the inmates in the salutation of our fathers. "Hail to you, kindly stranger," replied the housewife. "Come forward and take this seat. If it be not ill-mannered, may we ask whence you have come to-day? ... May the Possessor keep you in his own keeping, good man! You have left early and travelled far, and must be hungry." With this the woman raised her eyes towards her daughters standing demurely silent, and motionless as Greeks statues, in the background. In a moment the three fair girls became active and animated. One ran to the stack and brought in an armful of hard black peats, another ran to the well and brought in a pail of clear spring water, while the third quickly spread a cloth, white as snow, upon the table in the inner room. The three neighbour women rose to leave, and I rose to do the same. "Where are you going, good man?" asked the housewife in injured surprise, moving between me and the door. "You must not go till you eat a bit and drink a sip. That indeed would be a reproach to us that we would not soon get over. ... Food will be ready presently, and in the meantime you will bathe your feet and dry your stockings which are wet after coming through the marshes of the moorland." Then the woman went down upon her knees and washed and dried the feet of the stranger as tenderly as a mother would those of her child. ...

'In an incredibly short time I was asked to go "ben" and break bread. ... The table was laden with wholesome food sufficient for several persons. There were fried herrings and boiled turbot fresh from the sea, and eggs fresh from the yard. There were fresh butter and salt butter, wheaten scones, barley bannocks, and oat-cakes, with excellent tea and cream. The woman apologized that so had no "aran coinnich" – moss bread, that is loaf bread – and no biscuits, they being simple crofter folk far from the big town.

' "This," said I, taking my seat, "looks like the table for a 'reiteach' (betrothal), rather than for one man." '

Burns, who made a tour of the Highlands in 1787, leaves an enduring tribute to the virtue of hospitality in the race to which he was bound by blood and sentiment:

> When death's dark stream I'll ferry o'er –
> A time that surely shall come –
> In heaven itself I'll ask no more
> Than just a Highland welcome.

THE SCOTS KITCHEN

Elizabeth Robins Pennell   *1923*

An AUTUMN DINNER

*Mrs Pennell was a great collector of old cookery books and her book about her own collection (*My Cookery Books, *1903) is itself a collector's item. She also wrote about cooking, in a florid Edwardian style. It is agreeable to taste this, although more than the measured dose here would become soporific.*

Why sigh if summer be done, and already grey skies, like a pall, hang over fog-choked London town? The sun may shine, wild winds may blow, but every evening brings with it the happy dinner hour. With the autumn days foolish men play at being pessimists, and talk in platitudes of the cruel fall of the leaf and death of love. And what matter? May they not still eat and drink? May they not still know that most supreme of all joys, the perfect dish perfectly served? Small indeed is the evil of a broken heart compared to a coarsened palate or disordered digestion.

'Therefore have we cause to be merry! – and to cast away all care.' Autumn has less to distract from the pleasure that never fails. The glare of foolish sunlight no longer lures to outdoor debauches, the soft breath of the south wind no longer breathes hope of happiness in Arcadian simplicity. We can sit in peace by our fireside, and dream dreams of a long succession of triumphant menus. The touch of frost in the air is as a spur to the artist's invention; it quickens ambition, and stirs to loftier aspiration. The summer languor is dissipated, and with the re-birth of activity is reawakened desire for the delicious, the piquante, the fantastic.

Let an autumn dinner then be created! dainty, as all art must be, with that elegance and distinction and individuality without which the masterpiece is not. Strike the personal note; forswear commonplace.

The glorious, unexpected overture shall be *soupe aux moules*. For this great advantage it can boast: it holds the attention not only in the short – all too short – moment of eating, but from early in the morning of the eventful day; nor does it allow itself to be forgotten as the eager hours race on. At eleven – and the heart leaps for delight as the clock strikes – the *pot-au-feu* is placed upon the fire; at four, tomatoes and onions – the onions white as the driven snow – communing in all good fellowship in a worthy saucepan follow; and at five, after an hour's boiling, they are strained through a sieve, peppered, salted, and seasoned. And now is the time for the mussels, swimming in a sauce made of a bottle of white wine, a *bouquet-garni*, carrots, excellent vinegar, and a glass of ordinary red wine, to be offered up in their turn, and some thirty minutes will suffice for the ceremony. At this critical point, *bouillon*, tomatoes, and mussels meet in a proper pot well rubbed with garlic, and an ardent quarter of an hour will consummate the union. As you eat, something of the ardour becomes yours, and in an ecstasy the dinner begins.

Sad indeed would it prove were imagination exhausted with so promising a prelude. Each succeeding course must lead to new ecstasy, else will the dinner turn out the worst of failures. In *turbot au gratin*, the ecstatic possibilities are by no means limited. In a chaste silver dish, make a pretty wall of potatoes, which have been beaten to flour, enlivened with pepper and salt, enriched with butter and cream – cream thick and fresh and altogether adorable – seasoned with Parmesan cheese, and left on the stove for ten minutes, neither more nor less; let the wall enclose layers of turbot, already cooked and in pieces, of melted butter and of cream, with a fair covering of bread crumbs; and rely upon a quick oven to complete the masterpiece.

After so pretty a conceit, where would be the poetry in heavy joints or solid meats? *Ris de veau aux truffes* surely would be more in sympathy; the sweetbreads baked and browned very tenderly, the sauce fashioned of truffles duly sliced, Marsala, lemon juice, salt and *paprika*, with a fair foundation of benevolent *bouillon*. And with so exquisite a dish no disturbing vegetable should be served.

And after? If you still hanker for the roast beef and horse-radish of Old England, then go and gorge yourself at the first convenient restaurant. Would you interrupt a symphony that the orchestra might play 'God save the Queen'? Would you set the chorus in 'Atalanta in Calydon' to singing odes by Mr Alfred Austin? There is a place for all things, and the place for roast beef is not on the ecstatic menu. Grouse, rather, would meet the diner's mood – grouse with memories of the broad moor and purple heather. Roast them at a clear fire, basting them with maternal care. Remember that they, as well as pheasants and partridges, should 'have gravy in the dish and bread-sauce in a cup.' Their true affinity is less the vegetable, however artistically prepared, than the salad, serenely simple, that discord may not be risked. Not this the time for the bewildering *macédoine*, or the brilliant tomato. Choose, instead, lettuce; crisp cool *romaine* by choice. Sober restraint should dignify the dressing; a suspicion of chives may be allowed; a sprinkling of well-chopped tarragon leaves is indispensable.

It is autumn, the mood is fantastic: a sweet, if it tend not to the vulgarity of heavy puddings and stodgy pies, will introduce an amusing, a sprightly element. *Omelette soufflée* claims the privilege. But it must be light as air, all but ethereal in substance, a mere nothing to melt in the mouth like a beautiful dream. And yet in melting it must yield a flavour as soft as the fragrance of flowers, and as evanescent. The sensation must be but a passing one that piques the curiosity and soothes the excited palate. A dash of orange-flower water, redolent of the graceful days that are no more, another of wine from Andalusian vineyards, and the sensation may be secured.

By the law of contrasts the vague must give way to the decided. The stirring, glorious climax after the brief, gentle interlude, will be had in *canapé d'olives farcies*, the olives stuffed with anchovies and capers, deluged with cayenne, prone on their beds of toast and girded about with astonished watercress.

Fruit will seem a graceful afterthought; pears all golden, save where the sun, a passionate lover, with his kisses set them to blushing a rosy red; grapes, purple and white and voluptuous; figs, overflowing with the exotic sweetness of their far southern home; peaches, tender and juicy and desirable. To eat is to eschew all prose, to spread the wings of the soul in glad poetic flight. What matter, indeed, if the curtains shut out stormy night or monstrous fog?

A GUIDE FOR THE GREEDY BY A GREEDY WOMAN

Anonymous   *1726*
James Boswell   *1786*

THOUGHTS *on* DUMPLINGS *and* PUDDINGS

The Dissertation on Dumplings *is witty and ingenious;
perhaps the most amusing contribution from the 18th century
to culinary literature.
Dr Johnson's observations on puddings, as recorded by
Boswell, are an object lesson in organised thought and clear
expression. Johnson's reputation among food historians suffers
from his having ignorantly stated that Hannah Glasse's
famous cookery book was written by a man, an error made
worse by his male-chauvinist and incorrect observation that
only men could write good cookery books. But this passage is
on the credit side.*

216

The Head of Man is like a Pudding; and whence have all Rhymes, Poems, Plots, and Inventions sprang – but from that same Pudding? What is Poetry but a Pudding of Words?

The Physicians, though they cry out so much against Cooks and Cookery, yet are but Cooks themselves; with this difference only – the Cook's pudding lengthens life – the Physician's shortens it: so that we live and die by pudding – For what is a Clyster but a Bag Pudding – a Pill but a Dumpling – or a Bolus but a Tansy, though not altogether so toothsome. In a word, Physic is only a Puddingizing, or Cookery of Drugs: – the law is but a Cookery of Quibbles.

The Universe itself is but a Pudding of Elements, – Empires, Kingdoms, States, and Republics, are but Puddings of People differently mixed up.

The Celestial and Terrestial Orbs are deciphered to us by a pair of Globes, or Mathematical Puddings.

The success of War, and the fate of Monarchies, are entirely dependent on Puddings and Dumplings – for what else are Cannonballs but Military Puddings, or Bullets but Dumplings – only with this difference, they do not sit so well on the stomach as a good Marrow Pudding or Bread Pudding. In short, there is nothing valuable in Nature but what more or less has an allusion to Pudding or Dumpling.

A Learned Dissertation on Dumplings

Let us seriously reflect what a pudding is composed of. It is composed of flour, that once waved in the golden grain, and drank the dews of the morning; of milk, pressed from the swelling udder by the gentle hand of the beauteous milk-maid, whose beauty and innocence might have recommended a worse draught; who, while she stroked the udder, indulged in no ambitious thoughts of wandering in palaces, formed no plans for the destruction of her fellow-creatures – milk that is drawn from the cow, that useful animal that eats the grass of the field, and supplies us with that which made the greatest part of the food of mankind in the age which the poets have agreed to call golden. It is made with an egg, that miracle of nature, which the theoretical Burnet has compared to Creation. An egg contains water within its beautiful smooth surface; and an unformed mass, by the incubation of the parent, becomes a regular animal, furnished with bones and sinews, and covered with feathers. Let us consider – Can there be more wanting to complete the Meditation on a Pudding? If more be wanting more can be found – It contains salt, which keeps the sea from putrefaction – salt, which is made the image of intellectual excellence, contributes to the formation of a Pudding.

Journal of a Tour to the Hebrides with Dr Johnson

Theodore Child   *1890*
George Augustus Sala   *1895*
Henry Sidgwick   *1877*

THOUGHTS *on* SOUP: *on* SAVOURIES: *and on* DESSERT

*Towards the end of the 19th century and early in the present
one, a few American writers cautiously experimented with
gastronomic philosophising. Theodore Child was one such.
Here he addresses his powers of logical analysis to a problem
which must have bothered – and may still bother – other
people besides himself. On the other side of the Atlantic,
George Augustus Sala and Bentham (via Sidgwick) were
ruminating on the other end of dinner.*

Soup is really good only when it is eaten *hot*. Its warmth is an essential part of its excellence, and prepares the stomach for the important functions of the digestion of the succeeding and more substantial courses.

The soup-plates should be hot, and the soup-tureen should be heated before the soup is poured into it. At a truly scientific table the spoons and ladles ought to be heated.

Now, let us suppose a dinner of nine persons. If the host or hostess serves the soup, the last guest served will begin to use his spoon when the first served has finished, unless, out of politeness, all wait until the last is served, and then attack all together. If the soup is served from the side, and one or two servants pass the plates, the result will be the same. In both cases, during the time required to fill nine plates and pass them, there will be a loss of heat, and the beginning of the dinner will be wanting in unison. The best way is to serve the soup in hot plates immediately before the dinner is announced. Then the guests enter the dining-room, take their seats, and begin to dine all at the same time and in perfect unison.

DELICATE FEASTING

I venture to think that there is a mild kind of madness prevailing among people who like nice dinners touching savouries, and especially in connection with the stage of the repast at which the zests in question should be served. Over and over again have I said in print that when you have consumed a well-cooked dinner, and have passed gently and satisfactorily from the soup to the fish, thence to an entrée, thence to a joint of some game, thence to a special dish of vegetables, and finally to the sweets, it is in a sense monstrous to indulge in a savoury, the very taste of which must necessarily spoil your appetite for dessert. How on earth can you enjoy the exquisite flavour of peaches and grapes and pine-apples, or good sound British apples, when your tongue has only a minute or two previously been excited by cayenne pepper or curry powder, or some other condiment used in confecting these confounded savouries? Why do you eat them? Our fathers used to devour devilled toast and pick the burnt flesh from devilled bones after dinner and while they were drinking their wine, and they did so in order to provoke an artificial thirst which would stimulate them to drink more wine. But delicate ladies and moderately drinking gentlemen, who have not the slightest desire to swill wine after dessert, have surely no need of savouries at the end of dinner.

I know perfectly well, however, that when a lady has made up her mind to anything, that thing has got to be done; and so I have carefully selected some recipes for savouries. To discover them in the best sources of culinary information has been no easy task. They are almost entirely ignored by such illustrious masters of the gastronomic art as Ude and Carême. Even in a work so modern as Kettner's 'Book of the Table,' the late Mr. Dallas observes, on the subject of *hors d'oeuvres* or savouries, 'There was a time when these little articles demanded a good deal of attention, but they are now of the smallest account, and are little more than the trifles – prawns, olives, radishes, anchovies – which keep the customer occupied at the restaurant while the dinner he has ordered is getting ready.' Kettner's 'Book of the Table' was published about twenty years ago, but the fashion in savouries has changed in a most capricious manner since Mr. Dallas's time. If you dine at a grand hotel, say at the Albemarle, the Berkeley, or the Royal Palace Hotel, Kensington, your relishes – anchovies, radishes, olives, Italian salads, and what not – will be served as a prelude to your dinner; but at dinners in private life, the, to me, objectionable savoury comes between the sweet and dessert. In the name of common sense, why? When I have friends to dinner I feel compelled to submit myself to this silly fashion, simply because it is my endeavour to study other people's tastes rather than my own, and I shrink from laying down laws which I am well aware would be only reluctantly obeyed, if they were obeyed at all.

THE THOROUGH GOOD COOK

Bentham was strictly temperate in his diet: he ate meat but once a day, and then very moderately, and was almost a teetotaler. But the pleasures of the table were too important to be diminished by a stupid adherence to custom; and being particularly fond of fruit, he used often to maximise his prandial happiness by commencing with the dessert, before the sensibility of his palate had been impaired by coarser viands.

'Bentham and Benthamism in Politics and Ethics'
FORTNIGHTLY REVIEW, *May 1877*

George Lang   1971

An Ox Feast in Hungary

See page 197 for George Lang. Here he is quoting from a
historical novel by Lajos Zilahy, based on a 16th-century
manuscript.

Master Kigyó appeared, a short little wrinkled-faced man, so small that one wondered how he managed to contain so much knowledge. Brandishing his cherrywood stick, he issued hoarse commands from beneath his gray walrus mustache. He supervised every step in person, tested everything. He took the knives in hand, the platters, the spits, the crosspoles, and the pokers, even tasting the cakes of lard and the salt. He dismissed each item to its task with a cry of 'Good enough – let 'er go!' First he skinned the ox, after explaining that the head and the hoofs must be left in place. He slit the throat to make room for the spit, which was as thick as a telegraph pole and would come out at the tail after passing under the backbone. He cut a hole into the stomach of the ox, just large enough to receive a calf, which would replace the tripe, the stomach, and the lungs. But the kidneys were left inside. When all this was done they produced a quail larded with bacon. Master Kigyó took it in his hand and looked it over.

'Did you salt it on the inside too, Julie?' 'Salt it, love – of course I did! Don't ask so many questions!' 'Good enough – let 'er go!' and Master Kigyó handed the quail to one of the assistant butchers.

They placed the quail inside a plucked capon. Good enough – let 'er go! They put the capon in the stomach of a lamb, and the lamb was nestled inside the calf. Good enough – let 'er go! Now the calf was crammed into the stomach of the ox. The poor ox had never imagined it would sometime be so pregnant.

They drove the tremendous spit through the flayed beast. And now came the most difficult part. Kontyos, the estate blacksmith, came forward with five-foot-long iron spikes under the arm. They drove these through the backbone of the ox so that they penetrated the spit and came out of the belly. It was hard work that took expert skill. It was even harder to nail the legs of the ox to its shoulder blades so it would seem to be in a reclining position – for the ox would have to be served, in its entirety, from the center of the table. Finally it was secured. Twenty strong men were needed to lift the spitted ox onto the crosspoles. There a mechanism similar to that of a grindstone would turn the beast. Of course Csengös, the estate cartwright, had fashioned a wheel for the tail end of the spit, which was long enough so that the men turning the spit would be out of range of the blazing heat. They tried the wheel, and found it worked splendidly. Good enough – let 'er go! The two-thousand-pound ox began to turn.

'All right! Light the fire! Let's move! No loitering!' But Master Kigyó did not use the ai or i sounds. What he said was, 'oll rot! Lot the far!' But first the wood had to be stacked, and that took considerable finesse. The logs were placed on both sides of the crosspoles, none of them longer than the ox itself, and far enough from the meat so that it would be enveloped in heat but not touched by the flame. If only there be no wind! For if a breeze should strike up the whole arrangement would have to be moved to face it, and the whole business started from the beginning again. The horns and hoofs of the ox were wrapped in wet rags, lest they catch fire in the course of roasting. Just let the horn take fire, and then watch everyone run from the smell!

The women were melting the lard and boiling the salt in a large kettle. This mixture would be poured over the roasting ox. They were already tieing saucepans to the ends of brooms handles.

'Good enough! Let 'er go!'

They lit the bonfire. The sparks began to crackle, the dry oak logs popped angrily, and the smoke whirled skyward just as it had done once upon a time in Asia, in the ancestral home. Slowly the ox began to revolve to the tune of *Ladi-ladi-lom*, [popular song] for the arms of the turners unwittingly took on the rhythm of the music.

'Tha ox' had been revolving over a tremendous heat for nearly four hours. Now it slowly came to a standstill. János Kigyó doffed his hat and clicked his heels together before Count Dupi. 'Beg to report to His Excellency the Count – tha ox us done!'

They put the fire out on both sides, and removed the kettles as well to make room for the carvers. From the horns and hoofs they removed the steaming wet rags that had been periodically dampened during the roasting. Master Lusztig, the estate painter, stood with his brush and cup in hand, ready to spread gold paint on the hoofs and horns. When this was done, Master Kigyó personally tied the Dukay [the landlord of the estate] seal, with its eleven-pointed coronet, between the two horns. 'Good enough – let 'er go!'

Five wagon shafts were poked under the ox, and ten strong-fisted men lifted the enormous roast from the crosspoles. They put it on a wide table that Master Berecki, the estate carpenter, had made for this very purpose. The ox lay quietly on the table, its legs drawn under, like any ox when it settled down to rest, with the difference that this one had settled down to roast. And how it had been roasted! Its crackling exterior was iridescent with the most beautiful hues of rose-red and deep brown, for it had been continuously drenched with fat while it was cooking. There lay a ton of ox, with the Dukay seal on its forehead between the tremendous forked, golden horns, in Renaissance splendor.

'Bring the knives!' commanded Master Kigyó. And the women brought their clothesbaskets full of kitchen knives. Now came the final embellishment: hundreds upon hundreds of knives were driven into the ox. The multitude of black knife-handles made the ox look like a quilled beast of prehistory. János Kigyó offered Count Dupi a long knife, and when he saw the Count eye the ox indecisively, he whispered into his ear: 'From tha brosket, your Lordship, from tha brosket. Thot's the best!'

THE CUISINE OF HUNGARY

Elizabeth Mary Wright   1932

A BOARDING HOUSE MEAL

Thomas Wright was the editor of the great English Dialect
Dictionary. *This vignette by his daughter nicely reflects the
discontinuity of conversation at such an occasion.*

We had a new and amusing experience on the way to Minehead when we spent a few
days at Weston-super-Mare to see two aged maiden aunts of mine. They could
not take us into their house, and Weston was very full of visitors, so we contented
ourselves with a boarding-house. It was before the rationing system was established, for
though the food was extremely plain, it was abundant. The butter came to the table in
pound pats, and the elderly helpers who brought in the dinner almost staggered under
the weight of the vast fruit-pies in enamel pie-dishes. We all sat together round one big
dining-table. If any one was late for breakfast the hostess had already poured out his or
her cup of tea, and it was getting cold. We were a queer assortment of folk. There was
the High Church curate from London, who was addressed as 'Father'; the gloomy
Belgian refugee priest; the English clergyman with the stout wife who was discussed by
the others in whispers, they were sure she was 'a German', it was no good her saying she
was 'Dutch'; her daughter and her step-daughter; and the lady of a certain age with an
auburn wig. The last-named guest was always trying to drag up the level of conversation
at meals. She had a friend called 'George' whom she quoted continually to show the
kind of society in which she was accustomed to move. He was not a part of speech like
Sairey Gamp's 'Mrs. Harris', for I actually saw him once, walking out with the lady.
They had been one afternoon to see the caves at Cheddar. This gave a fine opening: 'My
friend George – he was nineteenth wrangler at Cambridge -- says that it takes a thousand
years for a stalactite to grow one inch.' 'Umph!' murmured the Belgian refugee, being
the speaker's nearest neighbour, and feeling some response was due from him. 'Maria',
said the German lady to her step-daughter, 'have you got your cheese?' and then to the
waiting-maid: 'Bring Miss Maria some cheese. She never eats meat.' 'Most vegetarians
are cranks, and they are always rather scraggy, aren't they?' observed Joseph Wright,
genially inattentive, and quite unaware that the lady next him was just such as he
described. 'You are eating nothing, Father!' This in a tone of anxiety from our hostess.
'Fact is,' replied the curate, 'I ate too many jam-tarts at the picnic this afternoon' – this
with as near an approach to a wink as befitted his cloth, directed towards the only young
lady member of the party. Joseph Wright liked to get his money's worth, but he never
liked to feel he was getting more than that. Before we left the boarding-house he said to
the proprietress: 'You feed us too well Mrs. —, you can't make it pay at the price.' 'Oh,
but, Professor', she replied, 'I *do* like to see people eat. If I could do just what I should
like, I should keep a Zoo.'   THE LIFE OF JOSEPH WRIGHT *vol. 2*

Barbara Santich   *1984*

FOOD *from* PIERROTS

The banquet which was the climax of the First Symposium on
Australian Gastronomy was an astonishing affair. I was the
solitary English guest and had planned to write a description
of it. However, as I drove Barbara Santich home afterwards I
realised that her reactions were superior – more structured and
with a greater sense of history – so kept my own disordered
thoughts to myself.

It is deep night as we arrive; the blackness is pierced here and there by the brilliant white of floodlights. The house is sealed and curtained; no noise escapes, there is no whisper of behind-the-scenes activity. Suddenly out of the darkness appears a white-faced Pierrot, leaping Nijinsky-like through the garden. He bows low, gestures to us to approach the main door, and then dissolves again into the darkness.

Entering the bright and animated scene of the foyer, already crowded, we experience momentary difficulties of recognition; citizens of the day have been changed into children of the night by gay and fanciful dress. Softly, intermittently, music wafts down from a quintet of Pierrots on the landing and evaporates into the atmosphere.

More black-and-white-costumed Pierrots offer apéritifs of pale dry sherry or pink sparkling burgundy, which is more popular and better expresses the mood of the guests, as excited as children before a birthday party. The dinner is late, and this unprogrammed delay intensifies the anticipation and suspense. Not even the organizers of the Symposium know what form this banquet will take; total control of the production has been handed over to Phillip Searle, former artist, now restaurateur and chef. All of us have a copy of the menu, but in this context its words cannot convey the total spectacle; our conditioned responses to the menu descriptions are far removed from the actuality we will soon experience.

Then, unexpectedly, another Pierrot bounds on to the stairs, the music and the crowd hush as he announces: 'Cooks, food philosophers, nutritionists, passionate amateurs, dinner is served!' Single file, we enter what was once the ballroom, now practically devoid of decor – simply blank walls, dim and muted lighting. Within the frame of the room, and in the form of a long rectangle with one open side, are white-covered tables, interrupted at pre-determined intervals by a square of black, the whole lavishly strewn with multicolored rose petals and roses. Nothing else on the tables, save the white napkin squares at each place – no intimation that a banquet is to take place. But from the doorway, our eyes light on the first item of the menu, displayed on one of the black squares: Jellied Seascape.

It is so realistic that no one is sure it is meant to be eaten – perhaps we are to be treated to something like a truite au bleu? We gaze at this large glass aquarium, murkily translucent, where seaweeds and sea creatures co-exist. On one wall a delicately delineated sea plant seems to move to its own mysterious rhythm, on another we notice the sinister suckers of an octopus groping towards the surface flotsam. One can admire it all, in a detached way, but the palate is wary of savouring nature undisguised.

We are directed toward the chairs and, once seated and at ease, we whisper with our neighbors, marvelling at the originality of the seascape, theorizing on the practical aspects of its creation, wondering what act will follow. We watch entranced as a sequence of mute Pierrots lay knives and forks, arrange glasses, pour wine: and we begin to realize that this evening we are captive, dependent on these pantomime characters for all our needs in food and drink.

From the ballroom alcove the musicians continue, their flute-like sounds evocative of medieval instruments. Along and across tables conversations continue until, abruptly, order is imposed by the soft beat of drums announcing the arrival of the dishes of the first service. Five of them – the Jellied Seascape is already in place – are paraded up and down between the two rows of diners, receiving spontaneous applause and exciting appetites. The platters are set down on the black squares and some of us, unable to restrain our curiosity, leave our places to take a closer view – of the steaming silver cauldron of consommé, in which float tiny wonton; of the large silver salver on which individual molds of lambs' brains are arranged, each enrobed in transparently thin slivers of zucchini, flanked by a little pile of delicate slices of tongue; of another huge tray, unadorned save for the solid, glistening block of truffle-coated liverwurst, across which is nonchalantly draped a pale and fleshy sausage of the same mixture.

We are offered servings from the dish nearest to hand, and for a while we are oblivious to any sensation but that of the food on our palates. Delicious, seductively delicious: the meltingly soft textures of the brains and tongues, the gingery sweetness of their sauce, the rich decadence of the liverwurst. After a temporary disappearance, the Pierrots return to the inner rectangle to re-parade the dishes and, as in a game of musical chairs, set them down in new places. The Jellied Seascape is broached and ladled into bowls; disappointingly, it is a textureless, semi-solid mass studded with pieces of scallop, its flavor interesting but bland after the vigor of the preceding dishes.

Now it is the interval. Plates are cleared from tables, wines poured. Some guests circulate, here pausing to comment, there appropriating a vacant chair to discuss, in hushed voices, the performance so far. Once more the musicians are heard, softly; they had been almost forgotten during the excitement of eating.

Again, there is a muffled roll of drums. Chairs are hurriedly occupied and the parade of the second service begins. Carried high aloft comes the platter of sliced roast suckling pig, crowned by the grinning head; then a snapper, poached in rice wine. Two Pierrots invite us to peer into a brown-glazed lattice basket, woven from strands of bread dough, in which lie pieces of goose and venison. Another platter passes, bearing the Mount of Pigeons, crisp and dark-skinned, supporting and supported by each other like a pyramid of circus acrobats. We applaud in admiration of these, and of the final platter, the magician's trick of quails cooked in bladders – little balloons that hold juices and aroma captive.

Less distanced now, the Pierrots are almost participating in our banquet. One Pierrot, inexpertly slitting open a bladder to remove a tiny bird, finds voice to comment. Others ask us, at the second tour of the dishes, whether we would like a piece of goose or venison, a serving of snapper. We in our turn, finding them less formidable, make so bold as to request a spoon of sauce, a slice of suckling pig. . . .

Indeed, the banquet structure is so far eroded that dessert seems to arrive unheralded, and is borne in by a Pierrot assisted by an ordinary mortal. It is a guest who comes to the rescue as the red-and-white carnival cone of ice cream starts to slide off its base. On another tray is a rough-and-tumble pile of fresh raspberries, encircled by tall cigarettes-russes cones, while a large slab of glass supports the mirror-surfaced expanse of blackberry trifle. There is no formality with dessert; it is each to his own now. One of the guests locates the coffee machine and starts coffee; another opens and offers an ice cold Tokay.

Slowly, the evening winds down. Addresses are exchanged, farewells kissed. The ballroom is in disorder, with chairs scattered, dishes piled up for washing, dessert leftovers here and there, an almost untouched plate of chocolates and nougat amongst unfinished cups of coffee. The performance over, cooks and Pierrots discard their roles and gather in a small corner for their own backstage party.

Reluctantly, we depart and promise to meet tomorrow, to exchange impressions of this fabulous feast, to relive our experiences, repeat our enjoyment. And we go our separate ways.

JOURNAL OF GASTRONOMY, *vol 1, summer 1984*

Jill Tilsley Benham   1987

TWO ARAB FEASTS

There is a long tradition of intrepid Englishwomen travelling
alone in the Arab world. No doubt everything is easier now,
but Jill Benham's culinary quests seem to me to be in the spirit
of this tradition.

Despite the soaring skyscrapers glittering with bronze and gold reflective glass, the Bougainvillia-bordered motorways, and cool green gardens jewelled with Indian roller birds, it is never easy to escape the desert in Arabia.

But then, no Arab wishes to. Those grains of sand which nestle in the velvet curtains of his air-conditioned limousine, and add an extra crunch to cardamom-scented sweetmeats, evoke pure nostalgia in his breast. Every weekend, tents spring up like mushrooms among the rolling dunes and *wadis*. Camp fires, crackling with acacia, provide an endless stream of black and bitter *qahwa* – a Bedouin coffee that make the Turkish type seem hopelessly effete – together with smoking heaps of *kufta kebabs*, and huge silvery pans of *marag lahem*; a thin but highly aromatic stew which, by tradition, must be large enough to feed friends and neighbours too.

Indeed this Eastern spirit of hospitality is all-pervasive. But today the Arab is far more likely to take you to a restaurant than invite you to picinic *en famille*, so visitors who fancy lolling on embroidered cushions, and sipping sherbets beneath a starlit sky must needs rely upon imaginative hotels.

The Inter-Continental in Al Ain, for instance, holds a regular desert feast in pukka Wilfred Thesiger country, just a short, if bumpy, mini-coach drive away. Like children let loose upon the first beach of summer, staid businessmen soon abandon shoes and socks, and push on through sand so warm and silky that they grunt with pleasure as it slides between their toes.

Leaving a posse of experts to set up an immaculate camp-kitchen, we clamber up a modest hill to watch the setting sun, and examine a tomb dug 3,000 years, or more, before Muhammed himself was born.

Nostrils begin to twitch. The evening breeze, slightly chill by now, is pungent with the heady scents of charcoal and roast lamb. We turn and rapidly descend towards a vast white tent, gorgeously furnished with azure-blue and orange patterned rugs, plump pillows worked with scarlet and with cornflour-coloured threads – and a display of food that would have tempted the Caliphal appetite of Haroun al-Rasheed himself.

For this is no simple Bedouin meal, no 'mutton grab' of rice and meat, but a feast of Levantine sophistication. Gulf Arabs today fairly dote upon the cuisines of Lebanon and Syria, with their Ottoman-Turkish overtones, and must have their *mezzeh* come what may.

An *hors d'ouevre par excellence*, the *mezzeh* on this enchanted night consists of vine-leaves, voluptuously stuffed with rice and spice, and the emerald-bright parsley and cracked wheat salad called *tabbouleh*. Deep fried florets of cauliflower too, (once bitten, always remembered), together with *hummous* and *muttābel*; sesame-rich purees of chick peas and smoky aubergine.

And then there are *sanbusak*; flute-edged half-moon pastries from the golden kitchens of Abbāsid kings. And salads of lambs' tongues, and *loubia bil zeyt*; green beans cooked and cooled in a garlic-charged olive oil.

Issuing, like naughty *ifrits*, through the flame and star filled opening of our tent, dark-eyed youths wield *kebabs* of every kind and colour. Skewered lamb, and chicken *tikka*, (marinaded to a hectic pink), sumptuous chunks of *hammour*, the king of Arabian fish, and shrimps of a size to make a lobster blush still more. Steak, too, and rice, white and saffron-yellow, from great chafing pans of softly burnished copper.

We begin to cast lascivious glances at baskets full of fruit. More refreshing these than the old-fashioned Arabic desserts. Those pyramids of *awaamat*; deep fried puff-balls soaked in sugar syrup, are notoriously sweet, as are those saccharin fritters, *balah el-Sham*, the 'dates of Syria'.

But, programmed automatically, the roundest member of our party pops one in his mouth – and the look of perfect peace which transforms his podgy face seduces everyone.

Even so, we seem to be committing no serious dietary sin, for they are admirably light on sugar after all. Crunching and munching in near guiltless bliss, we sing loud the praises of Muhammed Murphy, the hotel's executive chef. Having wooed and won a Lebanese wife, this amazing Irishman also embraced the Muslim faith. Yet culinary custom dies hard, and he cannot subscribe to his namesake's dictum that 'the love of sweetmeats proceeds from the Faith'. Too much sugar is too much sugar thinks Muhammed Murphy, and we all agree, and can't stop eating, and debate what improvements an Arab might make if let loose in a Catholic kitchen.

Another saying, not of the Prophet's, but one with which we would have certainly agreed, is that 'eating with a knife and fork is like making love through an interpreter'. Cutlery was, in fact, provided, but few of us bothered to use it and no one mourned its total absence from the next feast I attended – the Muscat Inter-Continental's traditional 'Omani Night'.

This had begun, for me, on the hotel beach a night ahead, when I watched a jointed goat, ensconced in aromatic paste and green banana leaves, being lowered into a sand oven. The next evening, suitably attired in flowing cotton *kaftan*, (my usual dressing gown), I walked straight from the 20th century into the days of Ali Baba and Princess Shahrazad.

Stentorian music shocked my ears. Men with drums and pipes of the type which once put Crusaders into panic flight, rose like phantoms from the dusk. They danced, arms unmoving, faces straight, in shimmering moon-illumined robes, (*dish-dashas* in vulgar parlance, *thobes* to the precise), brilliant turbans like a flock of parrots, clinging gamely to their heads.

Having rinsed my hands in perfumed water, (fingers being the only cutlery allowed), I wander through palm trees sparkling with little lights, and join a group already squatting round a cotton-covered palm leaf mat. Appetites sharpened by night air, we bribe complaining stomachs with buxom toffee-tasting dates, and listen, when the entertainers tire, to the whispering Arabian Sea.

Suddenly, an Olympian platter descends into our midst. It exhales ambrosia. So, this is *shuwa*, the Omani national dish of roasted goat and rice! We dip in, tentatively. We dig deeper, greedily. Conversation ceases. Our chins begin to gleam with grease. Indian boys appear with fresh green salads; we ignore them. We want goat, nothing but goat. Why haven't we tasted meat like this before? Jaws move rhythmically, urgently.

We begin to eye our neighbours with suspicion – are they faster eaters? Will there be enough? Should we discreetly hide a luscious lump or two, (or three), beneath some rice? We do, and taste the rice. Heavens above! Its almost better than the goat!

Impregnated with a sauce Escoffier might have envied, the portly grains explode with myraid flavours – dainty cardamom and clove, cassia and coriander, braving the urgent onslaughts of garlic and volcanic chilli pepper. Cashew-and-sultana sweet, tamarind-and-lemon sour, *shuwa*, we finally agree (all friends again), must surely be the finest dish in all Arabia.

'But have you not tried *quoozi*, made with a fat-tailed sheep?'

We turn, wolf-eager, to the lovely girl who is offering seeds of cardamom to sweeten our collective breath.

She smiles. 'They say that sometimes there is a feast of *quoozi* at ... but that's another tale.' And turning swiftly on a rosy henna'd heel, she fades into the shadows.

The big man on my left hitches his dropped jaw and sets it to work on the saffron *halva*.

'Talk about The Arabian Nights – I think we've just met Princess Shahrazad!'

He laughs uneasily, only half believing he has made a joke. 'Now, where's that dish of cardamom she brought?'

How very strange – it too has disappeared.

A TALE OF TWO FEASTS
[*forthcoming essay*]

Anonymous   *12th century*

The VISION *of* MACCONGLINNE

The land of Cockayne (where food abounds and luxury and idleness reign) is a familiar image, if only because of Breughel's well known painting. It has its parallels elsewhere, including Ireland. 'The Vision of MacConglinne', which is thought to date back to the end of the 12th century, is a weird tale in which widely disparate elements seem to have been conjoined. MacConglinne, a vagrant scholar (or gleeman?) and a man greedy for food, turns up in Cork, where he is bound to a pillar and tormented by having foods passed under his nose and consumed under his eyes, while being starved himself. The first night an angel came to comfort him, and on the following day he recounted this vision which the angel had manifested to him.

A vision that appeared to me,
An apparition wonderful
    I tell to all:
A lardy coracle all of lard
Within a port of New-milk Loch,
    Up on the World's smooth sea.

We went into the man-of-war,
'Twas warrior-like to take the road
    O'er ocean's heaving waves.
Our oar-strokes then we pulled
Across the level sea,
Throwing the sea's harvest up,
    Like honey, the sea-soil.

The fort we reached was beautiful,
With works of custards thick,
    Beyond the loch.
New butter was the bridge in front,
The rubble dyke was wheaten white,
    Bacon the palisade.

Stately, pleasantly it sat,
A compact house and strong.
    Then I went in:
The door of it was dry meat,
The threshold was bare bread,
    Cheese-curds the sides.

Smooth pillars of old cheese,
And sappy bacon props
    Alternate ranged;
Fine beams of mellow cream,
White rafters—real curds,
    Kept up the house.

Behind was a wine well,
Beer and bragget in streams,
    Each full pool to the taste.
Malt in smooth wavy sea,
Over a lard-spring's brink
    Flowed through the floor.

A loch of pottage fat
Under a cream of oozy lard
    Lay 'tween it and the sea.
Hedges of butter fenced it round,
Under a blossom of white-mantling lard,
    Around the wall outside.

A row of fragrant apple-trees,
An orchard in its pink-tipped bloom,
    Between it and the hill.
A forest tall of real leeks,
Of onions and of carrots, stood
    Behind the house.

Within, a household generous,
A welcome of red, firm-fed men,
    Around the fire.
Seven bead-strings, and necklets seven,
Of cheeses and of bits of tripe,
    Hung from each neck.

The Chief in mantle of beefy fat
Beside his noble wife and fair
    I then beheld.
Below the lofty cauldron's spit
Then the Dispenser I beheld,
    His fleshfork on his back.

The good Cathal MacFinguine,
He is a good man to enjoy
    Tales tall and fine.
That is a business for an hour,
And full of delight 'tis to tell
The rowing of the man-of-war
    O'er Loch Milk's sea.

THE VISION OF MACCONGLINNE

HERE *and* THERE

*Foods and dishes and ways of
eating which belong to a
particular place or country, be
it Afghanistan, Catalonia,
England, Indonesia, or (don't
miss this one) the homeland of
White Trash Cooking.*

Elizabeth David 1977

TOAST

An English institution. Some other writers have given it a
paragraph or so, but this is the only full treatment I know.
(See pages 32 and 114 for more of Elizabeth David.)

No bread. Then bring me some toast! *Punch, 1852*

"Toast" said Berry, taking the two last pieces that stood in the rack. "I'm
glad to get back to toast. And a loaf of brown bread that isn't like potter's
clay." *Dornford Yates, Adèle & Co., Ward, Lock, 1931*

It isn't only fictional heroes to whom toast means home and comfort. It is related of
the Duke of Wellington – I believe by Lord Ellesmere – that when he landed at Dover
in 1814, after six years' absence from England, the first order he gave at the Ship Inn
was for an unlimited supply of buttered toast.

In *The Origin of Good Habits* (1944), H. D. Renner makes an attempt to explain
the English addiction to toast. 'The flavour of bread', he says, 'can be revived to some
extent by re-warming and even new flavours are created in toasting.' This is very true,
but leaves the most important part unsaid. It is surely the *smell* of toast that makes it so
enticing, an enticement which the actuality rarely lives up to. In this it is like freshly
roasted coffee, like sizzling bacon – all those early morning smells of an intensity and
deliciousness which create far more than those new flavours, since they create hunger
and appetite where none existed. Small wonder that the promise is never quite fulfilled.
'Village life', Renner continues, 'makes stale bread so common that toasting has
become a national habit restricted to the British Isles and those countries which have
been colonized by Britain.' Surely England was not the only country where villages were
isolated and bread went dry and stale? I wonder if our open fires and coal ranges were
not more responsible than the high incidence of stale bread for the popularity of toast in
all classes of English household. For toasting bread in front of the fire and the bars of the
coal-burning range there were dozens of different devices – museums of domestic life
are crammed with them, Victorian cookery books show any number of designs – as
many as there are varieties of electric toaster in our own day; apart from toasters for
bread, there were special racks for toasting muffins and crumpets, and special pans for
toasting cheese. And there were, in the nineteenth century, eminent medical men
writing grave advice as to the kind of bread which, when toasted, would absorb the
maximum amount of butter. That buttered toast goes back a long way in English life,
and was by no means confined to country places where fresh bread was a rarity is shown

by the following quotation: 'All within the sound of Bow Bell', wrote Fynes Morison in *Itinerary*, Volume 3 (1617), 'are in reproch called cochnies, and eaters of buttered tostes.'

Buttered toast is, then, or was, so peculiarly English a delicacy – and I use the term delicacy because that is what in our collective national memory it still is – that the following meticulous description of how it was made, at least in theory, reads poignantly indeed. It is from the hand of Miss Marian McNeill, author of that famous work *The Scots Kitchen*, on this occasion writing in an enchanting volume, called *The Book of Breakfasts* (1932, reprinted in 1975).

'Sweet light bread only a day old makes the best toast. Cut into even slices about quarter of an inch thick. It may be toasted under the grill, but the best toast is made at a bright smokeless fire. Put the slice on a toasting-fork and keep only so near the fire that it will be heated through when both sides are well browned. Move the toast about so as to brown evenly. Covered with an earthen bowl, toast will keep warm and moist.

'If very thin, crisp toast is desired, take bread that is two days old, cut it into slices about three-eighths of an inch thick, and toast them patiently at a little distance from a clear fire till delicately browned on both sides. With a sharp knife divide each slice into two thin slices, and toast the inner sides as before. Put each slice as it is done into a toast rack.

'For hot buttered toast, toast the bread more quickly than for ordinary toast, as it should not be crisp. Trim off the crusts and spread the toast liberally with butter that has been warmed but not allowed to oil. Cut in neat pieces, pile sandwichwise, and keep hot in a covered dish over a bowl of hot water. Use the best butter.'

I have my own childhood memories of toast-making in front of the schoolroom fire. Although I fancy that more toast fell off the fork into the fire and was irretrievably blackened than ever reached our plates, I can recall the great sense of achievement when now and again a slice did come out right, evenly golden, with a delicious smell and especially, as I remember, with the right, proper texture, so difficult to describe, and so fleeting. Only when it was hot from the fire and straight off the fork did that toast have the requisite qualities. Perhaps young children are better qualified than grown-ups to appreciate these points. And perhaps that is why buttered toast is one of those foods, like sausages, and potatoes baked in their skins, and mushrooms picked from the fields, which are never as good as they were.

Nowadays my toast is usually made on one of those ridged metal plates which goes over a gas flame or an electric burner. This produces crisp toast, very different from the kind made in front of the fire, but in its way almost as good. These lightweight metal toasters are very cheap. There is no need to buy an expensive iron one. Rye bread or 100 per cent whole wheatmeal bread both make excellent toast, but for buttered toast a light white bread is best. I prefer to make this kind of toast under the grill, electric toasters being machines with which I cannot be doing. In this I must be in a very small minority, for electric toasters are one of the most popular of all wedding presents, and in May 1975

Which? published a report on no fewer than thirteen different electric toasters. 'Some like it well done,' declared *Which?*, 'others pale brown; some like it done slowly to give a crisp finish, others done quickly so it's still soft inside.' All of these pronouncements are no doubt correct, as indeed is the statement that 'you don't want your piece of toast to be black in the middle and white round the edges'. That is to say, I don't. But I know plenty of people who actually *like* their toast to be charred. Perhaps they prefer it charred at the edges and white in the middle, and I'm not sure how this would be achieved. Another of the report's dictums, 'however you like your toast, you want all pieces to be more or less the same', is one I don't agree with, perhaps fortunately, for it is not easy to get all your pieces more or less the same. Unless, that is, you have a caterers' toasting machine and caterers' sliced bread which between them produce what I call restaurateurs' toast, that strange substance cut in triangles and served with the pâté, and for breakfast, in all English hotels and restaurants. The English invention has in recent years become popular in France where, oddly enough, it goes by the name of toast, as opposed to real French toast which is called *pain grillé*, and is just what it says, grilled bread. That brings me back to the toast-making device I myself use, the metal plate or grill over the gas burner. Part of the charm of the toast produced on this device is that every piece is different, and differently marked, irregularly chequered with the marks of the grill, charred here and there, flecked with brown and gold and black . . . I think that the goodness of toast made in this way does depend a good deal on the initial quality of the bread, and the way it is cut. Thin slices are useless, and I don't think that white sliced bread would be very successful – there is too much water to get rid of before the toasting process starts, and steamy bread sticks to the toaster. Thickish slices are best, preferably rather small ones which can be easily turned with grill tongs. Like most other toast, this kind is best straight from the grill. 'If allowed to stand and become sodden, dry toast becomes indigestible. From the fire to the table is the thing,' wrote the delightfully named Lizze Heritage in *Cassell's Universal Cookery Book* (first published 1894). And if the toast is to be buttered, I suppose we must remember Marian McNeill's 'use the best butter'. What *is* the best butter? Unsalted, some would say. I'll settle for any butter that's good of its kind. The very salt butter of Wales can be perfectly delicious eaten with the right kind of toast (no marmalade for me), and here is Flora Thompson (*Lark Rise to Candleford*, 1945) describing toast with salt butter and celery, and toast with cold boiled bacon. Toast-resistant though I am, she makes me long for that fresh hot toast and crisp celery, a wonderful combination, and how subtle:

'In winter, salt butter would be sent for and toast would be made and eaten with celery. Toast was a favourite dish for family consumption. "I've made 'em a stock o' toast as high as up to their knees", a mother would say on a winter Sunday afternoon before her hungry brood came in from church. Another dish upon which they prided themselves was thin slices of cold, boiled streaky bacon on toast, a dish so delicious that it deserves to be more widely popular.'

ENGLISH BREAD AND YEAST COOKERY

Lynda Brown   *1985*

OATCAKES *in the* NORTH *of* ENGLAND

Quotable passages on oats and oatcakes abound, many of
them Scottish. I have chosen this one from the north of
England because of the interesting detail. When Lynda Brown
goes into something, she really goes into it.

The oatcakes that I am now able to buy come from Stanley's Crumpets in Barnoldswick, just over the border in Lancashire (though until the county re-organisation of 1974 part of Yorkshire, and still considered as part of the Craven district). They also make crumpets, potato scones, and scotch pancakes. Last summer the firm changed hands when the then owners, Mr and Mrs Petty, who had owned the business for 17 years, retired. They had bought Stanley's Crumpets after the war from the founders of the business, the Stanley brothers who established the business in 1943. It's very much a local firm, serving the local community. Deliveries are made, as they have always been to Earby, Colne, Burnley, and Nelson. In other words 'as far as you can get before dinner time'. At one time the Stanley brothers had two vans and then deliveries were made as far away as Todmorden and Accrington. Occasionally orders were sent by post, or people came to collect, which is how Stanley's products get to Skipton today. Crumpets still account for the bulk of the business, followed by potato scones and oatcakes. They also make some fine muffins.

The oatcakes themselves are made from approximately equal quantities of medium oatmeal and strong white bread flour, mixed to a batter with a little salt and water, and enriched with eggs. Just before baking, bi-carbonate of soda is added, 'about two dessertspoons per bucketful'. The eggs are Mrs Petty's own modification, brought about by necessity when the oatmeal suppliers started stabilising their oats. Although the oatmeal kept longer, it took the moisture out of them, which affected the batter and the throwing qualities to such an extent that trade dropped off by 75%. It wasn't until she started adding eggs that Mrs Petty found her way around the problem, finding the eggs also made the oatcakes tastier, improved the keeping qualities, and made throwing easier.

Although the recipe is very different to John James Leach's oatcakes, these, too, are a thrown oatcake and Mrs Petty took great pains to stress that the secret of a good oatcake lay in the throwing, a fact also confirmed by her successor, Mrs Wordsworth who trained under Mrs Petty before she retired. It is the throwing, she insists, which is responsible for the texture, taste, and overall quality of the finished product and which is why it is impossible to make an oatcake of this type at home without the necessary skill.

The bakehouse is housed on the ground floor of a range of old stone buildings, just off Barnoldswick's main square. It is not at all as one would imagine a bakehouse to be: sparse, no gleaming stainless steel or large ovens, a stone-flagged floor, a rack holding crumpet rings of various sizes for the crumpets and muffins etc, sacks of flour in one corner, a couple of benches, shelves fitted with hessian-type cloth for cooling the oatcakes on, and, in the far corner, a large iron-plated bakestone heated these days by gas jets, where all the cooking takes place. Straddled across the top end of the hot plate, resting against the wall, sat the canvas trolley. In essence this is a 2ft square continuous belt stretched over two pairs of wheels, the front ones being smaller than the back pair which run on rails straddling either side of the bakestone. It looks a bit like a rudimentary go-kart.

When I arrived, Mrs Wordsworth, a cheerful woman in her thirties, was already at work. First, the canvas was liberally dusted with the flour and oatmeal mixture with a circular sieve. Next, two ladlefuls of batter – thinner than I'd imagined, – were carefully spooned onto the canvas, about $\frac{1}{2}''$ in from the edge, so that they formed two saucer-sized circles, about $4''$ in diameter. Taking hold of opposite corners of the trolley, the mixture (so I was told afterwards, I couldn't detect the movement at the time) was first spread a little by a short jerking movement and then swiftly drawn across the hot plate. Within the twinkling of an eye, the oatcakes hit the hot plate and began to sizzle. They were now something like $12''$ long and $3''$ wide in the centre, the same characteristic elongated egg-shape. Immediately steam started to rise and bubbles began to appear on the surface; a warm, nutty aroma filled the air inducing an immediate and irrepressible craving to try one there and then, straight from the bakestone. I felt like an impatient child who couldn't possibly wait a moment longer. A sense of history too, for at last I was watching what I had previously only been able to read and muse about. After about a minute or so, the oatcakes, now nicely browned on the underside, were turned over with an outsize palette knife and moved along a little to where the bakestone was cooler. Another couple of minutes they were moved to the other end of the hotplate where it was cooler still, and then taken off and stacked to one side on top of each other, waiting to be swept with a stiff brush to remove the excess meal. Finally they were transferred to the cloth shelves to cool. Mrs Wordsworth worked quietly and methodically, again rhythm being all-important. She would expect to make 8–10 dozen oatcakes per hour.

It all sounds deceptively simple, but, as I was quick to discover for myself, is in fact far more difficult than my description would have you believe: The first problem is getting your batter to form two nice saucers. Mine wouldn't. Handling the trolley is even worse. It's easy enough but getting the oatcakes to come out right, and nice and even, proved well-nigh impossible. Neither is flipping them over as easy as it appears. They are still extremely fragile at this stage and if you don't work quickly, the oatcake is likely to tear. Even now Mrs Wordsworth doesn't consider that she can throw an oatcake as well as Mrs Petty.

Petits Propos Culinaires (PPC) *20*

Florence White   1932

TEATIME FARE *in* ENGLAND

Florence White was one of those few people who, between the
Wars, made a real effort to explore and record traditional
English cookery. What she has to say here about teas and the
fare prepared for them is delightful, and I especially relish her
final paragraphs. Who else would have debated in print the
propriety of using a gadget invented in America to help make
English cakes for tea?
Her observations about the various 'families' of cakes
reflect her wide knowledge of cookery in the various
counties and her ability to compare and correlate. A
thoughtful, earnest woman whose work deserves to be
better known.

These words conjure up pictures of the great halls of country houses with logs blazing and sizzling on the hearth; a table large enough to allow a man who hates afternoon tea to sit and spread scones with butter and home-made jam; a singing kettle; piping hot toast; and home-made cakes, dogs lying warming themselves in blissful happiness, never even troubling to stir as well-known footsteps are heard outside, and members of the houseparty and other friends come in, one after the other, exhilarated but tired after a splendid run with some well-known pack, or a day with the guns.

Or in summer time long trestle tables literally weighed down with cups and saucers and good things for tea out of doors for the consolation or encouragement of rival cricket teams; or between sets of tennis.

Or in farmhouses where one knows a good tea will be spread if one calls in at the right time.

Or – perhaps best of all? – schoolrooms in town or country where the best toast is to be had, and a cut-and-come-again cake of which one never wearies.

Recipes for homely favourite cakes, buns, jams and jellies and school tuck are given in this chapter; potted meats and fish, must be sought amongst the dinner savouries, ham and sausages amongst the breakfast dishes and some especially good things will be found amongst Local and National Specialities, whilst how to make Devonshire scalded or clotted cream cannot be divorced from apple pie although it is associated indelibly with Cricket Teas at Knightshayes, Tiverton, Devonshire when Blundell's School played some other Eleven, and whether they won or lost Blundell's boys piled thick rich cream on to thick slices of plum cake, or trickled golden syrup over substantial slices of bread and cream which they called 'thunder and lightning', or stuck a spoonful of luscious strawberry jam in the centre of a split Chudleigh already thickly spread with scalded (or as Londoners call it, clotted) cream before closing it with another half on top and digging their strong white teeth well into the chosen 'tuck'.

At Canterbury Huffkins can be provided instead of Chudleighs; at Hawkshead where Wordsworth went to school there may still be bought Whigs such as he loved and a special pastry cake filled with a sort of mincemeat resembling Cumberland Currant pastry. In Oxfordshire Banbury Cakes are the order of the day, and if you want to taste the real thing you must visit Miss Brown's shop at Banbury. She will tell you that some people say the original recipe for these cakes was brought by the Crusaders from the East; anyhow they are good, and it is interesting to note that Eccles cakes, Cumberland currant pastry, Chorley cakes, Coventry godcakes, Banbury cakes, Hawkshead cakes, Yorkshire 'Sally Sly', are amongst our oldest traditional Feasten Cakes, and that their only rivals to first place are the Darioles or Maids of Honour, or curd cheese-cakes for which Devizes, Melton Mowbray, Clee in Lincolnshire, Yorkshire and Richmond (Surrey) are particularly noted.

Again in *Memories of Three Reigns*, Lady Raglan acts as our gastronomic historian and gives us a vivid picture of country house teas in England in 1873.

'That tea-time! That was always a delightful hour in the country when we would gather beside a blazing log fire and retail to each other the news of the day. At one country house I remember that this meal was always served in the billiard room, because the men for what reason I could never imagine, liked to play billiards whilst we had tea.

'Everything was home-made, the bread and the cakes and the scones. And there was a particular delicacy associated with this place which I particularly loved. It was ginger jumbles, which were served all hot and crisp and sticky like treacle.'

Speaking of schoolroom teas she says:

'In those days hostesses used to encourage their cooks to become expert in some special dish which guests would afterwards associate with that particular house. My aunt's cook was famed for her gooseberry fool, and so we children used to be indulged with this particular delicacy at her tea parties served to us in dainty cut-glass cups.'

There is one instruction given in the recipe for making cakes that may well alarm us in 1932, and that is the length of time we are told to beat eggs! Moderns have neither the time nor the helpers necessary for such feats of valour, but we wished to know what effect such prolonged energy had on the cake. So we tested the recipe for an 18 lb wedding-cake that took us about four hours to make, and found that the prolonged beating and whisking of the eggs really made a better cake, that in short it was quite worth while.

So it might be; but life is not long enough, and there are other things worth doing. We therefore rang up Miss Caroline Haslett of engineering fame and asked her if she knew of a small electric gadget that would whisk one or more eggs. She did, and now we make this self-same cake in less than one hour!

All we have to do is to put an egg or more in a basin, adjust the whisk, regulate the

238

speed indicator, stick the plug into its fitment in the wall, and the egg whisks itself, while we sit down and read, or sew, and listen to B.B.C. talks, or music.

So the past and the present have clasped hands and never the twain shall part; and arm-aching produced by whisking eggs, whipping cream or making sillabubs is known no more. But the invention is American. Those cousins of ours are so clever.

I do not, however, see why I am not to use a useful gadget that we have not invented or made as yet in England simply because it is made in America; therefore I use my electric egg whisk gaily; after all, it is worked by English electricity, which, without it, would not be used . . .

GOOD THINGS IN ENGLAND

Ernest Matthew Mickler   *1986*

WHITE TRASH COOKING

White Trash Cooking *has to be seen in the original to be fully
appreciated, since the brilliant photographs (for example, of
the inside of a refrigerator) are an essential part of it.
However, even this unillustrated extract is probably enough to
get across the idea that the book offers welcome relief from a
diet of conventional cookbooks in which everyone is earnest or
skilful or both and every dish is the embodiment of peasant
wisdom/centuries of ethnic tradition/a great chef's
imagination/what-have-you [yawn]. You want to hear about
real-life food? Listen to Mickler. (See also page 300.)*

So you see, telling stories, laughing, and enjoying good food are all deeply rooted in our southern White Trash background. We'll tell any story to make it funny. And we'll bend over backwards to make a good meal: from cooking cooter (turtle) in its shell, to making Vickie's Stickies, to putting up Blackberry Acid in jars (hoping it'll ferment). But rather than runnin' around willy-nilly telling stories (which I could do all day long), it might be quicker to get to what I mean by White Trash cooking if, as Betty Sue says, we go straight to the kitchen and 'get it did.'

If you live in the South or have visited there lately, you know that the old White Trash tradition of cooking is still very much alive, especially in the country. This tradition of cooking is different from 'Soul Food'. White Trash food is not as highly seasoned, except in the coastal areas of South Carolina, Georgia, and North Florida, and along the Gulf coasts of Alabama, Mississippi, Louisiana, and Texas. It's also not as greasy and you don't cook it as long. Of course, there's no denying that Soul Food is a kissin' cousin. All the ingredients are just about the same. But White Trash food, as you'll see by and by, has a great deal more variety.

If someone asked me what sets White Trash cooking aside from other kinds of cooking, I would have to name three of the ingredients: saltmeat, cornmeal, and molasses. Every vegetable eaten is seasoned with saltmeat, bacon, or ham. Cornbread, made with pure cornmeal, is a must with every meal, especially if there's pot liquor. It's also good between meals with a tall glass of cold buttermilk. And many foods are rolled in cornmeal before they are fried. Of course nothing makes cornbread better than a spoon or two of bacon drippings and molasses. For the sweetest pies and pones you ever sunk a tooth into, molasses is the one ingredient you can't find a substitute for. And a little bit of it, used on the side, can top off the flavors of most White Trash food, even a day-old biscuit.

After ingredients, equipment is the next most important thing. As I've said before, there are no hard and fast rules. But skillets, dutch ovens, and cornbread pans (all of black cast iron) are the only utensils that give you that real White Trash flavor and golden brown crust – and that's what you're after. And don't be too concerned about keeping them clean. Netty Irene says, 'It's no trouble at all! All you gotta do is rench 'em out, wipe 'em out with a dishrag, and put 'em on the fire to dry out all the water. Then tear off a piece of grocery bag and fold it about two inches square. Dab it in grease and smear it round 'n round the bottom and sides 'til they're plenty covered. Let 'em cool and hang 'em on a nail.' Netty Irene also said that her mother would never use water on her black iron pots and pans, only dry cornmeal. She'd rub them until they were smooth. She said, 'Mamma never threw away the used cornmeal, so she always had another cake of cornbread seasoned and in the makin'.' Keep your black iron skillet in a good clean condition; it is as special to these recipes as is the wok to Chinese cooking.

Another real common feature of White Trash cooking that sticks out in my mind is that the recipes, because of their deliciousness are swapped and passed around like a good piece of juicy gossip, and by the time they make it back to their source they might be, and almost always are, completely different. Raenelle, Betty Sue's sister-in-law, says, 'If I fry down three onions, she's gonna fry down four. If I put in one pack of Jello, she's gonna tump in two.' So with every cook trying to outdo the other one, and with all the different tastes, these recipes change so fast it's hard at times to catch them still long enough to get them down on paper. I relied on old family cookbooks, yellowed letters, whispered secrets, and a lot of good hints straight from the kitchens of longtime southern cooks. But I have not written down the endless variations and elaborations on a single dish. And I have not revised the collected recipes unless I had to clarify a very confused situation – and there were a few.

I know you'll lay down and scream when you taste Loretta's Chicken Delight. And Tutti's Fruited Porkettes are fit for the table of a queen. Just how can you miss with a dessert that calls for twenty-three Ritz crackers? And then, there are recipes for coon, possum, and alligator. These ingredients can even be found in New York City, if you've got an hour and a good taxi driver. You'll be the talk of your social club or sewing circle when you prepare a Resurrection Cake that's guaranteed to resurrect when you pour on the whiskey sauce, or a Grand Canyon Cake or Water Lily Pie that, all going well, look just like their namesakes.

It's not hard to catch on to our ways. Even an awful cook will soon sop them up and become deathly accurate with the sweet potato pones and Miss Bill's Bucket Dumplins. How? No hard, fast rules. Soon you'll find out like the best of the White Trash cooks that there are many ways to fix the same thing, and before long you'll be preparing these dishes with your eyes closed, with the very basics of southern cooking just at your fingertips. I know you'll want to place this cookbook next to the Holy Bible on your coffee table (I know you've got a coffee table with Polaroid snapshots under the glass). And in the kitchen you'll become another Mrs. Betty Sue Swilley, in the true spirit of WHITE TRASH COOKING.

TUTTI'S FRUITED PORKETTES

1 pound sweet potatoes
12 slices canned pineapple
6 slices bacon, cut into halves
6 tender pork chops
6 tablespoons brown sugar

Select sweet potatoes to make slices a bit smaller than pineapple slices. Cut into slices 1 inch thick. Parboil the potatoes in salted water for 10 minutes. Place each chop between two slices of pineapple. Place slice of sweet potato on top of each pork-pineapple stack. Sprinkle each porkette with one tablespoon of brown sugar. Place bacon crisscross on top. Place porkettes in open casserole. Bake at 375 degrees for one hour or longer, depending on thickness of chops.

Tutti, Petie's grandma, said she 'learned to make her porkettes by using a Hawaiian recipe combined with Southern ingredients. You cain't git trashier than that.'

WHITE TRASH COOKERY

Sri Owen   *1986*

TEMPE

*Most of us have some vague idea of the problems presented by
the soya bean, and of oriental solutions to them, such as soy
sauce and tofu. But there is one such product, tempe, which is
peculiar to Indonesia and less well known. Sri Owen describes
it and what can be done with it.*

The soya bean contains not only protein but just about every vitamin and amino acid needed by the human body. The snags are that it is unattractive to eat and difficult to digest.

You *can* eat soya beans after simply boiling them in the pod – my school friends and I used to consume quantities of them as we sauntered idly in the direction of our classrooms or played truant to queue for the cheapest seats in the local cinema. They probably didn't do us very much good, however; and soya beans, fed to severely undernourished concentration camp inmates at the end of World War II, produced vomiting, diarrhoea and even death. One way to overcome this problem of digestibility is to extract parts of the bean in the liquid form, as soya milk. Another is to solidify the liquid extract in what the Chinese and Japanese call *tofu* and we call *tahu* – in English, bean curd. This has very little taste or texture of its own, but you can cook some delicious dishes with it. But Asians have known for centuries that the best way to deal with soya beans is to ferment them, to get some other organism to break down the long, tough molecules and the cell structures which the human gut cannot cope with. Fermentation in a liquid is generally easier to start and control than fermentation of a solid, and soya sauce has been brewed all over east and south-east Asia for at least a thousand years. It is an excellent cooking medium, and has helped inspire the cuisines of perhaps half the human race. The varieties and qualities of soya sauce make up a fascinating and important field of study which, as far as I know, no one has yet fully explored. But tempe is something else again.

Tempe is a fermented preparation of whole soya beans, which are bound together into a firm block or cake while still retaining their individual shape and texture. The active agent in this process is a mould called *Rhizopus oligosporus*, which by good luck makes the tempe attractive to look at and handle and gives it a pleasant, nutty flavour – though it still needs to be cooked. (It is only fair to add that tempe is a Javanese product and that people from Sumatra often dislike it; even the Javanese admit it is an acquired taste.)

Tempe can be cooked in many different ways, and will take the place of meat in a wide variety of western and eastern dishes, so that it is an ideal food for vegetarians in search of variety and a balanced diet. A popular dish, in my experience, is a stir-fried mixture of tempe and tofu (bean curd), with onions, garlic, *terasi* (shrimp paste), chillies, tomatoes and a little soya sauce. *Tempe bacem*, another deliciously savoury product, consists of pieces of tempe boiled with onions, garlic, coriander, ginger, *laos* (gakingale), brown sugar, chilli powder and tamarind water, and then fried. If tempe is indeed an 'acquired taste', I think this is a good way to acquire it quickly.

'Food and Society in Indonesia'
PROCEEDINGS OF THE KONYA CONFERENCE ON FOOD HISTORY 1986

Alexandre Dumas 1873

The MADELEINES OF COMMERCY

Dumas brings his great gifts as a story-teller to bear on
the speciality of this French town. An unforgettable tale.

As for the excellent cake which is called madeleine, and which well deserves the great reputation which it enjoys, there befell a little adventure to one of our friends which we are going to relate.

A few years ago, one of our friends was going to Strasburg. Since he was travelling as a tourist, he gladly stopped in the towns and villages through which he was passing, first of all to rest, and then to observe the different manners and customs of the inhabitants.

One day he got back on the road rather late, thinking that he would reach before nightfall the next town where he was to rest, but he hurried in vain; he could not see any sign of any sort of dwelling. Finally, towards eleven o'clock, he saw in the moonlight the dark and thrusting spire of a church.

Everything was dark and quiet, not a single light was still shining and our traveller was at a loss to know where he would find a good table to cheer his stomach and a good bed to rest his limbs, benumbed with fatigue.

Suddenly he saw through the night a glimmer which seemed to come out of the ground. He approached this ray of light, the only one which he could see, and which represented salvation to him. He knocked at a door which was beside him and from under which shone the gleam of light which made his heart beat faster. At first a grunting answered him.

He knocked a second time, but harder, and then heard a strange, seemingly subterranean voice ask:

'Who is there, and what do you want?'

'I am a traveller, plagued with weariness and dying of hunger,' answered the voyager, 'in the name of God, open the door, and you will not regret it.'

Then he heard footsteps approaching the door. Someone pulled back an enormous iron bar, the door opened and he saw a man whose wild face was completely besmeared with flour, and whose bristling hair and beard contributed even more to his frightening appearance; the man was naked to the belt.

'Come on in and hurry up,' said he to the traveller, in this same sepulchral voice.

Our friend did not feel at all reassured, and at one moment he rather wanted to turn back and go and knock at another door; but the man had replaced the iron bar, and there was no way of retreating, so he put on a brave face and entered a large room where there was a huge baker's oven giving off enough light to illuminate it entirely.

'Excuse me, Monsieur,' said the traveller very politely, 'I have just covered sixteen or eighteen leagues, almost without eating, could you get for me, on condition, of course, that I pay you, something to stay my hunger and to rest my body?'

'I only have my bed,' answered the man in his gruff voice, 'and as for something to eat we are not lacking that here; it remains to be seen if you will like it.'

'Anything will please me, if only I can eat something. Look, what do you have to offer me?'

The man went towards a cupboard, opened it, and took out a little basket in which were about a dozen beautiful, golden, oval cakes.

'Here,' said he to the traveller, 'just taste that and you'll have something to say to me.'

He put the basket on the table, near the traveller and, placing his hands on his hips, surveyed him.

Our friend took a cake and bit it hungrily; in a second he had swallowed it whole; he took a second, then a third, then a fourth and at each cake which he swallowed the man kept smiling with pleasure.

Finally when not one was left in the basket, he said to him: 'Well, what do you think of my "madeleines"?'

'Give me something to drink first,' said the traveller in a strangled voice.

Once more the man went to his cupboard and brought out a bottle covered with a venerable layer of dust. He uncorked it and then, taking two glasses, filled them and offered one to the stranger.

'Drink,' he said to him, 'I don't want to see you choked to death by my precious cakes.'

The stranger drank in one gulp what was an excellent Bordeaux wine, and then, stretching out his glass a second time, said: 'Your good health, my good chap, you have just given me one of the best meals of my life. But, tell me, what do you call these succulent cakes?'

'What, you don't know the madeleines of Commercy?'

'Am I then at Commercy?'

'Yes, and you may be sure that you have just eaten the best cakes in the world.'

Without entirely sharing the good fellow's enthusiasm for his cakes, the traveller was forced to admit that they were excellent and that, being in need, he had supped very well.

The man then offered him his own bed, saying that he would manage with a mattress. The traveller protested a bit, but finally accepted and went to bed, falling asleep directly. Next morning he breakfasted more copiously than he had supped the night before, which didn't stop him on leaving from providing himself with a certain number of madeleines, which the good man forced him to accept as a souvenir of the fright which he had felt at first.

The madeleines of Commercy are in fact famous. It is thought that their reputation was made by King Stanislas Leczinski, when he came to France.

Here now is the recipe which comes from Madeleine Paumier, pensioner and former cook of Mme Perrotin de Barmond.

Grate the zest of two little citrons (or two lemons or Seville oranges) on a sugar lump, crush the sugar lump fine, mix it with some powdered sugar and weigh out nine ounces of this mixture. Put it in a casserole with eight ounces of sieved flour; four egg yolks or six whole eggs; two spoonfuls of eau de vie from Andaya and a little salt. Stir this mixture with a spatula. Once the dough is worked, continue to stir it for only a minute. It is absolutely necessary to observe this rule if you want to have really good madeleines; otherwise the excessive workings of the mixture will have an adverse effect on the cooking and will incline the madeleines to be heavy, to stick to the moulds and to be ragged or to crinkle up, which would make this sweet look pretty sad.

Next, clarify ten ounces of butter from Isigny in a little casserole. As the milk progressively rises up, skim it off carefully. When it no longer bubbles, that shows that it is clarified. You thereupon decant it into another casserole and when it has cooled slightly, you fill one madeleine mould with it. You then pour this same butter into another mould and continue thus until you have done eight, after which you pour the butter back into the casserole. Once more you fill a mould with hot butter and pour it in turn in another eight moulds. Finally you do this twice more, which gives you 32 buttered moulds.

One must not turn the moulds upside down once they have been buttered, as they must hold the little bit of butter which has run back into the bottom of each.

Afterwards, you mix the rest of the butter into the dough mixture and then put it on a range at a very low heat. Stir the mixture so that it does not stick to the casserole and, as soon as it starts to become liquid, take the casserole off the fire, but without allowing it to become tepid. Then fill each of your moulds with a spoonful of this mixture and put them in the oven, at a moderate temperature.

DUMAS ON FOOD

Helen Saberi   1986

Meals *in* Afghanistan: *and a* Note *on* Tea

The author, an Englishwoman who worked in Afghanistan
and married an Afghan, wrote her book for two purposes: to
record the traditional ways of cooking and eating, and to raise
funds for humanitarian aid to Afghan freedom fighters. I was
very happy to be her publisher.
The clotted cream to which she refers is found elsewhere in the
Near East, for example in Turkey, and is indeed similar to
that of Cornwall and Devon. A local historian in Cornwall
has the interesting hypothesis that the way of making it was
introduced there long ago by Phoenician traders who came to
Cornwall for tin.

Afghanistan is a poor country but it is rich in traditions and social customs. Hospitality is very important in the Afghan code of honour. The best possible food is prepared for guests even if other members of the family have to go without. A guest is always given a seat or the place of honour at the head of the room. Tea is served first to the guest to quench his thirst. While he is drinking and chatting with his host, all the women and girls of the household are involved in the preparation of food.

The traditional mode of eating in Afghanistan is on the floor. Everyone sits around on large colourful cushions, called *toshak*. These cushions are normally placed on the beautiful carpets, for which Afghanistan is famous. A large cloth or thin mat called a *disterkhan* is spread over the floor or carpet before the dishes of food are brought. In summer, food is often served outside in the cooler night air, or under a shady tree during the day. In the depth of winter food is eaten around the *sandali*, the traditional form of Afghan heating. A *sandali* consists of a low table covered with a large duvet called a *liaf* which is also big enough to cover the legs of the occupants, sitting on their cushions or mattresses and supported by large pillows called *balesht* or *poshty*. Under the table is a charcoal brazier called a *mankal*. The charcoal has to be thoroughly burned previously and covered with ashes.

Food is usually shared communally; three or four people will share one large platter of rice and individual side dishes of stew *qorma*, or vegetables. Home made chutneys, pickles, as well as fresh *nan* usually accompany the food.

The traditional way of eating is with the right hand, and with no cutlery. Spoons may be used for puddings and teaspoons for tea. Because hands are used in eating there is a handwashing ceremony before meals and for this a special bowl and jug called a *haftawa-wa-lagan* is used. A young boy or girl member of the family brings this to the guest, and pours the water over his hands for him, the bowl being used to catch the water.

Tea

No Afghan cookery book would be complete without mentioning tea, *chai*, which is an important feature of the way of life. It is consumed in great quantities and I must say both the green and black tea are excellent. Afghan tea is particularly refreshing on the hot, dry summer days.

Tea is seldom drunk with milk but is often flavoured with cardamom. On formal occasions such as weddings and engagements, a special green tea called *qymaq chai* is prepared and drunk. *Qymaq*, which is like clotted cream, is added to the top of the tea. The technique for making *qymaq chai* is elaborate and it has a strong, rich taste. Another special tea is *sheer chai*, prepared in the same way but without the *qymaq*. Salt is sometimes added, and it is served with various biscuits or bread such as *roht* or *nan-e-roghani*.

The hospitality of the people can be almost overwhelming at times. A good example of this is the honour attributed to a guest being measured by the amount of sugar he is given with his tea – the more sugar, the more honour. Another Afghan custom is to have a first cup of tea with sugar, *chai shireen*, followed by another cup without sugar. This second cup is called *chai talkh.* Many people soak sugar cubes called *qand* in their tea which they then hold in their mouths as they drink.

Tea is often served with sweets, called *shirnee*, or the Afghan equivalent of sugared almonds, *noql-e-badomi. Noql* is also made with roasted chickpeas (*noql-e-nakhodi*) or apricot or peach kernels (sometimes called *noql-e-khastahi*). *Ghur*, a kind of lump sugar made from sugar cane, is also taken with tea, especially in the winter. Another custom often observed is the turning over of your cup when you do not want any more tea. If you fail to do this, the host or hostess will continue to refill your cup with fresh, hot tea.

Because tea plays such an important role there are many *chaikhana*, tea houses, in Afghanistan. Apart from serving tea from a constantly boiling *samovar* they also provide other basic food and requirements for the traveller, for instance a simple and basic soup called *sherwa-e-chainaki*. This soup is actually made in a teapot, hence the name, teapot soup. The tea served in a *chaikhana* can be either black or green and is sometimes served in glass tumblers, but more often in handle-less porcelain bowls, similar to the Chinese tea bowl. Each customer has his own small teapot plus a small bowl for the dregs.

Noshe Djan – Afghan Food and Cookery

Jeanne Caróla Francesconi 1965

PIZZA *and the* PIZZERIA

A Neapolitan author, whose book on the cookery of Naples is
the best I know, writes with emotion about the dish which set
out from her city and conquered the world.

Whiteness of marble both on the floor and on the walls, sometimes projecting or recessed to designate separate spaces for tables; marble seats, marble tables and marble 'bancone' (the big counter). This is how *pizzerie* once were and some still are, witnesses of past tradition. Among so much whiteness, touches of colour on the counter: the small glass bowls with green spots, full of mozzarella, tomatoes and basil, and the silvery glitter of the *arciulo*, the glass bottle for oil, its elegant and slender form ending in a very thin bill which allows only the thinnest thread of oil to drip. In a corner, the smoky oven, with its wide open mouth reddened by faggots and wood shavings.

In these surroundings we used to eat our pizza, our inimitable, wonderful creation, whose ingredients are an assemblage of all the main nutrients and which is a meal on its own. We Neapolitans, when deprived even for a while of our pizzas, really do miss them. Even when away from our city, should we read the prophetic sign 'Pizzeria', we are unable to resist the call, though well knowing that almost without fail that pizza will not be 'the real thing'. But it will not matter, we will enjoy it all the same, because it will bring us fleetingly home, to the Naples about which we are incurably nostalgic even if we have left it only briefly and for our pleasure.

Is it necessary to tell how a pizza is made? To describe the expert handling of the *pizzaiolo* (the pizzaman) as he flattens the small round of dough leavened with bread yeast into a perfect circle, thinner in the centre than on the edges? And the following quick movements as he sprinkles the measured amount of tomatoes, cheese, mozzarella and drips the oil? And the sharp knock by which the pizza, first placed on the shovel, will be made to slide into the oven, at the right temperature, and then turned so that each side is evenly exposed to the heat, and the edges dotted with burnt blisters? And then picked up again with the shovel and, with another skilful knock, deposited on the plate and placed still sizzling in front of the client who, waiting for it to cool, judges it by eye and, with anticipation, checks the baking and the seasoning and, if he is a real expert, folds it in four, book-fashion, and eats it with his hands in the classical way.

La Cucina Napoletana

Richard Beckett   1984

The AUSTRALIAN COUNTER LUNCH

A vivid description of a peculiarly Australian institution.

By the 1860s the great, free, Australian counter lunch had arrived. It was a phenomenon that lasted until World War Two. (After a lapse of some years after the war, pub food was revived but the word *free* had vanished forever.)

Counter lunches started quite simply, with bits of cheese, beef and damper being made available to anyone who wanted them. But the boom times of the 1880s saw the cheese on a stick turn into whole turkeys, roast beef, fried fish, salads and almost anything else one cared to sample for the price of a single drink. It was all good, plain, English fare with no frills. The 6d and 1/- eating-house owners, not to mention the temperance associations, were quite furious, but they were unable to stop the custom.

The amount of food, style of service and the customers themselves of course varied from pub to pub, but many men ate nowhere else. It became a boon to the single man with the price of a drink in his pocket, and many a family man with an appalling cook at home did better at the pub than in the bosom of his loved one.

The following account of a turn-of-the century counter lunch in the city of Adelaide was told to me many years ago by one of my grandmother's many brothers-in-law, a woodcarver by trade, now dead.

We used to knock off at midday from the works and go down to the local hotel. The free dining room was on the first floor. You could only get snacks in the bar at street level. Cabinetmakers used to work in coats and ties in those days, even in the summer. As you got to the top of the stairs there was a long table with trestles on either side. There was always boiled mutton, roast beef and sometimes pork – never lamb, no one ate lamb in those days, not in pubs anyway, lambs were too valuable. And then there were always great dishes of vegetables as well, potatoes and pumpkin, roast and boiled. There'd be greens, cabbage and silver beet, but I don't remember any salads. I don't think anyone really ate them in those days except at Sunday tea. You could take as much as you liked. The meat would have been mostly carved beforehand, but you could carve extra for yourself if you wanted to, and most days most blokes did.

It was *expected* that you'd have a pint of beer with your meal.

CONVICTED TASTES

The AUSTRALIAN MEAT PIE

A meat pie and tomato sauce has been named a 'national
dish' of Australia. There are many jokes about these pies. I ate
one in a university canteen in Sydney, and could see why. But
I never managed to eat a 'floater' in Adelaide, and cherish the
idea that they are better.
Michael Symons' thoughtful book has had quite an impact on
thinking about Australian food. In this passage he sets the
meat pie against a background of male attitudes; but I should
explain that the whole chapter, which includes 'Daintiness'
and 'Childishness' in the Australian culinary scene, paints a
broader and more complex picture than any one extract
would suggest.

Through his yarn-spinning hero, Billy Borker, the writer Frank Hardy revealed something of male attitudes in a story, 'How the Melbourne–Sydney Argument was Settled'. Two representatives arguing in a border hotel at Albury harped on such matters as the harbour bridge (an oversized coathanger) and the Yarra (the only river in the world that flows upside-down). When Melbourne Mick would say that Australian Rules football drew bigger crowds, Sydney Sam would call it 'aerial ping pong'. They'd turn to climate, Sam knocking the rain, and Mick responding that Melbourne enjoyed more sunny days a year. Of course, the border pub served both beers. If Mick said there was more alcohol in Melbourne beer, Sam would say that was why there were more alcoholics. Billy Borker tried settling the dispute by switching the beers. But they'd take one sip of the foreign beer and spit it out. Finally, Borker decided they'd send a sample of the best Melbourne and Sydney brews – marked A and B – for CSIRO analysis. Back came the telegram: 'Thorough test made – Stop – regret inform you both horses have yellow jaundice'.

That captured the male stereotype. The men were urban workers, but with a hankering after the bush, revealed by their fascination in horse-racing. Even their Sydney–Melbourne rivalry was based on the clash of different origins, competition for gold, uneven land booms, conflict over free trade and tariffs. Their uncritical acceptance of the CSIRO symbolised the rise of the expert and the state. And the whole thing floated from the 1890s on factory beer – beer which, if Frank Hardy's observation was correct, secretly disgusted us.

According to the stereotype, the men had basic eating habits, which flowed from bush origins. Back in the 1850s, William Kelly had noted a 'dead down' among gold-diggers on all 'made dishes' (our modern idea of complementary foods arranged on a plate), the men wanting a slab of what they knew to be meat, simply cooked. Visiting in the 1880s, Percy Clarke wrote about the 'universal habit of bolting of his meals', colonials boasting of this fast feeding and saying that a 'slow feeder is a slow worker'. It was an attitude to food which devised such nick-names for a camp cook as the 'doctor', 'greasy' and 'poisoner' and his mate as the 'slushy', to take examples in G. A. Wilkes' *Dictionary of Australian Colloquialisms*. The same approach continued in the mixed grill served in what became known between the wars as the 'Greeks', the cafe remembered in country towns. You dined even worse at pub counter-lunches. It was the tradition of the grace: 'bog in, don't wait'. Or an uncle who put his breakfast chop in his porridge, with the grunt, 'What's the difference, it all goes down the same way'. Or in more modern times, ABC journalists I knew who formed a Dirty Eaters' Club to dine appallingly in public. Its gastronomic height was believed to be reached in the Carpetbag Steak, beef stuffed with oysters, a combination also occurring in the United States, although I have not confirmed where it originated. Men also cooked over the fire at barbecues. And for the worker's lunch and after the football match, it became the meat pie and tomato sauce, although this was as truly Australian as the Holden car.

Not until the Second World War, or perhaps a little earlier, was the meat pie and tomato sauce mentioned as a 'national dish'. However, pies had arrived with the British, the Flying Pieman one of the many street vendors in our first towns. British cookery books in the early years of our settlement contained several variations. In his 1864 cookery book, our 'Australian Aristologist' quoted a medical opinion on the 'Danger of the Meat Pie' (not leaving a hole in the crust to let out poisonous gases). Writing about the top of Melbourne's Bourke Street in 1869, journalist Marcus Clarke described the coffee barrows, with urn kept hot by charcoal, and the stalls at which a pieman poked a hole in the crust with his finger and poured from a long-spouted can a 'gravy' of salt and water. A fellow customer reassured Clarke, 'Mutton's cheaper than cat'.

In the 1890s, Melbourne journalist 'Rita' recommended the meat pie for the packed lunch for men and schoolchildren. Here it replaced the big agrarian midday meal, destroyed as a family get-together by the separation of workplace, and classroom, from home. Tomato sauce was being bottled from the beginning of preserving factories, and at least by 1868. With the advent of automatic machinery, the strictures of the depression and the need for street comfort in the war, the meat pie and tomato sauce was accepted as a characteristic 'fast-food'. In Adelaide, the pie rolled over in pea soup became a 'floater'.

Pressures to conform were strong between the wars, but it would be wrong ever to consider men marching totally in step to coarse meals. Many genuinely loved Sydney rock oysters, yabbies or 'crays' boiled in a drum by the river, the weekend fisherman's catch, as well as a good T-bone steak. And it would be negligent to disregard among the men numbers of cultivators, quietly building their own houses, filling the backyard with cabbages and settling down, as Lawrence saw it, with a wife, cow, chickens and the

Pacific. Many were strict abstainers. But the dominant model of male behaviour was aggressively uncultivated. We made lazy eaters and sudden drinkers.

Against the rough male attitudes to food, formed in our early years, was increasingly pitted the adorning approach of a woman, expected – as childbearer, cook and shopper – to make the society decent. She represented gentility, parsley by the back path, little cakes, pots of tea and teetotalism. If the damper symbolised our first, male century, then now succeeded the pavlova. If the male stereotype was to emerge as Frank Hardy's Billy Borker and as Bazza MacKenzie, then the female counterpart was Barry Humphreys' Edna Everage, whose attitudes were moulded in times when a most desirable quality was 'daintiness'.

ONE CONTINUOUS PICNIC

Leopold Pomés   *1985*

PA AMB TOMÀQUET

*Of the relatively few books devoted to a single 'dish', one of
the most engaging, and humorous, is that by Leopold Pomés
(in Catalan) on the mainstay of the traditional Catalan diet,
Pa amb tomàquet. These extracts are drawn from his version
of its history and reveal his minutely detailed instructions for
preparing it.*

Nobody can exactly say when and where it all started. I believe that the beloved, familiar and daily bread and tomato has always been with us, because it has been linked to us in a very natural way throughout our childhood.

There is a widespread tendency in gastronomy to believe that most popular foods have no date of origin or, at least, don't have a chronological reference as to when this or that food reached our country or our community. The same goes for bread and tomato. The fact that our grand-parents, or even our great grand-parents, would heartily and simply share with us in the afternoon, makes us consider it almost as old as the world. Maybe our grand-parents lacked memory or perhaps, like for the author, their secretion of saliva was such at the moment of having our bread and tomato that their mind was completely obnubilated and incapable of making any kind of anthropological exercise. Let us then inquire. Our enthusiastic team of investigators has contacted many Catalan grand-parents and has even conducted a poll with the most 'sophisticated and efficient up to date systems'. Here is the final result of our investigation from the answers of 833.422 grand-parents consulted.

	AFFIRMATIVE	NEGATIVE	DOESN'T KNOW
Have you ever eaten bread and tomato?	833.420	1	1
Have you ever eaten a luke-warm surmullet liver salad, perfumed with non starched new potato?	3	833.419	

As one can easily deduce, given the revealing and spectacular results of our poll, the knowledge of our bread and tomato by our grand-parents confirms our first opinion: there is no clarification as to its origin.

Néstor Luján, known Spanish writer and gastronome, in an enlightening article, published on June 19th, 1984 in the Barcelona newspaper 'La Vanguardia', tells us that the first mention in Catalan literature of bread and tomato goes back to 1884, exactly 102 years ago. Néstor Luján then adds: 'Bread and tomato, invented by our peasants in order to soften and enliven, in summer, the loaves of stale bread and also to make use of the abundant amount of tomatoes at a certain period of the harvest, I believe cannot be considered multisecular. There are some things in gastronomy that we believe are very old but aren't at all. In cuisine, the tomato is relatively recent' ...

TOMATO: you need almost a kilo of them. By having a lot of them, you will be able to discard those too ripe or those that, on the contrary, have green or yellow seeds. They have to be very red and ripe but firm. Some people cut them in two and, by pressing with their fingers, make the seeds come off. We recommend you this refinement. Josep Mercader, the late great talent of Catalan cuisine told me that he considered a mistake to add sugar to the tomato sauce, as many people do believing that by doing so they sweeten the natural acidity of the tomato. He cut them in half and expelled the water and the seeds. Then he wrapped them in a clean cloth, making a small bag out of it and hung it on the refrigerator overnight. Thus the tomato would completely eliminate all its acid liquids and acquire a natural and wonderful sweetness. I have tried it many times and the results are surprising. For bread and tomato, the tomato skin is necessary since you need to handle it with your fingers.

THE OIL: very important! This is the great element that will bring us, with its golden transparency and its incomparable flavor, the voluptuous lubrication that will deliciously complement the taste and touch of the bread and tomato ...

THE SALT: you only have two possible choices: the refined table salt and the grain salt, or coarse salt. Some advocate coarse salt because they love biting into that salt grain when eating bread and tomato. I, personally, prefer the homogeneity provided by fine salt which is logically easier to spread. It seems as if the grain, due to its explosion of taste, is distracting.

Let us now proceed to the elaboration. If the careful selection of all these elements is essential, so is the following operation. Achieving our goal, which is gratification, depends on it. Our dish, our exquisite dish, offers, as most of them usually do, many alternatives: more dressing, less dressing, rub more or less the tomato, cut the bread in such or other way, etc. Personal taste is important in all of them. My dedication to this subject has made me experiment several and even maybe all possible procedures, and my voluptuous passion for biting into it an infinite number of times has made me select very rigourously the different ways of preparing it.

Cut the bread with a saw knife, trying to make very regular cuts. For this, we will start by the end part of one of the sections previously considered as 'optimum section' until reaching the other end. The slices must be 1, 3 cms thick. Put the slices aside. Cut the tomatoes with the small knife. Check their ripeness and their inner color for adequacy: they must be very red and their pulp, very tight. If their flesh is yellowish or somehow greenish, discard them.

Take a piece of tomato with your thumb, index and middle finger and rub the slice circularly until covering evenly the whole surface. Once painted or tinted in red, renew the operation concentrating on the crust. For this, pick another piece of tomato and generously coat the perimeter, but always with the slice facing you. It would be a mistake to coat the crust from the side. Never try to save on tomatoes. If the tomato we're using doesn't tint enough, throw it away and pick another one. Let us not fall in the stinginess or laziness that could make us say: 'There is so little left to do, I'll just rub a bit harder and that's it'. Don't coat the surface too much. It isn't necessary, as many people do, to spread pieces of tomato with the grater on the bread. The excess of tomato produces an unbalance. It cannot be spread as if it were jam. But in any event, the coating cannot be too thin. I believe that the exact point is when you reach an intense red tint all *over both surfaces*. This is very important. Both surfaces of the bread have to be intensely coated and tinted, thus softening the crumb and the crust. The flavor will then perfectly and evenly distributed.

So, once both faces are red, salt them. There are doubts as to whether put the salt before or after the oil. Those who prefer it before, argue that the salt gets impregnated and that the oil settles it. On the contrary, if salting at the end, the oil can, with its sliding flow, displace the salt towards the plate, which is logical.

Finally, proceed with the seasoning. Take the oil cruet. Its sprout has to be 10 cms away from the bread. Pour it slowly, elegantly and steadily, not by jerky flows. If generous enough, the golden lubrication with the golden liquid contributes to a sensorial success of our blessed enterprise. Once the first surface covered, turn the slice over and repeat the operation on the other face, with the same rhythm and generosity.

Once the first slice is prepared, we will proceed accordingly with the others and . . . quickly, to the table! A world of gorgeous bites awaits, in which bread has been enriched to a soft touch of wonderful flavor and texture. Each time we use our teeth, these fantastic tools, every bite will bring us a voluptuous sensation! Soft but full touches out of each bite that, by being divided into exquisite portions, will spread throughout our palate and jaws the short sprinkles of a sweetly flavored oil, resulting from its skilful mixture with the tomato!   Pa amb Tomàquet

Elisabeth Lambert Ortiz   1984

TORTILLAS

The author, who has lived and worked in many continents,
here describes the interesting aspects of an item typical of
Mexico, the country from which her husband comes.

The Spaniards named them *antojitos*, little whims or fancies, and to me they are perhaps the most exciting aspect of pre-Columbian Mexican cooking. We have some very good descriptions of the markets of old Tenochtitlán, now modern Mexico City, before the Conquest was completed, when the city was virtually untouched by the invaders. In his *Historia General de la Cosas de Nueva España* Fray Bernardino de Sahagún, a Spanish priest, tells, among other things, of the types of tortilla on sale in the market; it is enough to make one's head spin – with envy. That marvellous early war correspondent, Bernal Díaz de Castillo, a captain who was with Cortés before and during the campaign, gives in his memoirs, *Historia de la Conquista de Nueva España*, a remarkable picture of dining in Mexico, so we do know that there was a great deal more, now alas lost, of this cuisine. However, loss was soon balanced by gain, as post-Conquest Mexicans made good use of the foods the Spanish brought from Europe and Asia, and enhanced their *antojitos* with beef, pork, olives, almonds, raisins, and so on.

With the exception of *arepas*, the corn bread of Venezuela, tortillas are unique among breads in being made from a cooked, not a raw, flour. Dried corn is boiled with lime until the skins are loosened and the cooked, skinned kernels are then dried and ground to make the *masa harina*, dough flour, that is used for tortillas. Happily for anyone wanting to make them, it is sold packaged by the Quaker Company. The flour is mixed with water to a fairly soft dough, pressed on a tortilla press or patted into a flat pancake by hand, and baked on a *comal*, an ungreased griddle, for a minute or so. It is not possible to speak of a raw tortilla, only of an unbaked one. Tortillas for those who don't want to make them are available frozen.

Arepas are also made from a cooked flour, and since it was in the Valley of Mexico in 5000 B.C. that corn was first cultivated, not arriving in South America until about 1500 B.C., it is a safe bet that the technique of cooking the corn before making it into flour was established in Mexico long before Venezuela invented *arepas*. In any event they are quite different.

Tortillas or *antojitos* are made in a variety of shapes and sizes and with a variety of fillings. Sternly traditional cooks parcel the fillings out among the shapes with some rigidity. However, when we make such things, we should have the freedom to follow our own whims and fancies. A selection of *antojitos* makes a fine buffet lunch when accompanied by a dessert.　　　　　THE BOOK OF LATIN AMERICAN COOKING

William G. and Yvonne R. Lockwood   1983

The CORNISH PASTY in NORTHERN MICHIGAN

*The Cornish pasty belongs to Cornwall; of course. But it also
belongs to Cornish people, of whom many emigrated, and
there are now Cornish pasties which are the property of
Northern Michigan. The Lockwoods are, I believe, the first
authors to give a considered account of this phenomenon.*

It seems to us, after much examination of what data are available, that nearly all cases of the incorporation of immigrant foods into the American repertoire can be best understood by reference to a single continuum. Immigrant foods become ethnic foods, which are adopted by some people outside the ethnic group but living in the same local community. As this phenomenon grows, the food becomes a regional specialty, perhaps becoming de-ethnicized in the process. Some of these regional foods gradually become adopted at the national level. While we would not argue that this is the only route by which ethnic foods can be absorbed into the American mainstream, examples abound of foods at every stage in the on-going process. Substantial changes in the foodstuff may be involved as the process takes place; this is part of what makes it so interesting.

A good example (or, perhaps, just the example for which we have assembled the best documentation) is the pasty. Pasty, the national dish of Cornwall, England, was brought to the United States by Cornish miners. In its country of origin, pasty is a turnover of pie-like crust filled with variety of combinations: rice and leeks, egg and bacon, lamb and parsley, fish, venison, apple, and so on. However, in the multi-ethnic Upper Peninsula of Michigan, where Cornish were brought to develop newly discovered copper mines, the diverse Old Country Cornish pasty became standardized to a meat and vegetable combination. Concomitant with standardization, pasty diffused via the mines throughout the area to other residents. Newer immigrants to the Upper Peninsula looked to the Cornish as established American citizens. As mine supervisors and foremen, the Cornish had status and their habits and lifestyle were noted, if not imitated, as a model of American life. Pasty as an 'American' food was also adopted. This process resulted in the status of pasty as a regional specialty of the Upper Peninsula, rather than of the Cornish alone.

Finnish-Americans, the predominant ethnic group in the region, played a significant role in the diffusion of pasty. The first Finns began to arrive in the mid-1800s, soon after the Cornish. By the time of mass migration in 1880, some 1,000 Finns were already settled in the Upper Peninsula. When the newly arrived Finnish immigrants saw their countrymen, who had arrived some decades earlier, eating pasty, they had no reason to doubt that pasty was anything more than a regional variant of a Finnish food. In Finland *piirakka* and *kukko* bear resemblance to pasty, and the existence of these foods made adoption of pasty easier for those familiar with them. This similarity to Finnish foods also explains why some Finnish Americans came to believe that pasty is Finnish.

Pasty is as commonplace in the Upper Peninsula today as are hamburgers elsewhere. One can obtain hot, cold, partially baked, frozen, and day old pasties in bakeries, restaurants, bars, fast food outlets, and grocery stores. Originally a hand held food, pasty has been upgraded to plate and table service. This change from hand to plate enabled other changes such as a flakier crust, increased size, and variations in shape.

With secondary migration to other areas of the state and the nation, Upper Peninsula residents are now diffusing pasty to new audiences, and as pasty moves beyond the borders of the Upper Peninsula, it once again is diversifying. Whereas *the* Upper Peninsula pasty contains beef (some pork is optional), potatoes, onions, carrots or rutabegas, one is now beginning to find on the fringes and in other areas pasty with chicken, cheese, chili, and gravy, as well as vegetarian pasty. The Upper Peninsula pasty is now franchised in California, and it is also available in these new versions in Florida and a few other states. Although not questioned outside the region, these new variations on the traditional pasty are not accepted in the Upper Peninsula as the 'real' thing.

The submarine (aka hoagie, sub, poor boy, torpedo, grinder, hero, zepplin, musalatta, Italian sandwich or Garibaldi) is somewhat farther along the developmental scheme we have proposed. It was introduced by Italian-American workmen, probably in the late nineteenth century, but cannot be traced to any specific Italian origin and, as far as we can tell, there was never any equivalent in Italy itself. Other workmen adopted it from their Italian co-workers, and from them it diffused to the public at large.

Speedis, a specialty of Binghamton, New York, represent an early stage of the same process. They consist of small skewers of grilled meat. They are a common bar snack, and local hardware stores advertise 'speedi skewers' and butchers, 'speedi meat.' Many inhabitants of Binghamton do not recognize that speedis are derived from Italian *spiedini*.

In our own hometown of Fresno, California, we grew up eating beerocks – hamburger sized rolls filled with peppery meat, onions and cabbage. Everyone considered them 'German,' but after leaving Fresno and beginning to cook for ourselves, we tried in vain to find a recipe in German cookbooks. It was only much later that we realized that the 'German' community in Fresno was in fact Volga Deutsch (Germans who had settled in Russia prior to immigration to the United States) and that 'beerock' was an English corruption of the German corruption of the Russian *pirog*, a similar but not quite the same filled pastry.

'Food in Motion'
Oxford Symposium Documents 1983

YORKSHIRE PUDDING

On the whole, there are surprisingly few good historical
studies of the cookery of the individual counties or regions of
England. A shining exception is Peter Brears' book on food in
Yorkshire. Here is his account of that county's most
famous dish.

Of all the regional foods associated with Yorkshire, none can compare with the Yorkshire pudding, justly celebrated in poetry and prose by writers and performers as diverse as Stanley Holloway and Abe Clegg. Great mystique surrounded its preparation, and it was popularly claimed that it could only be made successfully by a native of the county. Light, slightly crisp, and served with real beef gravy, it was one of the county's greatest delicacies: 'There's nowt nicer when it is nice, wi' a sup o' gooid beef gravy – an' when ah sez gravy ah mean gravy, not weshin' up wotter – but ther's plenty 'at can't make a Yorkshire puddin' fit to eyt. They'll gi'e tha a gurt dollop o' clammy soggy stuff at looks an' tastes as mich like putty as owt, an' wi' gurt lumps o' raw flah i't middle; or happen it'll be same as a buffalo hide wi' black blisters all ower it'.

The Yorkshire pudding was originally baked in a dripping pan placed beneath the meat as it slowly rotated in front of a hot fire. As the juices dripped from the joint they were absorbed into the pudding, giving it a unique flavour.

The method is clearly described in Hannah Glasse's *Art of Cookery* of 1747:

> Take a quart of milk and five eggs, beat them up well together, and mix them with flour till it is a good batter, and very smooth; put in a little salt, some grated nutmeg and ginger; butter a dripping or frying pan and put it under a piece of beef, mutton, or a loin of veal that is roasting, and then put in your batter, and when the top side is brown, cut it in square pieces, and turn it, and then let the underside be brown: then put it in a hot dish as clean of fat as you can, and send it to table hot.

When ranges came into use, both the meat and dripping pan tended to be transferred into the oven, the Yorkshire pudding now being baked on one side only, instead of being cooked on both sides by the radiant heat of the fire. The usual recipe was as follows:

> 2 eggs; 4 oz flour; $\frac{1}{2}$ pint milk and water; pinch of salt

> Mix the flour and salt in a basin, and make a hole in the centre. Break in the eggs and gradually add the milk and water, beating the mixture continually

to obtain a smooth batter. Put a little dripping (hot from the roast if possible) into a dripping pan and pre-heat in the oven until smoking hot. Pour in the batter, and bake for 30 minutes at 400°F, gas mark 6, until crisp and brown, then cut into squares and serve immediately.

This basic recipe could be enriched by the addition of a wide variety of savoury or sweet ingredients, including:

1. 4 oz seasoned minced meat sprinkled over the batter when it had just been poured into the pan.
2. A small onion, sliced thinly and separated into rings.
3. A large onion, boiled, chopped finely, and mixed into the batter with a teaspoonful of dried sage. This was served with mutton or pork.
4. 4 oz Cheshire cheese, finely grated and mixed into the batter.
5. 2 oz currants mixed into the batter. This too was served with roast pork.
6. A large baking apple, peeled, sliced, and spread over the batter when it has just been poured into the dripping pan.
7. A large baking apple, peeled, cored and grated, mixed into batter.
8. 1 or 2 sticks of forced rhubarb cut in short pieces and mixed into the batter. This was served with a sweet white sauce at the end of the meal.

The plain Yorkshire pudding could also be spread with any of the following:

9. Treacle or golden syrup.
10. Raspberry jam.
11. Raspberry jam and malt vinegar, to give a fruity 'sweet and sour' taste.
12. Raspberry or blackberry vinegar.
13. Mint sauce.
14. Yorkshire ploughman's salad, described by Eliza Acton in 1845 as a tablespoon of treacle mixed with two tablespoons of malt vinegar and a pinch of black pepper, or:
15. Mint sauce salad, made with a handful of mint, finely chopped, together with finely shredded lettuce and spring onions all dressed with sugar and vinegar.
16. Parsley sauce.
17. Butter and sugar.

Although the Yorkshire pudding was cooked with the roast, it was traditionally eaten quite separately as a first course, the effect being to take the edge off the appetite. The motto 'Them as has most pudding can have most meat' was well known in families where meat was a great luxury. Squares of pudding left over from the first course, or specially baked to use up the surplus batter, could be served as a dessert with one of the sweet accompaniments listed above.

TRADITIONAL FOOD IN YORKSHIRE

Colman Andrews 1988

PAELLA

*Catalan cuisine, so important in the Middle Ages and so
distinctive today, has had less attention than it deserves.*

One cool, bright, early afternoon in January, I left my temporary quarters in El
Saler, near the marshes of La Albufera just south of Valencia, and drove northwest
to the little inland village of Benisano. If you know any Latin, the town's name might
suggest 'good health' to you, but what I was looking for wasn't a doctor or a mineral spa.
I was after the salutary effects of a genuine *paella valenciana* as prepared by one Rafael
Vidal, who had been dubbed by local gastronomes on one occasion as *Meior Paellero* or
Best Paella Maker of the entire Valencia region (a region where, as a Spanish restaurant
guide has pointed out, there seems to be a *paellero* under every rock).

Vidal's establishment, the Restaurante Levante, turned out to be a plain-looking,
under-lighted place on Benisano's main drag – at first glance, nothing more than a
rather dingy workingman's bar. But on a table in a little hallway at the back of the room
was a huge paella pan (itself called a paella in most of the *països catalans*, and a *paellera*
in the rest of Spain, but known here on paella's home ground, perversely enough, as a
caldero) probably four feet across, partially covered with a cotton towel. And beyond
the hallway, through a bead curtain, was an actual dining room – a bit brighter than the
bar, pleasantly if simply furnished, and almost completely full of customers, most of
them men and many of them in business suits.

Shown to one of the few remaining tables I was promptly addressed by a waiter.
'What will you have?' he asked. 'What have you got?' I answered.

'Well, paella, of course, for the main dish,' he said, 'but first you can have cuttle-
fish fried with garlic and parsley, deep-fried squid, or *bacallà* with red peppers.' I chose
the last of the three – a dish known locally as *esgarrat*, meaning 'shredded' – in fact a
bowl of roasted red pepper strips mixed with bits (shreds) of salt cod, dressed in good
olive oil enlivened with minced raw garlic – a dish that got my palate's attention right
away. Then came the paella ...

Had this been my first encounter with authentic *paella valenciana*, I would have
been shocked. To begin with it came not at all the way most of us imagine paella – in a
steaming-hot paella pan decorated with bright green peas and pieces of red pepper and
garnished with whole shrimp and mussels; it was simply heaped onto a ten-inch plate, at
room temperature. (That big *caldero* in the hallway contained the day's full ration of the
dish, cooked in the morning and scooped up as needed; most aficionados of paella prefer
it tepid, not hot.) More astonishing, though, would have been the paella's contents –
which were nothing more than little hunks of rabbit and chicken, some broad green

beans and pale yellow butter beans, a hint of tomato and onion, more than a hint of saffron, and rice, rice, rice. There were no peas or red peppers, no ham or sausage or meat of any kind, no fish or shellfish, period. Yet this paella was as historically and traditionally correct as it was delicious. This was a real *paella valenciana*.

Rice was brought to Valencia by the Moors in the eighth or ninth century A.D.; the region earned its reputation as Spain's great rice capital only after 1238, when Jaume I of Aragon, in an attempt to contain an incipient malaria epidemic, restricted rice plantings in Catalan-held territories to the marshlands of La Albufera, practically in Valencia's backyard. Because La Albufera is separated from the Mediterranean by a narrow strip of solid land, and because rice growers are after all farmers and fishermen, it was natural that early rice dishes of the region looked inland for raw materials

Today, of course, seafood has become de rigueur for most kinds of paella, in Valencia as in neighbouring Catalonia, which has adopted the dish and fashioned its own versions of it – and beyond the borders of Spain (for paella is the most international of all Spanish dishes) it is universally considered to be a seafood dish by definition. What is understood in Valencia, and usually understood in Catalonia, however, is that whether it contains seafood or not, paella is above all a *rice* dish – and it is ultimately good rice, not good seafood (or whatever) that makes a great paella.

As that erudite and charming specialist in Valencian cuisine Llorenç Millo has noted 'A paella can be as savory in the shade of a tree, out in the country, with the rice accompanied only by some snails and runner and butter beans as one served in the most luxurious dining room, adorned with crayfish and lobsters.'

Millo also offers five traditional rules (with a bit of a wink in his eye) for the proper enjoyment of this famed Valencian specialty: (1.) It must be eaten outdoors, preferably in the shade of an old vine or a wide-topped fig tree, and ideally when the mild noontime breeze that local peasants used to call *El Paellero* is blowing. (2.) It must be eaten only at midday – it being considered self-evident by Valencians that a properly made paella will be too rich and heavy for the evening meal. (3.) It must be served directly from the *caldero*. (4.) It must be dished up with a spoon made out of boxwood. (5.) The only proper topics of conversation during the consumption of a paella (it being assumed that those sitting around in the open air at noontime eating it are male) are women, bullfighting, and crops – and above all, political controversies and philosophical declarations are to be avoided. In this last context, Millo recounts this story about Valencia's most famous author, Vicente Blasco-Ibáñez (author of *Blood and Sand* and *The Four Horsemen of the Apocalypse*): One afternoon, after attending a political meeting at a small inland village near Valencia, the noted novelist was invited to help polish off a monumental paella. As he dug in, one of the locals, seeking to show off his intellectual knowledge to the distinguished guest, asked, 'Don Vicente, what do you think of Schopenhauer?' The author looked up from his plate, fixed the man with a stare, and responded, '*Schopenhauer?* Shut up and eat, man! Shut up and eat!'

CATALAN COOKING

Dr Yan-Kit So   *1984*

YUAN MEI'S ICED BEAN CURD

Among the numerous authors of books on Chinese cookery
there are three who especially engage my sympathy. One is
Yuan Mei, an 18th century poet who wrote the first
comprehensive Chinese cookery book. The second is Dr Cheng
(see page 299), in whose work erudition is married to style.
The third is Dr Yan-Kit So, who combines erudition with
outstanding practicality. This essay by Dr So happily
embodies a recipe from Yuan Mei.

Iced bean curd is one of the bean curd recipes from *Sui-yuan Shih-tan* (Sui-yuan Cookery Book), written in the late 18th century. The book, consisting of more than 300 recipes – categorized either according to main ingredients such as seafood, meat, poultry, vegetables and bean curd or to specialities such as *dimsum*, sweets and cakes – is the most comprehensive Chinese cookbook before cookery writing became popular in China in the 20th century. The author of this book, Yuan Mei (1716–1798), above all a poet and government official, was also a gourmet and *bon-vivant* who had at least four, if not half a dozen, concubines! He may have been the ranking poet of his times, yet to many Chinese he is remembered for his cookbook with its far-reaching influence down to the present day. So unique a work that it is compared to *Ch'a Ching* (Treatise on Tea), the classic handbook on tea by a T'ang scholar, Lu Fu, of the 8th century.

An ardent lover of food and wine, Yuan nevertheless had a delicate stomach so he preferred eating at home where the dishes were prepared to his liking. Not that Yuan would try his hand at cooking – no Chinese gentleman would – but for forty years, whenever he was well satisfied with a dinner at a friend's house, he would send his cook who would, humbling himself as an apprentice, learn to make the dishes. Back home, Yuan asked for the procedures and meticulously wrote them down, noting the different tastes and flavours from different homes. His cookbook, completed toward the end of his life in 1796, is therefore an anthology of recipes not only from his own cooks but also from those cooks of other upper-class Chinese families. As Yuan never tired of voicing his opinion on them, be it serious or gossipy, the recipes mirror his philosophy and predelictions on food.

It seems that Yuan was extremely fond of bean curd, for he lauded it as 'far superior to bird's nest' if it was 'well flavoured'. Seen from the chapter on bean curd, consisting of nine recipes altogether, he certainly spared neither time, trouble nor ingredient to flavour bean curd. This recipe, although it is not as well known as the one entitled Prefect Wang's eight treasure bean curd, which is much quoted by cookbooks and adapted in homes and restaurants, is nevertheless a summation of Yuan's definition of 'well flavoured' bean curd.

Like many other recipes in his cookbook, there are no precise quantities given in the recipe, so all the quantities given are adapted by myself. In a rather authoritative tone, in line with the admonitions and exhortations set out in the two introductory chapters of his book, Yuan tells one and all in shorthand language how they must prepare this dish:

> Ice the bean curd overnight. Cut into square pieces then blanch off the bean odour. Add chicken stock, ham stock and pork stock to the bean curd and stew. Before serving the dish at the table, discard the chicken and ham, etc., retaining only the fragrant mushroom and winter bamboo shoots. After bean curd has been stewed for a long time, it loosens up forming beehives, similar to frozen bean curd. Thus, stir-fried bean curd should be tender while stewed bean curd should be well cooked (for a long time) ...
>
> Never add stock seasoned with garlic, onion and ginger; otherwise the pure taste will be lost.

No other cooking fat has been given in this recipe, even though in some of the other bean curd recipes Yuan has specified the use of lard. If lard is used, this dish will be very heavy; I have therefore taken the liberty to use groundnut oil, the popular and more healthy cooking fat used for Chinese food today ...

It is a unique characteristic of Chinese cookery to use an exotic yet almost tasteless ingredient, cook it for a long time in the most concentrated stock so that the end result is an unsurpassed epicurean dish. In this recipe Yuan, using this technique, infuses the bean curd in concentrated stock in a similar way as one would cook bird's nest and shark's fin. As if to gild the lily, he specifies two other accompanying ingredients, the fragrant mushroom for flavour and bamboo shoots for a contrast of texture.

As for Yuan's insistence on purity of taste by forbidding the use of garlic and the like in the stock, he is representing the palate of his native city, Hangchow, a gastronomic centre since the 12th century. Unlike the people in north China, people living in east China dislike the odour of garlic and use it sparingly in their food.

If you wish to try the recipe above, I suggest you follow Yuan's instructions faithfully first and then try the following modification a second time. Add a large piece of peeled and crushed fresh ginger root (about one to one and a half inches or 2.5–4 cm) and 4–5 spring onions – no garlic though, please – to the bean curd; discard them, however, before serving. You will find that the taste is all that much more interesting without losing its purity. But then my taste is that of a Cantonese palate, which Yuan Mei would not approve of.

'Cookery: Science, Lore and Books'
OXFORD SYMPOSIUM DOCUMENTS 1984/5

Alicia Rios   *1987*

TAPAS

The author, besides being a brilliant cook, is well equipped to
write about the history of food in Spain and the psychological
aspects of Spanish food habits. The essay quoted here is one of
a series of such studies, and unrelated to the fact that tapas
have enjoyed a vogue in the USA during the 1980s. This
vogue has led to, or been created by, the publication of tapas
recipe books, so that people can give tapas *parties at home; but*
it will be obvious from what Alicia Rios says that such
activities have little in common with what she calls the art of
tapeo, *which can only be practised in Spanish bars.*

*T*apeo is a term used to describe the Spanish tradition of going out before lunch or dinner to mingle with friends while drinking an apéritif, and sharpening the appetite for the main meal ahead by choosing from the myriad of tempting appetizers (*tapas*) on offer in the bars throughout Spain.

The art of *tapeo* represents the perfect marriage between food and drink, because, unlike the more well known concept of food supplemented by good wine, in the case of the art of *tapeo*, it is not the wine which lubricates the ingestion of good food, but quite the contrary; it is the food which really acts as an accompaniment to the series of sips of good wine.

The art of *tapeo* is like a baroque, sybaritic game, as it pleases the five senses by means of the multifarious smells, the friendly pats on the back, the sight of beauty on the streets. It induces states of inspiration and delight, it gives rise to witty banter on trivial topics and the interchange of snippets of juicy gossip. There is a kind of irony and philosophy peculiar to this custom, like a treaty of coexistence accompanied by elegance and a generosity of the spirit developed to the ultimate possibilities. The *tapeo* is a peripatetic art which takes the form of a route; a path paved with chance meetings and random conversations.

The drink stimulates the appetite and aids digestion, and the food palliates the ethylic effects of the drink. The combination of these factors results in a perfect balance which is supported by the concept of physical space, as the *tapeo*, by its very nature, inherently involves a plurality of settings. It is impossible to imagine the art of *tapeo* taking place in a single session with no element of sequence or spacing. However good a particular bar may be, a good *tapeador* could never exhaust his possibilities in any one place. Movement is essential.

As well as the spacing effect of the various mouthfuls of food and sips of wine, and

264

the physical movement, conversation also forms a fundamental and essential part of the art of *tapeo*. If in the case of other meals conversation may be considered an obstacle or perhaps as an additional factor, verbal communication and the exchange of looks complete the concept of the *tapeo*. At times the *tapeador* has to try very hard to separate himself from his *tapeo* companion when he becomes lost in the pleasures aroused by the focus of his digression. As in a game played with counters, the portions of *tapas* are shared out mysteriously between snatches of conversation. On occasion, albeit rarely, the more voracious *tapeadores* have gone as far as to violate these ritual pauses between bites and sips when one surrenders oneself completely to raising the spirits because the enjoyment of the various different tastes is an inevitable and imperative pleasure for them. These lucubrations, however, are usually only interrupted by a furtive flirtatious compliment directed at an attractive woman passing by. The combination of conversation, compliments, – even if only about flowers – the art of peeling prawns and the sharing out of a portion of something is always impregnated with the smell of seafood.

And finally, within the framework of physical aspects, the perfect *tapeador* practises his art standing up, using the following reasoning as his alibi: 'Soon I shall have my lunch sitting down at the table. This is no time for the comforts of luxurious, plush bars.' Standing up at the bar, the *tapeador* can resort only to his elbows for comfort, as he tries to nudge a niche for himself in between the various plates on the wooden or metal bar, to then soak his elbows in pools of wine and vinegar.

It does not matter if a *tapa* is somewhat large, but this volume must be distributed in terms of height, and not of surface area. For example the *montado* – a piece of fried *morcilla* on a small slice of bread, speared with a cocktail stick, or perhaps assorted pickles on sticks, can be piled very high because they do not conflict with the requirement for occupying a minimal surface area. This phenomenon has various explanations. Let us consider first the ethical reasons, which are always connected with the respect shown with regard to the meal awaiting in the home. Food with a large surface area is reserved for the more intimate atmosphere of meals enjoyed with the family or friends. There are also various other fundamental reasons. The individualization of the portions is an important factor as it renders cutlery virtually unnecessary. The fork, for example, is only needed to spear the bite-sized morsel, and the use of the knife is not considered correct form, even if only to cut a sausage up into pieces. Cutlery has no place in the eart of *tapeo*, belonging to the environment of sit-down meals.

PETITS PROPOS CULINAIRES (PPC) 27

NOW *and* THEN

*The subject of food associated with occasions
brings up the broader topic of food and
religion. Indeed I see that all the items here
are of religious significance. Perhaps I
should have tried harder to find something
secular, like turtle soup at a Guildhall
banquet; but these would only have been
exceptions to prove the rule.*

Farga   *1963*

MEXICAN OCCASIONS

The Day of the Dead and Twelfth Night are two Mexican occasions with which special foods are associated. As with so many cultural things in Latin America, the Old World origins are plain to see but the journey to the New World has produced something different.

'DIA *de* MUERTOS' *(1st and 2nd of November)*

The offerings to the dead date back to the times of the Blessed Sebastián de Aparicio, who founded the tradition in the year 1563, on the 'Careaga' hacienda, in the vicinity of the suburb of Atcapotzalco. The missionary friars undertook to extend the offerings to other parts of the country. They found ready acceptance among the Indians for this custom (which had been practiced in other parts of the world since ancient times), for the Indians maintained a traditional veneration of the dead. Their offerings were based primarily on products and dishes which were favourites of the departed ones.

The theme of the fiesta stimulated the popular imagination tremendously, in the preparation of special dishes and also in their execution and variety. The setting and adornment of tables also drew imaginative attention, and the centerpiece was usually a small altar decorated with candles and flowers. Among the latter, the outstanding variety was the glowing **cempoalxochitl**, or flower of the dead, a native marigold. The victuals, fruits and tidbits displayed on the table were later eaten, accompanied by plain and flavoured **pulque**.

The artistic qualities of our people respond warmly to these activities, and they are displayed in the superbly skillful creation of small figures made of sugar, representing skulls, thigh bones, cross-bones, skeletons, devils, symbols of Death, and 'burials,' an entire tableau of a funeral procession, all done with great ingenuity, and contributing considerably to an upsurge in retail trade during these days.

Many tidbits and delicacies are prepared, with consummate skill and imagination, in an endless variety, in keeping with the long-standing traditions.

The table or altar is decorated with wreaths, festoons and streamers of colored paper and resplendent tin made into candelabra, incense burners, votive candle holders, and a thousand other fantasies decorated with openwork, fretwork and other classical motifs. The gastronomical display at the table may include many of the following: sugarcandy skulls of various sizes and expressions, **alfajor** of cocoanut, (a paste made of honey and nuts) **condumio** of peanuts, **charamusca** of brown loaf sugar,

jamoncillo of melon seeds, caramel **trompadas, pirulines**, aniseed rolls, 'crackers of the dead', jellied paste of quince, peach and guava; 'fish' made of pastry; coconut candies, milk macaroons, jelly drops of different flavors, **alegrías** of sesame seed, milk and almond bars, **calabaza en tacha** (pumpkin, baked in honey), **camote tatemado** (a sweet-potato confection), crystallized pumpkin, citron, **pepitorias** (brittle), **cacahuate** of squash and brown loaf sugar, figures made of almond sugar paste, **tamales** of various kinds, stuffed peppers, **mole poblano**, and a variety of 'breads of the dead' decorated with crusts shaped like cross-bones and with a rich flavor of citrus-blossoms ... eloquent examples of how extensive and varied is the cuisine of the country, and how vast its folklore.

All bakeries sell the 'bread of the dead,' **pan de muerto**, which is a kind of puffed yeast-cake, made with flour, yeast, egg, sugar, butter, lard, citrus-blossom water, grated orange peel, and aniseed, sprinkled with sugar and topped by the crossed 'bones'.

Rosca *de* Reyes

On January Sixth (Twelfth-Night), the Three Kings arrived with gifts at the manger where Jesus Christ was born. The Catholics celebrate this event by giving presents to their children. Although of French origin, the idea of assembling the family and friends on this date to eat a cake ring **(rosca)**, has taken deep root in Mexico: The **rosca** is made with flour and yeast, in the size suitable to the number of persons invited. Other ingredients are eggs, sugar, salt, citrus blossom water, grated lemon peel, and butter. A small figure of a child, made in porcelain or other material that will not melt in the baking, is concealed in the dough. (This is a substitute for a European custom of inserting a large bean, **haba**, a tradition that dates back to the Middle Ages.) The top of the ring is adorned with sprinkled sugar and with strips of crystallized fruit in various colors.

The **rosca** is divided into equal parts, and the person who gets the little doll is regarded as the ruler of the fiesta, to whom obedience is due in all the little rules which he makes to heighten enjoyment of the event. If the lucky one is a man, he chooses a queen and offers her a flower.

A sequel to this custom is the party which the king or queen of the fiesta must give at a later date for all those present. Very often the party is a **tamalada**, where **tamales, atole** and other typical Mexican foods are served.

EATING IN MEXICO

Maria Johnson 1981

BOILED WHEAT *for* ALL SOULS' DAY

*Maria Johnson, a Bulgarian married to an Englishman and
living in England, is preparing a* magnum opus *on Balkan
food and cookery. Here she describes a dish common to all the
Balkan countries but not to be found in recipe books.*

This sweet and aromatic, ancient wheat dish, possibly of pre-Christian Slavonic origin, was adopted by the Eastern Orthodox Church, and introduced into the cult of the dead. In the Balkans, the dish is variously known as *kolliva* in Greece, *koljivo* or *žito* (wheat) in Serbia, *kolivo* or *vareno zhito* (boiled wheat) in Bulgaria, *varena ženica* (boiled wheat) in Jugoslav Macedonia, *koliva* or *kolifa* in European Turkey and northern Albania, and *colivă* in Romania. The dish is brought to church to be blessed by the priest on All-Souls' Days. According to Orthodox canon law, All-Souls' Days are celebrated three times a year, and always on a Saturday.

Kolivo is also offered at Funerals and memorial services and in Macedonia and Turkey, boiled wheat is made to celebrate the appearance of the first tooth of a child.

Each Balkan country has it own traditional recipe for Boiled Weat. Here, I am giving the Jugoslav version, which can be prepared using ordinary, unprocessed whole wheat. This recipe was given to me many years ago by my friend Dušica Javanovič during my stay at her home in Belgrade. It has the same lovely flavour as the Bulgarian *kolivo*, but is quicker and easier to make.

ZITO (KOLJIVO)

(To make 20 dessert portions or about 50 small offerings)
500 g whole wheat
500 g shelled walnuts, coarsely ground
500 g vanilla sugar, sifted (made by burying several split vanilla pods into
the sugar, and keeping them together in a tightly-lidded container for
several weeks)
grated zest of 3 lcmons
3 heaped tsp ground cinnamon
150 g rusks, finely ground to the consistency of flour; a small packet of edible
silver balls used for cake decoration (optional)

Wash and drain the wheat. Put it into a large clean saucepan, add cold water to cover generously, put the lid on, and leave it overnight.

Early next morning, drain the wheat and cover it again with fresh water by at least 5 to 6 cm. Bring to the boil and simmer gently for about 2 hours. (The duration of the boiling process depends on whether the wheat is of the hard or soft type.) Top up with extra boiling water if and when the level falls below that of the grains. If any scum should rise, spoon if off. The grains are ready when they have all burst, and are soft enough to eat, though still sightly chewy. By the end of the cooking time, the liquid in the pan should be just to the level of the grains. Remove the pan from the heat and wrap it well with polythene and then with a small blanket. Leave to stand for about 5 to 6 hours.

Next, rinse the wheat with warm water and drain it thoroughly. Place a large sheet of plastic on a table and put over it several layers of newspapers. Cover the newspapers with clean tea towels. Spread the wheat over the towels and pat dry, using kitchen paper towels or a cloth. When dry, put the grains through a mincer or food processor, then add the walnuts, about 300 g of the sugar, the lemon zest and the cinnamon to the wheat, and mix thoroughly, using two large spoons, or a food processor with the dough hook attached. If you have to leave the mixture standing for any length of time, cover it and keep at room temperature.

Just before serving, or taking the wheat to church, form the mixture into a large flattish loaf, the size and shape of your serving tray. (Ideally, it should be a very large oval, silver tray with side-handles). Place the loaf on the tray and sift the rusk crumbs over it, pressing the crumbs gently down with a piece of folded greaseproof paper. Sift the remaining icing sugar evenly over the crumbs. Decorate the top with words or symbols, carefully drawn with the handle of a spoon. If you wish, fill the indentations with silver balls.

SYMPOSIUM FARE

Constance Cruickshank   1959

LENTEN OCCASIONS

Lenten Fare and Food for Fridays is a good example of the
sort of outstanding book which results when someone who
writes clearly and well settles down to deal thoroughly with
some well defined subject – and probably more for her (or his)
own satisfaction than for any other reason. I always enjoy
dipping into Constance Cruickshank's book.

The FIFTH SUNDAY *in* LENT

The Fifth Sunday in Lent is known as Passion Sunday, a name which goes back at least to Wyclif's day and presumably much further. It used formerly also to be known as Care or Carle Sunday; but this seems now to be quite forgotten, except possibly in the little rhyme:

> Care Sunday, Care away;
> Palm Sunday, and Easter Day.

Though the derivation has been debated, it is probable that both names, Latin and English, refer to the passion or suffering of Our Lord. This is the Sunday which begins the period of Passiontide and the deeper meaning of Lent. It is worth noticing in passing that the present use of the term Passion Week is comparatively modern. This name originally meant what we now call Holy Week. When this continental usage was introduced, the earlier name was taken to refer to the week following Passion Sunday.

The name Carling or Carlin Sunday has already been referred to. There is no doubt that the Fifth Sunday is the one best known for carlings. Perhaps this is partly due to the old tradition, still observed here and there, that inns should serve them free to their guests on this day. It is said that they encourage thirst.

Originally peas and beans were fasting fare, and Brand presumed that their connection with this day goes back to the Roman association of beans with funerals. I quote his deductions though they are open to doubt. 'In the old Roman Calendar so often cited, I find it observed on this day, that "a dole is made of *soft Beans*". I can hardly entertain a doubt but that our custom is derived from hence. It was usual amongst the Romanists to give beans in the doles at funerals: it was also a rite in the funeral ceremonies of heathen Rome. Why we have substituted peas I know not, unless it was because they are a pulse somewhat fitter to be eaten at this season of the year. They are given away in a kind of dole at this day. Our Popish ancestors celebrated (as it were by anticipation) the funeral of Our Lord on this Care Sunday.'

However this may be, by the eighteenth century carlings came to be regarded as matters of jollity. A passage from 1724 says, 'There lads and lassies will feast ... on sybows [onions], and riforts [radishes] and carlings', a reference which occurs also in an old Scots song. And we cannot imagine that those parties at the inns were occasions of great sobriety. It appears that the carlings which survived were a festive form of the original plain parched peas.

There are a number of theories about the origin of this name, in one or other of its forms. The Yorkshire people who observed their Carlin Sunday on Mothering Sunday, are said to have got the name from the word for old woman. A more usual derivation, from the other spelling, is that it comes from Care or Carle Sunday, in the way, suggests Brand, that presents from fairs are called fairlings, or as we should say, fairings.

Quite another explanation, again of this spelling, is that a ship was wrecked with a cargo of peas and the starving peasants seized the food and have ever after commemorated the event. According to this picturesque legend, the name carling comes from part of the boat's structure, which no doubt was also washed up. Some say it was an Australian boat, others put it back to Commonwealth days; but in sober fact the name was known well before that date. The first appearance noted in the *Oxford English Dictionary* is in Turner's Herbal of 1562, 'the perched or burstled peasen which are called in Northumbria Carlines'.

Perhaps it is no wonder that such an old and persistent custom should have such a varied appearance today. It must at one time have been very widespread. Scotland knew it and most of the north of England. I am told by a firm which supplies the peas, that the custom is still observed to a certain extent in Northumberland, Durham and parts of Cumberland and Yorkshire; though they say that the tradition has been much weakened since the break in the war years.

CARLINGS

Wash and steep the carlings for 24 hours. Then boil for 2 hours till they are soft. Drain and dry by frying in butter for a few minutes. Put into a bowl and mix with more butter and lots of sugar and add a small glass of rum. Eat while hot. They are delicious.   *Mrs Ivison, Morpeth, Northumberland*

It is not always rum that is added. Other spirits or wine can be used and not always that. The carlings can be served plain with butter, salt and pepper or with vinegar.

I have had one amusing anecdote from a writer who took a friend to a small local inn which still serves carlings, which are fried in big brass pans on Carling Sunday morning. Each person who goes in receives a small saucerful with rum flavouring. Afterwards the visitor was heard to remark that he didn't care much for the grey peas but he did enjoy the gravy!

GOOD FRIDAY

There are innumerable popular superstitions connected with Good Friday. The washing of clothes, for instance, is considered unlucky. Nor would showmen of old open a fair. As recently as the 1951 Festival of Britain, it was reported in *The Times* that the Battersea Fun Fair had a kind of dress rehearsal on Maundy Thursday, especially to avoid this. On the other hand it is believed to be lucky to sow parsley, and that baking on this day will be blessed. It is also considered lucky to break crockery, and in Devon people used to do so on purpose so that the pieces should pierce Judas's body. Other Judas customs arose in different places, and may still survive.

Good Friday has always been a day to be observed with special strictness. It is said that in Ireland in the last century country-women were known to refuse their babies the breast till midday; and rather later in date my own aunt remembers their Catholic maids who commonly observed the Black Fast by eating nothing at all, or only a little dry bread with water. The Roman Church, which has dispensed the general law of fasting, still maintains the fast on Good Friday and Ash Wednesday. The rules do allow for a certain amount of food; but I believe a stricter fast is still kept by many. Certainly it is the rule in Anglican religious communities.

In England, among the general public, normal Lenten dishes such as fish pie or salt cod and parsnips were retained as Good Friday fare for people who never observed the fast in other ways. Even today, many people eat fish on this day who never think about it on other Fridays of the year; and it is noticeable that in many areas fish shops are still specially opened when everything else is closed.

In some coastal parts it was customary to gather and eat shellfish on Good Friday. I have heard of it from three quite independent sources from places as far removed as Guernsey and the Isle of Man. In between lie Cornwall and Scilly Isles, both places which share this custom. I am much indebted to Mrs. Hawke who sent me some very interesting information which I can do no better than to quote as she sent it to me: 'a very old Cornish custom was "going trigging". This meant collecting shellfish. At a case at Bodmin Sessions 1838, concerning the taking of oysters at Helford on Good Friday, evidence was given that "trigging" was an immemorial practice on Good Friday in the days of Queen Anne. In the Isles of Scilly it is known as "winkling", and last year (1957) it was reported that Scillonians upheld the ancient customs on Good Friday and gathered winkles for the "well-known Winkle Tea".' In Guernsey till early in the century they used to cook and eat limpets on the shore. This repast was accompanied in Jersey by a *Gâche à Fouée* (a dough or breadcake eaten hot with plenty of butter) and in later times with hot cross buns.

In the northern counties, especially in the Lake District areas, there is the quite different tradition of the Herb Pudding. It is doubtful now whether anybody associates this with Good Friday or even with the Church at all; but the connection is clear in the local names for bistort, the principal herb, and it is obvious that this is the English version of the continental customs mentioned under Maundy Thursday. Everywhere the Church in her wisdom has hallowed and encouraged the prudent use of the 'spring-cleaning' herbs, as they are commonly known. An enormous variety of leaves are put into the herb pudding, the various docks, nettles, dandelions, Lady's Mantle, blackcurrant leaves, cabbage, kale, leeks, chives, mint – as one writer told me, 'in fact you can use any kitchen garden leaves except rhubarb'. She also went on to say that the ingredients for herb pudding can still be bought in Carlisle market at the right season ready for cooking.

One old name for this pudding was Passion Dock Pudding, from the Passion Dock or bistort (*Polygonum bistorta*), known also as Snakeweed or Adderwort. This is not to be confused with Herb Patience (*Rumex patientia*), which has larger leaves and is used as spinach, or with the Sour Dock or Common Sorrel (*Oxalis*), which has a sharper flavour; though both of these herbs can be used in the pudding. At some time the name 'passion' seems to have been transferred by popular etymology to bistort from Herb Patience, because of the association with Passiontide. There are probably still certain variations of usage in the valleys today. The local name for this plant in Cumberland and neighbouring counties, which is still used in a variety of forms, is Easter Giants or Easter Mangiants now thought to be from the French *manger*, to eat. Another traditional name in this area is Easter Ledger or Ledges. I have also found Wester Ledges, which has clearly developed from another local misapprehension.

Nowadays the herb pudding is commonly eaten with meat. It can be made in several ways. Usually there are oats or barley. The chopped leaves are mixed with the cereals and boiled or baked and sometimes both. An egg and possibly cream can be added after boiling. Here is a representative recipe I have received from the Yorkshire–Lancashire border.

Passion Dock *or* Herb Pudding

Groats   Nettles, docks, etc.   A little mint

Chop the leaves and mix all together and boil in a pudding cloth. The dock grew in patches in the meadow and were gathered when young.

'Yorkshirewoman'

This is the simplest and I am sure the oldest method.

Lenten Fare and Food for Fridays

Rinjing Dorje   1985

TIBETAN NEW YEAR

We already met this author on page 160. Here is a rather
different passage from his book, one of the many in which he
describes Tibetan occasions which involve special food customs.

The yearly cycle starts with New Year's Day. In Tibet this is called *Losar* and it is the biggest holiday celebration of the year. Lamas and monks work hard to prepare the monasteries for the ceremony. Outside they whitewash the monastery and dust and clean on the inside. Prayer flags are hung up all around the monastery, and brand new brocades from China are put on the statues of Buddhas and other deities. Most monks also receive a new set of robes from their patrons or family.

The pots and pans are glittering clean. Fine ash soap is used to wash the pots, and some of these big pots and pans have not been washed inside and out like this for a whole year. Even the stone steps leading up to the monastery are rubbed and oiled. Hundreds of butter lamps are lit, and bundles of incense are ready to burn. Whatever flowers one can find are put on the altar, and hundreds of holywater bowls are shined up until they sparkle and filled with fresh water.

Two piles of *kapse* are placed in front of the altar. *Kapse* is decorated with all sorts of luxury foods such as candies, dried fruits, rock-sugar, and nuts. Outside in the courtyard of the monastery there is a large pile of juniper, rhododendron, and other fragrant branches and flowers ready to light for use as incense during the ceremony.

Among the lay people, everyone is excited about *Losar*. They too clean the house, and sometimes whitewash as well. Everything is cleaned up and made shiny. The children are the most excited of all, as many receive a new set of clothing. Sometimes they also receive sweets such as rock candy, raw sugar (*buram*), or even hardened honey. People start preparations days ahead to be ready for the New Year's celebration.

I remember I always had a hard time falling asleep on the night before *Losar*. I was very anxious to wear my new clothes in the morning and to see everything all brightened up. Even the yaks' and sheep's horns are oiled and shined. The animals wear fancy collars and new bells are put on their necks. The men and women all wash their hair and braid it. They put on their jewelry and their very best clothes.

Early on *Losar* morning, the first day of the first month of the year, even before it gets light enough for anyone to see the lines on their palms, the adult men and women walk silently to the stream or lake where the villagers normally get their daily water. Along with their large water buckets, they carry bells, and cymbals. They fill up the buckets and carry them on their backs. As they walk home they ring the bells and play cymbals. The sound is like a big herd of animals coming home. When they arrive at the house, the grandmother and grandfather of the house bring out fresh butter in a large bowl, and take a pinch of it, and stick some on, right above the forehead of each member of the family.

Then everyone else gets dressed and goes into the house and sits down in a row. The oldest person in the family sits in the place of honor, at the top of the row of seats, next to the altar. The mother or grandmother of the family brings in the *chemar* (*tsampa* mixed with butter and sugar) and passes it around. Each member of the family takes a pinchful and throws it into the air along with prayers. They do this three times and eat the fourth pinch. This is to symbolize plenty for the grain harvest in the year to come. Next each member of the family is served with a bowl of yoghurt. This symbolizes a plentiful supply of products from the animals in the year to come. Since most Tibetans are either farmers or nomads, these prayers are very important.

Each person next receives a *derka*, a plate of *kapse* along with other treats. Everyone gets exactly the same amount of *derka*, even the unborn baby in its mother's womb is given a *derka*, which is saved.

Then the *cha* (butter tea) is served to everyone. The mother and daughter of the house are usually the servers. For this occasion the tea is made as thick as possible and is churned with lots of fresh butter and cream. There are old stories about how the tea is judged to be thick enough and best quality for serving. After the tea is poured into the cup, a coin is set carefully over the tea. If the coin floats without sinking, then the tea is proved to be good.   FOOD IN TIBETAN LIFE

Maggie Black   1985

SAINT AGNES' FEAST

St. Agnes, who was only thirteen years old when she was martyred, became immensely popular as the patron saint of all young girls who dreamed of a perfect marriage. In the North Country, especially throughout Durham, there was a special ritual on St. Agnes Eve. A pair of girls who wanted to dream of their future spouses had to abstain from food, drink and speech all that day. At night they made a Dumb Cake (doughy flatbread) with ingredients provided by their friends, who also had to take equal shares in baking and turning the cake and in removing it from the oven. The cooked cake was halved, and each girl had to carry her share to bed walking backwards, eat it and jump into bed. The solid dough supper after fasting and brooding on the ideal husband all day might well make any girl have dreams.

In nearby Northumberland they had other ways of stimulating the desired dreams. Here girls ate hard-boiled eggs, shell and all, filled with salt in place of the yolks. In fishing villages they might choose a salty raw red herring complete with its bones. Indigestion is a great aid to magic!   CALENDAR OF FEASTS

Lionel Stone   1982

The PASSOVER MEAL

*Orthodox Jews have one of the most strict set of dietary rules
and some of the most scrupulously observed food customs in
the world. Lionel Stone, brought up in an Australian
household of this persuasion, wrote a highly comprehensible
(and witty, but sympathetic) essay about all this, from which
the following passage on the Passover is taken.*

Exodus 12 and 13 prohibit the consumption of leavened food during the Passover week. Rabbinic authority has extended this text to include all comestibles derived from the fermentation (souring) of the basic cereal crops – wheat, barley, oats, rye, spelt, millet, rice and maize, whether intact or ground into flour.

Thus, not only is leavened (risen) bread forbidden, but precautions must be taken to ensure that neither the grain nor the flour become damp before the dough for matzos (unleavened bread) is mixed. This authority has ordained that cereals take 18 minutes to 'sour', and so all operations between the time water is first added to the flour and the baked matzo is removed from the oven must perforce be accomplished very speedily, with inspectors employed by the *Bayt Din* – and not the baker – to ensure that time is treated as being of the essence. Using modern equipment, each batch is mixed, kneaded, rolled flat and baked within 5 minutes. Thus after every three batches (15 minutes) production ceases while all the bowls, beaters, ladles, rollers, conveyors and oven peels are thoroughly washed and all unused dough eliminated.

Satisfied that all rules have been obeyed, and that the matzos are accordingly fit to be eaten on Passover, the inspectors seal each package; but such certification will be invalidated if careless household practice allows the matzos to come into contact with either foods which contain leaven or vessels which have held leavened food.

Matzo is a thin wafer, with absolutely no crumb, and should not be confused with *pita*, the standard thin bread of the Middle East. Matzo's lack of crumb is due to the steps outlined above to prevent the dough rising. The paucity of crumb in *pita* is due to primitive technique.

I recall the care with which all leavened goods were banished from my childhood home for the duration of Passover. All cereals, flours, yeast and baking powder were *ipso facto* victims of the anti-leaven syndrome. The dining table, kitchen dresser, pantry shelves and food preparation areas were scoured with boiling hot water; all the pots, pans and other cooking utensils, crockery, cutlery and napery in use throughout the year were safely locked away, complete with prominent labels which reminded us that they were not to be used until after *pesach* (Passover).

Theoretically, nearly all the utensils could have been made *kosher-le-pesach* (kosher for Passover) by hot water scouring, careful laundering and so on – that is to say, all items except those made of earthenware or porcelain, whose porosity made the rabbis conclude that they couldn't be made entirely leaven-free. But all in all, it was much simpler to reserve such articles for *pesach* use from the moment of their purchase as new items. Washing up was conducted in a large, metal baby's bath inserted into the meat side kitchen sink. The milk sink was blocked off for the duration.

There is no problem with wine and brandy, for both come from grapes which are not a cereal. But alcohol made from wetted grain – such a beer, whisky, gin and vodka – are out for the Passover.

Rabbinic authority ruled that cereal flours are incapable of leavening after they've been cooked – thus it is impermissible to use flour as a thickener for soup on *pesach*, but matzo meal may be freely used in cooking, as the flour was cooked during the course of baking the matzo. So it goes into matzo pudding, and dumplings.

The usual sharp distinction between meat and dairy remains, so the prohibition of real or suspected leavened foods is an additional requirement of the *pesach* period. In practice, we found it simpler to rule out dairy products, so we survived with just the one set of pots, crockery, etc.

This meant that we continued to eat kosher meat and poultry which was certified by the inspectors to be uncontaminated by any leavened foods. (Many of the 'small-goods' on sale in butchers' shops contain a little cereal, so the kosher butchers' shops needed to be specially cleaned for the Passover.) We also ate eggs, fish, tea, coffee, salt, sugar, and the full range of vegetables and fruits.

However, there was another problem. My people couldn't use packeted tea, coffee, sugar and so on, because in the days before World War 2 the adhesive most often used to seal packets was paste, which was wetted flour extract and therefore 'out'. Instead, larger quantities of these commodities were bought in problem-free containers – I still recall the tea in lead-lined wooden chests, net contents 14 lb, sugar in jute sugar bags, and the like. Of course, these foods do not deteriorate, and we continued to use them after the holydays.

The cereal content of *cholent* must, inevitably, be eliminated during Passover – so, more dumplings and more potatoes proportionately. Some communities would also forgo dried beans, just to be on the safe side.

The two loaves of fancily shaped bread which normally grace the holyday meal table are replaced on Passover by three matzos. The extra, third matzo emphasizes the importance of non-leavened food at this time. The meal ceremony of washing the hands and blessing the bread still pertains at Passover, and an extra blessing is pronounced for the benefit of the matzo. A piece is then broken off, dipped in salt and eaten as the usual preliminary to the rest of the meal. The normal grace is recited at meal end.

PETITS PROPOS CULINARIES (PPC) *11*

CHRISTMAS PUDDING

Our Christmas pudding, together with most of the secular
aspects of our celebration of Christmas, can correctly be
described as a 19th century innovation; but not a complete
innovation, since it has a long succession of antecedents.
Maggie Black succinctly describes its history.

All over England on Stir Up Sunday – the Sunday before Advent – some families still gather round the big bowl in which the Christmas Pudding lies glistening. Each member, even the smallest, gives the mixture at least a token stir, and makes a silent wish for blessing. The idea behind the custom is that the whole household should join in preparing for the year's most joyous festival.

This custom is quite a modern one, because the special association of Plum Pudding with Christmas only dates back to about 1836. But the pudding itself, like other boiled puddings, had been popular since 1617 when the pudding cloth was invented. Before that, so-called puddings were stuffings or else starchy, spiced mixtures boiled in a bladder like a haggis.

The real forerunner of Christmas Pudding was a meat pottage or soup, thickened with breadcrumbs and egg, flavoured with spices and dried fruit, and coloured bright red. It was called unromantically Stewed Broth, and it began its climb to fame in late Tudor times when prunes were first added to boiled mixtures. These dried plums were so popular that they gave their name to all other dried fruits. Thus curranty breads and cakes became plum cakes, and Stewed Broth became Plumb Pottage.

Soon, with the opening up of the New World and Eastern trading posts, dried fruits and sugar became cheap enough to make Plum Pottage a festival dish, even for the poor. Now a more solid, richer mixture or porridge, it changed its name again to Plum or Christmas Porridge. As such, well thickened, it became one of the first candidates for boiling in a bag or cloth.

The first cloth-boiled plum puddings seem to have contained no alcohol. However, George I on his first Christmas Day in England was served a rich Plum Pudding which had lost its meat, but kept its suet and had gained a large wineglass of brandy. In 1806 Mrs. Maria Rundell put a recipe for Common Plum Pudding with wine in it among her meat puddings. Ten years later, Dr. William Kitchiner created a Plum Pudding with brandy as – of all things – a Lenten dish. Far from being exclusively a Christmas treat, a handsome Plum Pudding had come to crown every parish feast or Harvest Home, tithe dinner or wedding breakfast.

Both rich and poor enjoyed Plum Pudding at Christmas. The pudding could be boiled in a pot over the family fire, so was cheap on fuel. It was a big treat to supplement the poor man's usually meagre beef or goose. It was in this role that Charles Dickens saw it. Good journalist that he was, he wrote it up as the central symbol of Christmas cheer and plenty, and found a receptive audience. The new urban middle class was seeking to recreate what they believed had been mediaeval Christmas revelry. Moreover, the concept and the dish were just to the taste of the young Queen Victoria's husband, Prince Albert. So Christmas Pudding became what we know it today.

CALENDAR OF FEASTS

Patience Gray   *1986*

The CHRISTMAS FISH of LECCE

A fish was one of the earliest and most widespread symbols of
Christianity. It survives in many forms and many places,
including an edible one from Lecce in Apulia, whose many
layers of symbolism are laid bare in this passage by Patience
Gray (see page 110).

The Almond has this connection with the Virgin, that it has long been considered to bear fruit without previous fecundation. This ancient belief, still held by Salentine peasants, is mentioned in a discussion of the *XXIème Arcane majeur du Tarot de Marseille* – the card representing the World, in which the central figure is enclosed in an almond-shaped vesica of laurel leaves.

So, in relation to the Christmas fishes made of *pasta di mandorla* at Lecce one sees in their point of departure, in the shape of the nut, the *vesica piscis* – also called *la mandorla* (almond), the divine nimbus, the aura of sanctity, the cosmic egg. The ritually made fishes celebrate the birth of Christ in conjunction with the era of Pisces.

The nuns of a convent at Lecce are famed for these confections, but live permanently withdrawn from the world, so I am not able to give their recipe in all its simplicity, in all its refinement. But the basis of these sublime creations is as follows.

A quantity of almonds are shelled (let us say ½ a kilo – 1 lb 2 oz – when shelled, of sweet almonds, but including 3 or 4 bitter ones). Covered for a moment in boiling water, they are rapidly peeled. Laid on a linen cloth, they are set to dry in the sun for 2 days. The shining white almonds are then pounded, a few at a time, in a stoneware or marble mortar to a very fine powder with a marble pestle.

Originally one supposes the ground almonds were amalgamated with honey to achieve a firm but plastic consistency capable then of being pressed into lightly oiled traditional fish-moulds made of pearwood, copper, zinc, tin and plaster of Paris, patterned with carp-like scales. Nowadays a quantity of caster sugar equal to that of the almonds is used, but it is incorporated in an original way: in a copper pan the sugar is melted by stirring over a very low heat, using a minimum of hot water to bring this about without burning, the almond flour is sifted in, stirring vigorously and continuously the while, and the pan is taken off the fire only when the mixture coheres and comes away from the bottom and the sides. It is then left to cool in a bowl until it is lukewarm.

When filling the oiled mould, a depression is made in the centre of the fish into which some pear conserve (*la perata*) is carefully spooned, then covered with more paste. *La perata* has the aspect of dark amber, both the fruit and its syrup being transparent and glazed.

When the fish is turned out, a coffee bean is pressed into its eye socket. As coffee was only imported in the 17th century, arriving in Venice in 1615 from Moka, and the fish stem from time immemorial – as do the almond cakes called *divino amore* at Gallipoli – one wonders what constituted the eye before that, a raisin perhaps.

Some adepts lay on top of the pear preserve a narrow layer of *pan di Spagna*, a refined sponge cake, impregnated with rum, surely a Bourbon intrusion at the time when Lecce formed part of the Kingdom of Naples.

The significance of the pear preserve dawned on me one afternoon when a Leccese friend, Laura Rossi, sitting under the fig-tree, complained of the price of pears at Lecce, their conserve being, she emphasized, *obbligatorio* (obligatory) in the making of the Christmas fish. This word *obbligatorio* – more often used with reference to religious duties than to culinary procedure – stuck in my mind. And then I remembered that some Greek Orthodox friends had brought an Easter offering of delightful aspect – a shallow wicker basket containing haricot beans wreathed round with acacia flowers and leaves and on it a little crown of newly sprouting thorny wild pear. In the Greek Orthodox Church the wild pear is Christ's thorn, His Crown.

Sometimes in spring a neighbour appears at Spigolizzi to graft onto the wild pear trees, that grow spontaneously on the calcareous hillside, the shoots of a cultivar which produce the small honey-sweet pears for *la perata*. Thus another aspect of the Christmas fish is revealed: the destiny of the Christ child, concealed in the stomach of a fish.

Holy lambs are made of *pasta mandorlata* for Easter, in the same way, their heads of painted plaster, with red and gold paper flags. It is said that one cannot enter into the World of Symbols without cultivating a certain receptivity: the Leccesi who are devoted both to truth and to *friandises* act on this advice literally when confronted with the delectable *pesce di Natale*.

Honey from a Weed

Peter Brears   1987

WHITSUNTIDE FARE *in* YORKSHIRE

The study of traditional food in Yorkshire by Peter Brears
includes an account of many festival foods. Here Charlotte
Brontë is invoked to help describe those of Whitsuntide.

Early on this joyous morn,
What beautious articles are borne
Through the streets with utmost care,
Teapots, urns, and chinaware,
Jugs of sweet delicious cream
Glitter in the sun's bright beam;
Great tin boilers you may see,
To boil the water for the tea.

Whit Monday was the great day for Sunday School Anniversaries when the scholars of both Nonconformist and Anglican congregations walked in procession around their village, singing outside the homes of leading members of the community. Sometimes they were accompanied by their own musicians, perhaps with a harmonium on a horse-drawn cart, or even a military band. Further flat carts might be employed to carry the younger scholars, but the Rev. Baring Gould preferred to rely on the stirring strains of 'Onward, Christian Soldiers' which he wrote to march his scholars up the steep Quarry Hill to reach Horbury Parish Church. Early in the century the scholars might have been fortified with ale and rum and hot tea, but from the 1850s the teetotal movement brought an abrupt end to all alcoholic stimulants.

While the walk was in progress, the ladies were busily employed in the schoolroom preparing the food for the patrons and teachers of the schools, and for the children, the tables being set up out of doors if there was a field near at hand and the weather was fine. The wealthier churches might have sufficient crockery to serve the entire gathering, but it was far more common to ask each child to bring a mug of its own, strands of coloured thread being wound around the handle to clearly establish its ownership. An excellent description of the whitsuntide school feast is given in Charlotte Brontë's *Shirley*.

At four, 'long lines of benches were arranged in the close-shorn fields round the school: there the children were seated, and huge baskets, covered up with white cloths, and great smoking tin vessels were brought out. Ere the distribution of good things commenced, a brief grace was pronounced by Mr. Hall, and sung by the children, their young voices sounded melodious, even touching, in the open air. Large currant buns, and hot, well-sweetened tea, were then administered in the proper air of liberality: the rule for each child's allowance being that it was to have about twice as much as it could possibly eat, thus leaving a reserve to be carried home for such as age, sickness, or other impediment, prevented from coming to the feast. Buns and beer circulated, meanwhile, amongst the musicians and church-singers: afterwards the benches were removed, and they were left to unbend their spirits in licensed play.' A century later, the same events were taking place in exactly the same manner (except for the beer), individual paper bags containing a range of potted beef sandwiches and buns being distributed at our chapel at Thorpe near Wakefield.

TRADITIONAL FOOD IN YORKSHIRE

Anita Bouverot-Rothacker *1982*

CHRISTMAS EVE *in* PROVENCE: *Le* GROS SOUPER

There is so much to be said about this traditional meal, its symbolism and its variations, that each course requires a whole chapter in Anita Bouverot-Rothacker's study. This passage comes from the chapter on desserts.

Then come the desserts – and further arguments. How many are there? Thirteen, states Ricard in *Le Gros Souper à Marseille.* 'This custom is without doubt the most celebrated and honoured of all Christmas traditions.' It was a most regrettable omission, he goes on, in certain books whose authors give us no details. Fernand Benoit also confirms that there are thirteen 'according to the Marseilles tradition': raisins, dried figs, almonds and walnuts, plums, pears, apples, citrus preserve, quince jelly, black and white nougat, *cachat* and *fougasse.*

Mistral himself does not indicate the number of sweetmeats in *Mémoires et Récits,* mentioning only one or two. Villeneuve correctly points out that 'the dessert varies in its splendour according to family resources' and Seignolle goes back to several different traditions to do with the number and composition of the desserts. Jouveau in *La Cuisine Provençale,* even if he does side with those claiming there were thirteen desserts, recognizes the fact that they were not immutable.

So, as you can see, there is a fair degree of confusion. 'Thirteen desserts was the tradition, but not everybody followed it'; 'there were not thirteen but several desserts'; 'thirteen is only a rough guide – there are more when finances permit'.

No unanimity can be reached either on the number or the composition of the desserts. Just as for the main course, people used 'this and that', whatever they had to hand. Hence the variations. However, there are three traditions common throughout Provence: fruit, nougat and a sense of celebration. Beyond this, customs such as the baking of tarts apply to a wide area (inland Provence) whereas others are very localised, often no more than family customs.

'Hereabouts [in one part of Provence] people would make thirteen desserts. Here it was walnuts, almonds, nuts, dried figs. The latter were known as "beggars".' In fact 'beggars' featured in all desserts. Many people from Provence will tell you that there were four beggars, but cannot agree either on their names or their meaning. According to Ricard, their name derives from the similarity between their colour and that of the monks' habits from the four mendicant orders. Walnuts or nuts generally were Augustines; figs were Franciscans; almonds were Carmelites; and raisins were Dominicans.

Fruit was something people got from their own property and which they kept for the *Gros Souper*, such as grapes. 'I well remember the grapes we put by for Christmas when I was a child. We had a vine of white grapes and a vine of black grapes which we kept especially for Christmas. Before the harvest we would go out and select the best grapes, those which weren't damaged, which were beautifully translucent, and we would put them in baskets. A layer of leaves, then a layer of grapes, then, when we got home we hung them up in bunches on hooks attached to the ceiling and left them there to ripen.'

To the statutory 'beggars' other fruit was added as desired. Around Christmas it was apples and pears practically everywhere, with melons in the Vaucluse and chestnuts at Collobrières and La Doire.

'And afterwards we would buy oranges, mandarins, and dates, known as African figs, but only when I was older. (Report from Sainte-Cécile). These fruits made their appearance earlier in Marseilles, since Millin records their presence at the beginning of the 19th century. 'Oranges form pyramids crowned with garlands of sweet smelling blossom from the tree which produced them.' In the country, they were not on sale until between the wars. Oranges were still a special Christmas gift presented to the children.

'Around these exquisite dishes, which nature has generously donated, pâtisseries were arranged, sweetmeats of all kinds, white nougat being a conspicuous guest.' (Millin). Before Christmas, in every family, the honey is heated. When it bubbles, pieces of sugar are added and grilled almonds are tossed until they begin to crackle. Then the mixture is poured into a mould lined with wafers. Then weights are placed upon it. The nougat is cut into bars while it is still warm, three or four hours later. In Marseilles you can find both black and white nougat.

Le Gros Souper

ODDITIES *and* PARTING SMILES

'Don't you know where milk comes from?'
asked a horrified Asian.
My oddity may be your norm. But there
should be something here to set anyone
twitching slightly in his or her cultural
straitjacket. To offset any discomfort,
I conclude with some Parting Smiles.

Gilda Cordero-Fernando   1976

FILIPINO DELICACIES

*I am not sure whether the Philippines constitute an unusually
rich territory for those who hunt exotic foods, or whether it is
just that Filipinos have written more about their foodstuffs
than other South-East Asians. Anyway, some quite strange
things are eaten there.*

Animals, said Brillat-Savarin, are limited in their tastes, some of them live on nothing but vegetables. Others eat only flesh, some feed exclusively on grain. Only man has been created omnivorous and everything that is edible is at the mercy of his vast appetite.

Exotic foods are eaten for higher enjoyment or strictly from hunger – they are coveted by the very sophisticated or by the very poor. Anything that flies or moves, the rural Filipino quickly swats, cooks and eats. His catholic diet includes the pupa of honeybees, birds' nests, fresh-water beetles, sea urchins, lizards, iguanas, pythons, octopus and field rats, all of which are described as 'very delicious – tastes just like chicken.' Many of our animals have become extinct. Danger stalks the few monkey-eating eagles that dare fly across the clearing – some hunter is sure to be watching below with a hungry eye. The tabon bird of Palawan lays only two eggs and one of them is sure to get egg-napped. Even man's best friend is not spared. The dog is part of the rural drinking scene – alas, he is the delicacy on the table.

Other Philippine exotica are easily acceptable to city gourmets such as the incomparable fresh-water *maliputo* and *tawilis* – fish caught only in the Pansipit River and Taal Lake of Batangas. The eel which is cooked in yellow ginger is just as much a delicacy here as in Japan. Perhaps the best example of the Filipino's indulgence of his palate is the *talangka*, a tiny crab whose red fat is squeezed out and salted. (Later it is heated over cooking rice and eaten with rice.) To fill one small jar with fat, however, requires the meticulous shelling and picking of hundreds of these tiny crabs and many a cook has gotten cross-eyed at the task. Man is, after all, the only creature who does not eat only because he is hungry...

Turtle eggs are a delicacy in Sulu where they are dug from the sand of the seashore where the mama turtle lays them. It is believed that turtles cry with loneliness at finding their nests robbed. The proper way to eat a robbed turtle egg is boiled. A small hole is knocked off one end of the soft-shelled ping-pong ball-sized egg and the delicious, slightly gritty yolk is sucked out.

Balut country – Pateros – and the neighboring Rizal towns have variations of the ubiquitous boiled duck's egg with the little black chick curled in it. *Balut* can be roasted by burying in burning rice husks with a fire on top. In the process of *balut*-making, the unfertilized eggs are removed and sold as boiled *penoy*. If the chick dies before it reaches the *balut* stage, the egg does not hatch and is called *abnoy*. These eggs are separated from the successful *balut* – and the eating of *abnoy*, they say, is what separates the men from the boys. The chicks are removed from the eggs which by now have an odor, and a rotten egg omelet is made out of the yolks and whites. This round omelet on a banana leaf is called *bibingkang itlog* and *balut* fiends swear that, like the *duryan* fruit, it has the stink of hell but tastes like heaven. *Bibingkang itlog* is traditionally eaten with last night's cold rice and is dipped in vinegar flavored with crushed garlic.

The duck egg whose chick attains *rigor mortis* just when it is about to hatch (therefore past the *balut* stage) is called *ukbo*. With a large chick inside and no yolk or white left, *ukbo* eggs are cracked, the shell thrown away, and the feathers of the duckling removed. The ducklings are cooked *adobo* style, fried, and returned to their stock.

Azucena or dogmeat is the popular *pulutan* (canape) of drinking bouts. In the Mountain Province, dogs are raised for eating, but in the depressed parts of the city where dog-eating is also a clandestine passion, dog-eaters scan the highways for dogs that have been run over. Or they find a family who wants to get rid of a fierce pet, or in desperation dognap one.

The dog is opened from stem to stern and its hair singed. The intestines are made into *tinumis*. The dog flesh is scrubbed and quartered. Some like to eat dogmeat raw, only slightly seared on the skin, and with a *sawsawan* made out of uncooked liver mashed with vinegar, garlic and onions. Others like their *azucena* fully cooked, *adobo*-style, with a handful of hot red peppers. Raw dogmeat is served with gin, and *adobo* dogmeat is served with beer. . .

To make *kilawing musang* or wildcat cooked in vinegar, place a banana on the roof of the house. Trap the wildcat in the act of stealing it. Subdue the wildcat, kill and quarter it. Stew in a pot with vinegar and a lot of hot pepper.

Take heart when meeting a python in the jungles of Mindoro. Overpowering it will assure you of a pretty good *sinigang*. The delicious taste of snakemeat is a cross between chicken and tunafish (and of course the skin makes a nice inedible bag). For dinner, trap an iguana as it feeds on young plants on the shore. This tender vegetarian makes a rather praiseworthy *adobo*. Only for the very adventurous is the eating of mountain rats, marinated in nipa vinegar with garlic, salt, peppercorns and the juice of a lemon, the pieces are speared on bamboo sticks and barbecued – the original *daga*-cue!

A delicate tongue and a strong stomach are required in the eating of the wormwood (*tamilok*) picked from *bakawan* driftwood in Agusan, Surigao and Davao. The wood is chopped up so that the worms, pink, about six to eight inches long, may be extracted, washed a little, and deposited wriggling on one's tongue.

'Table Exotica'
THE CULINARY CULTURE OF THE PHILIPPINES

Tom Jaine   1986

EATING BADGER

Most restaurateurs who go into print (sometimes with ghostly
aid) are effective in broadcasting their recipes but not
much else.
An interesting exception is Tom Jaine, who used to be at the
Carved Angel in Dartmouth with Joyce Molyneux (whither
my wife and I once went for a wedding anniversary dinner,
the only one out of 36 for which we have travelled more than
20 miles, and it certainly 'merited the journey', as Michelin
would say). Jaine's wide reading and eclectic interests are
reflected in what he writes and publishes; also, as here, his
thoughtful attitude to foods.

We are living through a period of rapid change in perceptions of what is and what is and what is not permissible food. This has been charted for the centuries since the Reformation by Keith Thomas, in his *Man and the Natural World* (1983). More recently, Stephen Mennell has discussed the same question in his *All Manners of Food* (1985). As our sensibilities increased or altered and we began to take a more holistic view of the world, so humanitarianism, perhaps a contrary tendency, also took hold. Great areas became out of bounds, especially to Englishmen: dogs, cats, song birds, horses. 'What! Robins! Our household birds! I would as soon eat a child,' exclaimed Mountstuart Elphinstone when travelling in Italy in the middle of the last century. As certain species were less palatable, so the slaughter of those that were left became less brutal. Flaying, polling, bleeding were superseded by the humane killer. We distanced the process, banished it from the shambles to the abattoir. As faith in our own after-life diminished so it dawned on many that death to an ox was the same as death to a human. Mortality being the bugbear that it now is, the question has to be answered: 'How can we kill anything?'

There are signs that increasing numbers of people would like never to kill, although that alienation that renders our society so difficult of comprehension means that millions of us are quite happy to witness death vicariously so long as the hand that wields the weapon is not ours. The result, gastronomically, is that meat itself becomes taboo or that its processing is so mechanised that we can fool ourselves that it never happened. Even hunters may avoid the consequences of their actions, so squeamish are they in the face of death. A fisherman brought us a 16 lb turbot the other day which he had been unable to kill. It takes skill and dispatch to cope with it humanely. He had left it in the bottom of the boat, doubtless suffering more than it would have done had he walloped it as he caught it.

The test of our attitudes towards such taboos came with the arrival on the kitchen table of a badger. It had been caught mistakenly in a fox trap, necessitating its destruction. We took a hindquarter. None of us had eaten this meat before, though badger hams have entered the folk memory of Englishmen. 'The badger is one of the cleanest creatures, in its food, of any in the world and one may suppose that the flesh of this creature is not unwholesome. It eats like the finest pork, and is much sweeter than pork.' So writes Richard Bradley in the early eighteenth century while including a recipe from one R.T. in Leicestershire for brining the gammons before spit-roasting them. Waverley Root calls badger the food of eighteenth-century English peasants seeking more succulent fare. He is accurate in this, for it was by no means dry, and had a pronounced layer of fat over the ham. Where we differ from all those people whose written comments we could find is in comparing it to pork or sucking pig. Lilli Gore for example, in *Game Cooking* (1974), commenting on the possibility or otherwise of eating bear meat, remarks, 'After I discovered what I thought to be delicious sucking pig was in fact a badger, I decided there and then to "suspend my disbelief".' We found that the most useful comparison was to mutton. The meat was dark, succulent and strong tasting, but in no way like pork, having a particular smell to it, just as does roast leg of lamb.

The ham was not large, weighing only two pounds. However, authorities had led us to expect something from four to eight pounds. We were assured that the animal was adult – its pelt would not have made us think it was anything else. The fear was that it would be dry and tough. Therefore, the method of cooking was to lard it first with herbs (mostly thyme) and then to marinate it with red wine, bay leaf, thyme and parsley, carrots and celery. It stayed in the marinade for the best part of a week. It was then pot roasted, after browning, with the marinade in a cool oven. It took much longer to cook than so small a joint should have done, upwards of three hours. It was not overcooked as a result and, although firm, was not tough. The fat, of which there was ample, was not much enjoyed. It had not been shown the open crisping heat of a hot oven.

The most informative book on badgers is Henry Smith's *Master Book of Poultry and Game* (n.d., *c.* 1950). This is a catch-all compendium, designed for the catering trade. He has instructions for curing and baking a ham, for a pie from the fore-quarters and for roasting the legs. The latter includes a seasoning of ginger and an accompanying sauce of horse-radish or gooseberry. He suggests making a gravy from the feet and the tail. I would like to know where he found his recipes. One has difficulty imagining a Trust House in the 1950s offering in its *table d'hôte* 'roast leg of badger with gooseberry sauce'.

The real question is whether we enjoyed the meal. I do not think we did. The taste was by no means unpleasant, although rich. However, the psychological difficulties in eating a truly wild animal weighed heavily upon us. Had we thought it some variant breed of lamb, delivered by the Rare Breeds Farm, we would have been interested and mildly enthusiastic. None of us has the stomach to consume wild things. Game birds no longer count as wild – the few that have not been hand-reared are soon included in the semi-domestic bracket by a quick elision of the facts. Venison has suffered the same process and is no longer viewed as a mere creature of the forest; has it not been emparked for centuries? So which wild beasts do we eat? We would not take squirrel, bear or otter; nor would we accept lark, thrush or blackbird. (The poser of thrush pâté is perhaps solved by the very fact that it is pâté.) Hares we do take and eat; they constitute the greatest exception. However, their kinship with rabbit (permissible vermin) acts against their interest. Even so, there is increasing evidence of people refusing hare.

COOKING IN THE COUNTRY

Dr André Nègre   1970

EATING IGUANA

There is a highly desirable category of cookbook which flourishes in remote places and can be recognised by the following characteristics: cheap, only on sale locally, and often reprinted; probably written by a resident foreigner; attractively rough-hewn in quality of production; bulging with local information, none of which has been edited out by anyone; and slightly zany in one way or another. A good example is Dr André Nègre's book, translated into English by Christine Nègre.

The following preparation originates rather from Guiana; for very few people eat this kind of animal, be it in the 'Saintes' where it swarms, or in Guadeloupe, yet so close to these islands. I do not think it is appreciated in Martinique either.

Why are these small animals submitted to such unanimous disspproval, so highly unjustified, whereas people are excessively fond of them in Guiana?

As a matter of fact, I am here talking of enormous lizards, the name of which comes from the Arawak Idioma 'Ioana', and which can reach the length of one meter; though quite hideous, they are inoffensive; they feed themselves only on young vegetal shoots (that is why they regularly spoil the unfrequent attempts at farming made by the inhabitants from 'Saintes') and on hibiscus flowers: no edible animal can boast of such a delicate food; man himself, if compared to this animal, eats filthy food, comparatively speaking.

I used to enjoy such animals when I was in Guiana, where people regularly and rightfully eat them; even in France, in Paris, I have been told that a 'Banquet de l'Iguane' (an iguana feast) takes place every year; and there, some gourmets, whose palates are thoroughly educated, and who do not worry about stupid prejudices, taste these delicious reptiles recommended by the Larousse dictionary.

But in the 'Saintes', in Guadeloupe and in Martinique, where people easily swallow some piglets that paddle all their life among the dirtiest, muddy places of the island, and where people really enjoy eating ducks that have been unceasingly floundering in stagnant pools or in noxious ponds, where people also taste those chickens that feed themselves on 'ravets' (that is to say enormous cockroaches), there is nevertheless an aversion to iguana and people pretend to be deeply offended when you speak of saddle of iguana prepared with a 'chasseur' sauce...

I remember having a sharp discussion with a poor small scrivener: his blotched and episcopal-amethist coloured nose turned to a cardinal purple colour at the simple idea of swallowing the leg of one of these so delicate animals...

However, at the beginning of the 17th century, R.F. du Tertre already wrote about them: 'I venture to assure that they are one of the best dishes of these islands, when prepared properly...' and he adds: 'as for me, I think that the weakness of these delicate people who, in front of some good food, let themselves starve to death out of mere caprice, is to be blamed in the same way as the extravagance of plump women who confusedly long for things that are sometimes most harmful to them'; and R.F. Labat, this West-Indian Curnonsky of the 17th century, added: 'The lizard's flesh has the same whiteness, tenderness, exquisite taste and delicacy as the chicken's.'

That is how matters stand; I think that the absence of iguanas in the gastronomic range of Guadeloupe is a serious shortage; on the eve of a touristic era which promises becoming a very important one, the traveller must have the opportunity of being offered things he does not possess in his own country, especially when these things are delicious; does not the tourist taste grilled grass-hoppers... which are not good, when in Morocco?... That is why I did want to insist upon this animal of which Parisian gourmets are so fond, in order to urge the reader in 'daring' to taste the flesh of an animal, the food of which is so delicate, and the outwards forms of which are, all things being considered, much more attractive,than the snail's, the frog's or the eel's.

All the red full-bodied, or sappy wines, which seem to have been specially created to go with game, will perfectly suit iguanas. And here I am thinking more particularly of Chambertin, which you must taste slowly, remembering Pierre Poupon's saying: 'To drink Chambertin at big gulps, at the bar of a "bistrot" is a mistake far more serious than to read Racine hurriedly in the Tube'. But all the full-bodied white wines, such as Alsace, Sancerre, Chablis, Pouilly, etc... will also go with this dish very well.

THE FRENCH WEST-INDIES THROUGH THEIR COOKERY

Jane Grigson   *1986*

CAUL FAT

*For a paper delivered to a symposium on 'The Cooking
Medium', Jane Grigson chose this subject, familiar to her but
exotic for many of her audience – though it had enormous
appeal and it was 'standing room only' in the lecture hall.
(See also pages 58 and 104.)*

The caul is a large web of fat that encloses the intestines, rather like an apron. It is not the fatty frill called mudgeon or mesentery that actually holds the intestines together – what the French call *fraise* – but a cloth-like semi-transparent sheet about a metre square, or a little less. If you see it at all at the butcher's shop, it will most likely be hanging in a greyish-yellowy-white droop, looking like a worn-out dishcloth. Unappetising. Something you would never think of asking for unless you knew its value and usefulness.

You will not see it in supermarkets. I suppose that the caul – which as far as cooking is concerned comes from a calf or a pig – usually goes along if not to the pet food factory, to wherever it is that they boil down pork fat for lard. The family butcher, the pork butcher is the place to look, or perhaps if you have a French butcher in the area.

Supposing you run a bit of caul fat to ground, you should soak it in warm water (with a splash of vinegar if it looks particularly unappetising or smells slightly odd). Then you will be able to stretch it out slowly, slowly, and its beauty will be revealed. Try to avoid tearing the transparent membrane between the web of fat.

Now you can appreciate the names it has been given. Caul used to apply mainly to the little netted caps that people wore. *Crépine*, which is the French word, is related to *crêpe* meaning both pancake and those kinds of crinkled cloth known as *crêpes* and *crêpe de chine*. *Toile* and *toilette* are also used for caul, if it comes from a calf, again a textile reference with *toile* more usually meaning cloth of one kind or another, cloth in general, or linen or canvas. *Toilette* has come to mean dressing, putting on one's clothes, but originally it meant a little cloth.

Having taken time for admiration and reflection, it soon becomes obvious that the caul is the most useful thing, a basting medium par excellence. Much better, especially in this country, than sheets of pork fat: in France and Germany and elsewhere in mainland Europe butchers pride themselves either on cutting delicate sheets of pork fat themselves or on having a wholesaler who will provide them with thin pork fat by the yard. Here you are lucky if you are flung a lump of fatty bacon with your brace of pheasants or partridge – and butchers sometimes wonder why so many people turn to vegetarianism of however muted a kind. Ask instead for a piece of caul fat to wrap the birds in. And if you have a fancy to bake a whole piece of calf's liver, it will be all the better for being enclosed in caul fat. This kind of treatment was given especially for meats that were to be braised in the past. The method was described as *en crépine – foie de veau en crépine* – and it was so much a matter of everyday kitchen knowledge that I have not been able to find a specific recipe for it. There are references to the practice that indicate that everyone knew what it meant, but no recipe that I can find headed *Quelque chose en crépine*.

The method was also used, instead of thin sheets of pork back fat, to baste pâtés. Carême uses it for his *fromage d'Italie*, one of those smooth rich pig's liver pâtés, more fat than lean, endlessly pounded by some poor kitchen boy. Interestingly he sticks to pork fat for the top – probably it was cut into beautiful patterns – and uses caul for base and sides. Once the fromage had cooled down, you warmed the sides and base of the metal mould very slightly, and, thanks to the caul fat, the whole thing turned out neatly. Once you get to the bourgeois kitchen, the caul is used to envelop the mixture completely, which is easy, even when the instructions are written by one of Europe's most famous royal chefs, Urbain Durbois. If you are a pâté-maker you will find caul fat ideal. Spread out the caul. Put a bay leaf or two, if appropriate, in the centre, right side down. Form the pâté mixture into a shape roughly the same as the terrine it is destined for and wrap it up in the caul. Cut away surplus cloth and put into the terrine, seam side down. The caul fat on top will cook to a rich brown webbing with the bay leaves showing through in a particularly appetising way. . . .

I should add that the English version in Wiltshire at least, and the Midlands, as well as the Welsh, have wrapped a chopped cooked mixture of pig's liver in caul fat to make faggots. The little round knobs are put close together in a gratin dish and baked in the oven. These can be very good, and provided a convenient way of using up unmentionable parts such as the lights and spleen. The French in the south make *gaillettes* which are similar in style, though a fairly high proportion of greenery is added. The leaves of chard for instance. In Brittany I have seen and bought *boulettes* which are pure sausagemeat cooked in the same style.

At least this pursuit of caul fat has led me to an interesting explanation of something that had vaguely puzzled me. Harslet, a large roll of bits and pieces with stuffing that one sees in pork butchers in Wiltshire at any rate, and I expect elsewhere. I took the name to be typically Wiltshire, by analogy with Archard, a surname of great respectability derived from the local pronunciation of the word Orchard. But no, I discover that it is a old derivation from the French word *attelet*, meaning a little skewer. The bits and pieces to be grilled, innards usually, were put on to wooden skewers and the whole thing was wrapped in a piece of caul fat, just as the best harslet is today. The caul fat basted the lean meat and provided a nice brown finish.

'The Cooking Medium'
OXFORD SYMPOSIUM DOCUMENTS 1985/6

Richard Beckett 1984

COCKATOOS *and* PARROTS

The standard 'bush joke' about making cockatoos edible is
faithfully reproduced by Beckett in his passage about eating
birds in Australia; but with an appropriate qualification, and
with much other interesting information.

One turns now to the parrot family. Given the bush culinary abuse that has been heaped on at least two members of that tribe – notably the galah and the sulphur-crested cockatoo – one is also surprised to note that recipes for them survived into the 20th century.

The standard bush joke about how to make a cockatoo or galah edible is to put either a stone or an axe-head into a pot of water, add either bird, and when the stone or axe-head softens, throw the bird away and eat the other material.

Unfortunately, like many other Australian sayings or jokes, it is not original. The softened stone and water tale has at least one of its origins in German folklore in which a hungry traveller talks a woodsman into giving him a nourishing meal by promising to make soup from a stone. He didn't, of course, and had chicken soup by sleight of hand instead, and was praised by the woodsman for his magic powers.

The earliest parrot pies would have been made from rosellas and probably would have been quite tasty during the fruit season when they descended like plagues on settlers' orchards. Once again, one is indebted to Mrs Pearson for her pie recipe.

8 paroquets, 4 eggs (boiled 10 mins, until hard and then put into cold water), Teaspoon of lemon juice, ½ lb bacon or ham, Little good gravy or stock, 1 lb of fillet of beef cut into thin slices, Rough puff paste.

Cut the birds into two, and rub well with butter, place the slices of beef in a pie dish and place on them the birds and slices of ham, cut in neat pieces the hard boiled eggs and add, then pour in a cup of well-seasoned stock; cover over with rough puff paste, decorate with cut leaves etc., from the paste and stick the legs and feet well cleaned and blanched in the centre.

This is a parrot pie very heavily disguised. With the addition of beef, ham, hard-boiled eggs and a good gravy, one could probably have been able to push the parrots to the side of one's plate and forget all about them.

Two more birds almost made it into the 20th century as recipes. The first was ibis. In the *Australian Cook and Laundry Book* published in 1897 Mrs Lance Rawson, after giving instructions of how 'gentlemen' should preserve game in the height of summer during a shooting party (clean the bird and stuff it with a mixture of coffee grounds and dried grass), went on to discuss this beautiful creature in very matter-of-fact terms.

This bird has a very objectionable odour and consequently is little used, but the smell is confined solely to the feathers and skin. Skin the ibis and when cleaned, lay him in vinegar and water for a couple of hours, and all the offensive odour will disappear, when he is ready to be cooked in any way you choose. If baked, he requires to be well-seasoned and constantly basted as the flesh is rather dry and it is also very dark.

Her own preferred recipe was to cut the flesh up and stew it with tomatoes, onions, herbs, sugar and pepper. It should be served, according to Mrs Rawson, garnished with slices of lemon.

CONVICTED TASTES

Peter Lund Simmonds 1859

RAT SOUP *and* OTHER ODDITIES

Simmonds' Curiosities of Food is still, more than a century later, the best available mine of information on the subject, except for his chapter on insects, which has been overtaken by Bodenheimer (see page 311). He must have been a voracious reader, and made good use of travel books, carefully noting his source in each instance. Here, a mention of rat soup in China leads him on to strange items of Chinese cookery in San Francisco and Hong Kong.

In China, rat soup is considered equal to ox-tail soup, and a dozen fine rats will realize two dollars, or eight or nine shillings.

Besides the attractions of the gold-fields for the Chinese, California is so abundantly supplied with rats, that they can live like Celestial emperors, and pay very little for their board. The rats of California exceed the rats of the older American States, just as nature on that side of the continent exceeds in bountifulness of mineral wealth. The California rats are incredibly large, highly flavoured, and very abundant. The most refined Chinese in California have no hesitation in publicly expressing their opinion of 'them rats'. Their professed cooks, we are told, serve up rats' brains in a much superior style to the Roman dish of nightingales' and peacocks' tongues. The sauce used is garlic, aromatic seeds and camphor.

Chinese dishes and Chinese cooking have lately been popularly described by the fluent pen of Mr. Wingrove Cooke, the *Times*' correspondent in China, but he has by no means exhausted the subject. Chinese eating saloons have been opened in California and Australia, for the accommodation of the Celestials who now throng the gold-diggings, despite the heavy poll-tax to which they have been subjected.

Mr. Albert Smith, writing home from China, August 22, 1858, his first impressions, says:—

'The filth they eat in the eating houses far surpasses that cooked at that old *trattoria* at Genoa. It consists for the most part of rats, bats, snails, bad eggs, and hideous fish, dried in the most frightful attitudes. Some of the *restaurateurs* carry their cook-shops about with them on long poles, with the kitchen at one end, and the *salle-à-manger* at the other. These are celebrated for a soup made, I should think, from large caterpillars boiled in a thin gravy, with onions.'

The following is an extract from the bill of fare of one of the San Francisco eating houses—

Grimalkin steaks	. .	25 cents.
Bow-wow soup	. .	12 ,,
Roasted bow-wow	. .	18 ,,
Bow-wow pie	. .	6 ,,
Stews ratified	. .	16 ,,

The latter dish is rather dubious. What is meant by stews *rat*-ified? Can it be another name for rat pie? Give us light, but no pie.

Mr. Cooke, in his graphic letters from China, speaks of the fatness and fertility of the rats of our colony of Hong Kong. He adds: 'When Minutius, the dictator, was swearing Flaminius in as his Master of the Horse, we are told by Plutarch that a rat chanced to squeak, and the superstitious people compelled both officers to resign their posts. Office would be held with great uncertainty in Hong Kong if a similar superstition prevailed. Sir John Bowring has just been swearing in General Ashburn-ham as member of the Colonial Council, and if the rats were silent, they showed unusual modesty. They have forced themselves, however, into a state paper. Two hundred rats are destroyed every night in the gaol. Each morning the Chinese prisoners see, with tearful eyes and watering mouths, a pile of these delicacies cast out in waste. It is as if Christian prisoners were to see scores of white sucking pigs tossed forth to the dogs by Mahommedan gaolers. At last they could refrain no longer. Daring the punishment of tail-cutting, which follows an infraction of prison discipline, they first attempted to abstract the delicacies. Foiled in this, they took the more manly course. They indited a petition in good Chinese, proving from Confucius that it is sinful to cast away the food of man, and praying that the meat might be handed over to them to cook and eat. This is a fact, and if General Thompson doubts it, I recommend him to move for a copy of the correspondence.' THE CURIOSITIES OF FOOD

Dr F. T. Cheng   *1954*

BEAR'S PAW

*Bear's paw has been acclaimed as a delicacy in various parts
of the world. Here is a Chinese appreciation of it. The author,
Dr Cheng, was once Chinese Ambassador in London, and
wrote some legal treatises. But his interest in food was
evidently just as strong. Ever since I acquired a copy of*
Musings of a Chinese Gourmet *it has been a favourite
book of mine.*

This must be the earliest delicacy known to the Chinese; for even Mencius, the great philosopher of pre-Christian era who lived about 100 years after Confucius, said: 'Fish is what I like, so are bear's paws; but, if I cannot have both, I will forgo the fish and choose the bear's paws. Similarly, I love life and I also love righteousness; but if I cannot have both, I will forgo life and choose righteousness.' (Mencius, VI, I, 10, 1) It is fast becoming a delicacy of only historical interest; for its supply is very limited and restaurants in these days often use, as its substitute, buffalo's feet, which, if well prepared, taste rather like bear's paw, and of which the identity can never be discovered by those who have not tasted the latter before or, though they may have done so, are no connoisseurs. In fact, it is chiefly a delicacy of the North and, generally speaking, can be properly prepared only by cooks of the Shantung or Honan Schools. The taste of bear's paw is unique. The nearest comparison is that it is like the fat part of the best ham, or rather much better, for it has not the greasiness of the latter. It is so smooth and delicious that it simply melts in one's mouth. It must be highly rich in nutritious properties.

The paw is wrapped in mud (clean mud of course) and then baked in the oven. When the mud becomes firm like clay, it is taken out and, when it is cool, the mud is torn off. This will automatically bring the hairy skin off the paw, and you will thus get the meat fit for food.

The next process is to simmer it to get it softened, changing the water frequently in order to get rid of its gamey smell and taste.

When it has become softened and 'tasteless', a condition that is essential, then cook it until it is tender, over a simmering fire with chicken meat, lean ham, and wine like sherry, with water just enough to enable the ingredients to yield a rich and thick gravy. When served, it should be cut in slices like ham.

MUSINGS OF A CHINESE GOURMET

Ernest Matthew Mickler   *1986*

'GATOR TAIL

We have met Mickler before on page 239.

The only place you can find alligator is near the coast or the inland swamps in the South. So if you're lucky enough to get a holt to an alligator tail, there's a section about a foot long just behind the back legs that's tender and juicy. You cut it in sections at the joints just like you would a pork chop. Salt, pepper and flour each piece of tail and then fry in hot grease until golden brown. Or you can barbecue it with Bosie's Barbecue Sauce. He had alligator tail especially in mind when he concocted it.

If you haven't eaten 'gator tail before, you're in for a surprise. It's gonna taste a little bit like chicken, a little bit like pork, and a little bit like fish. It's so good, you'll wanna lay down and scream.

WHITE TRASH COOKING

Berthold Laufer   *1930*

EATING CLAY

Laufer, whose Sino-Iranica *(an account of the early movements of foodstuffs between China and Iran) was a major contribution to food history, must have been a man of insatiable curiosity and boundless energy, which sent him down some odd side-roads. His survey of geophagy (earth- or clay-eating) for the Field Museum of Natural History in Chicago, where he was Curator of the Department of Anthropology, is still, to the best of my knowledge, the best and fullest. From its 100 pages I have picked just a few examples: mere nibbles, one might say, at the edges of clay biscuits.*

The fact that clay is eaten in India was known in Europe early in the nineteenth century. Curiously enough, the edible clay of India was then designated 'clay of the Mogol'. G. I. Molina (*Saggio sulla storia naturale del Chili*, 1810), therefore, wrote at that time that the Peruvian women are in the habit of eating pottery sherds as the Mogol women eat the dishes of Patna. This Indic pottery is described as being gray in color with a yellow tinge, known under the name 'earth of Patna' and found principally in the environment of Seringapatnam. From this clay were manufactured vases so light in weight and so delicate in shape that 'a breath from one's mouth was sufficient to turn them upside down on the table.' Water poured into these vessels assumed a pleasant flavor and odor; and the ladies of India when they had emptied them would break them to pieces, swallowing the sherds with pleasure, especially in the period of maternity.

The clay consumed by the women of Bengal is a fine, light ochreous-colored specimen fashioned into thin cups with a perforation in the center and then baked in a kiln. In other words, it is ready-made pottery which they consume and which emits a curious smoky odor. It is this particular odor which makes it such a favorite with delicate women. The cups are strung on a cord and sold by the potters at so many pieces for one pice. Formerly these cups were hawked about in the streets of Calcutta, but this is no longer customary. Such a street vendor of baked clay cups once figured in a Bengali play staged in a Calcutta theatre; she recommended her ware in a song, pointing out that her cups are well baked, crisp to eat and yet cheap, and that delicate ladies about to become mothers should buy them without delay, as eating them would bless them with sons.

*   *   *

The women of Spain and Portugal take pleasure in munching a pottery clay styled bucaro from which vases of a yellow reddish color are made; when dissolved in water or wine, it imparts to these a very agreeable flavor and odor. The bucaro clay is found near Estremoz in the province of Alemtejo, Portugal, and in the province of Estremadura. The almagro, a very fine clay which occurs near Cartagena in the province of Murcia, Spain, is mixed with powdered tobacco in order to render it less volatile and to give it that sweet flavor which is the characteristic of the tobacco of Seville. Mixed with powdered chili pepper, the same clay is frequently eaten in southern Spain. The word *almagro* (also *almagra* or *almagre*) is derived from the Arabic *al-maghra* ('red ochre'); this clay is still employed in painting and known in France as *rouge indien* ('Indian red') or *rouge de Perse* ('Persian red').

Deniker states that it is asserted by women that the eating of earth gives a delicate completion to the face and that the same custom has also been pointed out among women in several countries of Europe, more especially in Spain, where the sandy clay which is used for making the alcarrazas is especially in vogue as an edible earth. The Spanish word *alcarraza*, derived from the Arabic *alkurrāz* ('earthenware vessel, pitcher'), denotes a porous, unglazed earthenware jar for cooling the water; in the southwestern United States such a jar is commonly called *olla*.

GEOPHAGY

Robert J. May 1984

SOME FOODS *of* PAPUA NEW GUINEA

'Flying foxes', also called fruit bats, are eaten in many other
places too, and so are beetle grubs and spiders, but perhaps
sago grubs are special to Papua New Guinea.

FLYING FOX (*Dobsonia moluccensis*)

This large, fruit-eating bat is a common item of food in many parts of the country. Outside Wewak, it is not uncommon to see large flying fox nets hanging across cleared flight paths by the side of the road, and flying foxes are common items in the Wewak and Maprik markets.

Flying fox meat is a delicacy. The flesh is sometimes compared with chicken but is in fact rather rich and more like a game bird.

Usually the animal is cooked over an open fire so that the fur is singed off and the skin is removed before eating. Sometimes the animal is gutted before cooking. In some parts of the country the whole animal is boiled and eaten fur, bones and all (only the gall bladder being rejected). Fortunately I have never been offered flying fox cooked this way, but someone who has, described the taste as '... well, furry'.

* * *

Numerous other small creatures are collected for eating, mostly by children, though their contribution to the overall food supply is marginal. Generally they are scorched and eaten as snacks, though sometimes they are cooked and added to grated tubers, or cooked in sago. A few are eaten raw.

The sago grub (Pidgin *binatang bilong saksak; Rhyncosphorus feringinlus papuanus*) is one of the better known delicacies. The grubs, a beetle larvae, are about 5 centimetres long, fat and cream in colour. In sago producing areas, palms are sometimes cut down in the knowledge that the grubs will breed in the rotting pith, and the grubs are 'harvested' after a couple of weeks. Usually the grubs are either boiled or roasted over an open fire. In the Maprik and Angoram (East Sepik) markets, and probably elsewhere, they are often sold spitted and grilled like *satay*. They are tender and very sweet with a slightly nutty flavour. The adult beetle is also eaten.

The larvae of a number of other insects, including beetles, butterflies, moths, wasps and dragonflies, are also eaten. Wasp nests are sometimes cut down onto open fires, providing an earth oven in which the larvae are baked. The adult of a hawk moth and another large unidentified moth, are scorched and eaten, or in the Sepik, wrapped in sago leaves and smoked, and several species of grasshopper, cricket, stick insect, cicada and beetle are consumed in various parts of the country, especially by children. Alóng the Sepik River, at least, mayflies are eaten when they appear briefly in large clouds; they are skimmed off the water when they fall and eaten raw or put into sago pancakes.

Another delicacy are the large orb weaving spiders (*Nephila* spp.), which are plucked by the legs from their webs by the more intrepid, and lightly roasted over an open fire. Other spiders are also eaten, and Clarke records that the Bomagai-Angoiang (Maring) people of the central highlands eat a large hairy spider, which will bite when threatened; a case, it would seem, of biting the hand that it feeds.

KAIKAI ANIANI: A GUIDE TO BUSH FOODS, MARKETS AND CULINARY ARTS
OF PAPUA NEW GUINEA

Sir Kenelm Digby   *1669*

TEA *with* EGG

Sir Kenelm Digby, one of the few 17th century writers on food
whose work can be browsed through with pleasure, devoted
most of his attention to mead. Here, however, he finds space
for a pick-me-up of a different nature. If a Jesuit lately come
from China endorses it, it has to be worth trying!

The Jesuite that came from China, Ann. 1664, told Mr. Waller, That there they use sometimes in this manner. To near a pint of the infusion, take two yolks of new laid-eggs, and beat them very well with as much fine Sugar as is sufficient for this quantity of Liquor; when they are very well incorporated, pour your Tea upon the Eggs and Sugar, and stir them well together. So drink it hot. This is when you come home from attending business abroad, and are very hungry, and yet have not conveniency to eat presently a competent meal. This presently discusseth and satisfieth all rawness and indigence of the stomack, flyeth suddainly over the whole body and into the veins, and strengthneth exceedingly, and preserves one a good while from necessity of eating. Mr. Waller findeth all those effects of it thus with Eggs. In these parts, He saith, we let the hot water remain too long soaking upon the Tea, which makes it extract into itself the earthy parts of the herb. The water is to remain upon it, no longer that whiles you can say the *Miserere* Psalm very leisurely. Then pour it upon the sugar, or sugar and Eggs. Thus you have only the spiritual parts of the Tea, which is much more active, penetrative and friendly to nature. You may from this regard take a little more of the herb; about one dragm of Tea, will serve for a pint of water; which makes three ordinary draughts.

THE CLOSET OF THE EMINENTLY LEARNED SIR KENELM DIGBY, KT., OPENED

James F. W. Johnson 1855

EATING ARSENIC

Johnson's book, in two volumes, has a wonderfully rhythmic
set of chapter titles: 'The Beverages We Infuse', 'The Bread
We Eat', 'The Liquors We Ferment', and – 'The Narcotics We
Indulge In ', 'The Smells We Disklike', etc. This piece comes
from 'The Poisons We Select'.

In some parts of Lower Austria, however, in Styria, and especially in the hilly country towards Hungary, there prevails among the common people an extraordinary custom of eating arsenic. During the smelting of lead, copper, and other ores, white arsenic flies off in fumes, and condenses in the solid form in the long chimneys which are usually attached to the smelting furnaces. From these chimneys, in the mining regions, the arsenic is obtained, and is sold to the people by itinerant pedlars and herbalists. It is known by the name of *Hidri* (a corruption of *Hutter-rauch*, smelt-house smoke), and the practice of using it is of considerable antiquity. By many it is swallowed daily throughout a long life, and the custom is handed down hereditarily from father to son.

Arsenic is thus consumed chiefly for two purposes – *First*, To give plumpness to the figure, cleanness and softness to the skin, and beauty and freshness to the complexion. *Second*, To improve the breathing and give longness of wind, so that steep and continuous heights may be climbed without difficulty and exhaustion of breath. Both these results are described as following almost invariably from the prolonged use of arsenic either by man or by animals.

For the former purpose young peasants, both male and female, have recourse to it, with a view of adding to their charms in the eyes of each other; and it is remarkable to see how wonderfully well they attain their object, for those young persons who adopt the practice are generally remarkable for clear and blooming complexions, for full rounded figures, and for a healthy appearance. Dr Von Tschudi gives the following case as having occurred in his own medical practice: 'A healthy, but pale and thin milkmaid, residing in the parish of H——, had a lover whom she wished to attach to her by a more agreeable exterior; she, therefore, had recourse to the well-known beautifier, and took arsenic several times a-week. The desired effect was not long in showing itself; for in a few months she became stout, rosy-cheeked, and all that her lover could desire. In order, however, to increase the effect, she incautiously increased the doses of arsenic, and a fell a victim to her vanity. She died poisoned, a very painful death.' The number of such fatal cases, especially among young persons, is no means inconsiderable.

For the second purpose – that of rendering the breathing easier when going uphill – a small fragment of arsenic is put into the mouth, and allowed to dissolve which it does very slowly. The effect is described as astonishing. Heights are easily and rapidly ascended, which could not otherwise be surmounted without great difficulty of breathing. The Chemistry of Common Life

Juanita Tiger Kavena 1980

Culinary Ashes

The title of this item is irresistible.

Culinary ashes are made by burning certain bushes or trees until they crumble into ash. Creeks and Seminoles use hickory, and Navajos use primarily juniper branches. Hopis may use various materials, such as spent bean vines and pods or corn cobs, but Hopi women prefer ashes made from green plants, since they are more alkaline. They especially prize the ash from the four-winged saltbush (*Atriplex canescens*). This bush, which is also called suwvi or chamisa, can be found in abundance in the desert areas of the Hopi reservation. It grows in clumps similar to sagebrush and produces a very hard wood. When burned, green chamisa bushes yield culinary ashes high in mineral content. Dr. Doris Calloway, a nutritionist at the University of California at Berkeley, has done tests which show that old plants have only a fraction of the potassium, magnesium, and sodium found in ash made from green plants.

The Hopi practice of adding culinary ashes to corn dishes therefore raises the already substantial mineral content of these foods. In addition to increasing nutritional value, chamisa ashes enhance the color in blue corn products. When one is using blue cornmeal for any dish, the meal will turn pink when hot water is added, so Hopi women mix chamisa ashes with water to make an 'ash broth' which is then strained and added to cornmeal mixtures. The high alkaline content of the chamisa ashes create a distinctly blue-green color, which holds a religious significance for the Hopis.

Care must be taken when chopping down the bushes, as snakes, including rattlers, seek the relative cool of the shade of the bush. A hoe or shovel is used to clear and clean off an area approximately six feet square, where the cut bushes are stacked after removing any dried tumbleweeds that might be caught in the branches. The chamisa is piled about five feet high, and the fire is started. We use a pitchfork to move branches into the center of the fire to make sure that all is completely burned to ashes. When the fire has burned out and cooled down, the ashes are put into buckets or tubs, and then sifted to remove any twigs or sticks not burned. Chamisa ashes should be stored in a container with a tightly fitting lid.

The saltbush was also used as a laundry agent in times past. The women would wet the bush, then rub it between their hands to make suds for washing clothes.

Hopi Cookery

Jennifer Isaacs   1987

KANGAROO HUNT

The history, arts and ways of the Aborigines have been
thoroughly and sympathetically described by Jennifer Isaacs.
Her books on the subject, and not least her latest volume on
their foodways, are deservedly best-sellers in Australia.

In remote parts of Australia it is inevitable that living and working with Aborigines will entail going on a kangaroo hunt. On one such expedition I went bush for the day with Walter Pukutuwara and his family to get kangaroo meat for the family and, from my point of view, to gather sinews in order to make and photograph weapons. The short trip looking for one kangaroo turned into a day's epic drive. We set out from Amata in the northwest of South Australia early in the morning and having gone on an enormous loop to within sight of Ayers Rock and back, arrived in Amata again at 10 pm.

Admittedly this was an unusual trip, but it highlights the enthusiasm that remains in Aboriginal hunters when they have a car, a gun and a quarry in sight. The haul was around seven kangaroos, enough to feed most of the community that night. Despite my feelings of nausea at the carload of dead kangaroos, it was clear that the men approached the animals with reverence and that the procedures they followed were of great ceremonial importance and 'men's business'. Although they shared the meat back in camp, the women took little part in the kangaroo hunt, preferring to head off and dig for rabbits when the truck stopped.

When hunting kangaroos silence is usual, though sometimes whistles and signals communicate intentions from one man to another. People often work as a group, one man acting as a decoy while the startled animal stands motionless, staring. The others close in and freeze as the animal looks again. When speared or shot a wounded kangaroo is finished off immediately with blows to the neck. The animal is disembowelled the moment it is killed through a small incision made in the abdomen. The incision is then neatly skewered with a stick and bound in a figure-of-eight with the cleaned-out small intestine. The legs are dislocated and the carcass is either carried home on the hunter's head or, more frequently, taken to the waiting vehicle.

One interesting variation occurs in the Kimberleys, where at this stage the stomach, lower intestine and liver are removed, cleaned and boiled. The empty stomach is filled with fat and blood and rolled into a kind of black pudding. It is cooked in the earth oven with the kangaroo. The animal is tossed on to a blazing fire and turned several times until the fur has been singed and blackened. It is then removed from the fire and scraped so that the flesh is clean. The tail is usually cut off and placed beside the animal when cooking, though it can be left intact.

To prepare the oven a rectangular hole is dug about the size of the kangaroo to be cooked. A hot fire is made with plenty of wood in order to make a good supply of hot coals. The kangaroo is put on its back in the pit and the tail placed beside the body. The flesh is completely covered with hot coals, then with earth so that only the feet protrude. Cooking time varies depending on how hungry people are, and can be from three-quarters of an hour to four hours. If the hunters return late at night, the meat may be left in the pit overnight; in this case it is very well done.

When the animal is removed from the pit, the men gather to cut up the meat ritually. Women remain in the background waiting for pieces to be handed to them by their male relatives. This has been described as 'men's time'. In the desert the belly is opened and the rich blood soup is carefully drunk or poured into a billy and shared. The kidneys, heart and lungs are also shared. The meat must then be cut up by the hunter, each section going to an appropriate relative depending on his or her relationship with the hunter. It is quite common for the hunter to get very little himself. He must rely, in turn, on the success of a relative if he is to have one of the best sections of meat.

This success depends not only on skill but also on the capacity of the hunters to deceive their quarry. Aborigines are brilliant mimics, both verbally and physically, and imitate the calls of birds, people's voices and movements. Emus are caught by preying on their inquisitive nature as hunters imitate other emus visiting from parts far off. Geese are brought down by hunters imitating their 'honk, honk, honk' in high branches and are then attacked with stones and sticks. Hermit crabs can be brought out of their shells with the high-pitched 'drrrrr' sound of the tongue against the palate; the sound of a snake from a hunter's mouth will cause a bandicoot to leave a hollow log. Hand signals are an additional aid and the elaborate sign language recorded by people such as Walter Roth in northern Queensland at the turn of the century meant that, without speaking, hunters could communicate extremely well over large distances without alerting their quarry.

Hunting magic is frequently employed to ensure a successful hunt and the weapons themselves are often smeared with blood from a kangaroo. Many weapons are carved or painted in an act of ritual and faith. The decoration is not purely superficial but associates the weapons visibly with the ancestral spirits and gives them greater power and accuracy. Spear-throwers and spears may also be 'sung' to ensure that they do not fail.

BUSH FOOD

How *to* Cook *a* Husband

Many 19th century cookbooks, especially in North America,
contain a joke recipe. The joke is sustained longer in this
example than in most. The Ladies of Des Moines who
produced the book, in aid of their Missionary Sewing School,
must be acquitted of any suspicion of allowing a double
entendre *to enter into it, but it is avowed that the recipe was*
adopted from the wilder environs of Baltimore and one
(anyway I) can't help wondering ...

More than a decade ago in the Baltimore Cooking School, the following receipt for 'cooking a husband so as to make him tender and good,' was contributed by a lady, presumably of experience. We commend it to our lady readers:

A good many husbands are utterly spoiled by mismanagement. Some women go about it as if their husbands were bladders, and blow them up. Others keep them constantly in hot water; others let them freeze by their carelessness and indifference. Some keep them in a stew by irritating ways and words. Others roast them. Some keep them in pickle all their lives.

It cannot be supposed that any husband will be tender and good managed in this way, but they are really delicious when properly treated. In selecting your husband you should not be guided by the silvery appearance, as in buying mackerel, nor by the golden tint, as if you wanted salmon. Be sure and select him yourself, as tastes differ. Do not go to the market for him, as the best are always brought to your door. It is far better to have none unless you will patiently learn how to cook him. A preserving kettle of the finest porcelain is the best, but if you have nothing but an earthenware pipkin it will do, with care. See that the linen in which you wrap him is nicely washed and mended, with the required number of buttons and strings nicely sewed on. Tie him in the kettle by a strong silk cord called comfort, as the one called duty is apt to be weak. They are apt to fly out of the kettle and be burned and crusty on the edges, since, like crabs and lobsters, you have to cook them while alive.

Make a clear, steady fire out of love, neatness and cheerfulness. Set him as near this as seems to agree with him. If he sputters and fizzes do not be anxious; some husbands do this till they are quite done. Add a little sugar in the form of what confectioners call kisses, but no vinegar or pepper on any account. A little spice improves them, but it must be used with judgment. Do not stick any sharp instruments into him to see if he is becoming tender. Stir him gently; watch the while, lest he lie too flat and close to the kettle, and so becomes useless. You cannot fail to know when he is done. If thus treated you will find him very digestible, agreeing nicely with you and the children, and he will keep as long as you want, unless you become careless and you set him in too cold a place.

A COLLECTION OF CHOICE RECIPES

Elsdon Best 1942

CONFIT *of* RAT

The author of this passage produced a comprehensive series of monographs on Maori life and customs.
Here he writes about potting the Polynesian rat in its own fat
– a curious echo from the other side of the world of the confit
technique of the south-west of France.

The native rat ate many kinds of berries, including those of the *hinau, miro, kahikatea, patate*, and many other species of trees, shrubs, etc.: the *hua tawai* or beech-mast was apparently highly appreciated by the child of Hine-mataiti, and the period during which the mast was available was the most important period of the ratting season. The flower-bracts of the *kiekie* or *Freycinetia* were also much favoured by the *kiore*. These native rats were generally in good condition during the late autumn and winter, but fell off much in summer; they are credited with having been clean feeders. They were given to eating the bark of the *houhou (Nothopanax arboreum)*, as also do the *kaka* parrot and horses... When forest-foods grew scarce numbers of rats would betake themselves to the open lands, lands supporting merely scrub and fern, such lands as is described by the term *parae*. When the beech-mast came to an end then rats often sought such *parae* islands, where they lived in holes or burrows; when they had become numerous at such places the fern would be burned off, at least in some cases. After the fire natives would search diligently the burned area and dig the rats out of their holes; at such times quite a number would often be found in one hole...

When rats were to be potted they were, according to my Matatua notes, put in a large wooden bowl or trough *(kumete)*, and allowed to remain there for a while; if in good condition, as they generally were when taken, the fat would soon commence to exude from them, and when a quantity had so collected, then hot stones were put in it, and renewed occasionally. This caused more fat to collect in the vessel, while it also cooked the fat and rats together, or at least sufficiently so to please the Maori taste, never in itself any too fastidious. The rats were then packed in gourd or wooden vessels, and the melted fat was poured over them, this being the preserving agent.

FOREST LORE OF THE MAORI

F. H. Curtiss   1891

The JOCULAR APPROACH

F. H. Curtiss's comical cookery book is a slim one, but even so
he found the effort of keeping the laughter going too great, so
that many of his 76 pages can be read with a straight face.
However, at his best he was very funny (or so I think – I love
the idea of pouring red wine over spilled salt).

Should you be so unfortunate as to upset a glass of claret upon the table cloth, immediately sprinkle the stain liberally with salt to prevent it from 'setting.'

On the same principle, if you upset the salt, sprinkle it liberally with claret.

Should you fill your mouth with soup so hot that you cannot retain it, playfully get rid of it by giving an imitation of a garden hose in full operation. This should be only done as a *dernier ressort*, but it is better not to scald yourself so badly as to be forced to leave a good dinner and repair to a hospital.

In carving, should the bird slip from under your knife, do not appear covered with confusion, although you may be with gravy, but simply say to the lady in whose lap the bird has landed, 'I'll trouble you for that hen,' or words to that effect, and proceed with the autopsy.

It is no longer considered fashionable for guests to carry with them to large dinners a small pair of silver bellows with which to cool their soup, and a pair of little silver safety pins to fasten back their coat sleeves while dining, are no longer *en règle*. The fashion of fastening the napkin about the neck with a small silver chain no longer obtains in the best society.

Having finished dining, the napkin can be thrown carelessly upon the floor or laid at the side of the plate. It is not necessary to fold it into a cocked-hat and place it beside one's plate, as its ulterior destination is supposed to be the wash-tub.

Do not eat from the end of the spoon with a noisy imitation of a high pressure suction-pump. Tip the spoon sideways gently and let the contents gurgle – as it were – down the throat, not scraping the dish, as the chances are that other courses will be provided which will satisfy your hunger, unless you have just returned from a shipwrecked expedition, in which case a few crackers can be placed in the pocket to be eaten surreptitiously.

CLEAR SOUP

Take two pints of water, wash them thoroughly on both sides, pour into a dish or something and stir round the kitchen until tired. Dilute with ice water, cook until it comes to a boil. Have the boil lanced and serve.

Spring Soup

This is made from spring water; add cabbages and other vegetabes to suit. Par-boil (or ma-boil, if pa is 'detained in the City') for ten minutes in two quarts of red-hot water, or two minutes in ten quarts of water, as you please; strain at a gnat. When tender add a gill of fish. Serve to your guests through a garden hose. THE COMIC COOKERY BOOK

F. H. Bodenheimer *1951*

STRANGE FOODS *in* LAOS

My own experience of insect-eating in Laos was confined to what one might call conventional insects, the sort that were served at banquets at the Royal Palace, and to the sight of our gardener popping live cockroaches into his mouth. Bristowe (referred to in Bodenheimer's survey on the subject) was luckier (?) than I in this respect.

One of the best studies on insects for human consumption is a paper by W. S. BRISTOWE (1932 pp. 387–404) on his observations in Siam. On his arrival in that country BRISTOWE was told that the Laos ate insects. He collected much pertinent information and paid special attention to discovering whether the Laos really like to eat insects or eat them from economic necessity. He came to the conclusion that the Laos without doubt like the insects they eat. 'Some fetch high prices and the capture of others is fraught with considerable risk. What is more, so would we like them if they were suitably disguised and if we gave ourselves the chance of acquiring the taste. By ourselves eating spiders, dungbeetles, waterbugs, crickets, grasshoppers, termites and cicadas, we found none distasteful, a few quite palatable, notably the giant waterbug. For the most part they were insipid, with a faint vegetable flavour, but would not anyone tasting bread, for instance, for the first time, wonder why we eat such a flavourless food? A toasted dungbeetle or soft-bodied spider has a nice crisp exterior and soft interior of soufflé consistency which is by no means unpleasant. Salt is usually added, sometimes chilli or the leaves of scented herbs, and sometimes they are eaten with rice or added to sauces or curry. Flavour is exceptionally hard to define, but lettuce would, I think, best describe the taste of termites, cicadas and crickets; lettuce and raw potato that of the giant *Nephila*-spider, and concentrated Gorgonzola cheese that of the giant waterbug (*Lethocerus indicus*). I suffered no ill effects from the eating of these insects'.

INSECTS AS HUMAN FOOD

Philip Hyman

1986

When SNAILS *were* NOT EATEN *in* FRANCE

The British stereotype of a French person used to be someone who eats snails and frogs. Philip Hyman, a food historian with a relentlessly questing mind, shows here that in fact the snail has had an on-off-on career so far as French tables are concerned. This passage deals with a period when it was in the off phase.

Despite the clear place of importance attributed to snails in texts prior to 1560, the next 90 years saw the snail's fortune take a dramatic turn for the worse, culminating in a virtual banishment from refined tables for almost 200 years thereafter. The first hint of a problem can be perceived as early as 1606 when Joseph Du Chesne, a native of Gascony and a proud defender of that region's cuisine, wrote:

> In Italy and in Gascony, more is made of snails than in France. In the first two places, snails are considered both appetizing and delicious when well prepared. Indeed, snails are common and frequently eaten there, but in some parts of France people don't even know what they are; they are horrified at the idea that we eat them and cannot stand to see them eaten or even prepared.

Despite Du Chesne's insistence, we suspect that he may have been exaggerating the situation somewhat since only one year later another author (who was neither Gascon nor Italian) says that snails are 'bien bonnes' and describes several preparations for them (*Thresor de Santé* 1607).

Nevertheless, Du Chesne's remarks foreshadow those of 50 years later when opinions had changed. Nicolas Bonnefons, for example, wrote in 1654: 'I am astonished that men are so oddly constituted as to find something desirable in this disgusting food which is nothing more than a gastronomic extravagance. Regardless of how they [snails] are prepared, I can find nothing good to say about eating them. But,' he added prudently, 'since I want this work to be as complete as possible, I must inform the reader as to when they are best eaten ...' He then went on to describe how to prepare them for cooking, and to give several recipes as well.

With the exception of some snail recipes in a treatise ostensibly on Spanish cooking published in *Le Nouveau et parfait Maistre d'Hostel Royal* by Pierre de Lune in 1662, snails were totally absent from all French cookbooks of the 17th century. Their exclusion from La Varenne's *Cuisinier François*, the most popular book of the period, is particularly significant, and shows that Bonnefons' remarks reflected more than a personal opinion; snails were clearly out of fashion by the end of the 17th century. As Jean-Louis Flandrin has pointed out, this was a time when the seasonings most commonly used in the Middle Ages and the Renaissance, spices, were giving way to more 'modern' condiments. Thus it is not surprising to see some of the more 'exotic' food preferences of a previous generation being condemned along with them. Not only was the seasoning of food to change during the 17th century, but the choice of foods as well, and one of the first to go seems to have been the snail. Interestingly enough, however, frogs and turtles did not suffer a similar exclusion, since almost all of the books that omitted snails included one or two recipes for either frogs, or turtles, or both.

The movement away from snails was accentuated throughout the 18th century. Already in 1713, we read In *Traité des alimens de Caresme*, 1713: '[Snails] do not merit a place on our tables, however highly they may have been esteemed by the Greeks and Romans'. French cookbook authors of all kinds continued to avoid them, although some included an odd recipe, often expressing personal distaste as Bonnefons had done in 1654. In 1758, the anonymous author of the *Traité historique ... ou le Cuisinier Instruit* wrote:

> It's not that [snails] are in the least appealing as food, no matter how they are prepared, given the natural repugnance they inspire; but there are still some people who find them excellent, and for them I give the following recipes.

Two recipes followed which no doubt gave little pleasure to the author who had perfunctorily included them.

As the century progressed, the snail seemed to make a timid comeback, appearing in works whose earlier editions had excluded them. Take for example the *Cuisinière Bourgeoise*: this did not include them in either the 1746 first edition, nor in the greatly enlarged 1752 edition, but later, around 1769, one recipe for snails was added. Was this simply a concession to that sneered-upon public of snail lovers previously alluded to by other authors? Or was it a first indication that the snail's fortune was about to change? If we are to judge by the gastronome and historian of French taste, Le Grand D'Aussy, writing in 1782, the former was more likely the case. After describing how snails were highly esteemed in the France of the 16th century he added: 'One still sees them for sale in markets today, something which implies that there must still be people around who eat them'. Hardly a return to favor!

When the 19th century began, no one would have foreseen that snails would experience a dramatic comeback in the course of the next 70 years, nor imagined that this creature, virtually banned from a well-dressed table, would become one of the gastronomic emblems of France – and yet this is exactly what was to happen, albeit by no means overnight.

Grimod de La Reynière, father of the French gastronomic press, did not mention snails in either his 8 volume *Almanach des Gourmands* (1803–12) or his *Almanach des Amphitryons* (1808). Any thought of eating them was so far from his mind that he didn't even go to the trouble of saying he didn't like them. Not so a contemporary, Cadet de Gassicourt, who in 1809 had a character in a dialogue on the history of cooking exclaim, 'How could they [the Romans] possibly have liked that disgusting reptile [sic!]?' But the most significant proof of the snail's continued ostracism is found in a survey of Paris' best restaurants by Blanc, published in 1815. The menus from 21 of the city's finest dining places were reproduced, and not a single one served snails.

PETITS PROPOS CULINAIRES (PPC) *23*

Bridget Ann Henisch 1967

NOAH'S ARK: *The* FOOD PROBLEM

*Mediaeval writers and artists who tackled the theme of
Noah's Ark did occasionally show awareness of the practical
problems which Noah must have faced; but they had little
guidance to offer on how all the animals (and, for that
matter, Noah and his family) were fed. Bridget Ann Henisch
(see pages 18 and 206) deftly outlines the apparently
unanswerable questions.*

Whatever the tragedies outside, the commentators kept Noah and his family much too busy to notice them. Their main job was to see that everyone was happy, clean and well-fed, the men looking after the animals, the women caring for the birds. This division of labour is remembered in a picture of the disembarkation in the *Bedford Book of Hours*, where it is a woman who is gently setting free a duck. No one is straining himself; indeed, Noah is having a nap, perhaps exhausted by the very thought of the strenuous timetable drawn up for him. In a Jewish story, no animal was prepared to be accommodating. Each expected to eat its favourite food at its accustomed meal-time, and so Noah raced up and down, one moment with buckets of vineshoots for elephants, the next with broken glass of which, as all agreed, ostriches were inordinately fond.

Christian commentators were less indulgent to these fads and fancies. A uniform diet of figs and chestnuts was favoured by many, led by St. Augustine, who remarked with brisk optimism:

> Hungry animals will eat almost anything
> and of course, God ... could easily have
> made any food pleasant and nourishing.
>
> *The City of God, Book 15, Chap. 27*

The writer of the *Cursor Mundi* was not so sure, and liked to imagine the pleasure of the carnivorous animals when their teeth sank into the first tasty morsel after the Flood:

> These beestes were ful glad in mode
> Whenne thei hadde her kyndely fode.
> [These animals were delighted when they
> had their own proper food again.]
>
> *Cursor Mundi, 11. 1911–2*

Those who felt certain animals must have meat and could not be allowed to eye their neighbours, developed the theory that a special supply of sheep was loaded for them. This ingenious arrangement brought psychological as well as nutritional benefits: as the sheep were eaten, the Ark became roomier, and the irritations of close quarters were smoothed away. A Jewish storyteller partially solved the problem by making his lions seasick and unable to face more than a scrap of grass throughout the voyage.

Others dismissed the preoccupation with meat as irrelevant, in the belief that men and animals alike were vegetarians before the Flood. This was a popular idea, despite the unkind comment of Procopius that, if this were so, Abel had been wasting his time as a shepherd. After the Deluge vegetables were found to be less nourishing than before, and so God said that meat might be eaten instead, as a compensation and a reminder of the sin that had spoilt the world.

All worried about the vast quantities of food needed, and the consequent problems of storage and waste disposal in an already over-loaded Ark. Artists were much more relaxed, few bothering to squeeze in more than an occasional Lilliputian sack. Some tastefully arranged trays of fruit and vegetables lie unjostled in the larders. Under these, and inconsiderately far from the living quarters, are the *stercoraria* for dung and refuse.

MEDIEVAL ARMCHAIR TRAVELS

POUBELLES *de* TABLE

Just about every meal must end with the disposal of the debris,
so I close this anthology with a subject relevant to that. It is a
string of observations on the phenomenon of the poubelle de
table *(table garbage pot) which appeared in a number of*
issues of Petits Propos Culinaires (PPC). *It was my wife and*
I who initiated the series and thus set people in many
countries looking out for the appearance of a PDT, as the
object came to be known. And, as the last item shows, it fell to
us to find the weirdest specimen of all, which we still possess.

When touring the Languedoc and the Pays Basque recently we found that kitchen equipment and gift shops were all displaying 'poubelles de table'. These are pottery recipients with lids, average capacity about 2 litres. They invariably have 'poubelle de table' written on them. But there is a rare subspecies, much smaller, which is inscribed 'poubelle d'apéritif.' We never witnessed the purchase of either, but inferred from their ubiquity that sales must occur.

Buying a bottle of wine at a remote farmhouse in the Minervois region, the urge suddenly overtook us to pose in this back-of-beyond locale the question which we had felt shy of putting to busier urban people. 'Permit us, Madame, to ask you something unconnected with our purchase. Do you possess a poubelle de table?'

Oh yes, came the answer, they had become quite the fashion since 1980 or so. Daughter-in-law had presented one to her last Christmas. See, she would show it to us. So she did, lifting the lid off and displaying a few olive pits inside. Très pratique it was, according to her.

Can any readers tell us whether this item of equipment is really new in France, or a revival of something which used to be common; and whether there are similar things to be bought in other countries?

PAMELA VANDYKE PRICE writes: '... I first saw these things in 1977, when I had been staying in the Lot and, on returning to Bordeaux, my hosts and I walked round Condom after lunch. After that I was vaguely aware of them in many shops – usually of the "craft and gift" type, although there were some very smart ones in Bordeaux. I should imagine, therefore, that the things may have been introduced to Paris and the other cities – where I seldom go – somewhat earlier.

'It occurs to me that they may have originated because, in regions where fish and its subsequent debris is often served, the smaller tables in modern flats and many inexpensive restaurants simply cannot easily accommodate a large bowl for the bones and bits which otherwise is set in the middle of the table. Certainly my Bordeaux friends found the things somewhat unusual at that time so I suppose they may have been the latest gift idea. I do not recall ever seeing anything of the sort in any of the museums of displays of former table settings and therefore I assume that they are a fairly recent item; most of those that I have seen have either pottery or at least the sort of china that is "peasanty" in style, and I have a theory that one manufacturer got left with thousands of gherkin pots that he couldn't sell, so had an inspiration! (Like the one who invented the "Tom n' Jerry" to shift the quantity of mugs he was stuck with!)'

PETER LEWIS says: 'I can trace my first sighting to 1976: it was then as always in one of those smart shops in small French towns which advertise their "listes de mariage". I suspect that is the market they are made for, since they are generally en suite with pots for cornichons and olives and trays for cochonailles, sometimes even sangria sets. Functionally they must be inferior to the "brush and crumb tray" which many English couples got as a wedding present in the twenties. Their giant size alone makes them quite unputtable on the table. I suspect they are a gimmick (apparently hugely successful) of the ceramic gifts industry. The poubelle apéritif (which surely cannot be a *revival* of anything) seems to confirm this.'

D. JON GROSSMAN has these comments: 'No self-respecting French housewife would ever, before recently, have dreamed of having a "poubelle" on her table. The scraps are pushed aside on your plate, and plates are changed after every course, ... My modern son reports that poubelles de table are showing up on the tables of "clever, modern" females, "chez qui", he says, "on ne mange pas très bien". Now you know.

'The thing is new, nor can its name possibly be very old. "Poubelle" comes from the name of Eugène Poubelle, Prefect of the Seine from 1883 to 1896, who at the beginning of his administration established the requirement that Parisian housewives use the things. Dauzat (*Dictionnaire étymologique de la langue française*, 1938) informs me that Poubelle's ordinance was dated 15 January 1884. The word is therefore just under a century old, happy birthday to it. Littré died in 1881 (birth year of Picasso), so could not have known the thing (nor the word).

'I should really reword this. "Before recently" implies that a "self-respecting French housewife" *would* now love one of these things. Which is of course ridiculous. The dinner table is no place for cuteness. Eating is not a solemn enterprise, but it is a serious one. I also draw the line at paper bibs for eating lobster, which I place in the same category as poubelles de table.'

CAROLINE DAVIDSON reports sightings in another country: 'Poubelles de table have become very common in German hotels at the breakfast table. They are used as waste bins for egg shell, jam wrappers, ham fat, salami rind and bits of leftover bread and roll – the debris, in short, of a large German breakfast. There are two types, both made out of plastic: an orange one, labelled "Breakfast Things" (in English) and decorated with pictures of a coffee pot, coffee mug, a boiled egg in a cup etc., and a light brown variety labelled "Für Fische Abfälle' (for fish debris) and decorated with an apple, pear, strawberry, gooseberry and daisies set against a trellis background. The orange type doesn't say where it was made, but the brown is clearly marked "Made in Germany". There is no sign that these poubelles de table are used at other meals, although the reference to fish debris is suggestive in this connection, or that they have been adopted in German homes. I certainly didn't see any in kitchen equipment and gift shops and, inspired by your account of them in France, I did look quite hard.'

JOHN THORNE says: 'I have a few more comments on the subjet of poubelles de table. First, proving that kitsch knows no boundaries, the pot has arrived in the USA, as evidenced by the enclosed ad from *Bon Appetit*. [The ad is not reproduced. It shows two p de t, with the legend POUBELLE DE TABLE (translated as "Garbage of the Table"), and states that the articles, "made by a Hoosier ceramist", are available in buckwheat and brown for an informal table or white and blue with multi-colored flowers for a more formal setting. "Use it for rib and poultry bones, seafood shells and claws, or just corn cobs." The vendors are MeLange Folio Inc, 2115 Keller Hill Road, Mooresville IN 46158.]

'Notice that these p de t, although imitative of their French cousins, are actually made over here. One would have thought that there would be more cachet in importing the genuine French model, but I guess not.

'As Jon Grossman pointed out (*PPC* 12), poubelle in French means a regulation-sized dustbin (garbage can in the USA). But I find no source citing it as metonymical for its contents, meaning garbage, as the MeLange people suggest with their "garbage of the table". "Garbage can of the table" is more like it, although I suspect that poubelle has for the French a certain coy humour that simply doesn't translate into English.

'This pretentious foolery is all the more offensive because there's a good English word for table scraps which would make a fine emblem if any were necessary on the pot designated to hold them – ORT. "Evening orts are good morning fodder" (Ray's *English Proverbs*, 1678). "Ort" still survives over here; at least I have a friend who uses "orts and ort plate" with artless ease and who was surprised when I accused him of showing off his Shakespeare – it was just family talk.'

THE EDITORS finally announce: 'This subject has been laid to rest for some time, but an extraordinary discovery compels us to give it one more airing.

'Contemplating a miscellany of unsold goods in a household goods shop, closed down for ever, on the King's Road in Chelsea only a hundred yards from our editorial desk, we beheld a dusty carton which bore the astonishing inscription "Queen Anne, Poubelle de Table, Biscuit Box, Keksdose".

'We traced the owner of the former shop, had it opened up, and found within the carton a silver-plated object which was, unmistakeably, a biscuit container with a hinged lid. The makers are identified as a company called Mayell, and the product is certified "made in England". We bought it, and are left wondering whether any French tourists in England may have acquired specimens and put them to use in accordance with the French name. Ours works thus quite well. . .'

PETITS PROPOS CULINAIRES (PPC) *11, 12, 16, 21*

LET US TRY HARDER

As an envoi to my collection I choose a piece of poetry, printed overleaf. Although it ranges beyond the world of food and drink, that is where it starts and ends. Coming after an anthology which includes much information, this gently ironic poem is an appropriate reminder that, however hard we try, there will always be things we don't (but ideally would) know.

319

Jeremy Round   *1984*

UTOPIA

'. . . tea . . . contrary to the belief of the vulgar . . . is seldom drunk with food
in China'

                                        Paul Levy, Observer, 16 January 1983

Just once to get it all right!
To wake having had enough sleep, alert
To spring at a day of sufficient exercise,
Balanced diet, faultless personal hygiene,
And satisfying creative endeavour.

To use without exploiting, intelligence,
Skill, fine judgement, compassion, wit, and
Profound understanding. To arrive at evening
Physically tired, at peace, and looking forward
To a sexually and emotionally challenging few hours
Of complete mutal fulfillment.

To always have pens and paper
And stamps and envelopes and current addresses
In the house at the same time. To remember that *mer*
Is feminine, and not to say 'who' in sentences such as,
'Patricia will sit between Mandy and whom?',
Or wash mushrooms that should be wiped with a cloth,
Or use knives anywhere near lettuce.

Never to yield to the thrill
Of letting comparative strangers into the scandalous
Details of a friend's involvement with a Catholic
Priest, or say dishonest things for effect like,
'Who can bear Belgium for more than an afternoon?'

Civilizations pull across ages,
And we toil also, forsaking completeness,
That some day just imaginable, either no-one who doesn't
Will be thought vulgar, or everyone *will* know how
Seldom tea is drunk with food in China.

BIBLIOGRAPHY
AND PUBLISHERS'
ACKNOWLEDGEMENTS

Grateful acknowledgement is made by means of this list of those authors and publishers who kindly gave permission for their items to be reprinted. Every effort has been made to trace the copyright holders of the various pieces reproduced in this anthology; the publishers sincerely regret any oversights that may have unwittingly occurred.

ADAMS, Ramon J: *Come an' Get It: The Story of an Old Cowboy Cook*, University of Oklahoma Press, 1952.

ALLEN, Myrtle: *The Ballymaloe Cookbook*, 2nd edn, Eyre Methuen, London, 1981.

ANDREWS, Colman: *Catalan Cuisine*, Atheneum, New York, 1988. Reprinted with the permission of Atheneum Publishers, an imprint of Macmillan Publishing Company, and Barbara Lowenstein Associates. © Colman Andrews.

AULNAY, Nathan d': see OLNEY, Richard.

BADHAM, Rev Charles David: *A Treatise on the Esculent Funguses of England*, 2nd edn (ed F. Curry), Lovell Reeve, London, 1863.

—: *Prose Halieutics or Ancient and Modern Fish Tattle*, Parker, London, 1854.

BECKETT, Richard: *Convicted Tastes – Food in Australia*, George Allen & Unwin, Sydney and London, 1984.

Beeton's Field, Farm and Garden, Ward, Lock & Co., London, c. 1879.

BENHAM, Jill Tilsley: 'A Tale of Two Feasts' [forthcoming article].

BEST, Elsdon: *Forest Lore of the Maori*, The Government Printer, Wellington, New Zealand, 1942 (reprinted 1977).

BLACK, Maggie: *W. I. Calendar of Feasts*, W. I. Books, London, 1985.

BODENHEIMER, F. S: *Insects as Human Food*, Dr W. Junk, The Hague, 1951.

BOSWELL, James: *The Journal of a Tour to the Hebrides with Samuel Johnson, LL. D.*, London, 1786.

BOUVEROT-ROTHACKER, Anita: *Le Gros Souper*, Jeanne Laffitte, Marseille, 1982. (Extract translated by Paul Angus © Macdonald & Co.)

BRADLEY, Richard: *The Country Housewife and Lady's Director* (1727) and the same, Part II (1732), 6th edn, printed for D. Browne, London 1736 (reprinted by Prospect Books, London, 1980).

BREARS, Peter: *Traditional Food in Yorkshire*, John Donald, Edinburgh, 1987.

BROWN, Bob: *The Complete Book of Cheese*, Random House, New York, 1955.

BROWN, Gavin: 'Growers of the Big Gooseberries and the Gooseberry Clubs', in *Fruit Year Book*, no. 3, The Royal Horticultural Society, London, 1949.

BROWN, Lynda: 'Yorkshire Oatcakes, Past and Present', in *Petits Propos Culinaires (PPC)* 20, Prospect Books, London, 1985.

BUNYARD, Edward: *The Anatomy of Dessert*, Dulau, London, 1929.

CALVINO, Italo: *Mr Palomar*, Milan, 1983 (translated by William Weaver), Picador edn, Pan Books, 1986.

CAMBA, Julio: *La Casa de Lúculo, o El Arte del Comer*, Collección Austral, Madrid, 1937. (Extracts translated by Eulalia Pensado.)

[CAREY, Henry]: *A Learned Dissertation on Dumplings*, London, 1726.

Cassell's Dictionary of Cookery, London, late 19th century.

CHENG, Dr F. T: *Musings of a Chinese Gourmet*, Hutchinson, London, 1954.

CHILD, Theodore: *Delicate Feasting*, Harper, New York, 1890.

CLARK, Eleanor: *The Oysters of Locmariaquer*, Secker & Warburg, London 1965.

CLIFTON, Claire: 'The Search for the Blue Violet Salad', in *Oxford Symposium Documents 1984–5*, Prospect Books, London, 1986.

COE, Sophie: 'Aztec Cuisine', in *Petits Propos Culinaires (PPC)* 19, 20, 21, Prospect Books, London, 1985.

CORDERO-FERNANDO, Gilda: 'Table Exotica', in *The Culinary Culture of the Philippines* (ed Cordero-Fernando, Gilda), GCF Books, the Philippines, 1976.

CRUICKSHANK, Constance: *Lenten Fare and Food for Fridays*, Faber and Faber, London, 1959.

CURTISS, F. H: *The Comic Cookery Book*, Simpkin, Marshall etc, London, 1891.

DAVID, Elizabeth: Introduction to *The Best of Eliza Acton* (ed Elizabeth Ray), Longmans Green, 1968 (& Penguin Books, 1974 & 1986).

—: 'Mad, Bad, Despised and Dangerous', in *Petits Propos Culinaires (PPC)* 9, Prospect Books, London, 1981.

—: *English Bread and Yeast Cookery*, Allen Lane, London, 1977 (& Penguin Books, 1979).

DAY, Bunny: *Hook'em and Cook'em*, Gramercy Publishing, New York, 1962.

DIGBY, Sir Kenelm: *The Closet of the Eminently Learned Sir Kenelm Digby, Kt., Opened*, London, 1669.

DOERPER, John: *Eating Well*, Pacific Search Press, Seattle, 1984.

DORAN, Dr: *Table Traits*, Richard Bentley, London, 1854.

DORJE, Rinjing: *Food in Tibetan Life*, Prospect Books, London, 1985.

DOYLE, Sir Francis Hastings: *Reminiscences and Opinions*, Longman's Green, London 1886.

DRIVER, Christopher: *Twelve Poems*, Perdix Press, Salisbury, 1985.

DUMAS, Alexandre: *Le Grand Dictionnaire de Cuisine*, Paris 1873; translated and edited by Alan and Jane Davidson as *Dumas on Food*, Folio Society, 1978; Michael Joseph, 1979; Oxford University Press, 1987.

Dumplings, Learned Dissertation on: see CAREY.

EVELYN, John: *Acetaria – A Discourse on Sallets*, B. Tooke, London, 1699 (reprinted by Prospect Books, London, 1982).

FARGA, Amando: *Eating in Mexico* (translated by Jaime Plenn), Mexican Restaurant Association, Mexico D. F., 1963.

FERNIE, Dr W. T: *Health to Date*, John Wright, Bristol, and Simpkin, Marshall etc, London, 1911.

FISHER, M. F. K: 'Loving Cooks, Beware!', in the *Journal of Gastronomy*, vol 1, summer issue, American Institute of Wine and Food, San Francisco, 1984.

FRANCESCONI, Jeanne Caròla: *La Cucina Napoletana*, Naples, 1965. (Extract translated by Francesca Radcliffe.)

FREDERICK, J. George, and Jean Joyce: *Long Island Seafood Cook Book*, Business Bourse, New York, 1939.

GRAY, Patience: *Honey from a Weed*, Prospect Books, London, 1986 (and Harper & Row, and Papermac, 1987).

GREEN, Joyce Conyngham: *Salmagundi*, J. M. Dent & Sons, London, 1947.

GRIGSON, Jane: *Jane Grigson's Fruit Book*, Michael Joseph, London, 1982.

—: *Jane Grigson's Vegetable Book*, Michael Joseph, London, 1978.

—: 'Caul Fat as a Cooking Medium', in *Oxford Symposium Documents 1986*, Prospect Books, London, 1987.

GRIMOD DE LA REYNIÈRE, Alexandre-Balthazar-Laurent: *Almanach des Gourmands*, seconde année, 2nd edn, Paris, 1805. (Extract translated by Paul Angus © Macdonald & Co.)

HAMSUN, Knut: *Hunger*, 1890; Farrar, Strauss & Giroux 1967 (translated by Robert Bly); Picador edn, Pan Books, 1976. Reprinted by permission of Farrar, Strauss & Giroux, Inc.

HARDY, Thomas: *Tess of the d'Urbervilles*, London, 1891.

HARTLEY, Dorothy: *Food in England*, Macdonald, London, 1954. (Reprinted here by kind permission of Anthony Sheil Associates on behalf of the Dorothy Hartley Estate.)

HENISCH, Bridget Ann: *Fast and Feast – Food in Medieval Society*, Pennsylvania State University Press, Pennsylvania, 1976.

—: *Medieval Armchair Travels*, Carnation Press, State College PA, 1967.

HICKS, Alexandra: 'The Mysteries of Garlic', in *Oxford Symposium Documents 1984/5*, Prospect Books, London 1986.

HOLT, Geraldene: *French Country Kitchen*, Penguin, London, 1987.

HOURANI, Furugh: 'Laban, Laban', in *Petits Propos Culinaires (PPC)* 18, Prospect Books, London, 1984.

HOWES, F. N: *Nuts*, Faber & Faber, London, 1948.

HUTCHINS, Sheila: *Grannie's Kitchen – Recipes from East Anglia*, Granada Publishing, London, 1980.

HYMAN, Philip: 'Snail Trails', in *Petits Propos Culinaires (PPC)* 23, Prospect Books, London, 1986.

ISAACS, Jennifer: *Bush Food: Aboriginal Food and Herbal Medicine*, Weldons, Sydney, 1987.

JACKSON, Ian: 'Pear-mania – a History of the Pear' [forthcoming book].

JAINE, Tom: *Cooking in the Country*, Chatto & Windus, London, 1986.

JOHNSON, James F. W: *The Chemistry of Common Life*, vols 1 and 2, Blackwood, Edinburgh and London, 1855.

JOHNSON, Maria: 'Kolivo', in *Symposium Fare*, Prospect Books, London, 1981.

JOYCE, Jean: see FREDERICK, J. George.

KAVENA, Juanita Tiger: *Hopi Cookery*, University of Arizona Press, Tucson, 1980.

KENNEY, E. J. (translator and editor): *Moretum (The Ploughman's Lunch)*, Bristol Classical Press, Bristol, 1984.

KENT, Louise Andrews: *Mrs Appleyard's Kitchen*, Houghton Mifflin, Boston, 1942.

KURTI, Professor Nicholas: 'The Physicist in the Kitchen', lecture to the Royal Institution of Great Britain on 14 March 1969, in *Proceedings of the Royal Institution* vol, 42. (Reproduced by courtesy of the Director of the Royal Institution.)

LADIES OF DES MOINES: *A Collection of Choice Recipes*, Des Moines, 1903 (in: Szathmary, Louis [ed], *Fifty Years of Prairie Cooking*, Cookery Americana series, Arno Press, New York, 1973).

LANG, George: *The Cuisine of Hungary*, Atheneum, New York, 1971. Reprinted with the permission of Atheneum publishers, an imprint of Macmillan Publishing Company, and Penguin Books (UK). © George Lang.

LAUFER, Berthold: *Geophagy*, Field Museum of Natural History, Chicago, 1930.

LAVERTY, Maura: *Maura Laverty's Cookery Book*, Longman's Green, London, 1946.

LECLERC, Henri: *Les Légumes de France*, Masson, Paris, 1927. (Extract translated by Paul Angus © Macdonald & Co.)

LEVY, Paul: *Out to Lunch*, Chatto & Windus, London, 1986.

LOCKWOOD, William G. & Yvonne R: 'The Cornish Pasty in Northern Michigan', in *Oxford Symposium Documents 1983*, Prospect Books, London, 1983.

LUARD, Elisabeth: *The Princess and the Pheasant*, Bantam Press, London, 1987.

MAY, R. J: *Kaikai Aniani – A Guide to Bush Foods, Markets and Culinary Arts of Papua New Guinea*, Robert Brown & Associates (Aust) Pty, Bathurst NSW, 1984.

McGEE, Harold: 'Science and the Study of Food' in *Oxford Symposium Documents 1984/5*, Prospect Books, London, 1986.

McNEILL, F. Marian: *The Scots Kitchen*, Blackie and Son, London and Glasgow, 1929.

McPHEE, John: *Oranges*, Farrar, Strauss & Giroux, New York, 1967. Originally appeared in *The New Yorker*; reprinted by permission of Farrar, Strauss & Giroux, Inc.

MEYER, Kuno (ed): *The Vision of MacConglinne*, D. Nutt, London 1892.

MICKLER, Ernest Matthew: *White Trash Cooking*, The Jargon Society, Winston-Salem, North Carolina, 1986.

MITCHAM, Howard: *Provincetown Seafood Cookbook*, Addison-Wesley Publishing Co, Reading MA, 1975.

MONTANDON, Jacques: *Les Fromages de Suisse*, Edita, Lausanne, 1980. (Extract translated by Paul Angus © Macdonald & Co.)

Moretum: see KENNEY.

MORGAN, Dr Joan: 'In Praise of Older Apples' (based on a BBC broadcast, 1983), in *Petits Propos Culinaires (PPC)* 20, Prospect Books, London, 1985.

MOULIN, Léo: *La Vie Quotidienne des Religieux au Moyen Age*, Hachette, Paris, 1978. (Extract translated by Paul Angus © Macdonald & Co.)

NÈGRE, Dr André: *The French West-Indies through their Cookery* (translated by Christine Nègre), privately published, 1970.

OLNEY, Richard [Nathan d'Aulnay]: 'A Matter of Form; and One of Texture', in *Petits Propos Culinaires (PPC)* 2, Prospect Books, London, 1979.

OLSZEWSKI, Peter: *In Praise of the Humble Yabbie*, Angus and Robertson, Sydney, 1980.

ORTIZ, Elisabeth Lambert: *The Book of Latin American Cooking*, Jill Norman/Robert Hale, London, 1984.

OWEN, Sri: 'Tempe', in *Proceedings of the Konya Congress on Food History 1986*, Turkish Ministry of Culture and Tourism, Ankara, 1988.

PENNELL, Elizabeth Robins: *A Guide for the Greedy by a Greedy Woman*, revised edn, the Bodley Head, London, 1923.

PIERCE, Charles: *The Household Manager*, 3rd edn, Simpkin & Marshall, London, 1863.

PLAT, Sir Hugh, *The Jewell House of Art and Nature*, first published London, 1954; reprinted by *Theatrum Orbis Therrarum*, Amsterdam, 1979.

POMÉS, Leopold: *Pa Amb Tomàquet*, Tusquets Editores, Barcelona, 1985.

POMIANE, Edouard de: *La Cuisine pour la Femme du Monde*, Société du Gaz de Paris, 1932. (Extract translated by Paul Angus © Macdonald & Co.)

POPENOE, Paul B: *Date Growing*, West India Gardens, Altadena, California, 1913.

POURRAT, Henri: *The Roquefort Adventure* (translated by Mary Mian), Société Anonyme des Caves et des Producteurs Réunis de Roquefort, 1956.

RHETT, Blanche S. *et al*: *Two Hundred Years of Charleston Cooking*, University of South Carolina Press, Columbia SC, 1976.

RIDDERVOLD, Astri: 'Gravlax – Buried Salmon', in *Oxford Symposium Documents 1984/5*, Prospect Books, London, 1986.

RIOS, Alicia: 'El Arte del Tapeo', in *Petits Propos Culinaires (PPC)* 27, Prospect Books, London, 1987.

RODEN, Claudia: *A Book of Middle Eastern Food*, Nelson, London, 1968.

ROUND, Jeremy: 'Let Us Try Harder', in *Grand Piano (A Magazine of New Poetry)*, 1984.

RUMOHR, Karl Friedrich Freiherr von: *Geist der Kochkunst*, Stuttgart und Teubingen, 1822. (Extract translated by Paul Angus © Macdonald & Co.)

SABBAN, Françoise: *Un Savoir-faire Oublié: le Travail du Lait en Chine Ancienne*, Zinbun Kagaku Kenkyusyo, Kyoto University, 1986. (Extract translated by Paul Angus © Macdonald & Co.)

SABERI, Helen: *Noshe Djan – Afghan Food and Cookery*, Prospect Books, London, 1986.

SALA, George Augustus: *The Thorough Good Cook*, Cassell, London, 1895.

SALAMAN, Rena: *Greek Food*, Fontana Paperbacks, London, 1983.

SANTICH, Barbara: 'An Australian Banquet', in *Journal of Gastronomy*, vol 1, summer issue, American Institute of Wine and Food, San Francisco, 1984.

SHERIDAN, Monica: *My Irish Cook Book*, Frederick Muller, London, 1965.

SIDGWICK, Henry: 'Bentham and Benthamism in Politics and Ethics', in *Fortnightly Review*, May 1877.

SIESBY, Birgit: 'Blood is Food', in *Petits Propos Culinaires (PPC)* 4, Prospect Books, London, 1980.

SIMMONDS, Peter Lund: *The Curiosities of Food*, Richard Bentley, London, 1859.

SO, Dr Yan-Kit: 'Yuan Mei's Iced Bean Curd', in *Oxford Symposium Documents 1984/5*, Prospect Books, London, 1986.

SOKOLOV, Raymond: 'Peach Ice Cream', in *Oxford Symposium Documents 1984/5*, Prospect Books, London, 1986.

STONE, Lionel: 'Kosher Food', in *Petits Propos Culinaires (PPC)* 11, Prospect Books, London, 1982.

SYMONS, Michael: *One Continuous Picnic*, Duck Press, Adelaide, 1982.

SZATHMARY, Louis: 'The American Perception of Hungarian Goulash', in *Oxford Symposium Documents 1983*, Prospect Books, London, 1983.

THOMPSON, Flora: *Lark Rise to Candleford*, Oxford University Press, 1939.

THORLACIUS, Sigridur: 'Do You Know Skyr?', in *Petits Propos Culinaires (PPC)* 4, Prospect Books, London, 1980.

THORNE, John, 'Cooking Without Cook', in *Simple Cooking*, winter issue, 1986, Jackdaw Press, Castine, Maine, 1986.

TICKLETOOTH, Tabitha: *The Dinner Question*, Routledge, Warne & Routledge, London, 1860.

TROLLOPE, Anthony: *The Kellys and the O'Kellys*, 3 vols, Henry Colburn, London, 1848.

VERRAL, William: *A Complete System of Cookery*, published by the author, Lewes, 1759.

Vision of MacConglinne: see MEYER.

WALLACE, Alfred: *The Malay Archipelago*, first published 1869, 10th edn (London, 1890), reprinted by Dover, New York, 1962.

WARNER, William W: *Beautiful Swimmers*, Little, Brown & Co., Boston, 1976.

WATTS, Mrs Elizabeth: *Fish and How to Cook it*, London, 1866.

WEAVER, William Woys: 'When Shad Come In: Shad Cookery in Old Philadelphia', in *Petits Propos Culinaires (PPC)* 11, Prospect Books, London, 1982.

WHEATON, Barbara Ketcham: *Savoring the Past*, University of Pennsylvania Press, 1983.

WHITE, Florence: *Good Things in England*, Cape, London, 1932.

WILSON, C. Anne: *The Book of Marmalade*, Constable, London, 1985.

WOOLF, Virginia: *A Room of One's Own*, The Hogarth Press, London, 1929.

WRIGHT, Elizabeth Mary: *The Life of Joseph Wright*, vol 2, London, 1932.

ZOLA, Émile: *Le Ventre de Paris*, Librairie Charpentier, Paris, 1873 & reprinted by Gallimard, Folio paperback, 1979. (Extracts translated by Paul Angus © Macdonald & Co.)

ZUBAIDA, Sami: 'The Taste for Fat', in *Proceedings of the Konya Congress on Food History 1986*, Turkish Ministry of Culture and Tourism, Ankara, 1988.

NOTE *on* ILLUSTRATIONS

The illustrations that open each chapter of this book were adapted from/are pastiches of/were done in the manner of the following paintings and artists:

CHAPTER ONE (*The* COOK *and the* KITCHEN) – *The Table* by Pierre Bonnard.
CHAPTER TWO (*The* ORCHARD) – *The Cherry Pickers* by Berthe Morisot.
CHAPTER THREE (*The* VEGETABLE GARDEN) – *Still Life with Onions* (among others) by Paul Cézanne.
CHAPTER FOUR (FOOD *from the* WATERS) – *Window at La Goulette* by Albert Marquet.
CHAPTER FIVE (*On* HOOF *or* WING) – *The Bar at the Folies Bergère* by Edouard Manet.
CHAPTER SIX (FOOD *from the* DAIRY) – *The Cook* by Jan Vermeer.
CHAPTER SEVEN (FASTING *and* FEASTING) – *The Marriage Feast of Cupid and Psyche* by Guilio Romano.
CHAPTER EIGHT (HERE *and* THERE) – the odalisques of Henri Matisse.
CHAPTER NINE (NOW *and* THEN) – *The Reading* and *Around Vence* by Marc Chagall.
CHAPTER TEN (ODDITIES *and* PARTING SMILES) – *Son of Man* and *Personal Values* (among others) by René Magritte.
FRONT COVER – *Luncheon on the Grass* by Edouard Manet.
BACK COVER (PORTRAIT *of* ALAN DAVIDSON) – *A Portrait of Dr Gachet* by Vincent Van Gogh.

INDEX *to* CONTRIBUTORS